I HAVE FUN
EVERYWHERE I GO

I HAVE FUN EVERYWHERE I GO

SAVAGE TALES OF POT, PORN, PUNK ROCK, PRO WRESTLING, TALKING APES, EVIL BOSSES, DIRTY BLUES, AMERICAN HEROES, AND THE MOST NOTORIOUS MAGAZINES IN THE WORLD

MIKE EDISON

FABER AND FABER, INC.

AN AFFILIATE OF FARRAR, STRAUS AND GIROUX

NEW YORK

Faber and Faber, Inc.
An affiliate of Farrar, Straus and Giroux
18 West 18th Street, New York 10011

Distributed in Canada by Douglas & McIntyre Ltd.
Printed in the United States of America
First edition, 2008

Library of Congress Cataloging-in-Publication Data
Edison, Mike, 1964–
    I have fun everywhere I go : savage tales of pot, porn, punk rock, pro wrestling,
talking apes, evil bosses, dirty blues, American heroes, and the most notorious
magazines in the world / by Mike Edison. — 1st. ed.
        p.   cm.
    Includes index
    ISBN-13: 978-0-86547-964-7 (hardcover : alk. paper)
    ISBN-10: 0-86547-964-X (hardcover : alk. paper)
    1. Edison, Mike, 1964–   2. Periodical editors—United States—
Biography.   I. Title.

PN4874.E47 A3 2008
070.5′1092—dc22
[B]

                                                          2007047590

Designed by Jonathan D. Lippincott
Monkeys by Cliff Mott

www.fsgbooks.com

1   3   5   7   9   10   8   6   4   2

It ain't what you eat, it's the way how you chew it.
—LITTLE RICHARD

AUTHOR'S NOTE

Everything in this story is, to the best of my recollection, true, and happened as written. In a few cases I compressed or juggled the chronology to maintain the narrative, and occasionally stretched a point for a laugh. Like many punk rockers and professional wrestlers, I confess to being prone to hyperbole. Although others may recall events somewhat differently, while writing this book I spoke with many of the key players, who remember things mostly as I do, even viewed through the soft focus of time and strong drugs. Some names have been changed to protect the innocent and the guilty.

CONTENTS

I HAVE FUN
EVERYWHERE I GO

FLASH FORWARD:
THE SHAPE OF THINGS TO COME

The next person who suggests putting Bob Marley on the cover is going to be looking for a new job.

I would get in a lot of trouble for saying things like that, but seriously, Bob Fucking Marley? That's the best you've got?

If you have ever imagined a creative meeting at a magazine to be a bubbling cauldron of energy and hot ideas, with ambitious editors pitching stories and competing to get plum assignments, well, this wasn't it. My exhortations were greeted by grunts.

After years of pumping out seedy sex books and down-market filth, promoting the careers of devil-worshipping wrestlers and Bourbon Street strippers, I had finally scored my dream job—publisher of *High Times* magazine. What my grandma used to call "that dope rag."

Strangely, not everyone wants to work for a marijuana magazine, no matter how famous it is. But after years of cut-rate pornography, drugs were a definite step up.

There was talent in the room, but most of it had been stifled by years of stoner ennui, the unfortunate side effect of working for a pop culture perennial where free weed was a perk. One editor, whose eyes looked like hemorrhoids from years of staring down the length of a water pipe, thumbed through an old issue dispassionately. Another amused himself with a chocolate-chip cookie. The others had about as much interest in my pep rally as a monkey might have in a chess match. I should have brought them a bright red rubber ball to play with. Or a coconut. These guys knew how to make a totally excellent bong out of a coconut.

But the magazine was in trouble. Circulation was flagging. It seemed like they had run out of ideas. Bob Marley? He had already been the cover story. Three times. There wasn't a whole lot more to report.

When I came on board, the most recent celebrity to have been featured on the cover was Pancho Villa.

Pancho Villa?

Presumably this is why I had been hired—to lead *High Times* out of the grove of hackneyed pothead icons and dead Mexican folk heroes.

I looked around the room and measured my team. The fellow who had been eating the cookie was covered in crumbs. Everyone looked as if they were just waiting for the bell to ring so they could go to recess.

This was not going to be easy.

1

IF YOU WERE THAT GOOD, DON'T YOU THINK YOU WOULD HAVE MADE IT BY NOW?

I earned my first Big-Time Magazine Gig thrashing king hell out of my boss in the middle of the ring. It was not pretty, a bloody no-holds-barred Loser Leaves Town match in Gleason's gym. The bell rang at midnight. I squashed the bastard with my signature Heart Punch, smiled for the cameras, and sent him packing. Then I took my rightful place atop the masthead of *Wrestling's Main Event* ("The #1 Magazine for Mat Fans Today!") and moved into his vacant office on the eighty-second floor of the Empire State Building. I was twenty-two years old.

Wrestling is an odd beast. Even Roller Derby fans and Republicans look down on it. When I announced to my father that I was going to be working for a wrestling magazine, it so chafed his Ivy League sensibility that he seized up and began frothing like a man in the throes of a major neurological event. He made it clear that for the sake of everyone involved, we were never to discuss it again. Oddly, he always considered my career in professional wrestling a much greater *shanda* than my gutter-born livelihood as a filth-peddling pornographer. It cast a darker shadow than when I was the publisher of the notorious doper rag *High Times*. It made him sick to the point of trauma, and still, twenty years later, if I mention that I have been writing, watching, or working wrestling, he pretends he doesn't hear me and asks how the Yankees are doing, even in the dead of winter.

The existential Truth about professional wrestling, it has been said, is much like Dostoyevsky's aphorism for Faith: If you get it, no explanation is necessary, and if you don't, no explanation will do.

I was always astonished at how many otherwise hip people, especially my extended posse of punk rockers, potheads, and pornographers—people who loved all sorts of crap, culture vultures who worshipped whoopee cushions and women-in-chains prison movies—perpetually pooh-poohed professional wrestling.

What, were they afraid they'd get hooked? That wrestling was a gateway to harder sports? *Feh*.

But those of us in on the joke were having a blast.

It was 1985, the height of the first Hulk Hogan era, the epoch of the nascent WrestleMania. It was a good time to be in the business. Diane Keaton was seen at matches. MTV was saturated with the stuff. You couldn't give a God-fearing jobber a swinging neckbreaker without hitting a poster for Hulk Hogan and Mr. T, who, along with Cyndi Lauper, were going to take on "Rowdy" Roddy Piper and his axis of evil in the WrestleMania main event at Madison Square Garden. Muhammad Ali was the guest referee. Liberace would be the timekeeper, using a diamond-crusted piano-shaped watch given to him by Elvis Presley. He made his entrance with a chorus line of Rockettes. How could anybody resist this stuff? Even Andy Warhol showed up to watch. Vince McMahon, a visionary on par with Columbus, had turned his World Wrestling Federation, much to the chagrin of elitists and squares who never got it, into a media giant.

I prided myself on being the first "heel" editor. "Heel" is wrestling argot for bad guy. We call the good guys "babyfaces." (A "jobber" is one of the bums whose only job is to get his ass kicked.) I modeled myself after the great rulebreakers, outlaws who would pull a pair of brass knuckles, a roll of quarters, or a sharpened wooden tongue depressor out of their trunks to carve up and KO the good guy when the ref wasn't looking. It's tough stuff—wrestling teaches that sportsmanship is overrated. It is the only sport where you can kick a man when he's down.

I stole riffs from Stan Hansen—who became the most hated man in the game after he broke insufferable fan favorite Bruno Sammartino's neck in front of fifty thousand people at Shea Stadium—and from the Magnificent Muraco, who once beat the living shit out of a hapless opponent while eating a meatball submarine sandwich. I continually paid homage to the original Sheik from Detroit, the most dangerous man who ever entered the ring. The Sheik could metabolize a fireball—he could *throw fire*—and would use this gift to blind opponents. Add some old-school newspaper shtick lifted wholesale from the *Front Page* films, along with Perry "Don't Call Me Chief!" White, editor of *The Daily Planet* in the old Superman TV show, and you start to get the idea of how we rolled at *Main Event*. Wrestlers had gimmicks, why shouldn't editors and writers?

I hated Hulk Hogan. He was overtanned, officious, and omnipresent, wrapping himself in red, white, and blue and proselytizing to his army of teenybopper fans to stay in school and stay away from drugs. Frankly, he just wasn't my kind of people. I declared a personal jihad against him and the hordes of Reagan-era zombies who followed him, unwaveringly rooting for the babyfaces.

Jeremy, my boss at *Main Event*, was firmly entrenched in this coalition of self-righteous do-gooders. Our feud boiled in the pages of the magazine for months, until it exploded like a can of beer left out in the sun at the height of a Texas summer. How dare he paint my lifestyle black with his Saturday-morning-cartoon version of American morality! This was going to have to be settled in the ring, mano a mano.

After our match, unprecedented in the history of magazine publishing, Art Burns, a *Main Event* staff writer, offered this recap, along with a brilliantly gory photo spread:

> Mike accused Jeremy of being a "hack artist and Hulkamaniac."
> Jeremy called Mike "rule-breaking scum" . . . There was no
> quarter given and none asked for . . . Jeremy's bleeding head
> wound sapped him of strength . . . the only thing that kept
> Mike going was his passion for excellence in Wrestling Journal-
> ism . . . After the pinfall, Edison pounded his fist into Jeremy's
> face, "just as a reminder."

Booya!

Of course, *I* was Art Burns.

I was also Ted Pipe, Mick Wild, and sometimes Monica Lisbon. There were seven names on the masthead, and I was five of them.

Few other magazines would have tolerated the bad-guy editor shtick. But I was throwing high heat and having the time of my life.

Jeremy was an incredibly good sport about honoring the great wrestling tradition of "going out on your back"—dropping the title and pushing the next guy—especially since he was the pioneer who opened the door for all of this insanity. In his final editorial column for *Main Event* he wrote, underneath a photo of me voguing over his broken, supine body, "It's not easy to admit that you're a loser." Now that's what I call taking one for the team! Supplicating the kind of febrile ego that makes one want to be the editor of a guerrilla wrestling magazine could not have been easy. What a pro! Everyone should take a page from his book.

The Night of the Great Wrestling Epiphany—two years before I ran Jeremy out of town—began innocently enough with a few tabs of exceptionally good LSD, the paper blotter stuff that usually had pretty pictures of pyramids or dolphins printed on it. I was a freshman in the New York University film school. Jeremy was a year ahead of me.

I was hanging out at the East Tenth Street railroad apartment where our pal Jim was living. Jim had been my roommate at NYU, but he was now smelling up this hovel of off-campus housing with cheap wine of a despicably nasty vintage and nickel bags of brown Colombian dirt weed. I was still living in relative luxury back at the dorm, sharing a tiny room with a high-ranking member of the Young Republican Club and an extremely confused Puerto Rican drama student who was trying to come to terms with his own sexuality. You could call the vibe "tense." I spent as little time there as possible.

Jim was a wino/poet/superbrain from St. Louis, a guy who knew as much about philosophy and history as anyone you are likely to meet, a guy who had impeccable taste in the ridiculous, who loved equally Robert Johnson, Robert Rauschenberg, and *Romper Room*, except he couldn't figure out how to hook up the stereo or light the oven or pay the phone bill, and he was notoriously bereft of social graces and lifestyle-maintenance skills, like doing his laundry on a timely basis. Jim wore his hair halfway down his back and sported hopelessly out-of-date octagonal-framed eyeglasses. He was the only adult I knew who still wore Sears Toughskin blue jeans.

I was in awe of Jim's intellect, most of which could not find practical application. But he could distill the absurd from the mundane, and he truly loved professional wrestling. He was the first person I knew who had, in his own demented way, intellectualized it to an impossibly heady stature.

By the time the World Wrestling Federation show came on at midnight, we were soaring through the spaceways on the backs of those blotters.

I had not watched wrestling since I was a kid. My father would pointedly show his disdain even then, although like most eight-year-olds, I was unprepared to argue whether wrestling was actually real or fake. But even if it was fake, who gave a flying fuck? So was *Romeo and Juliet*. And people kept lining up to see that beaten warhorse even though everyone and his sister has known for three hundred years exactly how it ends.

They die.

But I am nothing if not a slave to the spectacle, as witnessed by my undying affection for Jackson Pollock, the Sex Pistols, and the space program, and if Jim wanted to watch wrestling on acid, it seemed like a safe bet.

The broadcast peaked dramatically with a match between the Masked Superstar, a highly skilled thug who wore a series of spangled red, silver, blue, and gold masks with a giant ★ on the forehead, and Hot Stuff Eddie Gilbert, the twerpy-looking protégé of then World Wrestling Federation champion Bob Backlund, a humorless good-guy pissant with a crew cut who flaunted his college wrestling skills and called himself the All-American Boy.

The Masked Superstar was managed by the Grand Wizard of Wrestling—a raving lunatic who wore a ridiculously loud plaid jacket, a supremely ugly tie, flare pants that looked as if they were handcrafted from fuzzy toilet-seat covers, horrid wraparound shades that brought into sharp relief the worst features of his molelike face, and a sparkly turban punctuated with a rhinestone dollar sign. Overall, the effect was one of a Martian who had just raided a Jewish retirement home in Miami. And he claimed to be one of the most intelligent men in the world. He was perfect in every way.

How could anyone, stoned or not, ignore the sublime beauty of this? The Masked Superstar? The Grand Wizard of Wrestling? His big move was something called the Corkscrew Neckbreaker. There was poetry everywhere!

The Superstar's idea of wrestling was to treat Gilbert's head like the twist-off cap on a bottle of Budweiser. For his part, the Grand Wizard exhibited all the symptoms of a man having a stroke. "Break his neck! Break his neck!" he spat, standing over his charge. The Masked Superstar gleefully complied.

It was all so completely insane, so colorful, so out of control, so ridiculous—how could this even be allowed to happen in a civilized country?—I was sold instantly.

The real kicker, though, came after a commercial for the Apex Technical School ("And when you graduate, you'll have a set of your very own professional tools!"), when Backlund came back on TV and began crying.

Not just crying. Bawling his eyes out like a little girl. *Oh, Eddie, you didn't deserve to be treated like that. Masked Superstar I'm gonna get you, you Big Bad Man. Grand Wizard, you are so evil, weep, weep, weep . . .*

This was the Champ? The Heavyweight Champion of the World?? The Standard-Bearer of All That Is Tough on God's Green Earth??? Whatta fruit!

This was all too much for my brain, which was now glowing like molten lava and threatening to erupt. I was laughing so hard that I was on the floor convulsing, crying harder than Backlund. Jim considered calling the paramedics—then he remembered that we were both tripping on acid, and let it go.

The next stop was Jeremy's cold-water flat on Twelfth Street and Avenue A, then still a busy corridor for Alphabet City narco-traffic. Like everything else in that apartment, the buzzer wasn't working, the wires probably chewed through by a mule team of rodents and cockroaches. To get into Jeremy's, we had to call from the corner and then wait for him to come down to let us in. Which could take a while, considering he had dropped the same acid we had.

It took about two seconds for the guy with the shotgun to appear.

It's funny how on LSD things can sometimes appear so clear. Like what William Burroughs said about "the naked lunch," that moment when you can see exactly what's at the end of your fork. In this case it was just about the ugliest mutherfucker I have ever laid eyes on, covered in scars and sweat and leveling a sawed-off shotgun at our heads, demanding to know what the fuck we wanted.

"It's cool," I offered. "We're waiting for our friend." I think I was pretty calm. Just a simple misunderstanding between some harmless college-boy acidheads and a heavily armed smack dealer. For a guy who was about to get his head blown off, Jim was surprisingly relaxed. Probably happened to him all the time back in St. Louis.

At that moment Jeremy opened the door. "Ah, here's our friend now!" When Jeremy saw what was going on, his eyes popped out of his head, just like in a Tex Avery cartoon, but he managed to play it smooth. "They're just coming up to see me," he explained matter-of-factly. It was a big moment. I could feel my balls climbing up into my stomach. The guy lowered the shotgun. "Damn!" he said. "You can't be hanging around here. I'm doin' business!" And he disappeared. My balls descended, joyfully.

"Holy fucking shit—" I stammered. "Holy fucking shit."

"Are you okay?" Jeremy was just as freaked as I was.

"What are you guys talking about?" Jim said good-naturedly. Apparently, he had been busy traveling the astral plane and missed all the excitement.

Jeremy's place was no more relaxed than the street had been. He had also seen Backlund on TV, and his reaction to this aberration (there is no crying in wrestling) was to throw everything not nailed down out the window, beginning with buckets of paint left over from eighty years of dirtbag tenants. He had the twelve-inch single of "Rapper's Delight" on his turntable with the repeat switch on, the perfect soundtrack for druggy urban frustration.

After that, throwing things out of Jeremy's window became a regular pastime for us. TV sets were a hot commodity, and Jeremy used to collect them, picking them up off the street when they were left out for trash and carting them up to his place to be hurled en masse at a later date.

Perhaps throwing televisions out of windows sounds trite to you? Do not underestimate the sound a nineteen-inch RCA Colortrak makes after being tossed down a six-story air shaft. Some things, no matter how many times they have been done—Beethoven's Fifth Symphony, fried chicken, and the Missionary Position leap to mind—still provide near-universal satisfaction when done right.

———

Inspired by the warm and fuzzy feeling fully realized only when watching a human bunny slipper like Hot Stuff getting his neck broken by an *artiste* like the Masked Superstar—not to mention the psychedelic bliss of sharing a near-death experience at gunpoint—I invited Jim to join the new band I was masterminding, which we eventually called Sharky's Machine, an homage to the preposterous Burt Reynolds cop flick.

Sharky's Machine was an experiment—pure, without regard to result. I had never even written a song before, and after years of bashing away at the drums, I had just bought my first guitar (a copper-top '59 Danelectro, single cutaway, the one with two pickups and concentric knobs, 130 bucks at We Buy Guitars) and was bending a handful of rough-hewn blues riffs into compact blasts of high-energy rock 'n' roll and then working them out on the drum kit, where I was most dangerous. My idea was something approaching a hard-core thrash band— filtered through the wildly distorting refractors of Captain Beefheart, the Stooges, and the Troggs.

Jim shocked everyone with how great a singer he could be, especially for a first-timer—crooning, hollering, getting the Iggyisms and the Jaggerisms just right, howling very deep-felt lyrics far too complex for a Sunday-afternoon punk rock band, digging into some incredibly soulful stuff, and shredding himself into a bloody mess in the process.

I conscripted Alec to play guitar, for no other reason than that he lived upstairs and owned a really big amplifier and was game, which at the time seemed to trump any real need for conventional rock 'n' roll chops or sense of swing. What I didn't realize was that he was a savant, a pundit on almost everything, a difficult guy to be around for any length of time. Alec is a nice guy, an intelligent guy, and can be very funny; he's just completely off the beam. After he graduated from NYU and became a cabdriver, he was quoted in *The New York Times* as saying that the only way to make cabs safe was to "put the passenger up front and the driver in the back with a shotgun."

But he was very enthusiastic about the project, and besides, I figured it wouldn't last, so who cared? I never thought this would exist past a couple of gigs and maybe some recording. How could it? We used to haul our gear to CBGB in shopping carts we stole from a supermarket on La Guardia Place.

Tonia, our bass player, ditto, was an unqualified rookie who could barely tune her instrument, but very sweet, and very earnest about wanting to be in a band (eventually she learned to ride herd over what could have easily turned into a relentless din)—and the only person we could find willing to put up with this group of musical misfits.

Sharky's Machine was a fucked-up mess right out of the gate. One of our first shows was at our NYU dorm, and it resulted in a swarm of security guards trying to turn off our shrieking amplifiers while Jim taunted the crowd. Tonia, who weighed about 110 pounds in her Doc Martens, got pulled into a melee with some Neidermeir-like asshole whose girlfriend had been on earlier, playing "Für Elise" on the flute. When I tried to break it up, he sucker punched me in the head.

This was the beginning of a nasty trend of violence surrounding the group. In this case it was a bunch of frat-boy pussies and business-school dickweeds. Later it would be a New Jersey biker gang (who adored us), various soundmen (not so much), and audience members who had been savagely attacked by Jim (with, in one inspired moment, the jagged end of a broken bowling trophy). Pro wrestling–inspired riff bashing and avant noise explorations like "The Devastating Samoan Drop" were more likely to inspire a hail of bottles than a shower of daisies. When we opened for the Ramones at Vassar College, shit started flying at us on the very first *note*. Someone even threw his shoes.

Yet somehow we managed to do pretty well on the European club circuit, eventually warming up for hot handers like the Mekons, Soundgarden, and Mudhoney. It happened this fast: we had just finished playing our set at the gloriously illegal No Se No dance hall lounge on Rivington Street, opening for art-damaged hippie producer Kramer and his band Shockabilly:

KRAMER: Hey, you guys are great. Do you want to make a record for my new label?
US: Uh, sure.
KRAMER: Do you guys want to go on tour in Europe, starting in Amsterdam in the fall?
US: Uh, sure.

My father once came to a Sharky's Machine show—probably the only one we ever played where you actually could sit down and order a drink at a table. I thought it would be a good opportunity for the old man to see what his firstborn was up to. I was very proud of the band

and extremely focused on being a Holy Terror behind the kit. I was delighted when *Maximum Rock 'n' Roll* compared my drumming to air-raid sirens.

The show was at the famed Folk City on Third Street, famous because Bob Dylan got his start there. We were on before Sonic Youth. At the end of our set, there was the usual dustup when I kicked over the drum kit, breaking a few chairs and some tables (not to mention a guitar, two mic stands, and several audience members), but that was our thing, and some minor-league rock mag even named it "show of the year." Later Dad would offer me his review: "I've seen your band, I've seen the way you throw your equipment around, and frankly, I don't call it music." A few years later he would add, "If you were that good, don't you think you would have made it by now?"

Living as we did on the front lines of the new rock'n'wrestling connection, Jim and I also began a fanzine, a photocopied cut-and-paste (the old-fashioned way: with scissors and Scotch tape) "post-scientific" journal for the punk rock and piledriver set—called *The Foreign Object*.

In its perfectly unevolved state—laid out, such as it was, on folded 8½-by-11 paper, typed on a battered Smith Corona electric, hand-lettered with Sharpies, and illustrated with photos snipped from "bona fide" wrestling magazines—*The Foreign Object* looked as if it were put together by a couple of highly delusional mental patients. We wrote elaborate fantasies about dining with wrestlers at four-star restaurants and top-secret conspiracies involving the WWF and the military-industrial complex, and we created bizarre formulas calibrated to unlock objective numerical indexes of wrestlers graded on a twisted scale of "charisma and brutality." Post-scientific, indeed. We were leaders in the deification of Vince McMahon, who was bending the medium with a bizarre cable talk show for wrestlers, cohosted with a lisping British poof named Lord Alfred Hayes. Vince was bringing the oeuvre to new levels of absurdity with segments dedicated to wrestlers cooking, dancing, and performing Johnny Carson–esque sketch comedy. The Canadian eye-gouge king Butcher Vachon was married on the show (mazel tov, Butcher!), beginning a long string of in-the-ring romances that invariably led to some sort of donnybrook, busted-up buffet, or other comic outrage. Even in "real life," wrestling was getting pretty far-out.

Not to be outdone by our roll-your-own entry into the publishing racket—and he was always a great one not to be outdone—Jeremy got an internship at a legitimate national newsstand wrestling magazine, *Wrestling's Main Event*. While other journalism students were chasing their tails trying to get in the door at *New York* or *The Village Voice*, Jeremy went down-market and made a Big Score.

We now had one of our own safely installed inside the fortified walls of Wrestling. How much longer could it be until we ruled the world?

It wasn't long before Jeremy parlayed his internship into an actual job and was working full-time as an associate editor at *WME*, putting his spin on everything. Soon I was writing for them under a fistful of pseudonyms and cranking out three or four stories a month. The takeover had begun.

And I was now an officially published writer.

As in a good New Jersey street brawl, it was "anything goes" in the pages of *Main Event*. We didn't go as far out into the realm of the absurd as we did with *The Foreign Object* (now defunct since we had gone legit), but we definitely pushed the boundaries of objective reality. For unloading post-scientific fantasies on what I imagine was a thundering herd of dumbfounded wrestling fans, I was paid seventy-five bucks a pop. But if you were to believe the world we painted, we spent our time on Lear jets drinking champagne with the Champ and going undercover to top-secret Soviet training camps that specialized in banned techniques—that is, when we weren't hopscotching the Orient in search of the Forbidden City of Professional Wrestling.

2

I KNOW IT'S HARD TO BELIEVE, BUT THERE ARE STILL PURITANS WORKING IN THIS BUSINESS

Bobo the Porn-Writing Clown was not a *real* clown; he was just a stoned clod in sore need of a makeover. He maintained a robust Bozoesque coif—a comfortably wide landing strip down the middle, and giant tufts of hair sticking out from the sides of his basketball-shaped head—and he insisted on wearing OshKosh B'gosh overalls, inappropriate for anyone past puberty who doesn't spend his mornings squeezing the milk out of cow tits. That his shoes did not explode was an unfortunate oversight.

By this time I had dropped out of NYU and had moved in with my girlfriend in a sixth-floor walk-up on Avenue B, while I entertained the idea of becoming a professional writer, whatever that meant.

Bobo moved in to the apartment below ours and invited me over to get stoned with him. My girlfriend would have nothing to do with Bobo, but being a good neighbor, naturally I accepted. He had an ancient pipe that he had been using since junior high school, one of those short little metal things that gets too hot to hold after just a few minutes. Jammed with the resin of the years and badly in need of a new screen, smoking it was like trying to inhale pot through a billiard ball.

He asked me what I did. I gave him the short answer, viz., my career as a college dropout and part-time post-scientific wrestling journalist. He claimed to be some kind of a writer, too.

Watching this guy spill beer all over himself while he burned his fingers trying to get stoned, I wouldn't have guessed he could have composed a lucid "wish you were here" postcard to his folks without setting it on fire, let alone write a *book*, but he showed me an *entire shelf* of sleazy paperbacks he had written. I was flabbergasted. There were about forty of them, titles like *Hard Hat Lover, Black Dicks for Debbie, Teenage Bootlicker, Mother Daughter Rapists . . .*

Mother Daugher Rapists? It was part of an incest series, which included other evergreens such as *Daddy Knows Best* and *Mom 'n' Sis 'n' Me Make Three.*

In the name of All That Is Holy, what had I stumbled upon? *Black Dicks for Debbie?* Just what kind of clown was I dealing with?

I was no prude. I was, after all, a Worldly Film School Dropout. But I certainly had never seen any pocket novels for incest fetishists, let alone met anyone who took pride in their authorship.

There were bondage books, transvestite books, "young debs," hot slave-girl horrors, tri-sexuals . . . *Tri-sexuals?* I didn't even know what that meant.

I cleaned the pipe with a paper clip and passed it back to Bobo, who gave it another go, this time more successfully (he looked at me as something of a miracle worker), while I continued to marvel at this licentious trove of literary wonder. *High-Heeled Husband. A Bra for Bobby. Spank My Pussy. Hot for Chicken . . .*

There was certainly something for everyone. I thumbed through a few of them, not quite knowing what to expect. Except for the shockingly crude covers—and the ad on the back cover for the Weekend Orgy Kit—they looked like, well, *real books.*

"Did you ever think about writing smut?"

"You actually write these things?"

"Yeah, like one a week. I know they're looking for people. You should give them a call."

The mind reeled. I had nothing against pornography, but I had never really given it much thought. Mostly I found it boring and just kind of dumb. I only occasionally looked at *Playboy* or *Penthouse.* I can be a pretty shameless onanist, even without pictures.

As for the writing, one reason I floundered at NYU was because I always had trouble mustering eight pages of academic blather about the "Myth of the Western" or "Revisionism in the Noir Cycle," which, in retrospect, is kind of pathetic, since all that was expected was to cough up a load of hackneyed egghead bullshit, and I usually excelled at such bullshit.

But writing for *Main Event* had taught me how to focus in thousand-word blasts. I was learning how to tell a story, learning which colors I could lift from Raymond Chandler, what tattoos I could swipe from Richard Brautigan, and what grammatical excesses to leave far behind. As freewheeling and loosey-goosey as it might have been, I was finding my voice. Mainly I had gained an enormous amount of confidence. *Main Event* had evolved into something of a writer's laboratory, and the results were far more successful than my overpriced private university. I looked at Bobo, now completely stoned and playing with the hooks on his overalls. I was pretty sure I could make the leap from men in tights to cheerleaders in chains.

"Can you type?"

"Uh, sure."

That job interview went well. After affirming that I was indeed a forty-five-words-per-minute man, I was seated in front of a battered IBM Selectric, the detritus of someone's failed business but in those dark days before the Mac Classic, still at the apex of writing machines.

"Set it up, boy-girl, and then bring the camera in close. Give me like a thousand words."

I wasn't really expecting to be auditioned on the spot, but I was up to the challenge. I put my paws on the keys and began banging away, determined to unleash a torrent of such unrivaled smut that I would be hired on the spot and quickly declared the greatest eroticist since Ovid.

I did as I was told. Jack and Jill were on the couch, lingering over a kiss. And then, like a hooker in heat, Jill goes for the ol' okeydoke and they're off to the races. The IBM typeball clicked and clattered. Sparks were flying. It sounded like an elevated train tearing across the South Side of Chicago. Who knew that I had it in me? She sucked, he groaned, she pulled up her skirt, her wet dum-de-dum, his hard blah blah blah . . . and Shazam! Twenty minutes later I pulled my sordid little vignette out of the typewriter. The roller mechanism whirred contentedly.

The editor who had interviewed me so efficiently gave it a good once-over.

"When can you start?"

Hooray! I was a pornographer! I couldn't wait to tell my folks.

First, though, I had to learn the rules. The editor spelled them out for me.

"We like plots. The books should read like *books*, preferably with a beginning, a middle, and an end. And nothing that couldn't really happen—no extraterrestrials having sex with Earth girls or anything like that. It has to be plausibly real. In the S and M books, nothing that leaves a scar, no wounds that don't heal. And no one dies. We like happy endings."

"Is that it?"

"No. No shit eating." He took a contemplative beat. "I know it's hard to believe, but there are still puritans working in this business."

Each book was 180 pages. Ten chapters per book, and each chapter was about four thousand words, but we counted them by lines. There were something like five hundred lines per chapter. A good tip was *never underestimate the dramatic impact of a one- or two-word paragraph.*

"Oh!"

"Don't stop!"

"Glubglubglubglub . . ."

"Mmmmmmmmmmmmmmffffff!!!"

Because that's what it looked like ripping down a page, and if you hit the carriage return often enough, you'd get to the end of the chapter in quick time. And that's what this was all about—grinding out these books at record speed. They had nothing against good writing, as long as it didn't get in the way.

Bobo wasn't kidding when he said he wrote a novel a week. People who had been doing it for a while—and didn't suffer from porn-induced psychosis or institutional burnout—could crank out *two*. By the time I was done, I had written twenty-eight novels, all attributed to "Anonymous." These books didn't even merit the clever pseudonyms that D-list hack writers customarily drape themselves in. But I could finish a serviceable book in under twenty-two hours: *Mandy's Shame, Rich Man's Sex Toy, Busting Susan's Cherry* . . . they were mine. Ditto *Cindy's Brutal Ordeal, Sex Farm, Class Virgin,* and on and on.

The Factory, as the space we wrote in came to be called, was above a storefront on Third Avenue near Thirty-eighth Street, down the street from the Pierpont Morgan Library. It was a nice open loft, with about half a dozen workspaces equipped with Kaypro computers. These were primitive metal boxes that looked like air conditioners, with text-only green LED screens, and no hard drive. We were always swapping five-and-a-quarter-inch floppy disks in and out of the two toasterlike slots at the front of them—one for the system, one for PerfectWriter, which was the software we used, and one to actually write the book on. They ran on a clunky operating system called CPM, which froze up all the time and wasn't good for much else besides writing dirty books. But it was an advance over the old electric typewriters, which were still the default technology of the publishing world.

In the back of the loft was another whirring, sputtering behemoth headed for the boneyard, the repro machine, which spit out reproduction-quality copy and stank of dangerous photochemicals. It was about the size of a Good Humor truck and needed to be fondled and sweet-talked if you expected it to work for you.

Basically, we ran a glorified typesetting operation. While I was crafting another masterpiece, their semiskilled house artist was rendering another museum-quality work for the cover. When I finished, the galleys were run out, packaged with the cover, and sent to a mob-run distribution company. They printed the books and flooded Forty-second Street with them for the raincoat brigade. They also distributed "rubber goods and marital aids." It was a different era, before the Internet, before VHS tapes were affordable technology. I think we sent about twelve books a week to the printer.

The Factory was run by a gay couple who worked upstairs from the loft and rarely came down. But they were nice as pie, and they paid every week, on time. When I started, I was making $250 per book, but that went up steadily, as I became more productive and consistent. After a while I was getting $430 per, not bad dough for a twenty-one-year-old dropout in 1985. (Plus, I was still writing the high-minded wrestling stuff. One could not live by smut alone. Spiritually, I mean.) And they let us invoice them in half-book increments, so if one week I wrote only half a book, I would still get paid. On the honor system. They were very good people that way.

They also had an enormous tabby cat with about twenty-five extra toes. His name was Handsome, but everyone called him Kitty Porn.

It was Christmas, and they had a lovely party for all their writers, which turned out to be a weird lot of young punks and old queens, lit majors down on their luck, and bored housewives who wrote prose of a previously unimaginable prurience, so depraved that even veteran smut writers blushed when they dared read it. The soiree was low-key but well catered, and queer as could be, with smoked salmon (the good stuff, not the pink plastic crap they serve at office parties these days), champagne, and ladyfingers. Everyone got a Christmas bonus, prorated on how long you had been there. I had only worked there for about three weeks, and had probably finished writing two books. It took a little while for me to really get up to speed. I think I got a hundred dollars, and I was over the moon.

I had to write every day, or I'd never hit the book-a-week quota. It meant at least acting like a professional writer and showing a little discipline. Hungover, no sleep, lazy, stoned, problems at home, felt like playing hooky and fucking off to the ball game—no matter what, I had to put my head down and write or I wasn't going to get paid that week. Worse, I'd lose any momentum I might have built up toward putting the polish on another groundbreaking paean to fuzzy handcuffs and butt plugs. You had to get up a good head of steam and drive hard from Chapter One until "they lived happily ever after."

To do this, you needed a guide of some kind. Like the man said, they wanted books with *plots*. Beginnings, middles, and ends. In academic terms, *a premise, a conflict*, and *resolution*.

To wit: Little Miss Muffet sat on her tuffet, eating her curds and whey. (There's your *premise*.) Along came a spider and sat down beside her (*conflict!*) and scared Miss Muffet away (*resolution!*). Of course, the story could have ended up with the spider sucking the brains out of Miss Muffet's head, or with Miss Muffet fellating the spider on top of the tuffet. But there you have it—everything you need to write your own bestseller.

All of these books, no matter what the perversion, fetish, or felony, were based on the same formula played in three acts, just like a nursery rhyme. It went something like this: Miss Muffet, always a bit fearful of the ways of the world and fearful of losing her virtue, starts out playing hard to get, before she finally acquiesces and gives it up to the spider. And then all hell breaks loose. For example, in *Busting Susan's Cherry*, Susan was, can you guess? A virgin! Did you guess that she was a very (very) *sexy* virgin? And that the fellas were just lining up for the honor of introducing her to the joys of womanhood? But Susan just wasn't ready. First base, second base . . . maybe some unsteady petting, a couple of fumbling blow jobs . . . And then one night, out behind old Mrs. McLeary's barn, or in the backseat of Zack's hot rod, or, well, you get the picture . . . and then . . . *she just can't get enough.* It's a slippery slope—one good fuck, and suddenly Susan is a raging slut on a full-time quest for summer sausage. By the end of the book, even the pimply-faced benchwarmers on the junior varsity badminton team were enjoying the pleasures of Susan's newly liberated loins.

It was always the same. Cindy didn't want to be tied up. "Oh, no. I'm not like that!" And then the Heavy Metal Band shows her the joys of bondage and barre chords—*and she just can't get enough.*

Each book was coded, depending on its particular niche. For example, YC was Young Cherries. LB was Lesbian Fantasies. IT was Incest Tales. Books were assigned according to a master production schedule, which presumably echoed the ebb and flow of a sophisticated marketplace and the demands of a discriminating readership. Everyone wrote everything; those were the rules of the house. I even wrote a couple of gay titles like *Frankie and Johnny* and *His Black Boyfriend.*

When I first got assigned *His Black Boyfriend,* I balked. What the fuck did I know about gay sex? "Well," the editor said, "you got a hole, and you got a pole, and that don't change. Now sit down and write your fucking book." Okay, Skip. Whatever you say.

I sat there and looked at the screen for a while, until inspiration came to me like a heavenly vision: *His Black Boyfriend* would be the adventures of Mr. T and Hulk Hogan—Tito and the Champ I would call them—and their match at the first WrestleMania, set against a greasy pastiche of locker-room ass play. After that epiphany, the book wrote itself. Fifty thousand words later, I was sitting on an interracial homosexual *obra maestra* that not only exploited the lovely chiaroscuro of black-on-white gay love through carefully crafted descriptive language and stunningly tender imagery, but also managed to pretty soundly bitchslap that chump Hogan.

And the hits just kept on coming. I had even made it into *Screw,* the notoriously obscene scum sucker of the publishing industry, which was always a lot funnier and hipper and more political than most people realized.

Writing for *Screw* was a gas. The paper was going great guns in those days: they had large, well-staffed offices and a bull pen of great writers. Their parties were legend. Al Goldstein, the founder, editor in chief, television star, corpulent media whore, and vociferous loudmouth, was like a rock star in the publishing world, and he was so filthy and reckless regarding whom he would attack in *Screw* and on his television show, *Midnight Blue*, that even other pornographers avoided him like a summons server.

I adored him. Goldstein was a renegade of the 1960s counterculture. He hated hippies but claimed the Yippies among his heroes. He was an old-school New York Jew, an admirer of Lenny Bruce and Groucho Marx, very smart and very funny. *Screw* was an inky weekly tabloid, part free-form Baedeker for libertarian hedonists, left-wing sex addicts, and hipster comic geeks, and part PennySaver for transvestite hookers. It seemed that they would print *anything*. They were fearless. Along with the most abject, unglamorized porn shots that would make any normal person puke (a reaction to the middle-of-the-road airbrush jobs in *Playboy*), the mag was filled with cut-and-paste composites of the president of the United States taking it up the ass and antiporn crusaders sucking cock (more than anything, Al hated hypocritical politicians and moralists), plus poison-pen hate rants against anyone who crossed Al wrong, from hot dog vendors to airlines. He had been arrested nineteen times on obscenity charges and found guilty only once, in 1971, for showing pubic hair in his magazine. He won a major lawsuit brought against him by Pillsbury after he had shown their Doughboy mascot shtupping the "Doughgirl." (Goldstein: "She had a yeast infection!") Thanks to Al, the right to parody corporate logos is now protected speech. Operating with more disregard for authority than even *Hustler* (which stole freely from *Screw*), and despite any discernible concern for the reader's ability to use *Screw* for nonprocreative acts, *Screw* pushed the First Amendment to its outermost limits. It was just the kind of rag I wanted to be part of. Considering the crap I was churning out at the Factory, I felt like a real corporate ladder climber.

The first thing I wrote for *Screw* was a *Star Trek* satire called "The Captain's Log." I followed that with a profile of miscreant punk rocker GG Allin, legendary for beating up audience members and defecating onstage.

GG was the Bizarro World Liberty Valance, a man whose reality scorched the myth. No matter how many stories were told of his excesses—the violence, the bloodshed, the onstage suck jobs, gigs that wound up with audience and star in the hospital or hoosegow—they could never approach the very real white-knuckle terror and bad vibes that were the invariable by-products of his shows. Even his best gigs rarely lasted more than a few songs before fights broke out, the power was turned off, and GG was making a fast exit to escape getting his head caved in by angry villagers wielding torches and tire irons.

Musically, GG was an unadorned between-the-eyes punk with a ringing theme of hard-core self-destruction, rough sex, booze, and drugs. His masterpiece, *Seven Songs About Ass-Fucking, Butt Sucking, Cunt Licking and Masturbation*, was a fucked-up, fuzzed-out mess, with hints of country and a full bouquet of extreme pain. The guitar solo in "Needle Up My Cock," a viciously high-pitched one-note workout, was particularly painful. "Drink, Fight, and Fuck" could have been the anthem for a generation.

There was always some young Turk who wanted to book GG and make his bones by promoting the most notorious man in punk rock. Everyone had heard the stories, but no one ever believed it would happen to them. And then the show would start, the shit would start flying, and everyone involved would be deathly sorry that they got out of bed that day. GG was the one man in show business who would alienate even his best fans. It usually took only a few minutes before someone in the front row would have a microphone-shaped hole in his head, his teeth on the floor looking for a new home.

Mykel Board, a longtime *Maximum Rock 'n' Roll* writer and fellow author of underground classics, had introduced GG and me the night of the infamous Cat Club show. GG's band for this fiasco in the making consisted of New York indie rock royalty, including members of Sonic Youth and Dinosaur Jr. They had barely finished the first number before GG was slinging shit and broken glass in all directions, the fire marshal was screaming for heads, and the audience was fleeing for the exits.

GG agreed to meet me in Boston the next week to do the story for *Screw*. (He lived in Hooksett, New Hampshire, a cow town near Manchester, where he occasionally drove a laundry truck—a job he loved, since it fed directly into his fetish for smelly panties.)

He met me at the bus station in a white Trans Am driven by one of his many scumbag sycophants. Between the two of them, they were wearing enough eye makeup to have supplied Tammy Faye Baker for twelve lifetimes.

We took off for the Combat Zone, Boston's sorry old strip of porn parlors and go-go bars. I took some pictures of GG in a dumpster trying to pleasure himself while looking at the pictures in *Screw*. Failing to accomplish the task at hand, he used the paper for more practical purposes.

Most other magazines would banish their freelancers to the far reaches of unemployment hell for even suggesting that they take pictures of the world's most disgusting punk rocker wiping his ass with their magazine. *Screw* encouraged it.

Afterward, we hunkered down in a bar to talk. GG was actually very charismatic, smart, and funny. He could be quite charming, even while smashing a beer bottle over his head for a cheap laugh. He was ecstatic about being in *Screw*. No one had ever written a serious article about him before. And we had a few things in common: we were both a lot more interested in the Rolling Stones and the New York Dolls, for instance, than in the prevalent punk rock of the day. We drank Jim Beam like water. We loved Hank Williams and worshipped Jerry Lee Lewis.

Beyond all of the outrage, GG actually adhered to a cogent philosophy of Rock 'n' Roll as Creator and Destroyer. It was rock 'n' roll that had made him a nightmare: he was everything Ma and Pa America ever warned you about. Fuck phonies like Alice Cooper or Lou Reed, GG Allin was *the* Rock 'n' Roll Animal. He believed this with his heart and soul, and despite his constant threats to kill himself onstage, he reveled in it.

We got good and drunk, and somewhere along the line we agreed that I should write some songs for him and play the drums on his next record.

Just in case I was getting ahead of my station in life, hobnobbing with aristocrats like GG, *Screw* also kept me on the peep-show beat, scouring Forty-second Street (then still known as "The Deuce") for the best and worst in gutter entertainment.

Once a month I'd take a walking tour of the neighborhood to see if any new filth palaces had opened or closed, and I'd adjust the Naked

City listings at the back of the magazine accordingly. If I felt particularly strongly about any establishment, I might dock it or award it another "erect penis," which stood in for stars in our ratings system.

In l'Age d'Or, before Rudy Giuliani whored the block to Disney, there were peep shows and dirty bookstores every few feet. Some places had actual live sex shows, mostly junkies trying (and failing) to get it on behind a Plexiglas screen. There were also "private fantasy booths," where, separated by a partition, one could enjoy the eclectic proclivities of one's very own stripper. Everything was paid for in tokens, twenty-five cents or a buck at a time. I remember reporting on the closing of the city's last "open window" peep show, where one was supposed to (presumably; I'm actually far too prudent to have ever found out for sure) interact with the "girl" on the other side of the window. If time ran out before stuffing another token in the slot, a metal shade would slam down like a guillotine. I shed a tear whenever I think of those days.

I was also writing a lot of letters, of the "Dear Penthouse" variety. You know the type: *Dear Penthouse, I never really believed the letters in your magazine were real until one day last week when I got on the crosstown bus. There was only one free seat, and it happened to be next to the prettiest girl I have ever seen. She was wearing . . .*

Letter writing was a great racket. I know a lot of people who got started in the business that way. First-person sexual adventures were common fodder in every men's mag on the stands, and I had met a few editors who needed stuff. It seemed like there were always column inches to fill, and I could churn it out fairly effortlessly.

Screw, of course, wanted complete filth, the sleazier and more outrageous, the better. I was paid fifty bucks a pop for a seven-hundred-word My Scene column, allegedly readers' tales of finding love in unexpected places.

My first story was written from the point of view of a Sinatra-loving cabbie who pretended to be a headbanger and wore a Bon Jovi T-shirt when he picked up slutty, spandexed hair hoppers coming out of heavy metal clubs. After that I was a college student who bought himself a crack whore with ten bucks in change. I picked up women at pro-choice rallies by pretending to "care," and I was a chubby chaser who would offer fat women food for sex. ("Come on back to my place, I've got some roast beef, a cheese log, some pies . . .") Nothing was too low, too base, or too sleazy for *Screw*. I have been a sex-crazed woman climbing the career ladder by blowing the board of directors, and a ninety-year-old man dry humping a ninety-year-old woman in a wheelchair. I have orchestrated drug-and-sex orgies with unwashed hippie chicks, and I got the best head of my life from a toothless homeless woman in exchange for a pint of cheap liquor.

When I had moved up the food chain and actually did write for *Penthouse Letters*, they always got my best stuff. For the money they were paying—two grand for a long letter—you had better believe it. I wrote "communiqués from abroad" and I always took my time with them, carefully plotting stories that arced over several steamy scenes in exotic scenarios before the Big Payoff. Even when getting into extremely graphic detail, I tried to avoid sex scenes that were purely blow-by-blow nonsense of the He-Did-This, She-Did-That variety. Ambience, texture, and thoughtful descriptions of the tactile experience, tastes, and smells were very important. What did her stockings feel like when you touched them? What did her perfume smell like—cheap, expensive, sweet, like Lysol? Or did she just smell of cigarettes and booze? How old was she? What kind of accent did she have? The dialogue rang true, colored with foreign phrases and local slang. The geography was spot-on. If I said there was a hotel on the Boulevard St.-Germain, you could count on its being there. All of these stories were based in some part on reality, on some adventure, some tryst that I had in my travels, and the stuff I made up I fact-checked scrupulously. It would take a couple of days to write one of these letters properly. I respected that paycheck, and I respected the editor who called on me to deliver a first-class job.

But by far the article I enjoyed writing most for *Screw* was a comprehensive review of condoms. A firsthand user's guide, this was the kind of research a young man lives for. I went to Rite Aid and grabbed one package of everything they had in the rubber department, which was a pretty surprising variety of studded, ribbed, lubed, extra-strength, extra-big, extra-lubed, colored, and flavored condoms, something for every taste. Plus, of course, the sheepskin models, which I always thought were pretty icky. My girlfriend was horrified when I came home with a giant sack of condoms and announced that I needed a research assistant. But not as horrified as the young Korean girl at the pharmacy who sold them to me. She looked at me as if I were some kind of monster when I dumped two hundred dollars' worth of prophylactics on the checkout counter. I just shrugged and told her I was having a party.

The girlfriend survived the extensive field test, although I do remember her laughing at me, probably just to keep from crying, when I modeled an exceptionally scary studded number that I thought had potential. I think I got paid $175 for that story. Plus the condoms, of course.

3

POSSESSION OF HASHISH IS PUNISHABLE BY DEATH!

I grew up, completely unsupervised, in a New Jersey suburb, just a thirty-minute train ride out of Manhattan. My parents separated, with extreme prejudice, when I was twelve, just in time to facilitate feverish teenage rebellion fantasies and an ugly predisposition toward anything offering even the remotest pleasures of mind expansion and liver damage.

They had no truck being together, my parents. My father was on a down-to-earth nature kick, collecting pricey Native American pottery and wooden ducks. My mother collected designer handbags and increasingly garish pantsuits from Saks Fifth Avenue. Neither of them had any taste. And they had nothing in common, except they hated each other. Well, they had their kids—my younger twin brothers, and me. But they weren't going to let a few bumps in the road like us get in the way of their shit storm and vitriol. My father put some things in a bag and moved to an apartment one town over.

My mother was left incapable of controlling her rage. Look up "acrimony" in the dictionary, and you'll see a picture of her, screaming my father's name and threatening to cosh him over the head with her trendy Prince tennis racket, the one with the oversize sweet spot. And my father really raked her over the coals. What she did for "acrimony," he did for "parsimony." Their settlement took *years*.

As if by magic, pot appeared when I was fourteen, illicit and plentiful and harboring promises of revolution and a better world far beyond my own. I couldn't wait to try it. I was working as a volunteer at a

March of Dimes–sponsored haunted house that was set up in a shopping mall. It was the biggest bunch of potheads ever assembled in the name of charity, a great gig for the nascent stoner. I loved getting high, putting on the faux Alice Cooper makeup, and greeting people with my overwarmed Bela Lugosi impersonation. We had one of those sound effects records with thunderstorms and creaking floors. There were black lights everywhere, lots of skull candles, and a real coffin that people would have sex in after hours.

Sometimes I would get to be a "plant"—a guy who walked in and paid with the regular tour—and at the end, in the execution room, I would get pulled out of the crowd and tossed into the electric chair. The strobe light would stutter and then black out, and my face and hands would glow from the clear glow-in-the dark makeup I was wearing. Someone would light a match and blow it out quickly to get the smell of burned sulfur in the air.

Working at the haunted house, I learned a little about makeup and stagecraft, and how to roll a killer joint. It was 1978, and conveniently, there was a head shop next door. In 1978 there was always a head shop next door.

Drug paraphernalia was at a wonderfully creative peak. There were Power Hitters, soft plastic canisters into which you would insert a lit joint and then squeeze a tornado's worth of smoke directly into your lungs. The best ones were festooned with ersatz band logos, like "Led Zeplin" or "Arosmith." The Buzzbee was a tribute to American engineering: it was a Frisbee retrofitted with a pipe in the center so you could take a hit and toss it to the next lucky player. The Concert Kit was first aid for stoners, a self-contained system of rolling papers, lighter, mini-pipe, extra screens, and roach clip. You wouldn't dream of going to the Bowie show without one.

Roach clips were de rigueur—either an alligator clip, the kind used in home electronics projects, with a large pink feather attached, or a pair of silver hemostats stolen from the local emergency room. And I shouldn't neglect the fine folks at U.S. Bongs, who were doing lovely things with acrylics that year. Their multicolored, multichambered water pipes (held together with miles of surgical tubing) were a marvel to behold. I longed to own one, but I figured it would be best if I got my own apartment first. A four-foot bong did not qualify as stealth technology, the first line of defense for the toker-in-training.

Fashionwise, patched jeans, rainbow iron-ons, and coke-spoon necklaces were what the well-dressed suburban burnout was sporting that season, and every head shop came equipped with a T-shirt press manned by a pimply-faced Yes fan trying in vain to cultivate a lip brow, as well as a display case of poorly crafted silver jewelry maintained by a flat-chested hippie chick who stank of patchouli and yearned to ride horses.

There was also, always, a collection of *High Times* magazines.

High Times was amazing, a ticket to a whole new world. One issue had a big tit covered in chocolate splashed on the cover, and featured a detailed story about drugs as aphrodisiacs. Typically, the centerfold unveiled mountains of Acapulco Gold, voluptuous blond hash balls from Nepal, shimmering slopes of Peruvian flake, or miles of Thai Stick. There were ads for "lettuce opium" and cocaine grinders; "peace pipes," "pinch hitters," and "snow screens"; *The Complete Psilocybin Mushroom Cultivator's Bible*; kits to make hashish from shake weed; Jimmy Carter "Presidential Snorters"; nasal douches; gram scales, high-end stereo components, sex toys, fake IDs, and the "Official Dealer McDope Dealing Game." I immediately developed a lifelong crush on the JOB rolling papers girl.

How could this even exist, this miracle of lifestyle journalism? I brought home a copy and put it under the mattress along with a few issues of *Penthouse* I had swiped from my father before he split. Porn and drug mags. Classic contraband. In my case it was prophetic.

I loved smoking pot. All that hoo-ha about opening the Doors of Perception was absolutely true: When you were high on marijuana, the absurdities of authority and hypocritical American morality were laid bare before your bloodshot eyes. Monty Python suddenly made more sense than the evening news. And Chips Ahoy cookies, when mashed into strawberry ice cream, could unlock the pleasure center of your brain. No wonder the government didn't want anyone getting stoned (except from drugs on their approved schedule, of course).

I got high every day—before school, after school, during school, whatever. There was no problem being stoned around adults; the teachers didn't care or were too stupid to notice, and my parents were never around. There was never anyone to scrutinize me when I came home, no evenings in front of the TV or "quality time" to kill my buzz. It's amazing I didn't contract scurvy when I was seventeen. For four years I survived on the frozen pizza my mother routinely left for my brothers and me to make "family dinner."

In the mornings, when I did see my mother, it was a nightmare. The yelling was unbearable, damaging, the bitterness and hatred palpable. Most of it was intended for my father, but since he wasn't there, it was aimed squarely at me, the largest male target within shouting range.

I felt bad for my mom. It couldn't have been easy with three kids. But the twins were preppy little cream puffs who never crossed the tracks, and I caught the brunt of it. (Years later, they would thank me for clearing the way for them, what with my Scorched Earth Policy. By the time they were old enough to come home drunk from some dim-witted prom, my mother would just groan in defeat.)

It was horrible, some mornings bordering on *Mommy Dearest* histrionics, with lots of screaming and crying and the occasional swinging of coat hangers. I promise, this is no exaggeration. I think my friends had an idea that it was unpleasant at my house, but they probably had no clue that this kind of anger and ugliness could exist in such a seemingly mundane Jewish home. It was no wonder that the first thing I did when I left the house in the morning was smoke a joint.

I also drank everything in sight and spent a preponderance of time getting wasted in the woods near our house. I snorted speed whenever I could score some—usually Black Beauties that I would cut open and crush into powder. A few times I woke up with my pillow covered in blood from cauterizing my nose with such cheap toxic crap (something I would definitely acquire a taste for). Then I would have to throw out the pillowcase and go to Bamberger's to try to find a matching one to replace it. Usually, though, I just chucked it, and the invariable result was my mother, even more confused and agitated than normal, screaming, "Where are all my pillowcases?"

There was a lot of pain in that house. Also hideous white carpeting and furniture that was just "for company," although none ever showed up.

My first hit of acid was a blue microdot. Later it came in different colors—pink, and orange—the legendary Double Barrel Sunshine. I loved it, although I am not sure that fifteen-year-olds have much business stumbling around the schoolyard on LSD.

By the time I was sixteen, I had found a decent group of similarly middle-class Jewish friends who had finally come around to the joys of underage drinking and smoking dope. Now I didn't have to spend as much time playing pinball at the shopping mall, looking for other delinquents who wanted to get wasted. I could just go over to someone's house—someone who my parents actually approved of—get ripped, and laugh at *their* parents' bad taste. That, too, was liberating.

We had prolific weekend beer-and-pot parties. It was amazing how in those days they would just give high schoolers beer. Here, kid, have a keg. Twenty bucks. Bring it back tomorrow.

After school we would get stoned and rehearse whatever band we had at the time. There were Jason and the Argonauts, the Tastebuds, and the Electric Bowling Trophy, named after a real, honest-to-goodness electric bowling trophy that had become an object of stoned fascination for us. We played Creedence covers, some Stones stuff, Elmore James, and the Who, for block parties and keggers.

We dropped acid and went to Grateful Dead concerts, which, depending on how strong and clean the acid was, could be pretty interesting. Certainly without the drugs it would have been a complete waste of time. But for a sixteen-year-old, a Dead show was definitely a happening, an open-air drug mart and freak fest. I liked it when Jerry Garcia sang slow, pained versions of Dylan songs, and when they got into a heavy, trippy vibe, even if most of Jerry's guitar solos were strictly for the birds, especially if you had been listening to Miles Davis or Ornette Coleman. And that other guy, Bob Weir, has got to be the Single Most Useless Guy in the History of Rock. He was never any good. But that's what my acidhead pals were into, and I was extremely enthusiastic about eating those little paper tabs of mindfuck, so I could definitely be counted in for the ride.

I discovered that we could get into the old Lone Star Café in Greenwich Village without ID, and I led the charge to see an incredible cavalcade of blues musicians: John Lee Hooker, Buddy Guy and Junior Wells (who were still a team), Albert King, and Albert Collins, and at Tramps on Fifteenth Street we would go see (my favorite) Big Joe Turner—the last of the great Kansas City blues shouters—and the sublime, fezzed slide-guitar master from Chicago, J. B. Hutto.

In the afternoons I got stoned and went to the Museum of Modern Art, a paradise of melted clocks and high-minded practical jokes perpetrated by an international drinking society of miscreants who called themselves Dada—their way, I figured, of flipping off the squares. They were my first heroes.

I also had another group of pals who weren't buying into what they called "that hippie blues shit." These guys were tougher and weirder. They wore spiked hair and had biker-style chain wallets. They were into pills and punk rock. The Bowling Trophy boys stayed as far away from them as possible—they *hated* punk rock. These guys were always bringing their guitars and amps over to my basement, where my drums were set up, to attempt Sex Pistols, Clash, and Ramones covers for an audience of ourselves. We took a stab at "Kick Out the Jams" one day, and I made my star turn putting a microphone stand through the drop ceiling. I covered the hole with an old Elton John poster that was lying around. I was starting to get some very big, very bad ideas.

Getting busted for smoking pot out behind the parking lot next to the school was inevitable. And now my mother was sure that I was the Bad Seed. To her suburban brain—easily addled by even the most harmless sort of teen rebellion (she began fibrillating wildly when I got my ear pierced)—I might as well have been caught hot-wiring her Caprice Classic with a dirty syringe. Of course it was my father's fault. She had never asked for Satan's Child.

After I got snagged smoking dope and was suspended for a couple of days (which I spent high on Valium I stole from my grandmother's medicine cabinet), there was a large-scale meeting with a team of guidance counselors, local drug pigs, and the funereal parents of about half a dozen kids who had also been caught in the act. My folks were making a rare "joint" appearance, ha, ha, which hadn't happened since my bar mitzvah, when under the cosmic weight of Serious Jew Guilt, they put on their game faces (and incredibly bad clothes) and tried not to kill each other in front of their icky gold chain–wearing friends who had ostensibly gathered to watch me become a man. My party looked like a mid-budget 1970s porno film, without the sex.

"We're here to educate you about the dangers of marijuana," began one smug, fat fucker, an obese guidance counselor who looked as if he had just finished eating a couple of seventh-graders with all the fixin's.

And then they proceeded to haul out every fear-mongering wife's tale about weed that has ever been propagated in the name of God and Country.

"Do you know that drug pushers put *heroin* in the marijuana so they can get your kids hooked on hard drugs?"

Oh, good Lord, was I really going to have to sit still and listen to this bullshit? "That's simply not true," I protested. This did not endear me to the gathered group of parents, self-righteous educators, and law-enforcement flunkies, now vibrating as one in a sick-making display of antidrug piety. I thought I was going to throw up. Or get my ass kicked by someone's mom.

A roly-poly police officer in a wrinkle-free blue uniform filigreed with shiny brass buttons offered this old canard: "Marijuana makes men grow breasts."

"That's not true!" I railed. I got the *malocchio* from every brain-washed parent in the room. I decided to keep my mouth shut before one of the cops shot me.

"Marijuana mutates your DNA."

"Marijuana makes you impotent."

"Marijuana leads to a life of crime."

This was getting tedious. The chief guidance counselor, an unen-durably pompous Bill Cosby wannabe with a V-neck sweater and a bow tie (and there is nothing worse than an administrator with a sweater and bow tie), who actually spoke with his nose at a 45-degree angle to the horizon, began his showstopping soliloquy.

"In Arab countries," he began, "possession of hashish is punishable by death!" Insert music here. "Because they know that marijuana and hashish destroy people's wills! Their will to fight! That is why Israel won the Six Day War."

At this point even my father knew he was being pissed on. "No," he chimed. "That's because we are the Chosen People!" And he marched out. The Israeli army would have been proud. I certainly was.

But there was so much steam pouring out of my mother's ears that her head sounded like the lunch whistle at the rock quarry where Fred Flintstone used to work. The rest of the room sat in awestruck silence, jaws on the floor.

Yeah, I was a dead man. It would be a while before I could hang out with any of those kids again. Like never.

But this was by far the coolest thing I have ever seen my father do, although now he claims not to remember it. For a moment there, he was my hero.

Given my high school transcript, now stamped with a scarlet "M for Marijuana," it was somewhat of a miracle when I was accepted into the New York University film school. But I had done very well on the SATs and was a Merit Scholarship finalist. That, plus a passel of Super-8 garden-tool murder movies I had made (not to mention my role as president of the Film Club, a half-assed dope-smoking consortium I had invented solely for beefing up my high school résumé) were enough for me to eke past the gatekeepers at NYU, which was a damn fine thing because it was the only school I had applied to. If I wasn't accepted, I was prepared to get a job and move into Manhattan anyway. Anything to get out of that fucking house. Forget all the drugs; my parents were really screwing up my head.

When I got the letter from NYU, my mother was relieved, but typically, she did not share my delight. This woman could find misery and strife in a rainbow. "I wish you would go to school for something you could use," she would tell me, and sigh with disgust. My father was quick to remind me that "no one ever makes it in the film business."

For some reason, the dean of the film department took a shine to me, and he would call me up to his office to chat fairly regularly. He told me that he thought I had talent and he wanted to encourage me. I had to be flattered. I don't think a lot of freshmen were getting face time with the dean. I think he liked that I was a musician—he had played B3 organ behind Otis Redding once, and I was very impressed with that, too. He was also an adherent of Meher Baba, the guru who did not speak for forty-four years and who counted Pete Townshend of the Who as his most famous follower. The dean had suggested that I might find some "answers" in Baba's writing, but frankly, I found more answers in *The Who Sings My Generation*.

The dean emphatically did not share my enthusiasm for films like *Dirty Harry* and director Don Siegel. "He is an *action* director," he would tell me patiently, as if he were speaking to a child, while handing me a book about Elia Kazan.

A lot of the stuff I was being marginalized for liking—surf music, punk rock, martial arts epics, gangster movies, gore fests, the talking ape genre—would later be co-opted by mainstream Hollywood and finally allowed into the canon by snooty cinephiles trying to keep up with their pop culture counterparts, but in 1982 at NYU, since I didn't think *Rules of the Game* was the best movie ever made and my father wasn't an industry Jew bequeathing me some sort of legacy as the next Spielberg, I was starting to get the notion that I didn't belong. It did not augur well that my idea for a winning student film was a violent skinhead zombie flick.

The star of my first picture would be my best pot-smoking buddy, Dave Insurgent, singer for anarchist "peace punk" band Reagan Youth.

Reagan Youth was hugely popular, one of the first and best of the New York City thrash bands. Befitting his role as a hard-core matinee idol, Dave's idea of prêt-à-porter was combat boots, a Che Guevara T-shirt, and chains hanging off of torn military fatigues, crowned by the kind of dreadlocks that only a nice Jewish boy from Rego Park, Queens, could cultivate. Onstage Dave led the charge, singing "We Are Reagan Youth," doing a rigid goose step, and tossing off Nazi salutes like the bastard child of Charlie Chaplin and Frankenstein's monster.

No matter how ironic it was meant to be, all that Sieg Heiling would not have pleased his parents, who were Holocaust survivors. Fortunately, they had no real idea of what Dave was really up to, except that when it came to contemporary preppy fashions, he had somehow missed the boat. He once took me out to Queens to meet them. Dave's mom made us Dave's favorite, fried eggplant, sliced thin and crispy. It was delicious. But the real highlight was his dad's home movies of professional wrestling from the early 1950s. He was so proud. He had come to America and had seen the great Gorgeous George at Madison Square Garden!

Gorgeous George, of course, was wrestling's first sissy superstar, a bad guy of Alpha Centauri magnitude. In the 1940s and '50s, when professional wrestling dominated the brand-new medium of television, he was the most famous man in America. He wore lavish fur coats and had a valet who would attend to his long blond tresses with a silver-handled horsehair brush and spray him with lilac perfume from an atomizer bulb. Fans packed arenas to watch him prance around and, they hoped, get his faggot ass stomped. He got so much heat from audiences that he had to travel with armed bodyguards. George was a direct influence not only on Liberace, Elvis, Muhammad Ali, and Little Richard, but also on Bob Dylan, who called him "a man as great as his race."

After the wrestling movie, over Dave's strong protests, Dad showed us his other great opus, a film of Dave's bar mitzvah, circa 1976. He may have been proud of his home movies of Gorgeous George, but looking at pictures of his son reading the haftarah and dancing awkwardly with a roomful of unformed teenage girls, he was so filled with emotion that he cried. When it was time for scenes of Dave in a leisure suit holding court at a papier-mâché monstrosity called Dave's Disco Bar, I considered joining him.

Everything in Dave's world was measured on his proprietary, Dada-esque scale of "hard" and "soft." All-natural Tripple Berry juice was hard. Mayor McCheese was soft. (Dave was a vegetarian, hence things like juice, sprouts, and tofu were "hard." His greatest fantasy was to pick up a girl at the cafeteria salad bar.) Dave was a big fan of 1970s rock stupidity, way ahead of his time in the stoner irony department. Who did I think was harder, Uriah Heep or Gentle Giant? Who was softer, the bass player in Kansas or the bass player in Styx? I don't think there is anybody on the planet who could answer those questions, let alone have the strength to ponder them. But indisputably, Joe Franklin was the hardest.

Joe Franklin was a batty old talk-show host with the pallor of a wax dummy and hair like a jerry-rigged carport. Incoherent and nasal, Joe sounded like someone's brain-damaged uncle who had been given a TV show because no one knew what else to do with him. He spoke. Like this. "Our next guest is Bigger than Big. He is Big, Big, Big, Big, Big." Tiny Tim had been a guest on the show "Many. Many. Many. Many. Times."

Joe was a nostalgia freak, the self-declared King of Memory Lane. Once upon a time, Joe would always remind his audience—his show had run since before the Jack Paar days of television—he had a kid named Barbra Streisand on the show. More recently his guests would be old-time talent scouts with wide ties and hair growing out of their ears, animal trainers, grade-Z cabaret singers, and an endless parade of self-promoting weirdos who worked on Times Square, where Joe had a real Broadway Danny Rose kind of office, jam-packed with memorabilia, decaying film reels, and eight-by-tens of every Big Star (and loser) on the planet.

Joe was worshipped by a cult of sallow New Yorkers who grew up festering in the blue flicker of black-and-white TV. The Ramones loved him and were guests on his show. Ditto "Weird" Al Yankovic.

Dave would call me at 2:00 a.m. and demand that I wake up and turn the TV on to see some retard of a magician whom Joe had introduced as "a legend in the business" before bringing out a bug-eyed hair weave of an algebra teacher who moonlighted at kids' parties. "This guy is the hardest of the hard," Dave would declare.

On Halloween, our freshman year, we went to a costume contest hosted by Black Sabbath. If you showed up at Tower Records appropriately dressed, you'd get to meet the band, and the winners would get tickets to their show. Dave went dressed as the Grand Wizard of Wrestling. I went as a member of the Sun Ra Arkestra, a costume I built around my bright green high school graduation gown, presciently saved for exactly this purpose, topped off with a solar space hat I built out of a bathing cap and a package of knitting needles. Our pal Paula came along as a freestylin' heavy metal queen, with some moose antlers duct-taped to her head. Naturally, they loved us.

This was the Black Sabbath B Team. Ozzy Osbourne had been tossed out, too drunk and fucked-up to carry on, and replaced by Deep Purple front man Ian Gillan. Bev Bevan, once the drummer for the Electric Light Orchestra, had replaced Sabbath stick man Bill Ward, who was in no shape to play the drums with a professional rock 'n' roll band.

Dave brought along a Bible to get autographed, and when we got up to the table to meet the band and have our pictures taken for *Circus* magazine, they were only too happy to comply. We had, by far, the weirdest costumes they had ever seen.

Ian Gillan scrawled his name, followed by original Sabbath members Tony Iommi and Geezer Butler. When Dave got to Bev Bevan, he stopped. "Hey," he asked, "weren't you in ELO?" Bevan beamed. Someone was paying attention! "Then you can't sign," Dave told him. "You are too soft." They gave us all tickets anyway.

Our movie (we never called it a "film") was going to be called *Rock, Rebel, Rock* and it would be a post-apocalyptic punk rock spoof of

1950s Alan Freed rock 'n' roll movies like *Rock, Rock, Rock* and *Go, Johnny, Go!*

Dave would play teen idol Johnny Rebel, which was just the most contrived, idiotic, and obnoxious name we could come up with for our "James Dean Meets the Mummy" character. The gist of our story was this: Sometime in the indeterminate future, in Anytown, U.S.A. (the name of a popular Reagan Youth song), a sleepy little hamlet whose mayor was a brain in a dish, and whose chief of police was a ventriloquist dummy hooked up to an ominous mainframe computer, rock 'n' roll was about to be made illegal. The town had been besieged by a horde of skinhead zombies, and Johnny Rebel and his band the Rebels were getting the blame. Empowered by the Spliff of Great Knowledge, Johnny takes on the Monsters and saves the town. The Evil Brain and Scary-Looking Dummy are ousted; rock 'n' roll, and the world, are saved.

When I pitched this project in our production class—it had to be presented in front of students and approved by the professor—I was met with blank stares. Apparently, brains in dishes did not resonate with NYU undergrads as much as, say, *E.T.* What's your budget? was the first question. Fair enough. Well, we had an allotment of film and equipment time that came with the class. That, and a few bucks I could scrape up to keep everyone fed on cold cuts while we worked (and some reefer for the Spliff of Great Knowledge) was going to be it. We were going to shoot "reversal film" to save money. This was not un-heard of for low-budget student projects. Reversal film meant that the same film that came out of the camera is what you would edit and pro-ject. Normally you would use "negative film," make a print and edit that, then cut the negative to match and make another print. I didn't have the money for all of that lab work, and had no idea how to raise it. This come-shot of a film, a blast of brains in dishes, zombies, teenage punks, and all-knowing Rastas needed to be made *now*. Why compli-cate things?

I remember one of the other projects pitched in that class. Some-one wanted to make a film about her grandfather, this great man who even at seventy-six years old got up every day to jog. The budget was ten grand. The class cooed, the project was immediately approved, and I wanted to puke. I asked the girl where she got ten grand to shoot a portrait of an old man. "From the old man," she told me. Duh. This was not my world. I told my father I could use some help. He told me I needed to grow up. Some encouragement would certainly have helped, but the truth is that I was totally unprepared for college. I was neither humble nor hardworking enough to make it work.

I spent the summer of 1984 driving the chase car in a caravan of hippies, punks, and freaks, and performing a "comedy" act strategically designed to piss them off.

It was Dave's idea to bring me along on the Rock Against Reagan tour, a spin-off of the Rock Against Racism tours, one of the last hurrahs of the Yippies, the late-sixties poster boys for radical politics.

The Yippies boasted such heroes as Jerry Rubin and Abbie Hoffman. In 1968 they ran a pig for president (they actually had a real live pig, a pink one, named Pigasus) and were instrumental in creating havoc that year at the Democratic National Convention in Chicago. Dave was great pals with their remaining crew, who usually holed up at their *Dr. Caligari*–like safe house on Bleecker Street. He took a lot of the militant idealism in Reagan Youth from their legacy of lunacy and their seemingly undying dedication to undermining the United States government. They also organized the May pot parade, Dave's very favorite day of the year. He loved to smoke pot. He called it "busting corn," as in "let's go bust some corn." We were always busting corn, more often than not in five-dollar increments bought from a fake candy store on Avenue C.

Since I'd grown up on a steady diet of punk rock and 1960s counterculture, a grassroots rock 'n' roll tour to jar American youth out of their comatose state—and put the rest of the country on notice—made perfect sense to me.

I was far more terrified of the ultimate tragedy happening as a result of Reagan's Cold War arms race with the Soviets than I ever have been in a post-9/11 world. Reagan may have seemed like a nice guy—he was subversively charming and aw-shucks polite—and he had undeniably astonishing charisma, as if they had invented television just for him. But behind the scenes he was a venomous, frothing fanatic, seething with hatred, blind to a global AIDS epidemic, and balls-deep in a gooey love affair with Jerry Falwell and the Moral Majority. Reagan was a warmongering, minority-bashing despiser of all people poor, hungry, or sick; an enemy of women's rights, civil rights, and especially antitrust laws; an anti-environment just-do-whatever-the-fuck-you-want whore for big business; a smoke-and-mirrors trickle-down supply-side huckster who ratcheted up the national deficit to galactic proportions with tax cuts, unchecked nuclear proliferation, and a little help from the "Star Wars" antimissile dodge. He fostered a mind-numbing might-is-right culture of greed where Beemer-driving douche bags in alligator shirts ruled the roost and having a brain was not merely frowned upon but considered a liability.

I am also fairly certain that he was responsible for all those crappy synth-driven power ballads that became the cornerstone of corporate rock in the early eighties, although I couldn't prove it.

The Rock Against Reagan main tour vehicle was a 1972 International Harvester school bus with most of the seats torn out and replaced with mattresses. It was a teenage stoner dream. When we got to the West Coast, there was never less than a couple of shopping bags full of weed on board, donated by the Humboldt County Growers' Association.

I was driving a Ford Escort that someone needed moved from Washington to San Francisco and, thankfully, was in no great hurry to get it there—a fine thing, too, since it shook violently at sixty-five mph. It had to be the most unsafe vehicle ever to hump an American highway. I could have crushed it with my hands like a paper cup.

Dave had conscripted me to open the shows for Reagan Youth after witnessing my latest NYU talent-show outrage. Posing as a twisted Borscht Belt comedian, I didn't tell jokes so much as I just drunkenly barked the most tasteless, offensive shit I could come up with. "A bum stopped me on the way to work. So I fucked him up the ass!" Bada-boom! I was bombed, as was my friend Cindy, who sat behind me with a snare drum, cymbal, and lipstick smeared all over her face, punctuating my idiocy with sloppy rim shots. After sodomizing the homeless, I moved on to a series of dead Jew jokes ("I got six million of 'em!"). The reaction was better than I ever could have dreamed: a nearly instantaneous tsunami of flying drinks, and my old friends, the best and bravest of NYU's rent-a-cop program, trying to restore order. When I got hit in the head with someone's keys, I stood up on a table, and stealing a line wholesale from Iggy Pop (cf. *Metallic KO*, the third-greatest live album of all time), declared, "I AM THE GREATEST." That pissed everyone off even more than the Holocaust crack.

I am a big fan of the riot in the theater—Igor Stravinsky pulled that trick in Paris in 1913 when he premiered *Rite of Spring*, and Tristan Tzara caused pandemonium at a Surrealist rally in the 1920s when he declared that he would write the greatest poem of all time by pulling words out of a hat. But they were *smart* people. I was just an obnoxious teenager trying to piss off a roomful of matriculating sheep. It was like ringing a bell.

Dave loved it. One of his main messages with Reagan Youth had always been *Liberate yourself. Don't react—that's what they want you to do. You are being handled. You are being controlled. Do not be manipulated. Think for yourself.*

Playing among a crowd of earnest, humorless bands and dyed-in-the-wool liberal speakers who all sounded like they were reading term papers or articles right out of *The Nation*, I was about as welcome as a yeast infection. I wielded my green madras jacket, slicked-back hair, and fat cigar like talismans of great power. In front of thousands of people at the July 4 Rock Against Reagan rally in Washington, D.C., the joke took on an evil political bent. After a few cracks about assfucking indigents and advocating for the chemical deforestation of Nicaragua and El Salvador, a real sore spot among leftists in those Reagan years, I'd move into my fail-safe material: "Wanna end Apartheid? Then just kill all the blacks!" Bada-boom! In this case, the rim shot was hit by Rick, the Reagan Youth drummer, an African American punk rocker dressed like a down-market Jimi Hendrix, which should have been a hint that this was all a great big put-on. But the drinks and bottles just kept on flying.

We pulled this stunt in front of enormous crowds. In San Francisco, outside of the Democratic National Convention at the Moscone Center, where the Democrats were busy nominating yet another pathetic, unelectable team of schlubs in Walter "Fritz" Mondale and Geraldine "My Husband Is Not a Mobster" Ferraro, thousands came out to see a free show and rally headlined by the Dead Kennedys. A few weeks later we'd do it all again in Dallas, outside of the Republican Convention.

San Francisco was the first time I ever saw disposable plastic handcuffs. There were massive—legal—protests in the street, but the SFPD had zero patience for any such shenanigans. The cops rode modified dirt bikes, ripping through the crowd, picking off protesters and tossing them in the jug with abandon. It was hard to believe that in San Francisco, a town so liberal it makes New York City seem like Nuremberg, the local gendarmes hadn't developed any tolerance for marches and dissent. They were out to squash the freak show and keep it off the nightly news.

On the way to Texas, in Taos, New Mexico, Dave, Reagan Youth guitar player Paul Cripple, and I dropped some acid and spent the night in the natural hot springs that shot under the Rio Grande, laughing under a starry, luminous night sky. No self-respecting acidhead would have failed to be moved by the experience.

It made us thirsty.

"Do you think this water is radioactive?" This wasn't that far from where they used to test atomic bombs.

"Sure, but no more so than *we* are at this point."

We thought about that for a while and then drank from the river. Still, a beer would have been nice, so we headed back to the school bus, where there was an outside chance there were a few cold ones left in the cooler. (At one point I was so stoned that I had convinced myself of the existence of a natural beer spring. You could see it, right?)

On the way, we ran into the Peace Pole Guy, an Age of Aquarius drug casualty with a Moses-like beard and a seemingly endless supply of tie-dyed shirts who had been carrying (what else?) a "peace pole" around the country, praying for nuclear disarmament and, I am sure, many other positive things. Many. Many. Many. Positive. Things.

I actually liked him, he was a good guy, nice and sincere, even if he was a harsh reminder of just how far out of the galaxy LSD could take you. When we had almost made it back to the bus, Peace Pole Guy pulled up alongside us in his RV. The sun was up by now, and it was quickly approaching the brutal midday heat.

"You guys want some ice cream?"

"Huh?" It was like a million degrees out there.

"We raided a supermarket and we've got tons of ice cream and it's melting. Try some. It's delicious."

And that's how we found ourselves, stoned and beautiful, in the middle of the desert eating strawberry ice cream. It really doesn't get much better than that.

———

After our odyssey in the desert, dropping out of NYU was easy.

I called my mother from a pay phone on the corner of Sixth Avenue and Thirteenth Street, across from Original Ray's Pizza. She cried, and blamed my father. Then I called my father. He wished me good luck in my future endeavors. Then I went and got a job as a liquor delivery boy.

That gig lasted about two weeks, during which there was just one too many rickety old alcoholic queens letting his ratty bathrobe fall open so I could get a good look at his withered hose, as if I might go for it.

I took any number of shit jobs. Telemarketing, loading trucks, whatever—the three hundred bucks or so I was raking in from *Main Event* every month certainly wasn't kicking a rock star lifestyle. But I was a lot happier out of school; at least I felt more in control of my environment. I certainly didn't have to answer to anyone.

And then Bobo the Porn-Writing Clown showed up, opening the door to a career in the skin trade.

With my newfound fortune and fame as "Anonymous," author of America's filthiest pocket novels—and as an ambitious *Screw* correspondent—I was able to really live it up.

I spent a lot of time drinking at the Dugout, a classic old man's bar, which was dirt cheap. Bob the bartender gave us a buyback on seventy-five-cent mugs of beer every third round without fail. The building on Third Avenue and Thirteenth Street was razed (along with the Variety Photoplay next door, the last real downtown porno movie house) to make room for an appalling cookie-cutter condominium, but you can see it in the beginning of *Taxi Driver*. It's where Robert De Niro first picks up Jodie Foster.

One of the relics who drank there knew I was a writer of sorts, and he would rib me on the dregs of my chosen profession. He was from Lowell, Massachusetts, and claimed to have known Jack Kerouac. "He was a drunk," he bellowed from his perch at the end of the bar. "His wife used to hide his shoes so he couldn't go to the bar. He didn't believe a word he wrote. He was an asshole. He voted for Eishenhower. Writers," he never failed to add, dredging wisdom from his mug of half beer and half tomato juice, "are all full of shit."

4

TOP SECRET ACTION

One benefit of being a gun-for-hire porn writer is that I could take off and the job would be waiting for me when I got back. No one ever missed me. No matter how deft I was at twirling these ripping yarns of young lust and sodomy, the porn business just kept on truckin' without the benefit of my viscous prose. This was an industry that never valued art over craft. No one ever wanted it "good," they just wanted it Tuesday.

A year after signing on with Kramer, the new Sharky's Machine record was finally out and we were stumbling around Amsterdam looking for one of those funny coffee shops we had heard so much about.

We had a few hours to kill, just enough time to get good and stoned and then catch the train to Brussels for our first show, opening up for Soul Asylum, who along with Hüsker Dü and the Replacements, were part of the great Minneapolis renaissance that threatened to take over rock for about ten minutes in the late eighties. But none of us had the vaguest idea of what we were doing or even what we were looking for. After walking around the Amsterdam Centrum for an hour, the four hundred drinks I had on the flight had finally worn off, and we had to get something to eat before I keeled over and drowned in one of the canals that crisscross the city. We ducked into the first friendly looking café we found.

I suppose we should have twigged right away, what with the Rasta tricolors flying everywhere and Peter Tosh on the hi-fi, but it didn't register in any of our jet-lagged, untutored American brains.

There was a little sandwich bar and a coffee machine. That's all I needed. I asked for a menu. At least everyone spoke English.

Expecting to see a list of sandwich combos, fruit drinks, perhaps my old friend the frozen pizza skulking around waiting to be snacked on, I opened the menu and hallelujah! A stately pleasure dome I did decree—Kubla Khan, meet Cheech and Chong!

The menu was peppered with a dozen varieties of hashish, with samples attached in mini-ziplocks. There was Katama Gold, Zero Zero, Special Abraxas, Sticky Fingers. There may have been some Thai Stick. Moroccan brick hash, gold pollen, Lebanese, Afghani—some in balls, some in narrow strips, some in puffy, turdlike patties—and at the bottom was a sample of the "Nederlander Homegrown," the only weed offered that day. It was bright green and stank wonderfully. One gram cost just a few guilders, about two bucks.

Years later there would be a multitude of brain-battering herb, superstrains of mind-boggling marijuana harvested locally in massive grow rooms that would rival the International Space Station in cost and technology, but in 1987 it didn't seem as if anybody there wanted to smoke the weed—it was all about the sweet and sticky hash. But we loved our reefer, and at that price, we were going to have a good old-fashioned pot party. And some milk shakes and sandwiches and coffee, please. Oh, all right, we'll try some of the Moroccan Black, some of that Nepalese Blonde that I used to gawk at in *High Times*, and perhaps we should try one of those space cakes?

Defying all odds, we floated out of there with our navigational systems intact, managed to find the train station, and caught the train to Brussels.

Our party in Belgium collected us as we spilled out of the train. You could have seen us coming a mile away. Four stoned Yanks with guitars. They should have locked us up. "Had a nice time in Amsterdam, yes? Good. Now we try some Belgian beer." That was another little continental wonder that no one had bothered to tell me about.

Keep in mind that in those unenlightened times, pretty much the only imported beer you would ever see in the States was Heineken or Beck's, perhaps the odd bottle of St. Pauli Girl or Grolsch. Certainly there was none of that crazy Pink Elephant stuff that rang the bell at thirteen-percent alcohol and made you want to take your pants off over your head. This Europe thing was really starting to work for me.

MIKE EDISON

The venue was an old theater, just gorgeous, the kind of place we would hardly be allowed in back in the States. When we got there, Soul Asylum was just finishing their sound check.

While we were beside ourselves with glee, half drunk and high like baboons, the Soul Asylum boys were a study in road burn. It was the first show of our tour, and it was their last. They had been on the road for months, and they just wanted to go home to Minneapolis, listen to their Prince records on the banks of Lake Minnetonka, and watch ice hockey, or whatever it is that one does in Minnesota. They just rolled their eyes at the four rookies in Sharky's Machine.

To make matters matters worse, Motörhead was playing down the street. There were about six people in the audience that night. I would have gone to see Motörhead, too. But the thing of it was, the people who did come actually came to see *us*. They had our record. They liked it. They got it.

Somehow the Sharky magic worked in Europe, where being a bunch of misfits was actually an asset that set us apart from the idiots who all looked and sounded the same, wrapped in off-the-rack rock clichés. We didn't have the most fans, but the people who came out to see Sharky's Machine were oddly loyal. They felt that they could adopt us as their own; and given a chance to play in front of an appreciative crowd who weren't trying to bluntly pigeonhole us into being a punk band or a thrash band or a fucked-up blues band, we could really shine. After Brussels, the gigs were fantastic, almost all well attended and successful. It was an unbelievable adventure. In every town there was something new, some strange German sausage or artisanal beer, a new way to roll a joint with seven rolling papers and a block of hash the size of a tangerine. Everyone was extraordinarily kind to us. We got wasted every night, wandering around medieval cities and waking up in strange places.

I was having the time of my life. We never worked from set lists, and I would holler out the songs from behind the drums, twirling sticks, throwing bombs, putting on a Muppet show with Jim, who on-stage was a like a level-4 hurricane.

Unfortunately, offstage, he moved about as fast as the Great Pyramid of Cheops, lugging around a gigantic fake-leather suitcase that he had come to college with, the clunkiest, most unwieldy piece of shit ever taken on tour with a rock 'n' roll band, all the more confusing since he never seemed to have any clean clothes. I think it was filled with books. But that was Jim.

Alec also had some baggage. He never learned to make friends with the soundman, which is rule number one if you want to put on a great show. Every night, before the sound check even started, Alec would warn the poor guy behind the board, "DON'T TELL ME TO TURN MY AMP DOWN." We'd be in the club for about five seconds and already there would be a confrontation.

Volume is a wonderful thing, and we took pride in being loud. When we were playing at the top of our ability and really cranking, the whole thing could sound like a jet plane taking off in the club. We never had the luxury of carrying our own tech guy, but once we got going, and the sound guy understood what we were up to, it really wasn't all that complex. Most of them were professionals and had been mixing live bands every night of their adult lives. A lot of them don't want to blow the ceiling off of their clubs. And every band turns up their gear after the sound check; it's the oldest trick there is. But you had to give these guys a little room and work with them and get a balance onstage, or you'd end up sounding like crap. And you could forget about the monitor mix. Piss off the soundman, and you were doomed.

Tonia was great at leveling the vibe, and generally everything went okay. Alec meant well. He cared. He wanted to sound mighty. But a twenty-minute sound check could turn into an hour's worth of group therapy.

There was another slight snafu. At one of our shows we met our Dutch record company—a teenager who worked out of his parents' basement. Nice kid—had a small business licensing American records for the European market. He told me that he had cut a deal with Kramer for *Let's Be Friends* and had sent him a bunch of dough for the privilege of licensing it and releasing it on his label. That was news to us.

This was my first experience in dealing with a record company, and since we were all pals, I thought everything was on the up-and-up. We had no contract, but as far as I was concerned, we had no secrets, either, and it was such a small operation anyway, it wasn't like we were going to get caught in the cogs of some conglomerate. Dutch record boy was as furious as I was that the accounting for the European release had somehow fallen through the cracks.

MIKE EDISON

The next day we were doing an interview, and I had a few choice words to say about Mr. Kramer. It took Kramer only twenty-four hours after that to track us down and get me on the phone at a sound check. He sounded miffed.

"Do you really think you could call me a 'ratfucker' on Dutch National Radio and get away with it?" he screamed. "Fuck you guys, you're off the label!"

But at that point it didn't matter. We had just played to a sold-out bacchanal of a gig at the Ecstasy club in Berlin, and the freak who ran the place was insisting that he release our next project on his label, LSD Records. Sounded good to me.

"Speedy Gonzalez," as he called himself, was in love with Sharky's Machine and had gone to great lengths to prove his affection. He had been working his ass off for weeks before we got there. The Ecstasy club was packed; there were people outside who couldn't get in. We were on the radio. There were Sharky's Machine posters all over town. We had never had that kind of reception or response.

One of the bartenders asked me, "Sharky, do you need any special kind of women?"

Oh, this was too good to be true.

As it turned out, I didn't need him to pimp for me. There were lots of beautiful, tall German women at our show and at the party afterward. They all wore tons of eyeliner and looked like Nico. That night there was lots of what Speedy always called "Top Secret Action." It is still too soon to talk about it.

Two months after we had blundered into that coffee shop in Amsterdam, I arrived home wearing the shimmerless halo common to anyone suffering from brain damage and exhaustion on a molecular level. Necessity demanded innovation, and the Edison Cure, an ever-changing R_X for rock 'n' roll overdose, was born: I slept for a few days, ate a few steaks and a boatload of green vegetables (what is it with Europeans and their aversion to food that photosynthesizes?), listened to some restorative John Coltrane records, got some sunshine, went to a museum, and washed out my eyes with modern art. In a few days I was back in the New York Groove.

Once again I was making ends meet cataloging sexual peccadilloes and submission holds, living large as a low-budget bon vivant. For a short while I joined the Lunachicks, an all-girl glam-horror band who would eventually become stars in an alternate universe of rock 'n' roll shock and awe, but at the time they were just getting started, blossoming nicely into their *Babysitters on Acid* phase.

Perhaps you remember the old horror story that was incessantly and oh so seriously repeated when I was a kid? A couple, out on a date, calls home to see if everything is all right. The teenager in charge responds, "Sure, everything is fine. The baby is almost done." And this is why drugs are bad: when you are high, you mistake toddlers for turkeys. And yet never forget to preheat the oven to 450 degrees.

Glammed-up dolls that they were, the Lunachicks had a strict dress code. I know a lot of guys who get all nervous and fidgety when it comes to putting on eye makeup and a feather boa or two, as if a couple of coats of Max Factor were going to turn them into Capezio-wearing queers with a fetish for poodles and leather pants. But I can dig it. If it was good enough for Elvis, it was good enough for me. Anyway, I've got a macho streak a mile wide, and there's not really much chance of me going offside on the play. If you have ever seen me tucking into a plate of ribs like a pit bull going at it with a chew rag, you might reconsider Darwin. It is downright *paleo*. Why would I fear a little eyeliner? As it turns out, the girls loved it. I'd put on a little glitter, and suddenly bombshells who dressed like Bettie Page wanted to come home with me so we could take turns tying each other up.

I played one or two shows with the 'Chicks, and then we all agreed that I wasn't woman enough for the gig. Anyway, I was just a fill-in until they found someone more gender appropriate. And Sharky's Machine was busy playing and working on new material while we waited for Speedy Gonzalez to come through with some dough to make a new record. Everything was groovy.

Except that I had finally burned out on writing porn novels. My trick bag was empty. Every word weighed a ton. *See Mike write. See Mike write porn. Porn, porn, porn.* I felt as if I were being sucked dry by a select genus of horny leeches thriving on the salacious lexicon of lowbrow literature. You try recasting "He plunged his pulsating meat puppet between the quivering layers of her moist scissor cake" for the eight thousandth time. It made me want to drink drain cleaner or stab myself in the throat with a salad fork. Anything to break up the monotony of another 180 pages of artless crud. It had gotten so bad that I had even done a "search and replace" for the names in a long suck-and-fuck scene I had written months before. Instead of Tony and Maria knocking boots, all of a sudden it was David and Michelle. I had finally hit rock bottom: I was plagiarizing *myself*.

It was a relief to deep-six the pulp fiction. But with the landscape unfettered by tales of nymphomaniac cheerleaders (and the men who loved them), I had a clear view of a bleak future. Twenty-two years old and already in the grip of a deeply existential blues. "Former porn writer" looked even worse on the résumé than "porn writer." Where was I going?

Not into outer space, that was for sure. That dream had exploded when the space shuttle *Challenger* came crying out of the sky with a schoolteacher on board and NASA immediately jettisoned their next civilian-in-the-sky initiative, the Journalist in Space program, which I had enthusiastically applied for.

Like all boys of my generation, I had lived vicariously through the adventures of the Skylab astronauts. What could be a greater fashion statement than a bright orange NASA jumpsuit, with Velcro on the feet so you wouldn't float around the cabin and bang into the science officer? This was surely the first step toward moon colonies and space stations staffed by bosomy space kittens dressed in tinfoil hot pants and antigravity go-go boots. Interstellar sex with Barbarella and all of her friends? That was the Sacred Covenant of Technology. That was the Future of Man.

The application for the NASA Journalist in Space program came in a really swell folder decorated with a graphic of a fountain pen soaring through the solar system, and I filled it out earnestly. Clearly, I was the right man for the job. I was, after all, a pornographer *and* a wrestling beat writer. Yes, it would have taken a little vision from the slide-rule boys down at Cape Canaveral, but as far as I was concerned, that was exactly the kind of pioneering spirit that made America great. Walter Cronkite was too old, and Peter Jennings, the prohibitive favorite, was Canadian. Unfortunately, I'll never know how close I came to making the short list.

With my career as an astronaut on hold, I had few choices. I began to consider the last refuge of a scoundrel: going back to school.

I had two years' worth of credits from NYU in the bank, and maybe it was time to capitalize on them. I hate leaving things unfinished, and by now, without the pitfalls of freshman life, I felt that I had enough self-confidence to get the job done right. I wasn't going for the beer. License to drink all night and bring girls home with me was no longer a novelty. I didn't care about making friends with other students, whom I generally wrote off as multislacking pussies who lived soft lives delaying reality. I thought that a degree would be a means to an end, furthering my career as a journalist. I could see myself causing a furor in the White House press pool or running around the poppy fields of Laos with a Nikon, getting the scoop on the Golden Triangle heroin trade for *Life* magazine. I decided to trade up from NYU and apply to Columbia University. And then I'd have a real shot at flying the space shuttle, just as soon as they got the kinks worked out of it and got back to the plan of putting a reporter in orbit.

Right.

Meanwhile, back on Earth, Jeremy had been officially coronated as editor in chief of *Main Event*, and I had moved up the ladder accordingly, to associate editor. I had been writing for the magazine whenever I was around, and four of my alter egos still jammed the masthead under "Staff Writers."

One of the first things I did was tear into a new column, The Heart Punch, a monthly manifesto of misanthropy and smart talk. (Pundits take note: my version of the Heart Punch was an homage to former WWF champ Stan Stasiak, and not Ox Baker, as is commonly believed, although Baker, too, is an enormously admirable individual. Legend has it that he *killed* two people in the ring with his Heart Punch. He wore a T-shirt that said YOU WILL HATE ME, and is the author of the only cookbook written specifically for those elite gastronomes who are also wrestling fans.)

The Heart Punch was my mojo. "Open up and bleed!" I wailed, stealing another riff from Iggy, and waging a one-man war against the lunch-box-and-action-figure era of family-friendly professional wrestling. Gimme some juice, baby! Brutality and bloodshed for all! I championed men who used primitive can openers to carve their names on their opponents' faces. I advocated sainthood for Dick the Bruiser. And I put Jeremy squarely in my crosshairs. I called him a milquetoast writer, an apple-polishing practitioner of puff-piece journalism, the hand puppet of the WWF publicity department. "I have had it with your editorial abortions!" I seethed. "You are a menace to the entire Fourth Estate!! You wanna butcher any more of my pieces, yer gonna have to get through me first!! In a cage, or by the railroad tracks . . . Loser leaves town . . . Winner takes all!!!"

Jeremy blasted back on his editorial page. "Edison is a disrespectful lowlife drunk. This morning he arrived in my office with a flowerpot on his head. There is only one way to settle this feud. I accept your cock-eyed challenge! I will edit your face with my fist! See you in the ring, slimeball!!!"

Jeremy took to wearing a green visor and a pinstripe vest. Except for the fact that he was twenty-three years old, he looked like an ancient newspaperman. I carried on like the victim of a botched electroshock therapy session.

One morning Sgt. Slaughter picked us up in his camouflage limousine and drove us to a television taping. Another day we were invited to see Liberace cut the gold ribbon in honor of the fiftieth anniversary of the Rockefeller Center ice rink. He was brought onto the ice in a chariot pulled by a dozen winged skaters who helped him onto an enormous throne so he could approve the exhibition of Olympic skaters. He was wearing a solid gold fur coat, if you can imagine such a thing, and his fingers sparkled with about a million dollars' worth of diamonds. There was a giant cake with a five-foot-tall marzipan skate on top. The whole thing looked as if it were art-directed by the same guy who did the old *Batman* TV series.

The *Main Event* office on the eighty-second floor of the Empire State Building was sparse and filled with the kind of office furniture you find at surplus sales. The space was cheap because you had to take two elevators to get to it—first with the tourists going up to the observation deck, which could take up half the morning, and then in a service elevator to get to the offices housed in a sort of no-man's-land around the building's heating vents and electrical infrastructure. But it was high up in the sky in the world's most famous building, and we loved it. Occasionally when we came to work there would be a giant inflatable King Kong hanging outside our window—put there to show off the building's simian legacy. It was hard to beat.

Main Event was owned by a bottom-feeding weasel of a publisher of indeterminate ethnic background, with a wide, lying smile and a pencil-thin mustache. He wore polyester shirts left over from his disco days and insisted we call him "Shuggie." He was not an easy guy to deal with, but he knew the shit end of the business. We wrote on Smith Coronas and sent everything out to be typeset. He laid out the magazines himself, reducing photos to scale on a copy machine "for position only" and slapping them down on art boards using a waxer, which coated everything with a thin patina of paraffin wax so you could stick it down and then easily pull it up again if the layout wasn't working. It was the ancient art of pasteup, and for all of his other shortcomings, he could compose a page in just a few minutes. He never really cared what we wrote, as long as we put popular wrestlers on the cover and filled the magazine with a lot of exclamation points.

It was around this same time that Vince McMahon, ever the hard-assed entrepreneur, decided to start publishing his own wrestling magazines, and he stopped giving press privileges to other writers and photographers. Since Vince owned Hulk Hogan, and Hogan pretty much owned wrestling, it made it even harder to stay in the game. Mr. McMahon is the Genghis Khan of show business—except with a better endgame.

I shot a lot of matches at Madison Square Garden from the seats, buying tickets from scalpers, and we covered a lot of action from other promotions who had yet to be squashed by Vince's onslaught and who needed the coverage.

But we were still on the outside looking in, in a very closed industry. We didn't have a whole lot of stroke in the biz. The other wrestling blats, like the TV Sports family of magazines, which included *Pro Wrestling Illustrated* and *The Wrestler* (and popular boxing slab *The Ring*), had been in the business for years and had indelible contacts and solid relationships with every promoter in the world. What they didn't have was a couple of stoned punk rock lunatics running the show.

One Mad Wrestling Brainiac we became close with was Kevin Sullivan, a heel with a devil-worshipping gimmick, who had enlisted me into his Army of Darkness to work an angle where he would actually battle Satan. (Sullivan had also been a star of *The Foreign Object*, in a feature called "Ring of Fire.") The idea was to write a three-part serialized story in which Sullivan would defeat his master, Lucifer, and come out walking on the Side of Light. We were going to "turn" him from heel to babyface in the pages of *Main Event*.

Sullivan was a smart, creative guy, and we were definitely ahead of our time—no one had ever done this kind of continuity writing in a wrestling magazine, and certainly nothing as weird as a battle with Satan, presented without irony.

> The final, life-draining rays of the scorching Florida sun danced off of his bloodshot eyes. He was about to face his toughest match . . . with Satan! He was tangling with the basest forces of Mankind, the ego and the avarice that percolates in the pious man as well as the most villainous wrestler . . .

After twenty-eight novels, you bet I could spin a cliff-hanger of good and evil.

> Next Month, it's no holds barred as Kevin grapples with the Darkness that lives in the hearts of men . . . Will he conquer the greed that drove him to follow the Devil? Can he save his immortal soul? Stay tuned for the exciting conclusion, only in "The #1 Magazine for Mat Fans Today!"

To make matters even more confusing, in the third and final installment, we actually had a picture of Sullivan posing with *Main Event*, reading about his epic battle in episode one, and pondering his plight as if he had no idea what was going to happen to him and he relied on us for news of his fate.

As a reward for my contributions as an acolyte in his Dark Army, Sullivan scored me a brief spot on that much-heralded gem of Saturday morning television, *Championship Wrestling from Florida*, playing "The Investigative Reporter." I put on a jacket and tie, tucked a big white card that said PRESS into my hatband, and interrogated him re his motives for forsaking the Forces of Evil. There are few things in the world better than being on television, because if it happens on TV, then it is *real*.

The Satan angle fed right into my feud with Jeremy. "It must be the time Edison is spending with Kevin Sullivan, because I have underestimated the darkness in his soul," Jeremy mused in his earnest, goody-

goody way. I railed back with a mouthful of vaguely satanic-sounding mumbo jumbo: "I will illuminate the Great Void of Professional Wrestling with my fiery Heart Punch!!!" The marks who read this shit went nuts. We received letters by the bushel, mostly damning us all to hell. It was awesome. There's nothing like a solid devil-worshipping gimmick to get that good heat.

When we finally made our date at Gleason's gym, Jeremy and I had both been sequestered in rigorous, top-secret training programs. Mine consisted of hoisting beer and chasing girls. Jeremy was more into drinking buttermilk and reading about Republican role models at the public library. But his blood was red, and it took only a few minutes before it was spilling onto the mat. He busted me open the hard way, with a mighty haymaker to the skull, and he choked me with the ropes. I couldn't believe it—he was *cheating*! Which just goes to show that you can never trust these moralizing do-gooders. They are dirty, dirty, dirty, every last one of them. Fed up with his phony babyface act, I hauled off and leveled him with a high-velocity Heart Punch right to the sternum, before delivering a few more fists to his head. But no matter how much I kept punching him, he wouldn't stop bleeding.

Main Event was now officially in the hands of a rulebreaker.

No one was more surprised than I was when the folks at Columbia gave me the green light and accepted my application. They were not fucking around with their groves-of-academia gimmick—that whole Ivy League shtick had really gone to their heads. At NYU the vibe was casual and easygoing, the side effects of a laid-back Greenwich Village locale straddled by Washington Square Park and an unwashed army of hacky sackers and fake beatniks. At Columbia, perched on a cliff in Morningside Heights, they were absolutely militant. And it actually looked like a school: a bunch of hoary neoclassical buildings surrounding a cookie-cutter quad. Actually, it was refreshing.

The first thing I had to do at Columbia was get past the expository-writing class, which I was told *everyone* had to take, no matter what school they transferred from. Apparently they didn't trust anyone to compose a term paper without first studying the Columbia Method. They definitely were not going to give me a pass based on two undistinguished years at NYU, but . . . I was a journalist, damnit! I was the brawn and the brains behind "The #1 Magazine for Mat Fans Today!" I was also the author of a series of saucy adult novels—although I kept that sordid little secret to myself. The patched elbows on the admissions staff who prided themselves on being at the forefront of political correctness might humor me with the wrestling stuff, but they definitely were not going to be sympathetic to the bard behind *Locker Room Slaves*.

Yet somehow they bought my act and gave me a pass on the expository writing, although I still got socked with a mandatory music humanities class. One can push these Columbia people just so far.

It was insufferable. Beginning with Gregorian chants and slowly meandering its way through the centuries, this was the very cliché of an Ivy League cocktail-party education. If I paid attention, maybe someday I could sound smart at a PBS fund-raiser.

I busted the prof's balls on a daily basis: *I'm sorry I was late, did I miss the discussion of Charlie Parker? Is today Chuck Berry day?? Can I write my paper about the use of contrasting harmonic modality and the boogie-woogie guitar in the mid-period works of Marc Bolan and T. Rex???*

At a liberal university fighting to stay on the front lines of multicultural curricula, I was not only livid that we did we not discuss any composers of color (here I am getting up on my soapbox), but I also posited that a basic knowledge of blues, jazz, and rock 'n' roll—America's only indigenous art forms—would be a lot more appropriate for a bunch of kids who might be able to apply that insight to music they *actually listened to*. He conceded my point and assigned me a detailed analysis of Bach's Brandenburg Concertos.

Actually, I like classical music, especially with a capital C. I love getting stoned and going to the symphony. It's just a goddam shame that an outfit as polished as the New York Philharmonic is stuck playing at a dump like Avery Fisher Hall, which looks like the departure zone of a midsize international airport and has the acoustics of a high school gym. Nonetheless, there is something to be said for 106 highly trained musicians in evening wear sawing relentlessly through a lumberyard's worth of fiddles, clanging away at a battery of kettledrums, and blowing their brains out through a forest of oboes and bassoons.

Add to that racket a lunatic in tails gesticulating wildly with a stick in his hand and the Bugs Bunny Quotient goes through the roof.

I never got less than an A on any paper I wrote while I was at Columbia. I used the same techniques that brought us such pocket classics as *Ding Dong Dildos* and *Marge Rides 'em All*. The formula was one of detailed outlines and lots of whiskey. I knocked the Brandenburg paper out of the park—the professor told me it was by far the best he had ever read. I am sure I was the only student who had capriciously compared the fast third movement and the following *menuetto* of the concerto in F major to an overheated gibbon smoking a post-coital cigarette after a swinging round of treetop monkey fuck. He had no idea with whom he was dealing: when I wasn't acing exams, I was still working behind the scenes, honing *Main Event* into a razor-sharp journal of Atomic Skullcrushers and Swinging Neckbreakers.

Somewhere in the midst of all this uptown hooey, GG Allin called. Against all odds, he had signed a legitimate record deal, and he wanted me to join the conspiracy, writing songs with him and slamming drums on the new album. With Sharky's Machine on hold between tours, I had nothing to distract me except my college education.

Homestead Records was Gerard Cosloy's label. Gerard had a reputation for putting out intelligent, quality recordings of hip, alternative rock bands. So I am not sure why he wanted to get in bed with GG Allin, a skid mark on the boxer shorts of the music business, who could cause havoc just walking down the street. I liked hanging out with GG, but I wouldn't want him as a business partner. He was a proven liability. I reckon Gerard thought that signing GG was going to kick his punk rock street cred up a notch. I'm pretty sure he regrets it.

Gerard's insistence on playing guitar in the band did not go over very well with GG. While Gerard was brilliant at putting out records, he had no place actually being on them, especially not in a group required to dodge bottles, one that ran the risk of being beaten half to death by angry fans—not to mention by the lead singer. This was a job for rock 'n' roll terrorists. In that spirit, I named the band the Holy Men, and we soldiered on. We drank prolific amounts of Jim Beam and ran around completely blind, generally making a spectacle of ourselves, pissing off Gerard and pretty much anyone else who was around us at the time. It was hard not to get caught up in GG's brackish behavior and aura of invincibility. I am sure I still owe a few people apologies.

The recording was a torrent of bourbon and noise. We did the whole thing, from basic tracks to a final mix, in two days. Not exactly Sinatra's *Songs for Swinging Lovers*. GG used a cheap handheld mic for the entire session, rolling around the floor as if he were onstage and not in a recording studio, and then, thoroughly drunk, insisting on overdubbing his vocals four or five times on every song. It sounded like a Wall of GG, though it certainly didn't approach the daunting quality of a Phil Spector record. The overall effect was a lot closer to the sound track from *The Exorcist* than anything by the Ronettes. The only thing GG Allin and Phil Spector have in common is that you could not trust either of them with a loaded gun.

The emerald in our crown was a cover of Charles Manson's ode to survivalism, "Garbage Dump," with its refrain *"That sums it up in one big lump."* The engineer was appalled. You can hear him at the end of the song, saying, incredulously, "You're actually gonna put this out?"

Back in the Ivy League, I scored enough A's to make it onto the dean's list, and you can bet Mom was pretty well chuffed. That changed quickly when, as an encore, I went off the reservation and once again joined the ranks of dropouts.

I enjoyed my stretch at Columbia. Between going to classes, pumping out *Main Event*, and getting fucked up with GG while making enemies all over town, it had been a very satisfying four months. But all I had actually learned was that I could do the work if I felt like it. Other than that, there was nothing I couldn't have bought for a few trips to the public library or an afternoon in a museum, and I did that anyway. At least at Apex Tech you got to keep your tools.

To supplement my paltry check from *Main Event*—I was now making about fifteen hundred dollars a month to put together an issue, including writing the bulk of it—I got a job at a record shop, Midnight Records on Twenty-third Street. It was a lot better than the gig I scored the first time I dropped out, delivering booze to perverts. Instead of smelly old men showing me their nut sacs, all I had to put up with was a nerdy gaggle of record-collecting geeks with Beatle boots and Prince Valiant haircuts. The improvement was marginal.

5

A VIOLENT MUTHERFUCKING PEOPLE

Out in the parking lot of Gilley's bar, in Pasadena, Texas, "Warlord" Jonathan Boyd was fumbling for his keys. He was fucked-up drunk and trying to do business out of the trunk of his Lincoln Continental. When he finally got it open he pulled out a championship belt. It was made of worn leather and heavy metal and it carried the weight of a thousand bloody matches won in a thousand sweaty roadhouse arenas. It was a totem of all that was great about Texas wrestling.

"I'm gonna put you over, mate," he told the kid, and handed him the strap. "Yer the new Texas Junior Heavyweight Champ." The kid beamed. He was a good-looking Mexican boy, and the fans loved him. He had been in the business for less than a year and already he was getting a promotion. So what if it was 2:00 a.m. in a parking lot, and the boss was bombed and could barely remember his name? Obviously, this was how it was done, or what the fuck else would they have been doing out there?

The Warlord's head looked odd. Blood shines black in moonlight, perhaps more so in Texas, and his skull shimmered with rivers of indigo from where the barbed wire had cut him. Earlier in the evening he had lost a gruesome main event. According to the match's stipulation, and there always was one in Texas, he was forced to wear a crown of thorns fashioned from razor ribbon, forcefully jammed over his bald pate, to further humiliate him in front of an arena of bloodthirsty Christians. He looked as if his head had been stuck in a food processor, and he was the scariest thing the kid had ever seen.

The Warlord patted the kid on the back and gave him some stern advice. "This is the old Southwest Heavyweight belt, so don't let anybody get too close to it until we can change it. If anybody asks, tell them you won it in a tournament in Mexico." Up until that point, there was no such thing as the "Texas Junior Heavyweight Champ." The Warlord, shitfaced and feeling magnanimous, had made it up on the spot. He stumbled and nearly fell back into the trunk of the Lincoln. I took his keys from him and carefully navigated us back to the motel, leaving the new champ in the parking lot, dazed. For a second there, standing in the Lone Star moonlight, his future looked bright indeed.

Running *Main Event* didn't have a lot of perks, but driving around Texas with the Warlord rated high. Jonathan was one of the original Kiwi Sheepherders, a brutal New Zealander tag team who chewed through the South in the mid-eighties. His career was presumed to be finished after a horrible car accident that had destroyed his back and busted both of his legs. The Sheepherders recruited a new man, and eventually became stars, working as the Bushwackers. Against all odds, Jonathan rehabilitated to the point where he could walk with a cane. Hobbling around, screaming at fans, he began managing all the heels in San Antonio. Eventually he made it back to the ring and took over the business. This guy was as tough as they come.

When I first met Jonathan, he was booking the Southwest promotion under a new name, Texas All-Star Wrestling. Their headquarters was the rodeo ring in Gilley's, the legendary "world's largest bar," a cavernous hall that smelled like stale liquor and cow shit (it burned down in 1989). "These are a violent mutherfucking people," he would tell me, speaking of the Mexicans and cowboys who would get fucked up on beer and fill the place on a Saturday night. "I'm gonna give 'em what they want."

The cards were filled with bloody gimmick matches from top to bottom. Dog collars and chains, steel cages, billiard balls dropped into tube socks—you'd see it all on one of his shows, climaxing with the Bloody Horror of the Barbed Wire Match. Every wrestler "got juice"— usually the old-fashioned way, by cutting their foreheads open with a razor blade secreted in their wrist tape. In a second there would be blood everywhere. And the fans would go crazy. There was always some hotted-up drunk who wanted to jump into the ring to defend the honor of a Lone Star Hero who had just been carved up by a filthy fucking foreigner like the Warlord—or worse, a mincing sissy like Exotic Adrian Street.

Exotic Adrian was the best of the post–Gorgeous George wrestlers working a swishy gimmick. He had incredible technical skills and could get unbelievable heat, especially in the South, prancing around like some kind of glammed-up freak show in pigtails and sparkly face paint. "I can hurt you so many ways you'll find new ways to scream!" he would coo at opponents before snapping their spines and skipping around the ring in faux faggoty delight. Whenever Adrian worked there was always some testosterone case who had to be put down by rodeo security, who were bigger, uglier, and meaner than the wrestlers. They had to be. So were the fans.

I also spent time in Philadelphia, the City of Brotherly Love, shooting matches promoted by the old National Wrestling Alliance, which was still trying to work the Northeast and got as far as Vince McMahon's backyard. Every show we saw there was fantastic, and you could count on lots and lots of juice. Tully Blanchard, one of the most gifted grapplers of his generation, was in a life-and-death feud with Magnum T.A. The Road Warriors, Animal and Hawk, would crush whoever stood before them. The great heel managers, Paul Jones and J. J. Dillon, always brought a full battery of ass-kickers. At the end of the night, Ric Flair, without question the Greatest Professional Wrestler of All Time, would defend his title, *the* title, in hour-long matches against Dusty Rhodes or Harley Race that were riveting from start to finish. It was the very height of the art form.

There has never been a wrestler so deserving of the accolades conferred upon him as Ric Flair. He is the Vladimir Horowitz of the turnbuckle, the Pablo Picasso of the pinfall. He is the Wayne Gretzky of the grappling world. There is nothing Ric Flair cannot do.

One of his greatest skills has always been his preternatural ability to "sell" his opponent. He could wrestle a toothbrush and make the toothbrush look good. He whipped crowds into a lather by begging for mercy—from men with a tenth of his talent. He is a testament to how great a sport wrestling is. He is an iron man. Every night his peroxide-blond hair would fill up with blood, his head would turn pink like a piece of bubblegum, and he would fall out of the ring, dripping gore, clutching the Ten Pounds of Gold—the coveted NWA Heavyweight Championship belt—and even though you knew he did this three hundred times a year, he always made you feel as though you were part of history.

And he was brilliant out of the ring. To be in a room with him was to know why they called it *professional* wrestling. He always carried himself like a true Champ. On the mat, he was a brutal egomaniac who would resort to anything to win, but after the match he was always totally approachable and generous with his time. When there were cameras or reporters around, he burned like a supernova. Any business would be proud to have a man like this represent them. I learned a lot from just being around him, soaking up the Championship Vibe.

Flair was always nice to me, as were all the wrestlers, with the notable exception of Dusty Rhodes, who was generally a dick. But no one ever made a motion to let me into the Secret Inner Circle until the Warlord invited me down to cover his personal brand of barbarism.

All of this goodwill meant nothing back at the office, where Shuggie was still demanding more and more for less and less. In addition to *Main Event*, we were now also doing a number of wrestling superstars picture albums—magazines of recycled photos and mini-posters, which needed a lot more love and care than you might imagine. As with a regular issue, I would have to draw up a "pagination," or "map," of the book, preferably with some sort of logical flow. Then I'd collect the material, which meant going through back issues and old files to find the best stuff (and stuff that hadn't already been reprinted, which became increasingly difficult the more of these retread books we churned out), write headlines and blocks of copy for each wrestler (and make it seem fresh), have it run out into galleys, and, after proofing it, traffic it to Shuggie, who was the art department. All told, it was a big job for one guy, but I was building some chops, and the books kept looking and reading better and better. Even though Shuggie may not have cared about anything except getting product on the stands as cheaply as possible, I took a lot of pride in my work.

I also expected to get paid. Shuggie kept giving me new jobs, such as these picture albums, for which I was supposed to collect an extra check, and I was glad to do it, but he'd drag his ass paying me. I was pretty much writing the entire magazine by now, and he owed me a dropout's fortune for all the photos I'd been snapping.

It is beyond me why he'd want to fuck around with someone whose new best pal was a drunk Kiwi called the Warlord. Hanging around with a bunch of ass-kickers in Texas had done nothing to damage my self-confidence, and I was not going to be intimidated by a rat fucker like Shuggie. He was one of those assholes who think they can make you feel guilty for wanting to actually collect what you've earned.

"Why you gettin' so angry? Didn't I give you a job? You're just a kid."

This went on for a few weeks before I finally saw red. I am like Billy Fucking Jack, very slow to anger, but when I hit the boiling point, you do not want to be around. I had flattened the last editor who got in my way, and now I was going to drop this mutherfucker like a bad habit. Except when I tore down Jeremy, it was a *work*. This was *real*, what we call a *shoot*.

"If you keep bothering me, I'll never pay you! I'll fire your ass!"

"You can't fire me. I quit!"

Didn't you always want to say that? I'm so glad I thought of it. A little bit of sugar to help the medicine go down. Because my next move was to take a swing at his head with a T square I had grabbed from the art table. He looked like a thermometer about to pop.

I measured him for another shot.

"I'll call security! I'll call security!"

"Yeah, whatever." What a coward. I thought for sure he'd fight back, but I really didn't want his blood on my hands. "There will be a check here tomorrow for three thousand dollars, all the money you owe me, and then I won't hire a lawyer, I won't sue you, and I will walk away without killing you," I advised him.

"You call first."

That sounded reasonable enough. I tossed the T square aside dramatically and headed for a bar. The next day the check was waiting for me. I left the Empire State Building walking tall.

Producing *Main Event* had been a humbling responsibility. I took seriously my promise to each and every one of my constituents, be they Nobel laureates or toothless hicks howling for Hulk Hogan. I know they counted on me, even if I wanted to rip their hero's lungs out with a pair of old ice tongs. But without that cross to bear, left with only a slacker day job peddling long-playing phonograph records to rockabilly nerds, I was free to get on with the care and feeding of Alec and Jim in *Sharky's Machine*.

Like a champ, Speedy Gonzalez had come through with the deutsche marks for our next record. And with Kramer out of the picture, we traded up for Wharton Tiers to record us.

Wharton had produced outings for Sonic Youth and Pussy Galore and was an instrumental part of Glenn Branca's swarm-of-bees guitar orchestras. I once saw Wharton playing on Branca's "Night of 100 Guitars," a free concert outside at the World Financial Center. There was an entire playing field of guitarists clanging away on hot-rodded electric six strings, each with its own amplifier. Wharton led the pack, pummeling a set of vintage Slingerland drums. The racket the guitars made was unbelievable, and Wharton was still about eighty times as loud as the herd, piledriving a modified Bo Diddley beat nonstop for nearly an hour.

He is also one of the most even-tempered men in the business and has a stellar rep for being a calming influence in the studio, where tempers can sometimes flare. But not even Wharton—with the help of Jimmy Carter, Dale Carnegie, and the Dalai Fucking Lama—could have brought peace to Sharky's Machine. He told me that in all the years of running his studio, we were the only band who got into an actual fistfight during a recording session.

Jim could be a complete fucking diva. For all of his vast talent, there was too little professionalism and too much cheap booze, which fueled his whole Sensitive Artist trip to intolerable levels.

During the recording, Jim was carrying on as usual, whining, whimpering, and wasting everyone's time trying to breathe subtlety into a song that sounded like a war between two broken lawn mowers.

At one point Alec just said, "Fuck him, just let him sing whatever he wants. It's not like we're gonna use any of this crap." Alec didn't realize that Jim could hear him through the talk-back mic. Jim threw down his headphones, stormed back into the control room, and delivered a vicious, openhanded slap to the side of Alec's head. All hell broke loose. Too bad we didn't get *that* on tape.

Not long after that, I made a spectacle of myself thrashing Jim in front of an audience of about two hundred people. It was the end of a long night of tedious opening bands playing indulgently long sets, which had pushed all of us to the breaking point, especially after hours of bored drinking. Just as we were about to go on, Jim refused to sing "Stray Cat Blues," one of our strongest numbers. A raucous, mean-spirited Rolling Stones cover, it was a fail-safe crowd-pleaser. "I no longer relate to it," Jim declared.

Oy fucking vey. What did I do to deserve this shit? Alec decided that we would just open the set with it. Once we started, what was Jim going to do? Neither of us predicted that he would spin on his heels and clobber me with the heavy end of an SM-58 microphone.

I leaped over the drums and flattened him. A crowd of concerned patrons pulled me off of him, and the show was officially over at the thirty-second mark, beating the old record set by GG Allin by a full five minutes. I felt bad about the whole thing for almost an hour.

Somehow, despite all odds, we made a good rock 'n' roll record, *A Little Chin Music*. The cover was a graphic painting of a batter having his head torn off by a high, inside fastball. We delivered the record to Speedy and booked a two-month tour of northern Europe, with a two-week stay in Berlin, where we were already slated to record another album for his LSD label.

Speedy was a man who made things happen. In 1988, before the Wall came down, Berlin—West Berlin—was the craziest town on earth. No one there slept, Speedy least of all.

It is hard to imagine, now that Europe is one happy family, that West Berlin was just a dot in the middle of the Soviet bloc, penned in like a goat at a petting zoo. The Wall was a surreal, ominous presence. The people who lived there, at least the druggy under-thirty crowd that I was running with, had a seriously conflicted love-hate relationship with it: there was empathy for their Eastern neighbors, who lived in the long shadow of Communist oppression, but everyone knew that if the Wall ever came down, West Berlin would be besieged by East bloc refugees, lines for food and basic services would be crippling, and West Berlin would lose every bit of exotic gravitas that had made it the center of glamorous sexual decadence for everyone from Marlene Dietrich to David Bowie. We were there just months before the fall, and no one had any clue that things might not go on forever this way.

Every time you left West Berlin to travel beyond the Wall into West Germany, you would have to go through a series of checkpoints and passport controls—first, the American military sector (e.g., Checkpoint Charlie), then West German customs, then DDR customs (Deutsche Demokratische Republik, a.k.a. East Germany). The East German border guards were master-race mutants, jackbooted and armed with oily black machine guns. Their uniforms, like their attack dogs, were designed, successfully, to inspire fear.

It was all very bizarre. On one side of the Wall were bars and cafés, and the Wall itself was covered in colorful graffiti. After a short stretch of a heavily mined no-man's-land fortified with spiraling clouds of razor ribbon, there was a new country, a Soviet satellite where no one had any rights and everything was painted gray. Guard towers popped up like middle fingers every fifty feet.

Leaving West Berlin, to go to, say, Hanover for a weekend gig, you would also receive a time stamp, so that when you crossed the East German border again to reenter West Germany, it could be verified that you were not lollygagging and, presumably, collecting intelligence. But there was nothing to collect except the crappy East German toilet paper at the primitive rest stops. It was of such inferior quality that Cain and Abel probably had a better time of it with raw papyrus. Otherwise, the highway was bordered by fifteen-foot hedges so you couldn't even see inside the country. There were no exits.

Travel to East Berlin was permitted—a one-day tourist visa cost about thirty bucks American, in return for which you would be handed a pile of East German scrip that was of a lesser quality than the toilet paper. The coins were made of tin. But none of this mattered since you had to spend all your money that day before you returned to West Germany and the only thing you could buy with it was beer and bratwurst. Exchanging dollars for a few pennies' worth of scrap metal was their way of bringing hard currency into the country. And of course, while you were a guest of the State, you were being watched by the Stasi. You had to be careful that no one tried to pass you a note or tried to talk to you about Hollywood movies, which were strictly *verboten*.

All of this made it a real pain in the ass to bring drugs into West Berlin, so they just made them there. Bathtub labs lurked in every corner of the city, cooking military-grade amphetamines. Beyond any truck-driver crank you might imagine, this was the shit that powered Wernher von Braun's best rockets. One good bump of shiny yellow crystals off the end of a switchblade could keep you going for days.

There were lots of blank-faced Berliners for whom years of tweaking on zoom dust had not had the beneficial effects of, say, a good nap and a bowl of Grandma's best chicken soup. While we were there, my policy was to eat and sleep once every few days, whether I had to or not.

We were staying in an apartment above the Ecstasy club in the swanky Schöneberg district. Every night there was another band, another party. Like professional wrestlers and high school teachers, about one in five was worthwhile. But there was always Top Secret Action in Kreuzberg, a bohemian district of anarchists and hard-core punks and artists nestled up against the Wall. The bars, many of which had blankets covering the windows to hold back the dawn, were uniformly shrouded in thick smoke from hash joints and were buzzing with booze and speed. Most nights I'd have to suck back a fifth of Jim Beam just to take the edge off.

Offstage and outside of the studio—where we spent our afternoons working—I had as little to do with the band as possible. I was having a great time without them, and was pretty much fed up with their amateur-hour bullshit. Alec was still infuriating soundmen all over Europe, and Jim was burrowing deeper into a wine-sodden wormhole dug with his inability to relate to anyone or get a grip on the basic responsibilities of a working band. How many gigs in how many countries do you have to play before you learn how to plug in a microphone? Or get a decent balance on your amplifier? It was maddening.

Tonia, however, was a winner. She fell in love with a nice German boy, and the next year she would end up going back to Berlin to marry him. She lived there for a couple of years, becoming something of an ambassador for baseball, teaching the American Pastime to punk rockers who wanted to start an inter-bar beer league. Later they moved to Massachusetts and began a family.

When we got back to New York after that tour, I was ready once again for the Edison Cure. I sent out for Japanese food, drank an ice-cold can of Budweiser in a steaming hot shower, and smoked a joint I had sagely left in my sock drawer for the occasion. After two months of zero time alone—except when I was squatting over some primitive European commode—I was ecstatic not to have to speak with anyone. No annoying bandmates, no idiots in brown leather pants who wanted to blame me personally for putting short-range nuclear missiles in Europe, not even any Fräuleins who, no matter how libertine and interested in my clipped Jewish wing-wang they might have been, had finally worn me down with their collective inability to conjugate English verbs. *Yesterday I go to Berlin. Tomorrow we make going for New York.* After two months, *my* English was getting soft.

Downtown, some of our friends' bands were playing, and I know we were expected to show up in our new guise of conquering heroes, but all I wanted to conquer was a plate of raw fish and some twentieth-century plumbing. The last thing in the world I wanted to hear was another loud electric guitar. I was ready for an adult dose of American television. Maybe I'd start with *Sesame Street* and work my way up to *Twin Peaks*.

Leave it to Alec to piss on my party of one. Once he was in a room full of boozy punk rockers who wanted to know how the tour was— and, naturally, if he got laid—he couldn't stop himself from leaking information like a Washington call girl with a bad coke habit.

"Jim and I didn't get any, but Mike slept with lots of girls."

I was just nuzzling up to my take-out sushi when the phone started ringing with ex-flames who wanted details. As if. I neither confirmed nor denied anything. Which somehow made them all hot to see me. That week I had dates every night with women just dying to repatriate me.

Perhaps I should be thanking Alec for a week of guilt-free sex? Fuck that. What happens on the road, stays on the road. It wasn't long after that I pulled the plug on Sharky's Machine.

Now I had no band and no job. While we were out on the road, another punk had taken my slot at the record store. Someone else might have seen the lack of livelihood as a problem. I am not one of those people.

6

LOUISIANA

I was twenty-four years old, and I had life kicked in the ass. I was in the backseat of a cab bouncing through New Orleans, watching the graveyards blur by, just like in *Easy Rider,* on my way to do a story for *Cheri* magazine on "the girls of the Big Easy."

Only a few days before, out of work and spinning my wheels against a bleak future, I had responded to an ad in *The New York Times* to work for a "men's sophisticate," which back in those days was the shibboleth for "porn rag."

When *Cheri* called back a few days later, I knew right away I had the job. They wanted someone who could travel and set up out-of-town trips to photograph, for instance, the Girls of New Orleans. No problem. I was a film school guy (okay, dropout, but they didn't have to know that right away) and therefore expert in organizing all manner of photo shoots. And I knew how to put out a magazine. Dig my stellar writing career—*Screw*, professional wrestling, and teenage bondage books. See? I was already in the gutter! They insisted that I come in right away for an interview.

I showed up at the *Cheri* offices at Forty-second Street and Second Avenue the next morning at 9:30 a.m. sharp, on time and drunk as a skunk.

It was my birthday, and when they called, I was just about to head downtown for some celebratory tippling. Having an important job interview the next morning did little to deter me; in fact, it only inspired me to new heights of inebriation. At 4:00 a.m.—closing time in New

York City—I was offering to buy drinks for everyone because "tomorrow I'm getting a job for a porn mag." The bartender told me to get out, go home, and get some sleep. I just kept drinking. In those days I insisted that sleep was for infants and old people and I would sleep when I was dead.

Anyway, I had nothing to worry about. I give great interview. Years of watching wrestling on TV had prepared me for pretty much anything. In fact, the first thing they said was, "Tell us about working at the wrestling magazine."

"Well," I said, without getting too puffed up, "I do everything—I write the stories, I assign photographers, sometimes I go to matches and shoot them myself. I write all the headlines and I spec the type; I bring it to the old Jewish man who typesets it for us; I read the galleys and make corrections and then bring it back to the typesetter for the repro proof. I shoot stats, lay out pages with the art director, write captions and pull quotes for space, write the cover lines, and let me tell you, when my name is on that masthead, I guarantee it is the best wrestling magazine money can buy." They told me to go home and get some sleep and come back the next day.

They hired me as an editor for 20K, handed me a company credit card, partnered me up with a short, dyspeptic Chinese photographer who called himself Wally Wang, and sent me on my way to New Orleans, my first assignment. "I can smell Pulitzer!" I declared to my fellow pornographers, who at that point were still wondering how I even got past the receptionist.

Driving toward the French Quarter, Wally wasn't nearly as happy as I was.

"Wally," I said, "this is fucking great. First thing we're gonna do is score some weed and maybe some coke and get some Dixie beer and start guzzling oysters. And then we're going to the strip club to meet the girls and set things up for tomorrow's shoot. We're Big-Time Magazine Guys from New York."

Wally was having none of it. "To you, this is New Orleans," he sputtered. "To me, this is Louisiana, and they hate my Chink ass. We're taking pictures and we're leaving."

Two days later Wally and I were still going strong with a couple of Bourbon Street strippers, both named Bunny.

The Superbowl was going to be in New Orleans that year, and our idea was, after doing a series of "nature pictures" at every topless joint in the Quarter, to throw a criminally sexy Superbowl soiree in a hotel room and then build a theme issue around our little fiesta.

Let me set the mise-en-scène for you: The Bunnys—dressed to kill in tearaway Saints jerseys and the kind of ultra-dynamite fuck-me pumps that no one not employed by Ringling Bros. could possibly walk on—are tipsy, horny, and . . . *bored*. Unable to distract their chuckle-head no-neck boyfriends from the turf battle on TV, they wander off to the bedroom to throw their own private party, one of those everyman's fantasy scenarios that the discerning gentlemen who buy these magazines think actually happen in real life. Whammo-zammo, and you've got yourself eight pages of four-color squack.

The Bunnys were very sexy but were never going to make it to the *Playboy* centerfold. I'm not even sure their names really were Bunny. But they liked to have fun. We were the Big Time Magazine Guys from New York, they were the Topless Dancers from the French Quarter, and everyone was very happy. We took good care of them; they were stars. They were going to be in a *magazine*—no trifling feat for a couple of girls from Jefferson Parish. They'd advertise themselves "as seen in *Cheri*," and they'd get top billing at the finest go-go emporiums in the land. The fact that we all got along so well was what my boss would have called a "perquisite," had he known the word.

The hotel room was about as low-rent as you could get. Everything was bolted down, including the Gideon Bible. In terms of production values, this wasn't exactly *Star Wars*. It wasn't even *Deep Throat*. More like home movies of the Kennedy assassination. We bought a case of cheap champagne and filled the bathtub with ice. The girls dropped some ecstasy. It may not have had the makings of *Gone With the Wind*, but we had all the elements for a successful shoot, or at least an extremely pleasant afternoon. Never underestimate the dramatic impact of a couple of D-cup strippers getting it on in football helmets and heels.

The key to these low-budget, on-location girlie shoots is *cheating*. It can't look like a cheap hotel room. If an alarm clock somehow shows up in a picture, you've just given away the secret to the trick. We're like magicians, and if you could see the shit-colored wallpaper and the generic lamp on the night table, you could probably smell the disinfectant, too.

So you shoot everything close. Play to your strengths, fill the frame with flesh. Tits, beavers, ridiculous toy football filling various orifices, girls soaked in bubbly tongue-bathing each other (that cheap champagne gets pretty sticky), colored streamers everywhere . . .

Colored streamers? Yup. And confetti. How dumb was that? Hey, it was supposed to be a party, and I thought it would add a little color. And in the end it did look pretty good. But as we were shooting and playing around with the girls, champagne was getting spilled all over the bed and the streamers were bleeding on the white sheets. The red ink made it look like a pig had just been slaughtered, but the blue was just plain unsettling. There was no way to explain it except maybe that a Smurf got whacked in there along with the pig. When the maid came in the next morning she looked as if she were going to call the police. Or the X-Files.

Up until that point it was probably the greatest weekend of my life. I had been driven to score some pot in a stolen Z-car by a hooker with a heart of gold. I was taken to a rodeo-themed gay bar by a spectacularly well-built go-go girl—she looked as if she had walked out of an R. Crumb comic and could crush coconuts with her thighs. It was the last bar open in the Quarter, and we were still thirsty. We were there for about half a drink before a guy in leather chaps grabbed my ass. My new best friend, the Amazonian go-go girl, knocked him out cold and then hurried us back to my hotel, where she took very good care of me—worried as she was that I might be upset about a guy in chaps grabbing my ass. And I got a blow job from another, somewhat more provincial stripper who took me into a back room and declared, "My first Jew!"

Cheri was owned by Drake Publishing (later known as Crescent Publishing Group), which also published *High Society, Celebrity Skin,* and, oddly, *Playgirl,* whose all-female staff of cock-and-ball peddlers generally thought that what they did was somehow more sophisticated than the smut we perpetrated.

Each of the men's mags had a slightly different niche: *High Society* was a pseudo-serious pornographic magazine and always had the best-looking photo sets, name porn stars, lots of girl-girl and boy-girl stuff. *High Society* was also the launching pad for *Celebrity Skin,* which fed on paparazzi titty-shots and 35 mm frames of now-famous actresses glommed from the nude scenes in the B movies they made before they hit it big. The idea for the celebrity stuff came right from *Hustler,* the ne plus ultra of porn mags, which had struck gold with the Jackie O. sunbathing shots in the early seventies. The rest was knocked off from *Penthouse,* right down to the idiotically pretentious, moneyed-sounding name. But in 1976, when *High Society* launched, local newsstands weren't overcrowded with a lot of high-quality "pink," and it caught on. *Cheri* was skewed more toward big-breasted, corn-fed American girls and lots of location shoots—i.e., the Girls of Wisconsin, the Girls of Michigan, etc., which is how they made their name. I got lucky with New Orleans. I could just as easily have been assigned the Girls of Hackensack.

The man behind the curtain at Drake was Carl Ruderman, a secretive, overtanned madman famous within the industry for being the "invisible pornographer." The one original spark to come out of Ruderman's brain was to hire yenta porn star Gloria Leonard as the magazine's "publisher." Of course she had little to do with the day-to-day running of the business, but it was a well-received put-on. Well-spoken, with an alluring air of open sexuality and elegance, she was the perfect front person and was instrumental in making Ruderman millions from the phone sex business.

Legend would have it that Ruderman was the genius behind the very first paid-for phone sex lines, an innovation that would put him in the same league as Alexander Graham Bell. A more popular version of the story is that he got the concept from an underling who had the idea to promote *High Society* with sexy phone messages read by Gloria. They started with a few lines and a few message machines, and the whole thing just exploded. Before long they had hundreds of lines and were charging by the minute. Ruderman then allegedly shit-canned the guy who actually thought of the gimmick and made a boatload from it.

Ruderman was filthy rich from selling sex, but unlike Goldstein, Hefner, Guccione, and Flynt, he stayed far out of the public eye, seemingly embarrassed at how he made his dough. He was obsessed with maintaining a smoke screen of manufactured respectability.

Everyone in the Drake office had to wear jackets and ties at all times, as if it were some kind of bush-league country club—a ridiculous conceit, especially given the fact that no one who worked there ever had to interact with the public on any professional level. We were twenty-something-year-old pornographers mostly getting paid shit, but Ruderman wanted to pretend that we were a "real" company. He wore four-thousand-dollar suits and fabulous silk ties that had been coded with tags on the back so he could get dressed in the morning without having to worry about clashing—allegedly he was completely colorblind, a sizable challenge if your business is publishing picture books.

When he came strolling through the office, people hid. He could be terribly intimidating. Personally, I thought he was funny. Completely off his nut, but funny. His spectacularly manicured fingernails actually sparkled, every silver hair on his head was perfectly in place, and he blurted non sequiturs while sucking on a fat, unlit cigar.

"Mr. Edison!" he would scream. "We've got to do some barnstorming! I want to hear ideas!"

"Yes, Mr. Ruderman. Brainstorming. Always *brainstorming*."

"That's right . . . barnstorming! Who's Trump fucking these days? Find out!" He was obsessed with Donald Trump.

"Uh, he's marrying that Maples girl."

"But is he fucking any *men*? That's what people want to know! Find out!"

In 1983, outraged that someone who was making a fortune sucking at the teat of the sex industry thought he could somehow remain anonymous and retain his precious standing in society, Larry Flynt made Ruderman *Hustler*'s Asshole of the Month and paid a five-hundred-dollar reward for a photo of Ruderman to run in the magazine.

The real brains of the operation at Drake was the editorial director, Carmine Bellucci, the *capo di tutti capi*, who led a somewhat retarded crew of miscast pornographers. Carmine had actually been on the front lines of publishing, editing, and producing girlie mags and movie-star scandal sheets, and was, unlike Ruderman, willing to get his hands dirty.

In the late 1970s and early '80s Carmine toured the country in a Winnebago with the legendary stripper Cheri Bomb. They would go from town to town doing shoots of local go-go girls and promoting *Cheri* magazine. It was quite a racket, and *Cheri* grew into a ridiculously popular title. If you take into consideration all the amateur porn and *Girls Gone Wild* stuff that came years later, Carmine was well ahead of the curve. Crescent bought *Cheri* and brought Carmine on as editorial director for the whole shop.

Carmine was the only one up there who really knew what he was doing. He understood the ins and outs of production as well as how to edit the "girl sets" and deliver the product. He was a smooth talker and a leader, and he could tell war stories about the early days of the business. He was slick, in his mid-thirties; he dressed well and had a game-show host's smile. He knew everyone in the business and could wheel and deal. Everyone at Drake looked up to him, not only because he was the boss, but because he carried himself like one.

Working under Carmine were his "captains"—Ron Ronson, Vincent Stevens, and Barry Rosenbaum—all just a few years younger than Carmine. Ron Ronson was the one who initially called me on my birthday and hired me the next day after getting the okay from Carmine. Previously he had worked on some square computer magazine. One day he decided he needed to do something "cool" so he signed on with a girlie mag. He was going through a very clichéd midlife crisis, which was doubly sad because he was only about ten years older than I. He pierced his ear and bought a motorcycle. It didn't work for me, though I suppose a gold hoop and a rice-burner pulled pussy in suburbia. But Ronson was a good guy, and he encouraged me. Eventually he helped me move up through the ranks of Drake.

Vince Stevens looked like a minor-league baseball player, tall, blond, and perpetually sunburned, and that's about all he had going for him. He was the nominal editor of *High Society*, Drake's flagship magazine, but Carmine was really pulling the strings, choosing the photo sets and going over every layout, blocking the sequences, setting the tone. Vince had never troubled himself with a purely original thought. There was no need to—being tall was enough to get by at Crescent.

Barry Rosenbaum, who worked on one-off titles, was a nice Jewish boy, a nebbish who probably would have been better off writing insurance claims than editing the kind of bathroom gazettes you read with one hand. Working at Drake had turned him into a complete head case, a victim of the near-deadly side effects of spending one's days in an erotic candy store.

Thanks to Ruderman's insistence on camouflaging our appearance, the office looked like any late-eighties pseudo-corporate maze of pre-fab cubicles with an unfortunate mauve color scheme, not like the headquarters of an officious gang of big-city smut peddlers. But underneath the hideous semigloss paint job was a superheated fantasy world of women in fuck-me pumps with perfectly formed pudendas, pouty lips, heart-shaped behinds, and traffic-stopping breasts. There were provocative photos everywhere. Every nook and cranny in that office was filled with porn. Every working surface was covered in wide-open beaver and ass shots. It was hard *not* to let it get to you: How were you supposed to look at these eye-popping models and then go home to your plain Jane sweetheart? No kidding—the women in these magazines were drop-dead gorgeous and photographed under the same exacting conditions used to launch lunar probes. We'd airbrush the covers, sometimes "blue the eyes," the idea being that azure orbs sold better than brown, but between the pages we never bothered. There was no need.

Rosenbaum let it get to him. In a world of über-women in slut shoes, he could no longer find "normal" women appealing. It was heartbreaking to listen to him. He was such a nice guy and took his job so seriously, really getting into the finer points of each photo, studying each model with gynecological precision. It was kind of creepy, actually, but he took a lot of pride in his work. Unfortunately, he could not separate his chosen profession from reality. "Edison," he would say to me, "I asked this girl to dinner and she had the nerve to show up wearing flat shoes. I didn't want to take her out after that." When one girl showed up on a date wearing flip-flops, he nearly had a coronary. He had psyched himself out so badly that he had no idea how to score. He became a neurotic mess. "Edison, I had to poop today after lunch. Later I have a date. Should I go home first and take a shower? I live like two hours away." How the fuck was I supposed to answer that?

The secret to working in such a highly charged environment lies a lot closer to detached objectivity than chronic tumescence. You obviously couldn't do your job walking around with a boner all day, but you had to enjoy the subject matter and be able to edit the magazines to the audience's taste. That's a very important lesson that Ronson taught me: *Know Thy Reader*. We'd see guys cater to their own coozeconscious connoisseurship, putting freaky punk-rock-looking chicks in a mag cherished by cheerleader-loving dolts—and then wonder why it didn't sell.

I love sex, and I love pretty women, and being in that environment liberated me from ever being intimidated by the kinds of women whom a lot of guys might be afraid to approach—models, strippers, A-list angels, fantasy girls. I'm not a real ladies' man. I'm a short Jewish guy with a receding hairline, and I've been rejected enough that even though it always sucks, I can deal with it because I like who I am. Some women want Brad Pitt, some women want guys like me (I try to go with the latter), and their relative good looks are not indicative of their kindness, sense of humor, or intellect, which is the ultimate turn-on. I always respected the women in our magazines and never looked down on them, but I never put them so high on a pedestal that they would be unattainable, either. I've dated women who look as if they had just leaped out of the centerfold, and women who to a man like Rosenbaum would be considered unexceptional, but they set me on fire. It's all an illusion. Once you learn that, happiness is just a shot away.

I liked all of these guys, but none of them were ever going to be feted as visionaries. Not surprisingly, they were very protective of their jobs and senior staff positions. They went out for lunch together every day and kept a good distance between themselves and the rank and file, who—beneath the stratum occupied by Carmine's Gang of Four— were *my* extended posse of twenty-something editors and art directors, the A Team who really put the pages together and got the books out the door.

Back in the art department were the young Turks we called the Happiness Boys: Gil, Kurt, and Braino. Gil was a good-looking guy with dark features. He looked like the son of a Greek shipping magnate and fancied himself some sort of Lothario. We'd be out drinking, and in five minutes he'd have the phone numbers of half the girls in the bar, which he would promptly lose after getting smashed on vodka. But it was inspiring to see him work. His greatest contribution to Drake Publishing was building a cardboard fort under an art table, where people could take naps after getting stoned at lunch.

Kurt was a talented painter who was there because he needed a job. He thought the whole place was absurd, and he just rolled with it. Braino was a punk rocker who later became a celebrated tattoo artist.

The editorial department was an equally mismatched group of miscreants. I wouldn't describe any of us as "normal," but certainly Spooner (he never explained how he got that nickname, but that's what he insisted we call him) was the weirdest. In fact, he was one of the weirdest guys I ever met, especially in the context of a porn factory, since he never showed any inkling of liking girls or sex. While the rest of us would discuss the relative pulchritude of the models in the most piggish manner possible, the best we could coax from Spooner was "Well, I *guess* she's hot." We all thought he was gay, except he wasn't cool enough to be gay. He was extraordinarily anal, which was actually a plus on a staff where no one was all that organized. Even his hair looked alphabetized. It was always perfect, as if it were designed by some great architectural firm and combed with a T square. Spooner would hang out with us after work, everybody really liked him, but after two drinks he'd be as drunk as a sailor on leave and we'd have to send him home to Weehawken, New Jersey, where he always kept his table set, like Miss Havisham in *Great Expectations*.

Next to Spooner, Chip was the boy next door. He was a fresh recruit from Norman, Oklahoma, where he used to race stolen cars at an abandoned air force base. He was never without his briefcase, which always contained about an ounce of marijuana and a handgun. He never went anywhere without his gun. One night he scared the living fuck out of all of us, firing it out the window of a car that was driving us back from a party. Chip loved smut and would go on to edit a number of porn mags and become Al Goldstein's ghostwriter.

Paul Proch (rhymes with "coach") was way too smart to be working at Drake. Brilliant but lost, he was trying to break into television and film writing and was constantly applying for jobs at art magazines, which invariably turned him down because his résumé itself was too much like the blueprint for a nonobjectivist installation, and his cover letters read like deranged manifestos. I have no idea how he got through the rigorous Drake screening process. He came with a gorilla costume, which he would wear in his office while he smoked cigarettes out of a long plastic filter. Naturally, we got along famously.

I ran my department like a workshop in Dada publishing. I bought everyone lab coats, clipboards, and stethoscopes to walk around in like it was a *M*A*S*H** unit. We armed ourselves with toy suction dart guns and had daily battles. In the mornings we listened to the *Make Believe Ballroom* on WNEW-AM. They played 1940s- and '50s-era swing and popular standards—lots of Frank Sinatra, Tony Bennett, Rosemary Clooney, Benny Goodman. In the afternoon we tuned in to a local heavy metal show that leaned hard on Motörhead and the first Guns N' Roses album. Despite the myopic weltanschauung of our employers, we had cultivated a real clubhouse environment where everyone pushed everyone else's creativity. If you were thin-skinned, you would not have lasted a second. The ribbing was rampant, and no one was immune. *Hey, Barry, did that belt come with those pants or did you have to buy it separately? Hey, Spooner, who does your hair, Frank Lloyd Wright?*

After work we went out and blew our money at a dizzying gauntlet of bars and after-hours dives, sometimes staying up all night snorting coke, just showering off before work. But we were always on time the next day, as was our usual breakfast of pizza burgers and chocolate milk shakes, which would arrive just as punctually. We had the guys at the Midtown Deli *trained*.

Carmine gave my guys a long leash because our work was good, we were motivated, and we didn't miss deadlines.

One enchanted evening we were out at the Irish bar across the street from Drake. We had been drinking for a while when we realized that the regular after-work crowd had turned into a creepy pickup scene. Unbeknownst to us, it was karaoke night, and the bar was suddenly packed with yuppie douche bags lining up to sing "Da Doo Ron Ron." The guys told me they would pay for all my drinks if I just got up and belted "My Way."

I had already absorbed a few martinis, so I was going for it. I gave it my best Sid Vicious, climbing on a table and warbling with a vibrato wider than the Jersey Turnpike. I was intent on being eighty-sixed from the place. I couldn't stand the crowd of jocks in blue shirts and power ties and the women who all wore Reeboks with their business suits (don't forget, this was the eighties).

By the time I got to the *"What is a man, what has he got?"* part, I had thrown my jacket into the crowd and was working on my shirt and tie. I was punk-rocking it hard, full tilt, at the top of my lungs, half naked, falling forward off of a table into a crowd of stunned nine-to-fivers. I was sure I'd be getting tossed. Except it backfired: dudes were high-fiving me, fat women were kissing me, and the guy in charge of the karaoke came running over and said, "That was great! You win!"

"Huh?"

I'd had no idea it was a contest. I was now a finalist for a ski trip to Vermont. They gave me an absolutely hideous sweater as a prize and told me to come back the next week, which I didn't. One must never do the same trick twice for the same audience.

7

YOU CAN BURN IT

Drake was a real paper mill. We put out something like eighty magazines a year, twelve issues each of our core mags—*High Society, Cheri, Live, Celebrity Skin,* and *Playgirl*—plus the *Best of High Society* and *Best of Cheri,* and a faux fashion rag called *Swimsuit* (like the *Sports Illustrated* swimsuit issue, but every month). Stuff came *flying* out of the production department. But all of it was knocked off from someone else's ideas, without regard or respect for the originality, adventurous spirit, personal risk, or culture shifts that spawned a sexually explicit vista within a truly free press.

Hefner, Guccione, Flynt, and Goldstein all understood that the simple act of putting out a porn magazine was a *political* act. Larry Flynt was *shot* for it.

I have always admired Larry Flynt. When it comes to defending free speech, he is as radically outspoken as he is irrepressible. In the early 1970s he showed up in court to face obscenity charges wearing the American flag as a diaper. Later he was held in contempt of the U.S. Supreme Court, whom he called, right to their faces, "eight assholes and a token cunt."

Whereas the *Hustler* knockoffs I had been working for had simply swiped the formula for producing pecker-popping squack rags, they never had the brains or swagger to use their platforms as bully pulpits and swing freely at the self-righteous, moralizing assholes who wanted to nanny the country. Larry, like Al Goldstein, said "fuck 'em all" and made legal history with his precedent-setting victory over pietistic

Moral Majority popinjay Jerry Falwell, whom he had depicted having sex with his mother in an outhouse. That case brought him once again to the Supreme Court, which had the wisdom to overlook his previous outburst. Its decision defended the right to parody public figures, a major kick in the balls to holier-than-thou celebrities and politicians who were now officially fair game for professional shit slingers like *Hustler* and *Screw*.

In 1978 Larry was shot by a sniper outside a Georgia courthouse where he was fighting obscenity-related charges. His injuries left him paralyzed from the waist down, making him the unimpeachable gold standard for First Amendment martyrdom.

There is still some speculation about who shot Larry and why. There have always been rumors that it was mob-related retribution for having begun his own distribution company—Larry was also one of the first distributors of *High Times*—outside the aegis of organized crime, which had traditionally controlled the sex industry. But the guy believed to have done it is Joseph Paul Franklin, a white supremacist driven to insanity by *Hustler*'s interracial fuck shots. Franklin, who confessed to the shooting while in jail (although he was never tried for it), became something of a star in the dark world of racist, ultra-paranoid right-wing survivalist hate freaks: the fellow who wrote *The Turner Diaries*—the book that inspired Tim McVeigh to blow up the Federal Building in Oklahoma City—dedicated another of his books to Franklin.

In 1989, soon after I was hired at *Cheri*, the Supreme Court ruled in *Texas v. Johnson* that flag burning is a protected form of speech. It was a great day for First Amendment advocates, a group to whom I believed we as pornographers not only belonged, but somehow represented the vanguard. *New York Newsday*, then the only New York daily that printed color on the cover, ran a brilliant photo of Old Glory in flames and the screaming banner YOU CAN BURN IT. I put it on the wall of my office, proud to live in a country that defended my right to Free Speech. In about five seconds I was told to take it down.

This was also the time of the Meese Commission on Pornography, a Reagan-sponsored study that unambiguously set out to connect the dots between pornography and violence. They didn't find what they were looking for, so they cooked the results. The final report said that without any evidence, the link between sexually explicit material and aggressive behavior is "plainly justified by our own common sense," and that's what they took to the American people. It was a frightening time: the Cold War was over, and the right-wing administration needed a new enemy. With the help of the Moral Majority and a virulent faction of antisex feminists headed by the indomitable tag team of Andrea Dworkin and Catharine McKinnon, they wanted to shut us down. You would think that anyone who did what we did for a living would have at least a passing interest in civil liberties and a sense of righteous indignation, but in our office, no one gave a fuck.

At Drake, there were no idealized conceptions of being muckraking journalists, Establishment-battling warriors of the Fourth Estate. There were no dreams of being next-generation Hefners, pop culture pioneers making lasting contributions to lifestyle publishing. The only belief system was to crank out these "me too" jerk-off mags and make Ruderman richer. Which is fine for a business model but somehow unevolved as a worldview. Even when slinging shit, there should always be a certain pride and nobility in enjoying the upper reaches of free speech.

Typical of the Drake experience was their stab at a higher-end men's mag, which somehow got strapped with the shockingly queer title *Hawk*. It featured the usual manly features about electronic gadgets and college football, some obviously gorgeous women, and adventure stories about extreme mountain climbing or some other equally testosterone-driven nonsense. It was undistinguished in every possible way, and without a point of view or a voice of its own, it failed miserably.

But I loved my job. I would have enjoyed a little more appreciation for the iconoclasm of the X-rated, but otherwise, putting out inconsequential slap rags was a lot of fun. And I was learning a ton—I hung around in the production department and sopped up everything there was to know about four-color printing from the ground up. I studied the sales numbers and every possible variable trying to figure out why some issues sold better than others. Common sense said that the cover was what sold the book—a lot of times the magazines were wrapped in plastic, so you couldn't even flip through them. We spent weeks picking the right girl and the right background color. Sometimes white sold really well, and then it wouldn't. It was impossible to tell. We carefully crafted cover lines and positioned them for maximum exposure, so that when the books were racked and you could see only the left side of the magazine, you could still read them. But clearly it was satisfaction with the entire package that helped build a loyal following, and our books were very consistent. You had to give a lot of bang for the buck, and you had to invest energy and joie de vivre in even the dumbest magazines or the reader could tell in a heartbeat. If you didn't care, why should they?

I watched Carmine pore over the layouts for *High Society* and *Cheri*—he would drive editors and designers nuts making them tweak and redo layouts. He had a great eye for girl sets. It was a competitive business, and he was not going to settle for anything less than approaching perfection in his magazines. And of course he was right. *High Society* and *Cheri* made boatloads of money.

I took a lot of my cues from Carmine. The way he managed me was brilliant. Some people like to be coddled, but I hate that namby-pamby bullshit. I'm a professional. Tell me what's on your mind. A lot of people disagreed with the way New York Yankees manager Billy Martin handled his pitchers (including most of the pitchers themselves)—*"Hey, asshole, throw strikes"*—but sometimes there is nothing else to be said. When I'm up on that mound, I don't want to talk about my problems at home, I want to get guys out. The important thing is that Carmine always treated me with respect, praising my good work and complimenting me when things were going well. I felt as though he was rooting for me. He was a hard-ass, but he wasn't dismissive. He engaged me, and when I disagreed with him, he listened. He answered all my questions about the business. He forced me to challenge myself and be better at my job. I was rewarded with raises and promotions.

My favorite part of the week at Drake was the Friday photo meetings, when we would vet piles and piles of photo sets that had been submitted for approval. In those days, a few years before *Penthouse* opened things up by going hard-core (and in the process almost going out of business, losing pretty much all of their national advertising after they started printing piss shots, perhaps to satisfy some bizarre Guccione fetish), there were some pretty strict rules that we had to follow. There was no penetration allowed. If a girl was touching herself and you couldn't see her fingernail, that was penetration, and it was not going in the magazine. No mouth-to-genital contact, no genital-to-genital contact. In the boy-girl sets, no erections. What constituted an erection? Anything more than a 45-degree angle between the body and the penis. Rosenbaum used to walk around the office with a magnifying glass and a protractor and some boy-girl photo he had fallen in love with, asking people if they thought the guy had a hard-on or not. (The myth is that this had to do with government censorship, but in fact the guidelines came down from regional distributors who wouldn't carry a magazine that had crossed some arbitrary line of decency, as if a partially obscured digit would lay waste to the Eastern Seaboard but seven girls bent over the hood of a Jeep Wrangler spreading their asses was somehow okay.) We would go through a hundred sets of photos in a few hours, cracking jokes about weird-looking tits or particularly robust genitalia, approving of the obvious knockouts, and howling when we spotted a hemorrhoid. These meetings generally brought out the worst in everyone.

Somewhere along the line, Proch and I developed our Post-Darwinian Theory of Publishing Evolution Based on *Planet of the Apes*. It was simple: the functionaries, that is the production people who spent their days trafficking material between the prepress shop where color proofs were made, our offices, and the printer, were the Gorillas. Since most of the grunts in the art department didn't know how to read, or at least didn't practice that sweet science, they were also Gorillas. Editors were Chimpanzees, the educated class, like Cornelius in *Planet of the Apes*. The more advanced art people, those who could recognize *type* as something more than just another design element to be pushed around, got to be Chimpanzees, too. Carmine, however, was an Orangutan, the ruling class, like Dr. Zayus. He was an adept who held secret knowledge. Rosenbaum, Ronson, and Stevens thought they were Orangutans, but they weren't; they were just spoiled Chimps. (Actually, Stevens was more like a Gorilla. Occasionally, lower apes were socially promoted based on good looks.) And of course Ruderman was the Lawgiver. There is never any mistaking the Lawgiver.

I was a good Chimp, and within a year I was promoted to special projects editor and running a handful of start-up books, including *Buxom*, maybe the silliest magazine of all time, written in an absurd over-the-shoulder-boulder-holder-jiggly-wiggly-major-M-cup-mammary-titty-fetish hep jive blather about bra stuffing, rib cushions, and lady bumps. It was a gas. For this nonsense I was now making thirty-four grand a year and not saving a dime.

I spent cash like water. Instead of a wallet I used ATMs and just took out whatever I needed. Thirty-four thousand dollars seemed like a lot then—after all, the rent for my top-floor apartment in a Harlem brownstone was five hundred a month.

I treated New York City as if it were my personal playground. I was dating a nineteen-year-old Armenian dominatrix who would bring me pita bread and string cheese for breakfast, and a twenty-three-year-old Jewish grad student who wore stockings and garters, listened almost exclusively to Billie Holiday and Bessie Smith, and harbored aspirations of being a poet; and I was carrying on with one of the *Playgirl* editors who worked upstairs.

How did women feel about dating a pornographer? Like my parents, they were just happy I was *employed*.

On an otherwise dreary Monday, Proch announced that we were going to Las Vegas. "Meet me at the Horse Around Bar Friday at three p.m.," he demanded. He was going to be coming from L.A., where he was trying to sell a script and shmooze some buddies of his who were television writers. We didn't discuss it again. He just assumed I would be there.

Okay, so we were taking a page out of the Gonzo playbook, and why the fuck not? We were twenty-five years old, and a pointless spur-of-the-moment trip to Vegas was the logical extension of our boozy Frank Sinatra obsession. Vegas was still ridiculously cheap: the flight was ninety-nine dollars, and a room at Circus Circus, home of the Horse Around Bar, was just twenty-five bucks. Ninety-nine-cent shrimp cocktails and $1.99 all-you-can-eat prime rib dinners were the order of the day. You could be a poverty-stricken pornographer stuck in Vegas and still die of gout like a seventeenth-century French nobleman.

At 3:00 p.m. on Friday I was in Vegas at the appointed locus. Proch was in his "experimental drinking" phase and was sitting in front of half a dozen cocktails including a grasshopper, a slippery nipple, a sex on the beach, and a few other trendy girlie drinks. I looked at his mixologist's nightmare and ordered myself the relatively sobering trinity of a vodka martini, ice cold with three olives, a Bloody Mary, also with olives, and a can of Budweiser. The bill came to $2.90.

The Horse Around is a revolving bar, built like a carousel, that overlooks the floor of Circus Circus, which is in fact a giant perpetual circus with dancing bears, tightrope walkers, scantily clad trapeze artists, fire-breathers, and a guy being shot out of a cannon. Hunter Thompson called it "what the whole hip world would be doing on a Saturday night if the Nazis had won the war." Thank God there were no monkeys. That would have been too much. The spinning bar itself was difficult to handle.

The best news (aside from the ridiculously cheap drinks) was that Redd Foxx was performing that night. As a dinosaur on the scene (the "party records" that his act was based on came out back in the 1950s), he had been banished to the Hacienda Hotel, so far down the Strip and away from the bright lights of Caesars and Circus Circus that it was practically in Oaxaca. Foxx and the Hacienda had nothing to do with the New Vegas that was beginning to creep in—only a few years later the city would be entirely family-friendly, but in 1988 such savagery had not yet become completely oppressive. The Strip was still seedy, and the Sands, Sinatra's place, had not yet been blown up to make room for a roller coaster. There were still hookers and drug dealers everywhere, what any sensible adult would consider "added value."

When we arrived at the Hacienda, my immediate reaction was to take a shower. The red vinyl booths were greasy, the chips dirty and worn. Even the air was slightly jaundiced. It felt forgotten, its cowboy motif hopelessly dated. It would meet a fate similar to that of the Sands: it was imploded in 1996 with eleven hundred pounds of dynamite to make room for an eye bummer called Mandalay Bay.

But Redd Foxx killed, finishing his set with the classic Ya Gotta Wash Yer Ass ("not your whole ass, just your ass*hole*") routine. He was filthier than the Hacienda's all-night coffee shop, and the crowd of low rollers loved it. At the end of the show Redd thanked a few people in the audience, adding, "I wanna say hello to my friend Evel Knievel. Evel, stand up!"

Evel did his best impersonation of someone standing up. After years of grinding his skeletal system into kindling, he was shaped more like a question mark than an exclamation point. But he got our attention, that's for sure.

If you can define a "hero" by how much your parents hated him, Evel Knievel was the single greatest man who ever lived. Fuck Neil Armstrong—Knievel jumped the fountain at Caesars Palace *on a motorcycle!* And the results were incredible. He rolled about a mile with half a ton of Harley-Davidson stuck to his head.

Everyone I know had attempted some sort of half-assed Knievel stunt when they were kids. I personally broke my nose and spent a day in the dentist's chair after going ass over teakettle trying to jump three Big Wheel tricycles on my Raleigh Chopper.

We had to meet Knievel. We had to pay our respects to a True American Original.

He was easy to spot in the crowd, dressed as he was in a perfectly Evel red, white, and blue spangled shirt, tight black jeans, and lizard-skin cowboy boots. He reeked of daredevil.

"Mr. Knievel," I said, "we're from *High Society* magazine. We wanted to say hello. We're huge fans of yours."

Evel stopped. He looked deadly serious, but he still carried the captain-of-the-football-team good looks, cleft chin and blues eyes, like a shell-shocked version of Paul Newman.

"High Society," he drawled. "Great magazine. I love the girls. Meet me at the Shark Club. Tell the guy at the door you're with me." And he was off.

Journalists such as we were, we found the Shark Club easily. It was a discotheque off the Strip that catered mostly to locals. Out-of-towners were asked to pay admission, but when we declared that we were "with Evel," the velvet rope was dropped along with the cover. Knievel's name commanded respect! (Thinking back, there may have also been a slight look of pity in the doorman's eye, although I really couldn't be sure at this late date.) I asked one of the bouncers if he had seen Evel. "Just look for the closest bar," he harrumphed.

There were five or six bars circling the dance floor, and sure enough, Evel was at the one nearest the door. "What the fuck took you guys so long?" he demanded. It had been ten minutes since we last saw him. We ordered beer and bourbon and got down to drinking seriously.

Knievel was with his "manager," whom we quickly nicknamed the Operator. A tall, handsome black guy with an incredible line of patter, he was keeping an eye on Evel, who was getting increasingly plastered with each successive round.

"Don't worry about a thing," the Operator kept telling us. "Evel likes you guys. That's all that matters."

"Evel likes us," Proch would intone, trancelike, while he sucked down increasingly bizarre combinations of liquor. "That is all that matters."

The Operator had worked with Muhammad Ali and had produced Muhammad's dental hygiene masterpiece, the absolutely mesmerizing album *Ali and His Gang vs. Mr. Tooth Decay*. (Highlights include an evil Frank Sinatra peddling molar-munching ice cream to children; Ali discussing the benefits of fluoride with Richie Havens; and "The Fight Song," which features Howard Cosell's play-by-play of the big match between Ali and his arch enemy, Mr. Tooth Decay. "We've got the stuff to run him away from here," says Ali, "just like I did George Foreman over in Zaire.") The Operator had also worked with Ali on some ill-founded merchandise schemes, like Ali Champion Brand Shoe Polish.

Knievel was in town for the opening of the Vegas Hard Rock Café, to which he said he had sold his Skycycle, the piece of shit he had banged into the side of the Snake River Canyon, etching forever another chapter of Knievel Heroics. He had a check he kept waving around for some crazy amount, twenty thousand bucks or something, claiming that he sold the Skycycle for a million dollars and that this was only part of the payment. But for some reason he was having trouble cashing it. We kept on drinking. Since no one in Las Vegas ever wants to hear about an uncashed check, I was paying for the drinks (and expensing them to *High Society*). We were telling dirty jokes, flirting with the bartenders, talking shit, and getting very fucked-up. "Evel," I said, "we gotta get you in the magazine. We'll build you a new Skycycle, you can jump over some girls."

"If you need anything in Vegas," Evel told me, "just call me. I'm at the Aladdin, room 1234. You can remember that. If *I* can remember that, you can. I like you guys." We drank to that. Quite a few times. Eventually Knievel became so drunk he could no longer sign autographs for the fans who would occasionally get the nerve to approach him—he kept getting stuck on the big "E" in "Evel." The bartender had to take his pen away. I promised I would call him.

The next day, after a horrifying food frenzy at the Circus Circus buffet, we rented a car and floated it over to the Liberace Museum and then to the Fred G. Sanford Junk Shop, where Redd Foxx was selling tons of his stuff to help pay off the IRS.

It was kind of sad to see him in a storefront selling boxes of crap. I don't want to get too far into the politics of the IRS and foulmouthed black entertainers, but they really did fuck Foxx, swarming on his house like a SWAT team with a vengeance, in front of television news cameras, with Redd cordoned off and watching helplessly in his underwear. I guess that taught somebody a lesson.

But he was very nice to us, and we walked out with some of the junk that the IRS had passed on—a case of twenty-year-old cans of Redd Foxx hair spray, some absolutely hideous ceramic candleholders in the shape of ducks wearing top hats (from the Foxx living room? I could only imagine what the rest of it looked like), and some *Redd Foxx: The Man, The Entertainer* paperbacks which he signed for us. Then I called Knievel.

Evel sounded paranoid when he answered the phone. "Who's this?" he demanded.

"The boys from *High Society*."

"Who's with you?"

"It's just us . . ."

"Are you sure?"

I didn't quite know what to make of that. I looked around. I didn't see anyone. I told him I was sure.

"Call me when you get to the Aladdin. I'll meet you at the bar downstairs."

When we got to the bar, we called, as instructed. Again: "Who are you with?" "It's just us." "Are you sure?" He told us to wait for him.

The Knievel who appeared was not the same man we were with at the Shark Club. He was wearing a blue oxford shirt and half-moon glasses and looked as though he had aged forty years since the night before. The Operator was with him.

Knievel bellied up to the bar and ordered a Budweiser and a shot of bourbon. "What the fuck are you drinking?" he asked me.

"Just beer. I'm driving."

"Fuck that. Drink bourbon. I saw you last night, Edison. You're out of your fucking mind, like me. You're crazy."

Me, crazy? This is the guy who tried to jump thirteen double-wheeled buses at Wembley and ended up bouncing about thirty feet in the air. This is the guy who thought he could fly a contraption called a

"Skycycle" over a canyon. He had broken his neck more times than Mother Teresa had said the Holy Rosary. I ordered some whiskey.

We pitched Evel our idea for him to write a column for *High Society*, and he loved it. "Do you know," he told us shrewdly, "why women with big breasts are stupid? Because it takes so much blood to operate their tits that their brains can't function properly." Sure, *that* made sense. "Listen," he told us, "I'm not a doctor, but I know plenty of them, so you can believe me.

"And you know what I hate? *Actors*. You know why? Because that's all they can do . . . *act*. What I do is *real*. Fuck George Hamilton. What does he know about being me? All actors are bullshit. I hate fucking George Hamilton. Fuck him."

After just a few drinks he was visibly drunk. He was still waving his check around, asking the bartender if he could cash it, and trying to pick up every cocktail waitress in the place. His basic technique was to holler, "Hey, do you wanna sleep with me tonight?" The girls failed to rally around for a Touch of Evel, and it quickly became obvious that he had been hanging around the hotel for a while now, working the same material, and everyone was getting a little tired of his routine.

Pretty soon he insisted that I drive him and the Operator to the Mirage, presumably so he could wave the check around at a fresh audience. I had a few in me, but I was game. I very carefully aimed the rent-a-car down the Strip. Knievel rode shotgun. "It is better," he proclaimed, paraphrasing Teddy Roosevelt, "to do mighty things and win glorious triumphs, even though checkered by failure and defeat, than to live in that gray twilight of those poor spirits who enjoy neither victory nor defeat, because they don't have the balls to try either one."

I managed to get the car back safely to Circus Circus, and the next day we left for New York. When we called him a few days later to get cracking on his column, he was nowhere to be found, and the women who answered the phone numbers he gave us weren't all that willing to help us, or him.

In those days Proch and I liked to cruise hotel bars for cute tourist chicks (with a zero percent success rate), and one night we ran into the Operator, who had been nice enough after our Vegas jag to send us some of that Muhammad Ali shoe polish. Now our feet looked just like the Champ's.

"The boys from *High Society*!" He grinned. He was happy to see us and invited us to join him for a few rounds. The entire time we were drinking, he was riffling through his little black book and trying to find a date, getting up every few minutes to use the pay phone. He must have called about twenty women. He was striking out miserably and getting increasingly desperate. Finally, he just took us to dinner.

He had a car waiting, and we went to this great soul food restaurant way uptown. The dining room was designed like a basketball court—an all hardwood floor with foul lines and a basket at one end—and there was a small jazz combo playing. We ordered fried chicken, collard greens, candied yams, mac and cheese, and biscuits and gravy, and we drank spiked lemonade in Ball jars.

"Evel is very busy. But he likes you boys," the Operator reminded us.

"That's all that matters," added Proch.

Apparently, Evel was working on another canyon jump, but this time Evel was going to get paid *not* to do it. People would call a national prayer line and try to convince him to call off the stunt and save his own life. Each call would cost a couple of bucks. Eventually Evel would see the light, and America would be spared the tragedy of another dead hero. It sounded like a good plan. I know I would have called.

"He was never going to make it across the canyon the first time," the Operator confessed. "We knew he wouldn't make it after the prototype failed. But he was supposed to land softly in the middle. The fucked-up thing is that Evel can't swim. He was terrified he was going to drown."

Finally the Operator connected with one of his girlfriends. He picked up the check and disappeared into the night, leaving us with our fortified lemonades, dreaming of Snake River and knowing in our hearts that Evel liked us. What else could matter?

8

THOSE TITS ARE TAKING FOOD OUT OF MY CHILDREN'S MOUTHS!

Life as a Chimp was good. But no matter how much savoir faire I may have shown composing the mot juste to accompany Veronica from Santa Monica, it was still knuckle draggery of the lowest order. And I aspired to walk . . . erect! It probably didn't help my quest to evolve that I was still wading in the muck and mire of the mat world and free-lancing for a handful of wrestling magazines, generally considered the La Brea Tar Pits of the literary landscape.

But that giant lumbering doofus Hulk Hogan kept on selling tickets, and the blats needed writers. In my eyes he was still the human equivalent of Big Bird—outsized, yellow, and dumb as a summer squash. I think the Cookie Monster would have taken him in a fair fight. Hell, Ernie and Bert had more genuine pathos than Hogan—but Hogan had just body slammed Andre the Giant at the Silverdome in Detroit in front of the largest crowd of all time. He wasn't going anywhere for a while.

Somehow I convinced my friend Ron that we needed to go see Hogan get gored by "Macho Man" Randy Savage inside a steel cage at Madison Square Garden, and he had bought four tickets—for him and his girl, and me and a date to be named later.

The week before the show, with still no name on my dance card, I went downtown to see local champs the A-Bones play. Their gigs were always a party, and I figured maybe I'd have some luck there. Before the show started, I was bemoaning to their singer Billy Miller that I could not find a young woman to accompany me to the Steel Cage

Match, even with its promise of two half-naked men ripping each other's flesh across four walls of chain-link fence. You could imagine his shock. He offered me this:

"We do a dance contest thing toward the end of the set, and we usually give away a record or something. Why don't we make it Win a Date with Mike Edison to Go See Wrestling?"

So this was what I had been reduced to: a dive-bar door prize being auctioned off to whichever local tosspot could manage to do the Twist for two minutes and fifty seconds without falling on her ass. Truly, this was the nadir of my romantic life. Had I no pride? I made my outrage clear and protested noisily until Billy bought me off with a couple of beers.

Actually, there were plenty of chicks there, and my prospects looked good. Everyone was drinking and having a good time. It was a distinct possibility that some cute girl could win me and not even know it until it was too late. In fact, I was counting on it.

When it was dance contest time, Billy announced the prize, and while I sheepishly beamed from the side of the stage, every woman in the place fled the dance floor, leaving two brutish guys in leather jackets pumping their fists. To add insult to injury, they weren't even interested in *me*, they just wanted to see the cage match. Bastards.

However, an incredibly attractive girl came up to me afterward and said she would love to go see wrestling with me, but there was no way in hell she was going to dance for it.

Rhea was a living doll. She was sass-mouthed and whip smart. She wore her long brown hair in girlish bangs. When I met her, she was wearing a clingy rayon shirt—"the fabric of the future," she assured me. She worked in a bar and could finish the Sunday *New York Times* crossword puzzle. I was bonkers for her. And I was over the moon to have a real girlfriend for a change. It just wasn't dignified for a professional porn monger to be running around chasing skirt like a horny teenager.

Not to mention that Rhea made a great gun moll. We went to the Jersey Shore on vacation—one night pretending we were a square married couple and staying at a fluffy bed-and-breakfast, and the next, pretending we were married, although not to each other, and staying in a sleazy motel with a water bed and mirrors on the ceiling.

It was a great time to be in New York City with little real responsibility. We got dolled up and went to jazz clubs, slurping dirty martinis until the music was a blur. We got loaded and went to see our friends' sleazy punk rock bands, invariably winding up in Chinatown at five in the morning, eating razor clams in black bean sauce for breakfast at Wo Hop. We went to see Frank Sinatra at Radio City Music Hall, and he forgot the words to "My Way." I was starting to get the idea that anything could happen.

The Lismar Lounge on First Avenue was part of an East Village that doesn't exist anymore. To give you an idea of just how noisome and unholy a place this was, it was the only club GG Allin was actually invited to play *twice*.

Upstairs was a dark, divy bar and downstairs was an indestructible, musty cave where bands played. Off to one side was another dank room where you could get a little relief from the racket and, if you were drunk enough and willing, wind up making out with a stranger. For the *High Times* Christmas party, which I had managed to get invited to via my *Screw* connections, it had been set up with rows of chairs, two by two across, like a commercial jetliner. If you sat down, a pretty girl playing a coffee-tea-or-me flight attendant would bring you a balloon filled with laughing gas.

There was tons of pot being smoked, and probably about half the people there were tripping. Someone offered me a hit of acid, but I thought it would be impolite to accept and not drop it on the spot. To me, that was just common LSD courtesy. As I got to know the extended *High Times* crew and their stoner sycophants, I realized that a lot of this supposedly sharing family of unreconstructed freaks were just self-centered drug sponges who wouldn't share the burning embers of a shake-weed roach with you unless they could confirm that there was a bushel of free pot in the next room, and they wouldn't think it at all gauche to take a few tabs of free party-favor blotter and stuff it in their pockets, wrapped in the cellophane from a cigarette pack, for later.

It shouldn't have come as a surprise that *High Times* always had a lot of terminally unemployed squatter types hovering for a free taste of some centerfold weed, or whatever other holiday treats were being dispensed. Tonight there were space cakes, LSD, magic mushrooms, and joints being tossed around like candy corn on Halloween, plus the nitrous tanks, all of which, when dangled like a carrot, would taunt the deep-seated druggy avarice in even the most mellow stoner.

John Holmstrom was neither greedy nor mellow. John was the founder of *Punk* magazine, one of the greatest, funniest magazines ever. He was also the executive editor of *High Times*.

Most people don't know about the seemingly incongruous blood bond between *Punk* and *High Times*, and a lot of that has to do with the more rainbow-hued editors at *High Times* who were always looking to polarize punks and hippies and rewrite their own history. The truth was that *High Times* had always embraced punk rock—it was the first national magazine to put the Sex Pistols on the cover. More recently, the magazine had been cast as some sort of One Love Fuck Fest for the retrograde dopers who thought Jerry Garcia was still a relevant force. But John was proof that once upon a time, the Revolution was real.

John started *Punk* with Legs McNeil in 1976 and was responsible for miles of trendsetting artwork—the great caricature covers, the comics that littered the magazine, and the charismatically hand-lettered interviews that went on for pages, featuring every punk rock superstar (Dead Boys, Ramones, et al.) and proto-punk legend (New York Dolls, Lou Reed, Iggy Pop, etc.) extant. *Punk* was Great and Stupid and Big because the people who created it were having the time of their lives.

The *Punk* interview style was a complete departure from the false idol worship that dominated the slick rock mags of the day. *Punk* was transparent. The wall between "star" and "fan" had been torn down, and what was left could be as shrewd as it was gleefully retarded. If the phone rang or the dog ran into the room during the interview, that could make the final cut. Sometimes the interviews were unabashedly confrontational, sometimes they read like pranks, but the coolest bands were always in on the joke. *Punk* was also keen on shooting outrageous *fumetti*—photo funnies—the most ambitious and gorgeous being "Mutant Monster Beach Party," starring Andy Warhol, John Cale, Joey Ramone, Lester Bangs, Debbie Harry, Peter Wolf, and Edith Massey. It was a masterpiece, the very apogee of trash culture and, as such, a thing of great power and beauty.

High Times was founded by Tom Forçade, a big-time pot smuggler who was always more of a radical than a paisley peacenik. "There are only two kinds of dealers," Forçade used to say. "Those who need fork-lifts and those who don't." He fell into the first category.

In 1969 he helped start the Underground Press Syndicate, a left-wing wire service providing news to college and renegade papers that didn't trust the Establishment media. Forçade had worked with Students for a Democratic Society (SDS) in the 1960s and was rumored to be knocking knees with its terrorist wing, the Weathermen. By 1970 he emerged as a Yippie.

The Yippies knew well that "if you threw a brick at a politician, you would be put in jail, but if you threw a pie at him, you would be put on the evening news." Forçade made the news in 1970 when he testified on behalf of the Underground Press Syndicate before a congressional commission on pornography. Dressed as a priest with a wide-brimmed Quaker top hat (one of his favorite gimmicks), he accused the commission of running "a blatant McCarthyesque witch hunt." When one bureaucrat objected, Forçade let loose "the only obscenity is censorship!" and nailed him with a cream pie.

Forçade often said that he "never met a drug he didn't like," but he *loved* marijuana. He started *High Times* in 1974 with twelve thousand dollars made from a smuggling run, and in no time they were selling hundreds of thousands of issues a month, all the more romantic since he was running the operation out of a secret flophouse while avoiding a subpoena in a drug case.

High Times was unabashedly based on *Playboy*, right down to the Boy-oh-Boy centerfold. Like Hefner, whom he admired, Forçade had found an audience that shared his new-world outlook and was clamoring for attention. *High Times* was the fast train to a hip and hedonistic lifestyle. An infamous paranoiac who imagined CIA plots swirling around him—and in reality, the FBI had been keeping tabs on him for years—Forçade also suffered from severe bipolar disorder and profound seasonal mood swings. His demons would eventually become more than he could bear, and in 1979 he took his own life.

Part of Forçade's genius was that—contrary to the strident hippies who surrounded him—he identified punk rock as a significant youth movement. Despite vociferous protests from staffers, *High Times* put Johnny Rotten on the cover. The same issue featured an editorial by Patti Smith. A few years later, after Forçade's death, Joey Ramone joined the fray with his own opinion page.

So the legend goes, Tom came into the *Punk* office, put his big ol'
cowboy boots up on Holmstrom's desk, and drawled in his radical
twang, "Son, how'd you like to be famous?" In short shrift John found
himself on a plane to Atlanta to see the Sex Pistols.

The Pistols U.S. tour was a disaster, yet it wouldn't have worked
any other way. Avoiding music and media capitals New York and Los
Angeles for hostile redneck bars in Oklahoma and Texas—where they
played under a hail of bottles flung by redneck shit-kickers come to
stomp the punk menace—they finally self-destructed at the San Francisco hippie palace Winterland, in what is often cited as the worst rock
concert in history. During the tour, Forçade was alternately rumored to
have kidnapped Sid Vicious or simply to have lured him away with the
promise of a Big Bag of Smack so Forçade could use him as a bargain-
ing chip for a film of the tour he was planning to make. John wrote the
Sex Pistols tour story for *Punk*, which Forçade would continue to back
with money he was hauling in from *High Times*.

I was a huge fan of *Punk*, and I was still under the spell of *High
Times*, cast back in my hazy adolescence. As a longtime student of the
lifestyle they promoted, I was exceedingly interested in joining their organization.

You cannot imagine how flattered I was when Holmstrom recog-
nized me from my photo in *Main Event*! He was a huge wrestling fan
and was into my whole "bad-guy editor" shtick. We immediately agreed
that I should write a column for *High Times*.

Although I hadn't gotten into the porn racket to position myself as
any kind of literary outlaw, it made perfect sense to me that if I was in
the skin trade, writing for a dope magazine was not going to hurt any
cachet that I might have been cultivating as a New Bohemian Action
Journalist.

Now I was on the drug beat. My column was called Shoot the
Tube, a free-form affair about politics and television. I loved writing it,
loved working with John, loved stopping by the *High Times* office and
getting stoned with the editors (except John, who wasn't a pothead). It
all felt so *illicit*.

John illustrated one of my first columns, a riff on a presidential address about (what else?) the drug plague threatening our children. As
evidence that no one was safe, George Bush (the First) had brought
with him a bag of crack cocaine that was purchased just blocks from

Capitol Hill. He held it up for the cameras, his face twisted into a horrible WASPy scowl that said "I smell poo." I suppose the nation at large was horrified, but I thought it was the most idiotic thing I had ever seen. If he had really wanted to score some coke that badly, surely someone in the White House could have hooked him up.

The conceit of the story was that I was watching Bush's show-and-tell in a bar with an old wrestler pal who was now retired and considering going into politics—a scenario that turned out to be prophetic when Jesse Ventura became governor of Minnesota. (N.B.: He was big on feather boas and glitter, too, and it didn't seem to hurt his career.) To illustrate the story, John drew a terrific comic of me slugging mugs of beer with my imaginary rassling friend, with the president on TV in the background. The guy who did the Ramones' covers was now drawing pictures of me! And in a magazine I used to have to hide from my parents! My star was definitely rising, although it was of such a pathetically low wattage that no one else seemed to notice.

I made some mistakes when I first started writing for *High Times*. Early on I declared, "the Simpsons are not funny." It was after their first Christmas pilot, which, I think we can all agree, did not even hint at what the show would become within a few seasons. Now I'm as big a fan as anyone, but the early shows were so clunky they couldn't even qualify as diamonds in the rough. I mean, really, the series didn't fully take off until the animation tightened up and they stopped writing Bart as cute-stuff on a skateboard and Homer grew into his role as the Great God of Duff-Powered Dysfunction instead of just aping Walter Matthau.

Okay, so I fucked up. I'm still eating that one.

One of the columns I was most proud of was about Dan Rather, who, early on in his career, arranged to be shot up with heroin in a Texas cop house for a story he was working on, so he would know what it felt like to be high on dope when he was writing about it. In an interview with *Ladies' Home Journal*, he confirmed the experience and added somewhat cryptically, "I can say to you with confidence, I know a fair amount about LSD."

Well, I went to town with that and encouraged all journalists who wrote about the dangers of drugs to go out and get wasted on the subject matter of their choice. I figured they just might like it, and change their tune.

After the column came out, *High Times* got a call from a syndicated call-in radio show who wanted to have me as a guest. It was the beginning of my career as a media whore. I did the show on the phone, and it was broadcast nationwide. I figured they were impressed with my courageous style of offbeat *reportage* and wanted to congratulate me on my brave point of view. Of course, when I got on the radio, I was attacked mercilessly as the scourge of youth, a devil worshipper, and one caller accused me of killing his daughter, who had died of an overdose. It was brutal, but I learned one more important lesson: always be prepared, write your sound bites ahead of time, and stay on point. When the Republicans figured that out, they began to dominate American politics.

The phone rang and it was bad news. Dave Insurgent was in the hospital. He had been beaten, savagely, after a drug deal gone wrong. They clobbered him with a bat. He was in bad shape.

I had not seen Dave in a while, not since we had worked on another student film together. Maybe it had been a year. But that was normal—we'd go great lengths of time with only the occasional phone call to discuss the homeless person claiming to be a child star who was featured as a guest on *The Joe Franklin Show* that night.

Dave was taking a film class at the New School in Greenwich Village, and he was intent on capturing his vision of a modern-day Babylon run by a right-wing government, depicting religion as pure crowd control—a loosely hewn spin-off of the ideologies he had been spouting with Reagan Youth. I was cast as Satan, manifest as a riot cop. I had a truncheon, a crash helmet, even a plastic shield. High-quality stuff. I have to admit it was fun to wear, especially when he had me beating up on Birkenstocked pacifist protesters. We filmed in a vacant lot on Avenue C. The old Hispanic ladies, watching *la policía* beat up a longhair, were not amused, and they yelled at us the entire time.

The costumes were an extension of Dave's new fetish for ridiculous stage gear. After two terms of Reagan, he had changed the name of his band to House of God, and carrying on in his overblown, ironic bombast (predating *Spinal Tap* by years), he began wearing supremely expensive stage costumes bought at a religious supply store. Where he once goose-stepped, he now offered benedictions over the mosh pit, dressed like the pope, with a three-foot-tall miter and gold-adorned robes. He looked like a cross between an extra in *Monty Python and the Holy Grail* and a seriously misguided heavy metal star. Pushing the gag over the top, he insisted on writing absurdly pompous, multipart songs, like "In the Beginning (Parts I, II, and III)," ostensibly designed to mock seventies prog rock excess, although I have a sneaking suspicion he really enjoyed it for its own sake. Whatever the case, it was a wildly costly joke that very few people besides Dave would ever understand. I thought it was hilarious, but it would probably have been enough for us to get stoned and talk about it. Bringing it to the stage in front of an audience of perplexed punk rockers who wanted to hear Reagan Youth songs may have been taking it too far. But that's one thing I loved about Dave. He was certain of what he thought was funny.

Unfortunately, some very ugly drug dealers did not share Dave's sense of humor, and they had left him for dead. Somewhere along the line he had developed a nasty heroin habit. I knew that he was snorting junk sometimes, I knew a lot of people who did, but I never saw him strung out.

Dave was also dealing, moving large quantities of weed. Those papal vestments didn't grow on trees, after all. However, he was a lousy drug dealer, and, breaking one of the cardinal rules of the game, was doing the drugs he was supposed to be peddling. To make matters worse, he had copped a completely cavalier attitude toward his suppliers, allegedly telling them "you'll get paid when you get paid"—a recipe for disaster. Dave was in the hospital for weeks. After that he moved back with his folks to recuperate. This was a far cry from the relative bliss of Dave's Disco Bar.

When I got the news about him, I felt as though my head was going to split open. How was a twenty-five-year-old acidhead pornographer supposed to parse that sort of drug violence? I cried.

Everyone who plays with drugs knows there are consequences, from hangovers that can be squashed pretty easily, to the chronic stoner malady of lost keys (my rule has always been that if you are too stoned to find the keys, then good, because you are obviously too stoned to drive), to cocaine psychosis and bad trips. Dave had a helluva ride the night we went to see Black Sabbath and dropped some acid that we had been told was "very mild." It was not. It was of the brain-scrambling variety, and all those strobe lights flashing in the form of a giant crucifix to the dark grind of "Iron Man" and "Electric Funeral" had been too much for him to handle—for anyone with a central nervous system, really—but he was the only one petrified that we were all going to be punished by God for our heavy metal indulgence. I just laughed my ass off.

Getting his brain tossed for real, however, was not on the agenda—at least not until he developed a heroin habit and started playing grab-ass with some people who were very serious about their business, and then all bets were off. It was certainly a harsh reality check, but so distant from any lifestyle that I would ever embrace that it did not jar me out of my own bad habits, which were basically full-bore hedonism. There were those mornings when I'd wake up next to my girlfriend in a room littered with empty coke bindles and rolled-up dollar bills, strewn with jazz records and special jellies, and peppered with a seething maelstrom of liquor bottles and spent birth control. But it was all in the name of fun, and so, ultimately, harmless. I am not stupid, but no matter what I saw happening around me, I was still very much convinced of my own immortality. I was crushed by what had happened to my friend, but he was living on another planet, and I wasn't going there. Eventually I got a call from Dave. He was in good spirits and cracked a joke about Joe Franklin or the Grand Wizard or Liberace—one of our favorite things—but it rang hollow. He didn't seem quite right. It worried me when he tried to shrug the whole thing off, but then again, maybe he was just being brave. It was hard to tell.

Back at Smut Central, the locomotive that was my career kept on rolling. I had been promoted to Orangutan and was now editor in chief of *Live!*

Live! was originally a *Cheri* spin-off featuring "live nude girls," but now the orders from the Lawgiver were to make it more outrageous and go after *Hustler*.

I don't think *Hustler* was too worried. The jewel of the Flynt Empire, it had a giant staff, infinitely deep pockets, and a mad genius publisher who wanted to push the envelope beyond any established limit and was willing to take a bullet for it. Their photography made *Architectural Digest* look like a supermarket circular. They had their own soundstage. Even the *paper* they used made you want to cream. They were, truly, the Industrial Light and Magic of Poon. We were two editors, Proch and I, and one aristocrat of an art director, who, although talented at pasting wide-open beavers into centerfolds, did not want to dally with lowbrow literature like ours, no matter how much fun we were having. He wore tasseled loafers and aspired to work for an ad agency.

Looking back, our magazine was pretty corny, but it was as good spirited and as well executed as it could have been, given our limited resources. I littered the pages with cartoons and gag panels and really tried to make it a high-energy porn *experience*. We "discovered" a female recording engineer who insisted on recording bands naked (as usual, we shot everything *close*); we threw a blue smock and a handlebar mustache on one perplexed staffer, gave him a pair of scissors, and coronated him as the Pussy Barber of Beverly Hills, putting him in a photo shoot and claiming that he "coifed all the quim on the Coast."

One innovation I brought to Drake was the use of violator dots on the cover. A "violator dot" is the black dot or box that would cover the naughty bits in an advertisement, anything from boobies to crotch shots or insertion, like the black bars that go over someone's eyes when you want to hide his identity.

Traditionally, covers were shot with the models either wearing lingerie or covering their nipples and nether regions. But because they were so contrived, most covers looked static and dull. My idea was to take shots from the regular set, girls all hotted-up and in full repose, and conceal the parts we couldn't show with starbursts or creative type, so that basically we were putting full nudity on the cover and just being clever about it. We were right on the edge, and my bosses were extremely unsure about the new tack. Although I'm sure my *Live!* covers had nothing to do with any sort of revolution, these days you see it all the time. It was bound to happen. It's pretty much the Wild West out there, and you can show just about anything short of a money shot, as long as you Photoshop it to just this side of a crime.

We also started printing *real* letters, holding a mirror up to the psychoses of a porn-loving public. Generally speaking, the stuff that came in the mail was more akin to arts and crafts at the state funny farm than anything resembling adult correspondence. We just photocopied it and ran it "as is."

I HAVE FUN EVERYWHERE I GO

The pages looked as if they were lifted from a textbook in abnormal psychology: letters from prisoners written in crayon; lunatic ravings addressed to centerfold girls care of the magazine, almost always featuring a rural route as the return address; incredibly detailed confessions of adoration ("I love the way you cut your nails" . . . "I love the dimples on your toes" . . . "The freckle behind your left knee is making me crazy"); equally detailed expressions of what physical acts the writers might like to perform, along with their *precise* measurements. Apparently, the men of the Illinois state correctional facility, if they are to be taken at their word, are so massively endowed they should be setting world records left and right. One regular writer began every letter with the declarative "I AM A BLACK MAN!" And there was always a preponderance of mash notes sent from military bases, all of them so less than literate that you'd shudder when considering that this was the United States' first line of defense.

For some reason, people like to tear out the pages of the magazine and send them along with their notes. Often, everything from subhuman doodles of penises to gooey marriage proposals is scribbled on the pages with Magic Markers. Sometimes the photos are torn up—there are a lot of broken hearts out there.

My all-time favorite letter was just a list of one man's possessions: *I got a truck, Ford . . . I got a TV, 26 inches . . . I got a tool belt . . .* There was no explanation, just a lonely soul taking inventory. Years later I read this letter over a soundtrack of jungle drums as part of a found-poetry art project.

But with a skeleton staff and zero budget (we were stuck using everyone else's leftover girl sets, so no matter what we did, it was always going to look second-rate) and a stifling, self-realized corporate culture that put the kibosh on any risk taking, it was never going to break out and become a big title.

Every day I went to work, and it was more of the same: Rosenbaum freaking out about some girl he met and soliciting me for lifestyle advice. "Hey, Edison. My balls are sticking to my thigh. Do you think I should switch to boxers?" Ruderman continued prowling the halls, barking non sequiturs: "You call those tits, Mr. Ronson? Those tits are taking food out of the mouths of my children. You can do better." After work we were at the bar. Every so often something would happen to keep my complacency at bay.

Like the night I got stabbed in a White Castle.

The intelligent person will want to know what the hell I was doing in a White Castle in the Bedford-Stuyvesant section of Brooklyn at four in the morning, which in 1988 was no safe haven for Ivy League dropouts.

I was hungry.

For those somehow not already initiated into the cult of White Castle, allow me to explain. A White Castle is a prefabricated white tile building, the sort of modern architectural wonder that became popular in America after being spotlighted at the 1939 World's Fair. Except for the low-rent turrets and the blue gothic lettering of the logo, a White Castle looks like a men's room turned inside out. But within lives a world of culinary pleasure that can be found nowhere else.

Charles Mingus once said, "If God made anything better, he was saving it for himself." He wasn't talking about food, but you get the idea. A White Castle burger is about three square inches of grade-A beef perforated with exactly five holes. White Castle orthodoxy maintains that the holes are for a better-cooked burger and that they actually cost the company more to produce this way. ("The holes are extra!" boasts a classic White Castle promo piece.) This slice of heaven is cooked on an open steam grill, smothered in suet and onions, then nestled into a formfitting square bun, *manna*, that has also been lurking on the grill, absorbing all the ambient goodness. The result is like a slightly soggy meat petit four. It is poetry written in grease. The double cheeseburger is so exceptional in texture and taste, so hedonistic by any contemporary societal standard, that it should be outlawed. In the Church of Sharky we use them as communion wafers.

That night, Rhea had dragged me to some lame-o loft party in Bed-Stuy thrown by one of the out-of-luck actresses who worked at her bar. I hadn't had a chance to have dinner, but I was told there would be food there, and knowing that my girlfriend would never lie to me, I had no reason to worry. When we got there, I was offered some organic carrot sticks.

That's the kind of shit that makes me crazy. Come to a party at my house and you are going to be fed—and well: my miniature porcini risotto cakes will make you weep. So unless you are tripping on acid and have mistaken me for a gerbil, do not invite me to your house and offer me a fucking carrot stick. I don't give a goddam if it was grown by

Gandalf the Great on the sunny side of Magic Mountain, don't do it. At least there was some vodka there, which, in lieu of dinner, I drank like a parched hog.

By the time these veggie-munching thespians were ready to break up their fruity little fiesta, I was hearing voices in my head. That happens sometimes. In this case they were telling me that there was a White Castle nearby. I was being *summoned*.

You cannot ignore that call. I was with Rhea and a friend of hers, and we had hired a car service to get us back to Manhattan. Bed-Stuy was a crazy, dangerous neighborhood, and if you had any concern for your personal well-being, you did not wander there late at night. I implored the driver to find the White Castle with all possible haste.

The Bed-Stuy Castle lit up the ghetto like a porcelain angel. I hopped out of the car, ran into the restaurant, and got in line before the bulletproof screen that protected the young artist working the spatula. The girls waited in the car. They wanted little to do with this mission, and if they had really been on their game, they would have talked me the fuck out of my quest. Nothing good was going to come out of a drunk white boy trying to score a sack of old-fashioned hamburgers in that neighborhood at that time of night.

I ordered my food. In those days, I always went with some combination of eight burgers, which, after years of 4:00 a.m. Castle runs, I had established as the Human Vomit Threshold. Eight Castles were the ticket to gastronomic nirvana, but one toke over the HVT and you'd be ralphing in a wire basket and have to start all over from scratch. I believe I went for two double cheeseburgers, two cheeseburgers, and two "Castles," the basic unit of currency. I did the math again in my head to make sure. Eight. Plus fries, natch. I paid the man and moved to the pickup line.

My order appeared in a huge paper bag. I grabbed it and was about to trot back out to the car and the ensuing prandial orgy when I was shoved back against the wall, hard. The guy doing the shoving was not fucking around. He had a blade in his hand, now flashing quickly toward my mouth. He jabbed me in the face, catching the bottom of my upper lip and pulling the weapon back, spraying my blood all over both of us. He stuck his hand in my pocket—I was in shock, frozen—grabbed all the money I had on me, about sixty bucks, and pushed his way out through the door.

I did what anyone would do. I chased him down and punched him as hard as I could in the head with my free hand—in the other I was still holding on to my sack of White Castles, which I had now paid almost seventy dollars for and was not about to give up. He looked at me, confused. Maybe I wasn't supposed to do that, after all.

The girls—horrified into sobriety by the sight of a drunk Jew running out of a White Castle, spurting blood like a fountain and pounding Bed-Stuy's Most Wanted with a series of sloppy roundhouse fists—began screaming holy bloody hell. Rhea's voice cut through the din in my head. "He's got a knife!" This was not a fight I was going to win, and I backed off. But hitting him felt good. My money isn't free.

The girls were not happy. They took me over to the police station, but there wasn't a lot to do there. They were never going to catch the crackhead who cut me. I ate one of the double-cheesers, spraying more blood with each bite and doing nothing to help keep the knife wound clean of infection. The girls looked as if they were going to be sick, so I sent them home. There was an ambulance waiting outside, on its way back to the hospital. I needed to be sewn up, and the cops told me in no uncertain terms to get in.

I took the burgers with me.

Luckily, most of the damage had been done on the inside of my mouth. I took about fifteen stitches between my gums and top lip, and the doctor did a tremendous job. Years later there is still a decent ridge of scar tissue there, but just a hairline on the outside.

I made it to work on Monday, in pain and with my face so swollen that you would have thought I was storing golf balls for winter. I looked like a combination of Elvis, circa August 1976, and Screwy Squirrel, circa always. At some point Carmine pulled me aside and told me I should stay out of White Castles in bad neighborhoods. Oh, how I wanted to thank him for that gem, but I kept my mouth shut. It hurt too much to talk, anyway.

The wisdom of my White Castle run aside, I was still a higher primate, and making the dough (for the time) to prove it: I was up to forty thousand a year now, double the salary I had been hired at two years before, but it was starting to be a grind. The Happiness Boys were burned out, and I was sick of supposedly "senior" editors acting like retards whenever a porn star or stripper came into the office. It was embarrassing. And Proch was drifting, spending all his time writing his own stuff and jamming magazine work in at the last minute, like a kid doing his homework in homeroom. I was told to fire him. It sucked, but it was inevitable. I'd been covering for him out of loyalty to a drinking buddy, but everyone knew he was making little effort. It's not as if he didn't see the axe coming, he just didn't care.

I was beginning to wonder if this was really what I wanted. I loved my girlfriend, but more and more I felt sucked into the vortex—work, drink, fuck, sleep, repeat. It wasn't bad, but being "content" is just a nice way to say "dying slowly," and I was starting to get that wanderlust again.

The great thing about playing the drums is that you get to hit things with wooden sticks, yet no one yells at you. With some extra dough I made writing *Scream Queens*, a *Celebrity Skin* spin-off about topless horror-movie starlets, I bought a new set of drums, silver sparkle Ludwig Super Classics. After work I'd rush home to Harlem to get stoned and bang on them, pretty much what I used to do after school when I was fourteen. It was cheaper than therapy.

That's how it went for a while until on an otherwise ordinary day at the shop, scribbling girl copy and trying to distill reason from a photo set of two girls getting it on in a Laundromat, my old pals the Raunch Hands called, with the kind of empathy unique to those of us doomed to sabotage our own lives.

The Raunch Hands were a proto-garage band of amphetamine-crazy juiceheads who once upon a time had chewed up the competition and seemed headed for great things. I had known them since my first days at NYU. The guitar player, Mike Mariconda, was also an NYU student, and we used to drop acid together and listen to *Trout Mask Replica*.

The band got started in 1984 and was quickly signed to a label, but it got caught in the gears of a record-company merger and was dropped before it made the big time. They had their day in the sun with a few good records, crisscrossing the country, and they had even played at Radio City Music Hall. Those days were over, though. Like Ric Flair used to say, "You show me someone with potential and I'll show you a future champ who's now working the graveyard shift at 7-Eleven." But they still drank more, took more speed, and fucked more girls than anyone I had ever known, and they had hung on to a sizable following of like-minded enthusiasts overseas, where quality and charisma tended to trump passing trends.

They had asked me to join twice in the past two years—they were apparently brutal on drummers—but every time they called, I was still riding the novel confluence of having a girlfriend and a job at the same time. I suppose I should have been grateful—it would be a long time before the stars would line up like that again—but I was getting bored with all that happiness.

They promised delights that most mortals will only dream of— exotic drugs and super women, Top Secret Action that would make my hijinks in Berlin pale by comparison. It was time to come in from the cold, they told me. We would get right to work on a new album and then go to Japan, where we would be greeted with flagons of rice wine and offered sexual delights previously known only to emperors and kings. Then we would skyrocket across Europe, through France— where the women wore frilly underthings and lived to pleasure touring American musicians—and Spain, where bronze-skinned women yearned for New World pleasures. We would drink our way through Belgium, lay waste to Germany, and smoke everything in Holland. I carefully considered what they had to say. Then I went into Carmine's office and quit my job.

9

MADE IN JAPAN

"WHAT THE FUCK IS WRONG WITH YOU?"

Rhea was steamed.

"You quit your job, you're up giving up your apartment, you're joining a rock band, and you're going to Japan—*and it didn't even cross your mind to ask me what I thought?*"

No whimsical explanation about following my muse was ever going to placate her. She was all set to play house with me. It seemed like the next logical step, and although we hadn't really discussed it, she had gone so far as to shop for old jelly jars for me to drink Jim Beam out of, just like in the George Jones song. When a girl does that for a fella, it sends a pretty clear signal. Naturally, my reaction was to flee the country.

The Raunch Hands' timing was sublime. Up at Drake, the bloom was definitely off the rose. A year before, I could have spent an entire morning joyously composing cover lines, egging myself on to new heights of licentious lyricism and glee. After putting the finishing touches on a sophisticated turn of phrase like "Soaked Panty Face Squat," I'd be so pleased with the radiant levels of sibilance and internal assonance that I could breathe into a mere five-seventeenths of smutty haiku that I'd spend the rest of the day dancing around my office like the star in my own cherry blossom pageant. These days I was just waddling through a swamp of cheap alliteration ("Bagging Betty's Bouncing Boobs," "Sex-Crazed Sluts Snack on Poolside Snatch," etc.)

and spending my downtime aimlessly pondering the fate of twenty-five-year-old pornographers.

I was crazy about my girlfriend. Hell, not being everyone's cup of tea, I was grateful to have one. But I was starting to have reservations about the long-term possibilities of dating a career bartender. She made fat money, about eight hundred bucks a week, cash, a lot more than I was making at my fancy-pants publishing gig. And she had a great employer who had a health-care plan for all of his employees. It was tough to beat. There was no reason for her to ever leave, except that in five years she'd still be working in the same bar, pouring boilermakers for the same assholes. And that takes its own toll: a gaggle of gin-blossomed gargoyles arguing about the '74 World Series for the fourteen thousandth time is not a soaring testament to the human spirit. She was already beginning to show the dim pallor of a lifer. A change of environment would have done her a world of good, but she wasn't going anywhere—not making that kind of dough while working only four nights a week; it was a trap. Sartre would have had a field day with that setup.

When I told Carmine that I was off to Japan to play the drums, he was decidedly more enthusiastic about my decision. "I like your work," he told me, "but you're getting bored, and I have no place to put you." He also appreciated that I did the right thing—I told him I was leaving as soon as I knew, instead of just giving him the usual two weeks' notice before I shipped out. In fact, I gave him almost two months' warning, plenty of time to restaff without going nuts.

"You've been great to me," I said, not too solicitously, "and I am not going to leave you in the lurch. I want to finish the books I'm working on and give you time to get someone else while I'm still around to show them the, uh, *subtleties* of what we do here." He loved that.

The best part was that I was now a lame-duck editor, and within a month after I announced that I was leaving, I had very little to do except oversee the next fool who had my job. I didn't even have an office to work in, since the new guy had already moved in. Carmine was happy with me floating through the halls for only a few minutes each day to make sure everything was ducky. Actually, without a desk anymore, me being around and killing time with the Happiness Boys was more of a pain in the ass for him than anything else. Meanwhile, every cartoonist and local stripper I had ever been nice to and had featured in one of the books wanted to take me out for a boozy lunch, and who was I to let them down? Work had turned into a movable feast. At some point I was told to stop coming in. But they kept on paying me. I left on the best possible terms, and years later they were still tossing me free-lance work.

Rhea had calmed down and we were enjoying our time together, sleeping in, and having lunch at B&H Dairy every day before she went to work. I would do a quick pop-in at the office and then go off to re-hearse and record with the Raunch Hands. At the end of the night I would pick her up at the bar and we'd go drinking in the East Village. It was a sweet schedule, but clearly the calm before the storm.

The Raunch Hands had a different approach to making records than Sharky's Machine. The first thing they did was start with a giant mess of cocaine, a great, sprawling slick of white powder that was left out in the studio for anyone to hit when they felt they needed a lift. It was replenished frequently. Somehow, this was included in the record-ing budget. I was amazed. For liquid refreshment I brought along a portable bar, a gimmicked-up doctor's bag fitted with a set of liquor bottles and a cocktail shaker. I filled a bucket with ice and kept us in drinks the entire time.

Mike Chandler, the Raunch Hands' prodigiously drunk singer, took it all in stride.

"As you get older," he told me, "the clubhouse gets better." He punctuated this by knocking back a full shaker of Tom Collins in one gulp, ice cubes and all. I hear Babe Ruth liked to drink 'em that way, too.

After the childish tumult of Sharky's Machine, this was a dream. The four Raunch Hands—Chandler, Mariconda, bassist George Sul-ley, and me—got along famously. And these guys could play. Unfortu-nately, there is just no good way to explain the amped-up attack of dirty boogaloo and between-the-eyes guitar assaults that the Raunch Hands perpetrated on the public. You have to hear it, you have to live it.

To help drive these monsters over the top, I employed a new snare drum, a military-grade Sonor with a brass shell that weighed about as much as the Liberty Bell and sounded like a thunderclap every time I hit the backbeat. It could cut through a barrage of artillery fire or a wall of loud electric guitars and saxophones. It was more like a weapon than a musical instrument.

Mean little monkeys that we were, Mariconda and I innovated a dangerous new technique, now commonly referred to in European conservatories as "throwing the fireball." It is the musical equivalent of carpet bombing. In the past, this was sometimes called a "rave-up." The Yardbirds and a few others had attempted it with mixed results, but we had escalated the attack to near genocidal levels.

We also carried a mercenary saxophone player with us. He was undeniably talented and entirely capable of launching flamethrower blasts of yakkety sax, but he needed to be beaten periodically to keep his personality disorder in line. He called himself Dan. He had wide shoulders and was always bent over his horn like a vulture. I called him Asshole. I'm pretty sure his mother did, too.

All sax players have mental deficiencies, largely because they spend their lives blowing through narrow brass tubes, and all that pressure backs up into their heads, stretching out their brain tendons. In the case of Dan, the result was not only massive damage to his cerebral cortex, which made it difficult for him to remember what band he was playing in—given his onstage shtick, I am guessing he thought it was Sha Na Na—but also a massive Jewfro, which grew from his skull like an azalea bush and made him look like a fuzzy kosher lollipop. At least he knew enough to wear a hat.

He played brilliantly in the studio, but on gigs he made us all insane, overblowing his parts and mugging like a Muppet at a toga party. I rode him mercilessly for his frat-boy bullshit. It would take only a few days into the tour before I got called into the van for a meeting of the Secret Inner Circle.

"You gotta take it easy on Dan." I have rarely seen Mariconda so serious. I was a little taken aback. "It's hard to find a guy who plays baritone as well as tenor and will put up with *us*," he explained. "Look, I don't like him either," he added flatly. "I also don't like having diarrhea every day on tour. But I've gotten used to it."

"Are you comparing Dan to diarrhea?"

"Yes. I am."

Well all right, then. George gave me a reassuring pat on the back as I was climbing out of the van. "Don't worry, Sharky," he told me. "I got the same talk last year."

By the end of the tour, Mariconda had apparently had enough and had begun to amuse himself by replacing the six-thousand-dollar

Selmer saxophone in Dan's case with a rusty sledgehammer, a Mafia-inspired warning that had the desired effect of scaring the shit out of Dan, who suddenly became very careful to kill the honky jive dance and blast his parts exactly the way Mariconda had written them. Mariconda definitely has a way with sax players.

As we got closer and closer to our trip to Tokyo, Rhea was getting more and more agitated. Things had been going well, but now we were fighting all the time.

The band was going to Japan for two weeks, back to New York for a few days, and then off to Europe for about two months. And then, as far as I knew, I was coming back.

She confronted me. "I know what you do when you guys are on the road. Alec told me what you were like with Sharky's Machine." (I knew I should have killed him when I had the chance.) "If you go on tour with the Raunch Hands, don't expect to see me when you get back. You're either on the bus or you're off the bus."

I don't negotiate with terrorists. I left for the Land of the Rising Sun wearing snakeskin boots and Ray-Bans.

The party started on the flight to Tokyo. Along with the Raunch Hands was our art director, underground comic artist Cliff Mott, an avuncular punk also quick to mop up the cocktails or whatever other accelerants might be lurking around.

I had been up partying all night and crashed as soon as I hit the plane. When I woke up a couple of hours later, somewhere over the North Pole, ready to enjoy the hospitality of the fine people of Japan Airlines, I was told very politely that they had run out of sake.

Run out of sake?? In the first three hours of a fourteen-hour flight???

I looked over at my crew, who were drunk as skunks and laughing hysterically. They had drunk so many little bottles of sake in such a short period of time that they had been cut off. Apparently, no one had ever drunk like that on a plane before, and there was genuine concern from the flight deck over the possibilities of an international incident.

I did what I had to do. I went into my carry-on, changed my shirt, put on a baseball cap and different sunglasses (I always carry two or three pairs), changed my seat, and did my best to pretend that not only was I not with these round-eyed Satans, but that I, too, was appalled at their loutish American behavior. I didn't fool the stewardess for a second. Of course they had not run out of sake; that was just the polite way of saying "no more." Once I had convinced her that I was going to play it suave, she took mercy on me and gave me a few drinks, the whole time nodding her head in subtle but palpable disgust at my companions, who were howling in boozy mirth at the pink Japanese vomit bag. I clearly had a choice—drink free sake or hang out with my friends. I went for the sake. It was going to be a long tour.

On our last night in Japan, I had sex with a beautiful Japanese girl in the hallway of the Star Hotel in Tokyo. I wasn't given much of a choice.

Since the first day we arrived in Tokyo, Halloween 1990, it had been like *A Hard Day's Night*—if, instead of four lovable mop tops, it starred Godzilla, Mothra, Rodan, and King Ghidorah.

We were met by fans at the airport and whisked to a costume party where an all-girl band dressed as Playboy bunnies was playing "Louie, Louie." At the hotel that night—aided by members of Supersnazz, the four cutest girls in all of Japan, who played a charmingly inept version of American garage sludge—we learned that the tea makers in every room were also good for superheating magnums of sake. It wasn't long before we were playing Punk Rock Samurai, waging fire-extinguisher wars dressed in our complimentary kimonos.

The gigs were spectacular. In Tokyo, we played at the Jam Club with the 5.6.7.8's, who were later featured in *Kill Bill*. In Nagoya, we played a tiny room on the sixteenth floor of an office building—space was at such a premium in Japan that sometimes nightclubs were housed alongside dentists' and lawyers' offices. It was by far the single hottest room I have ever been in. Even the walls were sweating. There was no use trying to work our normal show, a twenty-song marathon. We ditched the "pussy pleasers"—the striptease numbers and slow drags—and cut it down to the most bulletproof of the lot, a twelve-song hit-it-and-quit-it set that we branded "The Nagoya Destroya." That night, people were fainting.

After every show there were rowdy dinners for us, fifteen or twenty people at long, traditional Japanese banquet tables. We'd kick off our shoes and kneel or sit cross-legged in front of low tables. Fortunately, I was prepared for this and had come with a wide selection of pimped-out hosiery. Only losers got caught in Tokyo with white tube socks.

The tables were reserved for a predetermined amount of time—say three hours—and it was "all you can drink" for that period, plus whatever food set we ordered, which usually started with *shumai* and *gyoza* (shrimp and pork dumplings) and then moved on to piles of perfectly greasy *tatsuta age* (fried chicken) served with hot mustard, piles of charred *yakitori* (grilled skewers of chicken, pork, onions, garlic, and whatever else the chef had lying about) with crushed hot pepper and lemon wedges, and then the sashimi, which always got a round of applause. We'd settle in, and cases of Kirin beer would just seem to materialize, with a dozen or so flagons of hot sake and cups and glasses for everyone. In Japan it is considered rude to fill your own glass and also rude not to pay attention to your neighbor's glass. When you see a beer glass or sake cup that is less than half full, fill it up. The beer and sake just seemed to disappear, and then another sortie of bottles would overtake the table. It was like the world's most civilized drinking game. Everybody was getting smashed. There was never an empty glass on the table. Everyone just kept drinking and saying *arigato*—thank you— and bowing politely to each other while filling each other's glasses. Which made for quite the revelry among drunks.

The very first night, after about an hour of this game, I looked up and got an eyeful of Chandler and Cliff Mott dancing on the table. Inexplicably, Mott had fish cakes covering his eyes. He was playing peek-aboo with a delighted audience.

Our Japanese hosts were convinced that this is what Americans did when they were drunk and happy in restaurants, and soon, just to be polite, the girls from Supersnazz were on the table doing the Fishcake Dance, too. What they had not realized was that Mott and Chandler had drunk so much sake—which, as anyone who has ever gone the distance with a few hot liters of the stuff will tell you, has a pronounced psychedelic effect—and were now hallucinating so wildly that they were reliving their senior proms, albeit with fried seafood patties. Not only would this be considered a faux pax in most of postcolonial America, it would definitely get you tossed in the klink for "drunk and disorderly" anywhere else in the Western world. And yet this behavior was received with great enthusiasm by our new friends. Any other reception would have been *rude*.

Every night, after a festive round of table dancing, which had become firmly established as a ritual (for all I know, they are still doing it in Shinjuku ward), the party would carry on at a bar. Another quaint Japanese custom is to dispense with the formality of *drinks*, in lieu of the whole bottle. I'd sit down, and *kerplunk!* there'd be a fifth of Jim Beam in front of me. I felt like Jack Palance in *Shane*.

The practice in these bars was to buy a bottle. They'd put your name on it, and they would hold it for you for when you came back. No one was expected to plow through that much liquor in one sitting. The bottles we were inhaling were left by tourists and businessmen who the bartenders knew for sure would never be back, so they just gave them to us. There were no complaints from our camp, who were hellbent on raising the Japanese per capita liquor consumption that week.

After the bars, the hard cores would stagger back to the hotel to carry on. By this time we'd have lost most of the gang to attrition, but there were always those who could make it till dawn.

The only place to get more beer at that time of night was from one of the vending machines that famously pepper the streets of Japan. You could get anything from a Japanese vending machine: socks, pornography, motor oil, you name it. And everything seemed to have its own Zen koan inscribed on the package, translated into English as only the Japanese can do. A package of toothpaste offered "Hygiene for good fun and clean!" One night we bought a bottle of Scotch that promised "this whisky to create a new lifestyle." We drank it very seriously.

These robot storefronts dispensed not only normal-size cans of beer but also monster-size four-liter barrels. You had to put a lot of coins in the slot to get one, but it was worth it just to hear the sound it made when it came dropping down through the machine—not that dissimilar from the sound a TV set makes when it hits the ground after being tossed from a Japanese hotel window.

On our day off, our hosts were very kind and brought us to Kamakura, the ancient capital of Japan once ruled by shoguns. Surrounded by mountains on three sides and open water on the fourth, it is a natural, bucolic fortress, famous for its beautiful temples and shrines. In the center is a towering bronze Buddha, the most famous of all the Buddhas, and not because Bob Dylan put it on an album cover. In the fifteenth century a tsunami wiped out the temple that housed the statue—which is ten stories tall—and the entire town around it, but the Buddha did not move an inch. It is a giant, humbling presence.

It was a calming day. The perfect opportunity to center ourselves and find a little peace among the chaos. We even saw Zen archers practicing at their monastery.

And then Dan had to go and make a spectacle of himself, making an offering to the Buddha by lighting a joss stick and praying. He was like one of those pathetic Jews who cross themselves when they visit Notre Dame as tourists, just to look as if they belong. You can spot these assholes from a mile away. One of our Japanese friends told us that it was very embarrassing, but he could not tell Dan, because that would be rude. So he politely told us, so *we* could mock Dan.

The last night we were there, one of our Japanese friends had gone to great lengths to score us some weed—they knew we liked it, so once again it was the honorable thing to do. This was no trifling feat. The drug laws in Japan are brutal, even for reefer. When Paul McCartney got busted bringing in a Ziploc's worth of grass in 1980, they made an example of him.

"I was taken to the narcotics headquarters, handcuffed and a rope tied around me, led along like a dog," McCartney said at the time. "It was like *Bridge Over the River Kwai.*"

They kept him "in a box" for nine days and didn't spring him until United States senator Ted Kennedy intervened. McCartney was facing seven years.

If that's how they treat the Beatles, you can imagine what they might do to one of the Raunch Hands. But there we were in the Star Hotel with a big ol' baggie of the stuff, fashioning pipes out of cigarette packs, beer cans, weird Japanese tampon applicators, whatever. They may have found the herb, but rolling papers remained elusive.

Someone told me that the Japanese were "very hungry for marijuana." I believed it. Every one of our rooms was filled with young punks dying to try the stuff. Which is why I found myself entertaining a dalliance in the hallway. There was no other place to go.

There were high-quality drugs in Japan, smuggled from Thailand, but that wasn't the weed we were smoking. This was some sort of homegrown, or it was found growing in the wild somewhere on a hill in Hokkaido. Whatever it was, it was by far the worst marijuana I have ever smoked. It tasted like peat moss stir-fried with miso paste and dung. It had zero psychotropic effect, but we smoked it and complimented our hosts on their good taste. It would have been rude not to.

When we got back to New York a few days later, I had the idea that the story of our trip, ending with the irony of the lousiest pot in the East, might play well in *High Times*. I called Holmstrom and gave him the pitch. He told me that since it was basically a story about a band, I needed to talk to Steve Bloom, who was, to the chagrin of people of taste everywhere, the music editor.

I knew Bloom from hanging around the office, and we were always friendly enough, but he was one of those anachronistic lemmings who still thought that the Grateful Dead was a happening band. Doubly embarrassing, he was the only journalist in the world who thought that punk was a passing fad and that disco was cool.

But he gave me the green light to scribble the story, and as usual, I was very proud to be working for America's Premier Doper Rag.

Three months later, when I read my story in the magazine—*High Times*, like most monthly magazines, has about a ninety-day lead time—I began to experience a swimming sensation in my head. I knew that Bloom was a bumptious hippie, but what I didn't know was that he was the bungling vivisectionist of decent prose.

My story had been put through some type of remedial stoner Cuisinart and had come out as pothead pabulum. Where once there had been descriptive and well-crafted sentences that amplified the exigencies of Japanese drug quests and hallway trysts, all lovingly cast to capture the rhythm and ecstasy of a rock 'n' roll orgy, there was now baby talk. Bloom had destroyed any meter or cadence and had chopped any complex or compound sentence into grade-school declaratives. *Noun, verb, object.* His linguistic hegemony was astonishing. *High Times* was once famous for publishing autodidacts like William Burroughs and Ken Kesey, but Bloom's idea of literary rebellion was an independent clause. I'm not saying that my piece was ever going to be a benchmark in counterculture journalism, but when I filed the story, it was pretty good, and now it read like a *Dick and Jane* primer for first-graders. I couldn't even show it to my friends without fear of them laughing at me. My porn novels stood up better.

I was not the only one whose prose would suffer for his ham-fisted editing style—good writers gave up on *High Times* rather than deal with Bloom, and he scared off a lot of new talent whom he could send off crying with his uninformed dogma and strict adherence to a set of rules that would baffle squares, let alone druggy literati.

But wait. There was another problem.

Remember how our Japanese friends risked life in a labor camp to score us what turned out to be the positively crappiest reefer ever smoked by an American? When the story came out, somehow the locus of the situation had changed to New York City, and *I* was buying *them* the world's worst pot.

I was mortified. It didn't make any sense. I called Bloom right away.

"What happened to my story?"

"It's better this way."

"It reads like it was written by someone who is having a hard time grasping English. And now it's not even *true*. If there is one thing I know, it is how to cop drugs in New York City. There is no way I would be buying dirt weed, and even if I did, even if this actually happened the way you rewrote it, I certainly wouldn't be bragging about it in *High Times*. I look like an idiot. Don't you think you should have consulted me on this?"

Bloom exploded. Besides having no respect for his writers, he also had a serious anger-management problem. I backed off. It wasn't worth getting into a fight with a guy who was potentially so stoned that in five minutes he'd forget what we were arguing about in the first place.

It would do me well to keep all this in mind years later, when I became his boss.

When the tour started up again, hitting Berlin was kind of homecoming. Some of my old pals from the Sharky's Machine days showed up to see the Raunch Hands, and just for nostalgia's sake, I snorted a nice bump of bright yellow crank from the end of a Chinese butterfly knife. The adventure was off to a lovely start.

But we were exhausted—we had played Tokyo on a Saturday, had done a one-off show in New York, and now were on our third continent in less than a week. On the second night of the tour, a Sunday, we were stuck in some German cow town playing a *jugen Centrum*—a community youth center. These were the kind of gigs we sometimes booked on off nights, Sundays and Mondays. We'd get paid and fed, and we'd have a place to stay. It beat not playing.

It wasn't so bad. The youth center served beer and catered to teenagers and twenty-somethings who had no better place to go at night in a small rural town. A lot of people would come out for the shows. We did all right, plowing our way through a good set for an appreciative if not overwhelmed crowd of punks who probably would have preferred a hard-core thrash band. They dug the energy, but the James Brown and Dick Dale covers meant nothing to them.

Within five minutes after playing, Mariconda was asleep in the backstage area. Everyone was wasted tired, but there were still a few cute girls fluttering about, eager to talk to the Americans, and George and I hate to disappoint. Plus sometimes kooky shit happens in small towns. You can have a perfectly mundane weekend gig in Paris and a Wednesday-evening bacchanal in the backwoods. That's the thing about being on tour—you never know.

"This place is closing soon," the cute girls told us. Sisters, I think. They liked us, that's for sure. "You should come with us. Our friend has a pub, and we have the keys."

"Huh?"

"We have the keys to the pub."

Every time someone in Germany says something like that to me, I am more and more inclined to forgive them for the War. I took her by the hand and brought her to the backstage area, where Chandler was now also sleeping on a couch, catty-corner to Mariconda, and snoring vociferously. The poor lads, they were so tired. They really needed their rest. I wasted no time in waking them up.

"Tell them what you just told us."

"We have the keys to the pub."

One thing is for sure, you don't have to tell these guys twice that when pretty girls say they have the "keys to the pub," it is best in every circumstance to follow them. And they had friends.

The pub turned out to be the one bar in town, a superbly well-stocked tavern turned after-hours club for five Raunch Hands and five of their newest and bestest pals. Chandler was climbing the walls. Literally. There was a ladder used to get the vintage brandy off the very top shelf behind the bar, and he was on it like a duck on a June bug, tossing bottles down to me like Nerf footballs. I have never been to ancient Rome, but I imagine this is what it was like on a good night.

The next morning, I was interrupted in the Raunch Hands van by the sound of Chandler pounding on the door. It was hard to hear him over the ruckus we were making, and for a while we pretended that he wasn't there. But he was very insistent. I rolled down the window. I tried to tell him that I was busy, but he graciously handed me two cups of hot coffee and my day's per diem. "C'mon, Sharky, we gotta go. You've got five minutes."

Now this was how to run a tour. I'm holding everyone up, turning the van into my personal rumpus room, and Chandler rewards me with catering and cash. Even the girl was impressed. I liked traveling with these Raunch Hands. And this was only day two of a two-month tour.

It wasn't long before we were fully into the rhythm of the road. One night in Belgium, George set a pizzeria on fire. At the time, Mariconda was dancing on the table, reliving Japan, and I was hacking away at a version of "Night Train" on a piano I had dragged in from the barroom. I guess George thought some flames would add a little panache to the act and hadn't quite realized just how much damage could be done with a standard-issue Zippo.

In France, Chandler was trying to pick up a beautiful Frenchwoman—and her barely legal daughter—when suddenly she was clomped in the chest with an orange that had come sailing across the club, which exploded on impact. She looked as if she were going to die. More sticky citrus shrapnel came flying in all directions, along with rock-hard bits of baguette and gooey lumps of Brie, the results of a food fight Mariconda had sparked backstage that was now spreading like nuclear fallout. Ten minutes before, he had threatened to kill an incompetent soundman ("You don't know me, I'm from New York, and I will cut you"), and in another ten, the place would be covered in vomit and broken glass. Everyone fled to safer ground. Two nights later, the woman—and her daughter—came back, undeterred, and tried once again to charm Mr. Chandler, but by that point he had wisely written them off as a couple of psychopaths.

On that tour I also got another chance at opening for the Ramones, at a five-thousand-seat sportatorium in Rennes, France. It went a lot better this time. There was a local band on before us who took the heat from an impatient crowd. We were second-billed as "Special Guests from New York City," and we killed. I watched the Ramones from the side of the stage and realized that the famous "1-2-3-4!" count-offs shouted at the top of each number had absolutely nothing to do with the tempos of the songs themselves. The Ramones lived in their own world.

Things really reached a peak of decadence and absurdity when we played at a pink stucco spaceship on the beach near Alicante, in the south of Spain.

At dinner before the show, we were warned, "Eat well, because after this you will not eat again, or sleep, for two days." This from a guy whose favorite stunt was snorting speed off the hoods of moving cars, so we listened to him.

It was our driver's birthday that night, and it was the first time I had seen "Feliz Cumpleaños" written out on a large mirror with cocaine. That was a trick that never got old.

The "spaceship" was a monstrosity of a discotheque that looked like an extraterrestrial birthday cake that had crash-landed on the beach at the peak of Franco's regime and had been abandoned ever since. Inside, it was covered in dust and cobwebs, bottles everywhere, the detritus of a party that had ended years before. It must have been one hell of a fiesta. And now, even though they had reopened the place and it was about ten o'clock and we were supposed to play at midnight, there was still no one making any move to clean up.

Aside from the guy who claimed to be the promoter—and there was no reason to believe that he was who he said he was except that he gave us dinner and some drugs—the place was empty. There was no sound system and no sign of the band that was supposed to play before us. The "promoter" shrugged. "Relax. If they feel like playing, they'll come. Everything will be all right. Have another line. Have a drink. Welcome to Spain."

Slowly, almost imperceptibly, a few people showed up with brooms and began cleaning off the dance floor and clearing the stage. Like a bizarre outer-space ballet, speaker columns floated in, the bar opened, and people began drifting toward the mother ship a few at a time. All that was missing was the waltz-time sound track by Strauss. By 1:00 a.m. the first band was on. By 3:00 a.m., when we finally played, the place was packed and rocking. By 6:00 a.m. we were out on the beach playing baseball—Chandler and I always brought gloves and a ball on tour—and smoking cocaine cigarettes, because it was too windy to snort powder.

Leaving Alicante and heading back north toward Madrid, we had a pretty good drug collection going. Mariconda consulted the kit bag: there were a few tabs of acid, a golf ball–size chunk of hash, various white pills . . . and, dang! No more coke or speed.

"How the hell am I going to stay awake then?" I asked him.

"Maybe you should think about getting some sleep," he told me sternly, like a TV doctor. "Take some of these codeine pills. They'll help."

"They bother my stomach. Do you think they'll work if I crush them up and snort them?"

"Nah, I already tried it."

I took a pass on the codeine, but after two days of partying on the mother ship, I didn't have much trouble passing out. I may even have dreamed.

Far flung from the colony of extraterrestrials that were running things in Alicante, Madrid was under the control of a group of Earthlings who called themselves the Pleasure Fuckers.

The Pleasure Fuckers were Spain's premier rock 'n' roll band, the Raunch Hands' Iberian counterparts in a universe of punk rock excess and hedonism. Their reputation for eating, drinking, snorting, smoking, fucking, fighting, and playing harder and louder than anyone else on the peninsula was well earned.

The Pleasure Fuckers were fronted by a three-hundred-pound Basque man who went by Kike Turmix. (Kike, pronounced KEE-kay, is a common nickname, short for Enrique. Turmix was the name of a popular line of blenders.) Turmix was legendary not only for inhaling vast amounts of drugs and superhuman amounts of vodka, but also for his gastronomic proclivities. In Basque country in the north of Spain, where Turmix was from, everything was Bigger than Big—the people, the steaks, the drinks. For sport they had boulder-throwing contests.

Turmix also carried a reputation in Spain for being an early adopter, the first to play new American bands on a radio show he once hosted, and later booking them into the territory before anyone else had the bright idea. The Raunch Hands were part of that wave.

Upon arriving in Madrid, we were greeted by Turmix and the Pleasure Fuckers and immediately whisked to a neighborhood bar and fortified with a banquet of tapas—not a "real" meal, just something to sharpen our incisors before the *entrecot* we would enjoy after the sound check. Nothing in Spain was ever done in half measures.

Lavished before us were delicately fried baby squid; inch-wide anchovies that had been vacationing in olive oil and garlic for what must have been weeks; roasted red peppers stuffed with tuna; *jamón serrano*, paper-thin ham carved from the leg of an overnourished pig that sat right on the bar (just the leg, not the whole pig); *gambas a la plancha*, shrimp that had been covered in salt and seared on an open grill; plus bits of chorizo, Manchego cheese, ripe olives, and bottles of voluptuous Rioja wine.

Then we got around to the *carajillos*.

A *carajillo* is something of a miracle, a blood-confusing speedball of a coffee cocktail, the true Breakfast of Champions but also the perfect riposte to any of life's little hiccups, day or night.

The proper *carajillo*, the *carajillo quemado de coñac*, involves some tricky pyrotechnics. First, the cognac is poured into a glass, usually a wide, thick-bottomed job, and then a goodly amount of sugar is added. The cognac is steam-heated on one of those well-appointed, brushed-metal coffee-making contraptions—just as you would steam the milk in a *café con leche*—and then set on fire. Thick black coffee is dripped slowly onto the burning cognac without extinguishing the flame. The result is one hell of a sugar, booze, and caffeine jolt, and the whole thing tastes like a dream.

While Turmix was a study in corpulence, albeit one with sharp sideburns, the other Pleasure Fuckers were tall and thin. Norah, who pounded rhythm guitar, was sexy and tough and could drive all night long, navigating the van through the Pyrenees on a head full of hashish and God knows what else. She threw a mean punch and could drink even harder than Turmix.

Norah, like Mike (our Spanish friends thought every other American was named Mike), the lead guitar player, was from Southern California, and the two of them together brought some sunshine—no matter how aggressive it was—to a down-and-dirty high-energy band. Mike was six feet plus, blond and blue-eyed, and a jubilant guitar player who tore spectacularly musical riffs out of an old Gretsch rockabilly box played through a Marshall stack.

Barnaby played bass. Barnaby is from London, and suspiciously posh, but he plays it down. He is suave and charming and obviously didn't pick it up slumming in Camden Town. Clearly somewhere in his lineage was a peer of the realm, or at least a member of the Drones Club, but he preferred the Pleasure Fuckers' hedonistic lifestyle of wanton rock 'n' roll stupidity, sex, and drugs. They were a formidable team.

The only weak link in the chain was the drummer, who could play but was clearly not one of them. You got the idea he was slumming it—he had some obvious prog rock tendencies, like needlessly peeling off triple flamadiddles and quarter-note triplets in the middle of straight-ahead garage punkers—and was only Pleasure Fucking for the perks. What they obviously needed to complete the package was an ass-kicker from New York.

After dinner we were treated to snootfuls of Dexedrina, which came in bright orange amphetamine capsules that could be legally obtained at a *farmacia* with some odd sort of doctor's script that was given only to truck drivers. There was also a guy who sold them in Retiro Park. The genius of a Dexedrina cap was not only its high-octane oomph, which rivaled anything in Berlin, but the insidious fact that it was *time-released*. Drop a Dexedrina, and you could drive from Spain to Sweden in a straight shot, with a fresh bump of chemical zoom being pushed into your bloodstream every two hundred kilometers. And you could crush them up and snort them, and they worked like magic, although you'd have to be careful not to get orange powder on the outside of your nose. It made you look stupid.

We were in love with Spain. Every night the parties just got better and better. The food was spectacular. Drugs seemed to fall from the sky. Everyone was warm and friendly. The women were drop-dead gorgeous. Mariconda suggested that we move there. It seemed like a good idea at the time.

10

FIRST-TIME LESBIAN
HOUSEWIFE CONFESSIONS

The decision to relocate to Spain was never debated. We were going. Resistance was futile. We had no idea where we would live or if we could actually make a living playing music. One fact was irrefutable: none of us spoke Spanish. And yet, caught up in the whirl of undying optimism that somehow rock 'n' roll would solve all of our problems, none of this mattered. According to Mariconda's master plan, when the Raunch Hands got back to New York from this tour, we'd get right back in the studio to make the next record, and then we'd get back on the road to support it. And then, like Christopher Columbus through the looking glass, when we landed in Madrid, we would park the van and colonize. I am sure that if we had stopped to think about it for more than ten seconds, we never would have left New York.

The title of our new record, *Fuck Me Stupid,* was inspired by the Billy Wilder film *Kiss Me, Stupid,* starring Dean Martin as himself. A thinly veiled avalanche of double entendres wrapped around the story of a prostitute and two mentally ill songwriters, when it was released in 1964, it was decried as the filthiest movie of all time. Christian groups and decency fascists worked hard to shut it down, and Wilder came close to being run out of town on a rail. Along with *The Big Combo,* an overheated noir about a hate-filled mob boss, and the first twenty minutes of *Full Metal Jacket,* which we understood to be a primer on how to deal with saxophone players, it was our favorite.

The cover of *Fuck Me Stupid* was built around a piñata that we had stuffed copiously with drugs and booze—dozens of trumpet-shaped joints, plastic mini-Baggies stuffed with white powder, and lots of tiny liquor bottles, the kind you get on airplanes.

It was a ridiculously expensive prop. We blindfolded our sexbomb of a model and told her to have at it with a baseball bat. Wally Wang took the photos. On the back cover of the record the piñata is shown busted open, the contraband spilling out of its guts. Things were looking good. We were ready to move.

And then George the Bass Player began speaking in riddles. "Do you really think this is such a good idea? What are we going to do when we get there? Where will we live? How will we make money?" It was as if George had been Born Again and had accepted Common Sense as his Savior. Somehow, somewhere, he had gotten it into his head this crazy notion that sending a band of druggy boozehounds to the capital of European nightlife armed only with their sodden wits and some battered musical gear might not be the most sovereign plan on the table. The rest of us were baffled. Why would he even *think* about looking over the edge of the cliff before leaping? That was not how we did things. But his mind was made up; he was not going to move to another country on a whim. He would do the tour, and then he was going back home.

What had happened was that George had gone and got himself *married*—to Tomoko, the bass player of the Supersnazz—whom he had been pursuing since our tour of Japan.

I have no idea how George managed to import Tomoko to New York. She was as sweet as pie, but the language barrier was fraught with crater-size deficits. I can only guess that they spoke some sort of secret bass player's jive to each other, developed after years of wondering why their guitars had only four strings.

That summer in New York was a blur of drugs, whirlwind romance, and first-time lesbian housewife confessions, the last of which I was scribbling for my old colleagues at Drake to help make ends meet.

You can imagine the setups: the ladies had the notion to take sexy pictures of each other to give to their husbands for Valentine's Day, but once they slipped into the lingerie, well, one thing led to the next, and before you knew it, the tickle fight was on. Or the girls got together one afternoon to look at the porn videos their husbands thought were secret. "What do they see in this stuff anyway?" By the time they got through the first bottle of Chardonnay, they had discovered a whole new side to themselves. And so on.

When I wasn't fabulizing tales of desperate housewives' girl-on-girl action, I was babysitting Party Horse, who had just broken up with his girlfriend and whose remedy for everything was to snort ten Cadillacs' worth of blow.

Party Horse was a Wall Street dropout who had made scads of dough and was now on permanent vacation. He was one of us, but on a bigger budget. Given his endless supply of funds, we hit the danger zone pretty quickly. He'd drop a couple of eight balls on the kitchen counter and we'd be off to the races.

I always won the Who Can Stay Awake the Longest contest, but after seventy-two hours it was a joke. By that time our conversations had deteriorated into a swamp of cokehead neologisms:

> ME: *Squee bop.*
> PARTY HORSE: *Squiddly boodly bop.*
> ME: *Spivity spiva wang?*
> PARTY HORSE: *Ugga bugga!*

It was Party Horse's idea to fly George and Tomoko to Las Vegas to get married. We were hanging out with them at Flannery's bar on Fourteenth Street, Friday night around closing time, 4:00 a.m. Tomoko was heading back to Tokyo that Sunday. She had been in New York for a few months now, and Party Horse wanted to know why they hadn't got married while she was here. George shrugged and said they couldn't find a good deal to Las Vegas. I don't know how serious he was, but when I saw the light go off over Party Horse's head, I knew we were in trouble.

"Let's go right now. Let's get you guys married. I'll take care of everything. It'll be my wedding present to you. I'll get on the phone, and we'll be on the next flight. Tomoko, what airport is your flight leaving from Sunday, and what time do you have to be there?"

I have no idea how George explained this harebrained scheme to Tomoko, but before I knew it, they were in a cab to Brooklyn, back to his place to pack her stuff quickly. She was going to make the return flight from Vegas to New York to Tokyo without going back to George's apartment.

Somehow we all met at the ticket counter at JFK, Party Horse waving his Amex card around like a magic wand, and were on a plane to Vegas in about an hour.

When we landed, we got a room at the Flamingo, and I got out the phone book and found the Elvis Presley Wedding Chapel. They were booked that afternoon until three o'clock. We took the first open slot and were instructed to stop on the way at city hall to get the marriage license.

While we waited for George and Tomoko to take care of business, which took about fifteen seconds, I read the Nevada state wedding regulations. I was glad to see that people under the age of sixteen who wanted to get married needed a note from their parents. There should have been one about requiring more than thirty seconds' notice before flying across the country to get spliced in an insane last-minute wedding funded by a lunatic millionaire who had been awake for three days, wired on dummy dust, and half drowned in gin and beer.

The Elvis Presley Wedding Chapel looked like the mutated offspring of a Baptist church and a House of Pancakes welded onto a drive-thru hamburger joint. When we got there, there was a ceremony in progress. A large Hispanic family ("large" in both senses—there were many of them, and they were conspicuously obese) was celebrating the nuptials of someone's daughter. It was all very strange. I didn't take them for Elvis fans—all the women were wearing shiny off-the-rack bridesmaids' dresses with puffy sleeves, and the men were wearing powder blue tuxedos. Except for the Elvis impersonator, also conspicuously overweight, it looked like a normal wedding, unless of course they were practicing a level of self-conscious irony too subtle for me to detect. In a town of Quickie-Mart weddings, I had no idea why they chose this place. Maybe it was the bargain rates. Maybe they just wanted a fat singer who wouldn't make the bride self-conscious about her own expansive figure.

When it was our turn, we consulted with the minister about what kind of wedding would be best for George and Tomoko.

"Our Basic Wedding is fifty dollars," the minister explained. "The Elvis Wedding is another fifty, and that is what most people go for."

"What does the Elvis wedding include?"

"Well, Elvis here," he said, motioning to the tub in the white jumpsuit who was sitting on a bench reading a take-out menu, "will sing you three songs of your choice."

Party Horse was having none of it. "For twenty bucks couldn't he just take some Darvon and leave us alone?"

The minister didn't laugh. "You'll need rings," he said, clearing his throat. "These are our top-of-the line. They're twenty-five dollars each, and I think you will agree that they are very weddinglike." We agreed. They were very weddinglike. "They usually last a few years, and then you can get new ones." We took two.

I made some noise about being an ordained minister myself—back in the better days at Drake, Proch and I had been ordained by the Ministry of Salvation Church, Inc., a mail-order ministry that charged five bucks for a divinity degree—figuring I should somehow help officiate the proceedings. The minister shut me down, and fast. "What, are you a rabbi?" Mutherfucker had me nailed. And there was no way he was going to share his gig. "Do you have a license in the state of Nevada?" he asked me, solicitously. We both knew the answer. "No? What a shame. You can watch."

So there we were, Tomoko in a miniskirt and T-shirt, George in a Schott Perfecto leather jacket, motorcycle boots (his dress boots, I suppose), and baseball cap, with Party Horse and me standing behind them to witness this Holy Union.

The preacher went on about the blessings of matrimony and then asked George and Tomoko to face each other and hold hands while Leo sang a song.

Leo was the black guy you got if you didn't want to cough up the dough for Elvis. He was at the back of the chapel, sitting behind a cheap Casio keyboard that was propped up on a wood-veneer stand to make it look like a real organ.

"Some say love, it is an ocean . . ."

When Leo began warbling "The Rose," something snapped. I couldn't help it, I started laughing uncontrollably.

Usually I cry at weddings. It's true. I am very sentimental. I will weep openly at a particularly moving long-distance commercial. Grand Displays of True Love always get me choked up. But Leo had gone too far. I had the same reaction to him that Ted Nugent had the first time he heard reggae: my brain just rejected it.

I could see George shaking, trying not to start laughing, too. Forget about Party Horse; he looked as if he was about to shit his pants. He was turning beet red, and white, coke-flaked snot was dripping out of his nose. Poor Tomoko. I am sure that as a little girl growing up in the Japanese countryside, she did not picture her wedding day this way.

Come to think of it, I am not even sure she knew she was getting married, at least not for real. One second she was in New York, the next she was watching Party Horse haggle with a fat hillbilly and having Leo serenade her with Bette Midler's greatest hits.

At some point the minister pronounced them man and wife and we got the hell out of there and headed back up to the Strip to celebrate. We went to the Mirage, the last place I had seen Evel Knievel, and knocked back a few sugary frozen drinks in what had to be the most disappointing wedding reception since Butcher Vachon's new bride got clobbered with a cream pie on Vince McMahon's talk show. Actually, that was the honeymoon, too, since the newlyweds had to be back at the airport in a couple of hours to get Tomoko back to New York so she wouldn't miss her flight to Japan. It was all so horribly romantic that I went back to the hotel and puked.

After a summer doing research with Party Horse for a thesis on Toxicology and Sleep Deprivation in Humans, I needed to get back on the road with the Raunch Hands, just to calm down. This was the trip that was going to land us in Spain, and spirits were running high.

Thankfully we had jettisoned Dan the sax player and had hired Pete "The Other White Meat" Linzell for blowing duty. I love Pete. He's a bit of a pastry puff, soft around the middle and always the last guy in the van, but he plays ace saxophone and has a great stage persona, laying back until it's his time to shine, and even then, he never tries to upstage the singer. Everyone really liked working with him.

We were lucky to have a day off in Paris, and Pete and I were staying with a girl we knew who wanted to take us around and show us the sights a little bit. Pete wanted to see the Eiffel Tower. Not my first choice for a day off in Paris, but I let them talk me into it, and I ended up having a really good time. The Eiffel Tower, by the way, is *brown*. I think everyone expects it to be silver or gold, like the pencil sharpener your aunt brought you back from Paris when you were in sixth grade, but it is painted a decidedly fudgy-looking brown. Someone ought to write them a letter.

While we were there, Pete bought a black souvenir baseball cap with *Paris* written on it in Day-Glo pink script. The *i* was a little Eiffel Tower. It was without a doubt the gayest thing I had ever seen in my life, and Pete's shit-eating grin wasn't making it any more palatable. "Wait'll Mariconda sees this." He beamed.

"Pete," I warned him, "Mariconda sent the last sax player home in tears."

And sure enough, there was steam coming out of Mariconda's ears when Pete wore it onstage and refused to take it off. Chandler, taking a page from the Dave Insurgent playbook, declared it "harder than hard." It was nice to see a sax player who could razz the guitar player, especially since in the tough-guy department he was more like a Hershey bar than a crowbar. That took some balls.

It was another great tour, forty-five shows in seven countries in fifty-five days. At some point our drug collection had sprawled out of control and we were holding a baggie filled with fistfuls of multicolored, unidentifiable pills. Clearly, these were the uppers, downers, screamers, and laughers that had destroyed the best minds of our generation, but which was which? There was only one way to tell. Mariconda and I began some research of our own. By the end of the tour I felt like one of the "replicants" in *Blade Runner*. A month later, when someone asked me how the tour was, all I could do was intone, like Rutger Hauer at the end of the film, a moment before his brain finally stops functioning, "I have seen things you people wouldn't believe."

After the last gig in Hamburg, the three Spain-bound Mikes raced off. Mariconda was off to Holland to produce some band or another, and Chandler was going back to Paris to rendezvous with his new girlfriend, a huge-breasted dental assistant who was undeniably attractive but who would turn out to have the soul of a dragon—even her mother called her *La Gatita Mala*, "the Bad Kitten." I was also going to stop in France for a few days, to take this year's version of the Edison Cure, hosted by the Charming Promoter Girl, who lived in the southeast of France, not far from Perigueux. After our various adventures, we would reunite in Madrid and begin The Next Phase.

The Charming Promoter Girl lived in a little village perched on a steep hill, surrounded by a six-hundred-year-old wall. It was like a fairy tale. "You must come to visit me," she had insisted. "My little town is so sad." It's true, there was nothing happening there, which is why she got into promoting rock shows a few towns over, where there were enough young people to make a go of it. But where she lived was perfectly isolated and calm. It may have been lonely living there, but I think she liked the dark romance of medieval melancholia. She would put on a gig a couple of times a month and spend the rest of the time reading comic books and tending to the garden behind her little house that lived in the shadows of knights and castles. She was as petite as she was charming, but the night we met, she saved me from getting my ass kicked by a drunk who had been getting in my face after a gig. It was some asshole who had too much to drink, trying to be a Big Man and fuck with the band—I reckon there's not much else for the Huguenots to do these days—and I tried to walk away. But there was no easy escape, as the bar was crowded and he was determined to knock my block off. The Charming Promoter Girl just sidled between us and, using some sort of feminine magic, dismissed him. And then she took me home with her.

It was a good place to take the Cure. It seemed to be raining all the time, and everything shimmered with storybook antiquity. Every day we walked down the hill to have lunch in a stone bistro. We ate rough-hewn country pâté and thick onion soup with *confit du carnard* and drank hearty red table wine. Then we'd climb back up the hill and through the wall, explore the ruins, take a hot bath, and spend the evenings cooking and snuggling in front of a fire while listening to the Duke Ellington cassettes I had been storing at the bottom of my bag for use as an end-of-tour brain salve. Like a lot of French intellectuals, she was enchanted by American detective novels from the 1940s, so one day we took a trip to a decent bookstore and I showed her my favorites. After a week I no longer felt like an android in a science fiction movie.

When I got to Madrid, job one was to find an apartment and then figure out how to pay for it. I had about a thousand U.S. dollars in my pocket.

For the first few nights I crashed at various Pleasure Fuckers' houses in the center of town in a neighborhood called Malasaña. (The name sounds pretty grim—*mala* means "bad" in Spanish—but it is actually named after Manuela Malasaña, a teenage heroine in the Spanish uprising against Napoleon's troops in 1808.)

Malasaña sprang up around Calle Palma, a strip of rock 'n' roll bars in the center of town, a few blocks north of Puerta del Sol. Every bar had a DJ spinning records. That's the way it was done. There was no such thing as a jukebox in Spain. Even tossing a CD on the house hi-fi was considered déclassé.

There was another music bar every few meters: El Flamingo, La Vaca Austera, and, around the corner, the Tupperware and the legendary La Vía Láctea (The Milky Way), all blasting punk and garage rock. And there were dozens more on top of those. Across the Plaza del Dos de Mayo was El Sol, which had a sprawling patio in front of the bar. In the summer, everyone you ever met in Madrid would be there drinking Mahou, the preferred local beer. It was the punk rock version of European café society.

The Pleasure Fuckers were the kings of Malasaña. Every week Turmix spun records at various bars, holding court in the DJ booth, chopping giant white lines, and inhaling pints of vodka and orange soda.

At the end of the night we herded over to the Agapo, a dive that didn't even bother to open till 1:00 a.m. The bathroom was just a hole in the floor. You had to be pretty careful when you were drunk—and there was no other possible explanation for being there—or you'd end up knee-deep in some truly nasty bog water.

When we arrived in 1992, Malasaña was still wide-open. Hashish was smoked freely everywhere—the sticky black Moroccan was ubiquitous and plenty cheap—and most of the bars were functioning coke dens.

When the Raunch Hands were on the road in Spain, Turmix would come along on the dates he had booked, and he made sure that we ate in spectacular restaurants. Each region offered its own specialty, and we were as eager to try everything as he was to order it for us. In Valencia, we ate the traditional paella of chicken, rabbit, green beans, and red pepper. No seafood in that paella—that would make it *paella de mariscos*, and while it is also worth traveling across the Atlantic for, it's not the real, authentic *paella valenciana*. The locals could be downright militant about it. Later I would discover *fideuá negra*, which is like paella, only instead of being made from saffron rice, it is made from thin rice noodles and stained black with squid ink. In León we ate the *morcilla*, the powerful blood sausage, best sliced and grilled and, paired with the devastating, near-indigo Ribera del Duero wine, a combination decidedly not for the weak. At least one Raunch Hand woke up with the sheets covered in the stuff. In Galicia, in the northwest, just above Portugal, the *mariscos* were abundant, and we'd feast on *langostas*, *centollas*, and *nécoras*—crustaceans that looked positively prehistoric. We'd wash down that whole mess with young green wine drunk from wide, shallow cups that always seemed to refill themselves.

Before every show, there would be sparkling lines of dust to get us going, and again before the encore, and then the *marcha*, the Spanish pub crawl, would begin. Every city, even the smallest pueblo, had at least one world-class rock 'n' roll bar, a decadent cave run by the local lunatic-slash-connoisseur. In some places, like Alicante, it seemed that an entire barrio was dedicated to Johnny Thunders and the Ramones.

Later we would discover that Turmix's largesse was not so much generosity as it was embezzlement. Being the booker, he had been doing business at the end of the night with the local promoter and then paying us himself. A lot of times we'd have pulled in a thousand dollars at the door and he'd tell us he collected only five hundred. And we'd still be chipping in for the drugs, for the party, for the extra round of exotic, spiny-backed lobster. We had no idea that Turmix was making a small fortune, by punk rock standards, on our backs. A few years later it became clear to everyone that this was the way he did business, and bands ran to find new Spanish bookers. But back then, still in the dark about his transgressions, we were flying like intercontinental ballistic missiles jacked on rocket fuel, and we never looked back. How much better could life possibly be?

The only rule was *always bring your sunglasses with you*, because at some point you'd be walking out of a bar and facing the sunrise, and then two things would happen. One, you'd be miserable because your drug-addled brain would not welcome recalibrating for daylight and would punish you mercilessly; and two, everyone would make fun of you because you were stupid enough to forget your shades, and then you'd *really* feel bad.

We had been advised that it would be very difficult to find apartments in Madrid. It was like New York or Paris that way, or at least that is what we were told. But against the *mañana, mañana* attitude that permeated a country that shut down in the middle of the day to take a three-hour siesta, a band of hustlers from New York City had no problem getting things done. We asked around and, pretending to be exchange students, checked an off-campus housing board at the local university. In just a few days I was moving into a place in the trendy

Moncloa district, sharing with a couple of real students. My part of the rent was U.S. $280. It was a nice flat. A family had lived there before, and my bedroom had been their little boy's and was decorated with choo-choo train wallpaper. The landlord offered to tear the paper down and paint the walls for me, but I liked it just the way it was. Mariconda had also found a place right away—rooming with a twenty-something-year-old acidhead who kept him up all night having loud sex with his girlfriend. That was a good thing, too. What with all of our sax players back in the States annoying other people, Mariconda needed someone to piss him off. It actually makes him happy.

Chandler, however, had gone missing.

Always a prolific drinker, Chandler had been moving south toward "unreliable." And then he was just gone. Later, after days of phone calling and the kind of worrying that would have been applauded even by a seasoned pro like my grandmother, we found out that he had fucked off to Majorca with his girlfriend. It would be months before we saw him again.

With the Raunch Hands' plans having gone the way of the Spanish Empire, Mariconda immediately joined a local band and began gigging with them. I just hung around doing a whole lot of nothing and enjoying the days—a favorite Spanish pastime.

Sometimes I spent my days at the art museums. The Prado is home to Hieronymus Bosch's super-psychedelic triptych *The Garden of Earthly Delights*. It depicts, among other joys, a tableau of a half-tree/half-frog astronaut creature preparing to devour a naked woman; an angry rabbit torturing a man trapped inside of a giant drum; bird-headed monsters measuring their prey; men holding their ears as musical instruments crash down around them (and one fellow bent over with a flute up his ass); and someone vomiting into what looks like the loo at the Agapo. I spent a lot of time meditating on this masterpiece, trying to work out whether I simply enjoyed his depraved vision for its own merits or whether I related to it on a more profound, personal level. Obviously there were a few things I still needed to work out.

When the Pleasure Fuckers came by and gave their pitch for me to join them, I agreed without hesitation. Their mercenary drummer had bailed, his name forever to be cursed, and I had two weeks to learn the set before my debut at Espárrago Rock, the annual asparagus festival in Granada, in front of about five thousand craven Pleasure Fucker fans. It would be a smash.

And thus began the New Spanish Revolution. The Fuckers gigged constantly—for the next three years we averaged about a hundred shows a year—and had the same fireballing aesthetics as the Raunch Hands. Every Thursday we'd pile into the van for a weekend's worth of shows. If we weren't in Catalunya, tearing up Barcelona and Figueres (where Dalí was born), we'd be in Andalucía, hitting Córdoba, Sevilla, and Jerez. We tore through La Mancha, Extremadura, Valencia, Asturias . . . there was no region in Spain that was immune from our attack. This was an action band: the campaign never stopped. To paraphrase Ulysses S. Grant, we were a verb.

We took off across France and made the European circuit. A lot of old Sharky's Machine and Raunch Hands fans came out to see me with the Pleasure Fuckers, and it was extremely rewarding to know that someone was paying attention. We played up and around the Adriatic Sea, in Italy, and at a heavy metal club in the war-torn former Yugloslavia, in Croatia. After that show we ate fresh venison and went to a casino and played blackjack.

Under the European Community, Europe was a lot more open than it had been in the Sharky's Machine days, when we would be rifled by customs agents pretty much every time we crossed a border. In the old days, the rule was to always get rid of any and all drugs before we left one country for the next. Which meant that some days we were more fucked-up than others. No one would actually throw the drugs *out*.

With the new European Union, we'd roll up to the border and almost always get waved through. So we became a little less vigilant. We were never holding anything on our persons, but if you needed a little pick-me-up, inside the big boom cymbal stand back in my trap case would not have been a bad place to look. But no one was ever interested in searching us. They didn't even want to see our passports. Until we got to Austria, where they were so delighted that Team Pleasure Fucker had finally arrived that they rolled the van up over a mechanic's pit so that a task force of narcotics agents could search the underside of the vehicle while their colleagues sniffed out the interior.

The Austrian customs squad looked as if they had bought their uniforms at a Third Reich going-out-of-business sale, and I have seen smaller and less fevered crews working the pits at Indy. One guy was taking some sort of sample from the inside of the windows with a bizarre rubber suction device connected to an LED readout, which would apparently tell him if there was any residue left from the forty thousand joints that had been smoked in there. None of us had ever seen that before. It was horrifying. If they said, "Jawohl! Our THC measuring device has detected the presence of Illegal Action," it was going to be pretty hard to refute. I just hoped that thing had been set to "zero" before they started.

Another ambitious young government charge was emptying the ashtrays; still another was vacuuming the seats and carpet, looking for evidence. This was not good. We had already given the van a good once-over ourselves, but who knew if there was a stray roach or a speck of powder between the seat cushions? There could have been a body under the bench seat for all anyone knew. All sorts of kooky things went on in that van.

Having struck out in the interior, they motioned for us to open up the back. At that point we had two worries: one, the cymbal stand, which contained enough speed to keep the Vienna Philharmonic wired through an entire *Ring* cycle; and two, the huge amount of merchandise we were carrying—boxes and boxes of Pleasure Fuckers CDs that had been printed in the Czech Republic, which we were hauling back to Madrid. Forget about jail—if they forced the issue, we would have to pay several thousand dollars of duty on them. Turns out they weren't that smart. Creepy drug cops never are.

They started unloading the van. The Pleasure Fuckers backline was no joke: HiWatt and Marshall guitar amps, an SVT bass amp that dwarfed Turmix, guitars and drums, all in heavy-duty road cases. It was a lot of work, and they did not look amused. They hauled everything out, including about twenty boxes of CDs, until they found what, apparently, they had been looking for the whole time: an egg-shaped set of Russian nesting dolls, painted like Communist leaders.

You know the kind—on the outside was Yeltsin, and then you'd open it up and there would be Gorbachev, and then Brezhnev, all the way down to Lenin. It was a souvenir somebody had picked up in Prague and had thrown into the back of the van.

The Chief Customs Dude shook it knowingly. The dolls rattled conspiratorially. Evidently this was where we kept the stash. He motioned for Austria's Finest to gather 'round and watch him unveil the bindle of high-grade smack that was going to make him Employee of the Week. He dramatically twisted Yeltsin open at the waist to reveal . . . the next doll! Of course there was nothing to be found. By the time he got to Stalin, the Chief had been exposed as an idiot in front of his posse of no-neck henchmen, and the dolls were laid out in order, like Mother Goose and her Commie Children. We were all cracking up at their Keystone Kops routine (actually, more like *Hogan's Heroes*), until the Chief, tomato red and about to burst like a stuffed cabbage, yelled something in *haute Deutsche* that obviously meant "get the fuck out of here." Meanies. They didn't even have the decency to put the dolls back together.

But the van was cleaner than it had been in months.

11

THE CREATURE FROM
TEMPLE BETH SHALOM

GG Allin died last night. The phone started ringing early this morning, first with people from New York wanting to know if I had heard the news, and then people from various fanzines wanting to interview me about GG. I had been in Madrid for about a year, and hardly anyone from New York ever called. Now it seemed that everyone wanted to talk to me. I politely declined. I didn't feel like throwing any meat to the animals.

GG was last seen tumbling down Avenue B in the East Village, buck naked (except for his combat boots), covered in his own filth. Moments before, he had been performing in a dump called the Gas Station. And as usual, after a few numbers they shut the power off and threw his ass out onto the street, where he was followed by the horde of sycophantic punk rock clowns that usually hovered around him, proclaiming him as their deity. Later he went to a party and snorted a bunch of heroin. He woke up dead.

I never knew GG to be a hard-core junkie. I'd seen him shoot dope, but he was just showing off. He never once said to me, "Hey, let's cop some drugs." He hated pot, but would pretty much do any other drug that was offered to him. He had no boundaries. He would try anything on a bet. He was impervious to pain and he was not afraid to die. All of this made him terribly dangerous but also wildly attractive. No sane person could ever come close to his complete disregard for his own well-being. And he could play it as a joke—like putting his head through a glass window for a cheap laugh.

The second time we played at the Lismar Lounge, an idiot fan looking to score some points gave GG some dope to snort, and it was a disaster. He was so out of it he barely performed, and instead rolled around for a while, getting tangled up in the mic cord. And then we all went home. That night GG committed the ultimate crime: he was boring. Heroin is really good for that, which is not the only reason why I never touch the stuff, although it's one of the best.

Years later VH-1 named GG's final gig the fourth "freakiest concert moment ever," topping other "freaky moments" like Alice Cooper being pelted with a pineapple upside-down cake, and Quiet Riot gigging at a nudist camp. And that is exactly why I didn't feel like talking to a bunch of fawning fanzine geeks before GG was even buried: people who didn't know him always treated him like a cartoon, and I was sick of it. *Freaky?* Fuck you. A man was dead.

He had a lot of hangers-on, but I don't think he had a lot of real friends he could trust or talk to on a level beyond his public persona. He was too funny and too smart to take himself too seriously, but sometimes he needed to be reminded. In front of a crowd of adoring fans he would strut like the leper messiah, but when he was getting shitfaced with me over a bottle of Jim Beam, we could just laugh about what an incredible asshole he was.

He had been promising for years to kill himself onstage—the ultimate rock 'n' roll death. Instead he ended up an accidental overdose, passed out on someone's couch—the ultimate rock 'n' roll cliché. He had always said, "With GG Allin, you don't get what you want, you get what you deserve."

When I heard the news, I was certainly not surprised. The only shock was that he lasted as long as he did. He was thirty-six. His stories of being beaten up after gigs—by angry "fans," by cops, by frat boys who came specifically to kick the shit out of him—were legend. I had played only five or six shows in his band and *my* life had been threatened on several occasions. One night in North Carolina some angry concertgoers followed us to our motel with baseball bats. It was a bad scene—you know you are about to enter a world of pain when GG's the one calling the cops.

GG Allin was a classic American Story. He grew up in a log cabin in New Hampshire without electricity. His father named him Jesus

Christ Allin. "GG" was short for "Jesus," what his brother Merle called him when they were kids. (Later his mother changed his name to Kevin so that he might have a shot at a normal childhood, but it didn't quite work out that way: Kevin used to go to school in drag and was routinely beaten up by rednecks and jocks.) His father was a religious kook who never let anyone speak in the house after dark.

GG called me often from the Michigan correctional institution where he had been incarcerated for two years on an assault charge brought by a woman he'd had sex with. I liked getting his calls, always collect. That was a long stretch, but GG told me that it saved his life: "I was a wreck, physically and emotionally. I had to get off the street." According to GG, and I believe him, the sex was rough but 100-percent consensual. The women that were attracted to him were not looking to hold hands in the park. While the judge acknowledged that there were inconsistencies in the woman's account, ultimately GG pleaded guilty.

GG's mistake was that he later wrote a fan letter to John Hinckley, the fellow who shot Ronald Reagan. When the Secret Service ran GG's name through the computer, standard procedure for vetting correspondence with would-be presidential assassins, the thing coughed and sputtered and lit up like a pinball machine. For the good of God-fearing citizens everywhere, they mobilized a task force and tossed GG into the clink. According to GG, "The public defender they gave me might as well have been working for the prosecution. He hated me."

The last time I saw GG was at Rhea's house. Rhea liked GG and had insisted that I invite him over. He had been out of jail for less than a year and was in New York to do a gig with Dee Dee Ramone—also a man of questionable judgment.

We were on the roof, barbecuing. It was a pleasant scene: both of us wearing aprons and tall chef hats, flipping burgers, and hamming it up for a bunch of friends who had come over for an afternoon cookout. GG was all up in arms over John Waters's latest flick, *Hairspray*. He thought Waters had sold out. "I liked it," GG confessed, "but it wasn't what I go to a John Waters movie to see." He asked me if I wanted to be on the guest list for the show the next day, and I told him I wasn't going. "We're having a nice time. It was really good to see you. Why would I want to ruin that vibe by going to one of your gigs?" He laughed. "Yeah," he told me, "yer prob'ly right."

A few weeks after I got the news about GG, the phone started ringing ominously again. Dave Insurgent had committed suicide, just days after his girlfriend was murdered and his father had killed his mother in a freak accident. It was too crazy. None of it made any sense. I wept like a baby.

It was summer in Madrid, and hot. Most of Spain, including the other Pleasure Fuckers, had taken off for vacation. Without a lot of money to travel or a family with a beach house to crash in, I was sweating it out in the city. It wasn't so bad—at least it was quiet. But that also meant that there was no one around to whom I could eulogize my friend. So I got drunk by myself on the cheap Spanish brandy that had been haunting the back of the cupboard. It was a hangover in a bottle, a bad mistake, but it got me through the night.

Since he had gotten out of the hospital after taking that beating, Dave had not been quite the same. I hardly ever saw him. I bumped into him a couple of times, but he was always in a rush. He'd still call occasionally to tell me to turn on the TV to check out *The Joe Franklin Show* that night, and we'd have an entirely unironic laugh about how hard Joe was and make plans to hang out, but never would.

After he recuperated at home with his parents, Dave had started using drugs again. For a while he was trying to make a go of it with his new band House of God, but Reagan Youth fans weren't that eager to sign on to his confused attempt at ironic hard rock and hippie heavy metal. He was a believer, though, always a believer, and he followed his own star. I thought he had gone off the deep end with the new band, but I had to respect him for being true to whatever muse he was chasing, even if it was hopelessly naïve. Dave's newfound love of the Grateful Dead was a recipe for punk rock disaster, but he never gave up trying to foment an awakening. He wanted to jar the country out of its apolitical slumber, yet in his own state of druggy free fall, he forgot why the first attempts at Hippie Takeover had failed: drugs ask great questions but don't necessarily provide a lot of answers. Even tripping on Owsley's finest, Revolution takes a lot of work, a virtue for which most idealistic hippies, or punks, will never be famous.

But it wasn't Dave's trippy idealism that did him in—the plain fact was that he had become a stone-cold junkie.

He was a nice Jewish boy with parents who doted on him and struggled to make sure that he had every advantage they had been stripped of by the Second World War. His father, Ronald Rubinstein, had grown up a fairly well-off Jew in Poland who would spend summers in Vienna visiting relatives. He was able to escape the Nazis, but heading east instead of west, he was snagged by the Russians and found himself toiling in a labor camp until the end of the war. Not knowing who in his family had survived, he then traveled to Palestine—what would soon become Israel—to be with other displaced Jews. It was there he learned that some of his cousins had made it to America.

In New York, Dave's dad focused on reclaiming the good life he had enjoyed growing up in Poland. He had a job as a lithographer for *The New York Times* and later owned an antique shop in Manhattan. He didn't get married until his late forties, when on a trip to Israel, he met Giza, also in her forties. They moved to New York, tied the knot right away, and had their only son.

By the time Dave was a teenager, his parents were nearing sixty, blowing any normal generation gap ridiculously out of proportion. They were more like grandparents, and Dave's friends used to make fun of Ronald for wearing Bermuda shorts with black socks and garters.

Where Ronald and Giza saw the Holocaust and their experience as an inspiration to work hard, and to provide their son with a good education and every opportunity that America offered, Dave saw their values as just so much middle-class bullshit—no matter what the cause, his parents had been conditioned to think that way, programmed by Big Brother, brainwashed.

After his recuperation, Dave had apparently enjoyed enough teenage rebellion to last a lifetime and had reconciled with his folks. But he couldn't stay off dope, and he began dating Tiffany B., a twenty-two-year-old prostitute from Louisiana who would turn tricks to keep them in drugs. He told his friends that he was happier than he had been in a long time. He was crazy about Tiffany. She didn't judge him. She was great in bed.

One night Dave and Tiffany were hanging out on Allen Street. She was looking for a quickie so they could get some money to score some junk. She got in the car with a john who was cruising the block, and they took off. When she didn't come back, Dave called the cops. They told him to get lost. A few days later the driver was pulled over because his rear license plates were dangling. Tiffany's body was in the trunk. The John was Joel Rifkin, and Tiffany was his seventeenth and final victim.

As if this wasn't unthinkable enough, two weeks later, Dave's dad ran over his mother with his car. He was backing out of the driveway. She was bent over, pulling some weeds out of the sidewalk, and he didn't see her. She died in the hospital that same day.

Friends who saw Dave at his mother's funeral say that he was in agony and would not leave his mother's side, even when the casket was lowered into the ground. One person said that Dave wanted to jump in with her.

It was another two weeks later when Dave, worn down by years of drug abuse and unable to cope with the loss of the two women who loved him unconditionally, ate a bottle of sleeping pills. He was buried next to his mother.

Jewish law prohibits suicides from being buried in sacred ground, but Dave's death was called an accidental overdose. Allegedly he left a note, but his father refused to read or acknowledge it. There is no doubt in the mind of anyone who knew Dave at the time that he took his own life.

When I eventually got all the details of Dave's death and the events leading up to it, I felt as if someone had sucked all the air out of my lungs. GG's and Dave's deaths both made me deeply homesick for New York—suddenly I felt very detached from my old reality. I didn't even know whom to call about Dave. By the time I got the first call, he would have been in the ground. I didn't know anyone in his close circle anymore; since college, our friendship had existed in its own space.

I cried and drank and paced and wondered what to make of all this. Was there blame to be handed out?

Fuck. GG was a smart guy, and he had a death wish. Dave was an intelligent man, trying to liberate the masses, but he needed help, he was an addict. Still, he must have known that fucking around with heroin dealers was not a wise career move. Having his head caved in should have been fair warning.

What a colossal waste. Dave and I were the same age, our birthdays only a month apart. I suppose his death should have made me confront my own mortality, but I believe we control our own destinies. I finished the bottle of brandy instead and woke up in a heap.

I mourned deeply and quietly, and I said a prayer for my friend. Sometimes when I see Joe Franklin on TV, I get a little misty. Everyone just assumes that I'm nuts.

Living in Spain is a powerful balm. The days slink by punctuated by the baited semicolons of long siestas and the open ellipses of endless *marcha*, and after a while I was able to put Dave's story into a place where I felt I could guard his memory and still remain "liberated," as he would have said. Dave would have been the first one to rail against knee-jerk reactions to cautionary drug stories, and I was with him all the way.

For my birthday party that year, I re-created the piñata from the cover of the Raunch Hands album. I found a toy store that had a bunny-head piñata and loaded it up with hash joints, mini-bottles of booze, and some of Malasaña's finest marching powder, along with the kind of crap one usually finds in a piñata: toys, candy, squirt guns, confetti, etc. When it was busted open, about twenty people dove head-first in a pile to retrieve the goodies. It was silly and celebratory, and it was the best thirtieth birthday party a fellow could ever have.

I had also finally gotten a good handle on my Spanish and didn't feel so much like an outsider.

The best way to learn a language, of course, is in bed, and I was lucky to have met a dreamboat of a girl who didn't speak a lick of English.

I didn't quite catch it the first time she said *"quítame mi sujetador"*—it means "take off my bra"—but I didn't have to be asked *"¿Tienes un profiláctico?"* twice before I was knocking over the bottle of wine on the night table, scuttling for the condoms. I was well on my way.

Unfortunately, once I got to prattling, she dumped me in a hurry. After many happy months of pillow talk that consisted mostly of pointing and smiling, when we actually started speaking, she discovered that we had absolutely nothing in common and gave me the high hat.

For a while I dated a Latin professor who had a fetish for the Ramones. She taught by day and punk rocked at night. She was like a superhero. We used to play Scrabble in Spanish, which was perfect for me because there was no shame in losing. Naturally, when I finally won a game (just lucky—I pulled *oxígeno* on the first turn), I got to gloat to all the citizens of Malasaña the glory of my victory, the Greatest Upset in Scrabble History.

After that I hooked up with a twenty-year-old stunner of a heavy metal chick who had a thing for Americans, but after busting me for listening to Frank Sinatra, she tossed me for a long-haired punk with a nose ring and full-sleeve tattoos.

Meanwhile, Mariconda had met a totally sweet, *normal* girl, Susana, whom he had every intention of marrying. He was more centered than I had ever seen him.

Chandler had reappeared, still under the dark shadows of profound alcoholism and La Gatita Mala, and was planning to move back to New York to make a go of it and marry her. Later, sadly, it would become clear that she was just riding him for entrée to the States, but that would still make three married Raunch Hands. And me. Damn. I thought I was the catch in this bunch.

In lieu of holiday romance, Party Horse had come to visit me for Christmas and we had jetted off to Morocco on another spur-of-the-moment adventure.

We were sitting in the Agapo getting hammered. It was late. The sun was threatening to come up, and in the midst of some drunken shit talk he declared that we were "going to Fez to get a fez."

"You have your passport and sunglasses?" He was in fine form. "Good. That's all you need. Let's go to the airport." And off we went. Africa, after all, was only an hour away.

A fez, of course, is the lid of choice for your Freemason, Shriner, or retro lounge act. Jeff and Akbar from Matt Groening's *Life in Hell* comic always wore fezzes. It was an important part of my shtick, as well. After all, the Grand Wizard of Wrestling, not to mention Sun Ra, was quite fond of them.

Fez, the city, where the hat obviously comes from, is in the heart of Morocco, well off the beaten path. Tourists go to Marrakech, a hippie mecca, and Casablanca, a resort that flourishes in the cinematic glow of Humphrey Bogart. It seems like the only westerners who go to Fez are on assignment for the National Geographic Society.

The old part of Fez is the medina, a walled city built in the eighth century. Inside the walls are shops and businesses and palaces and mosques, all spiraling upward in a gorgeous, towering cochlea of Arab culture. The streets are only a few feet wide and, without a guide, impossible to navigate. They say it is the largest contiguous car-free area in the world. But if you are not careful, you can be run over by a goat.

We flew to Tangier, at the northern tip of Morocco, where, it's true, everyone works for the CIA and speaks eleven languages. There was no way we were going to be able to find our way across northern Africa on our own, so we took the advice in the guidebook I bought at the airport and hired a driver to take us on our hundred-and-eighty-mile journey to buy some sporty headgear.

We were about twenty miles outside of Fez when we got pulled over by some sort of highway control who wanted to see our papers. Not content with American passports, they took a peek in the trunk, where we had stashed our battery of duty-free liquor. When we left Spain, we didn't know much about Moroccan culture, but we were betting we weren't going to be served any cocktails in the heart of a Muslim country. We bet right. Four bottles of vodka lighter, the highway cops let us continue on our way. The driver just shrugged. That was the cost of traveling on the king's roads.

The next day, we entered the medina with a hired guide who took us to an old, bearded vendor to buy our fezzes, a couple of maroon-colored numbers with swanky tassels. At this point Party Horse declared unceremoniously that we had gotten what we had come for and that now we had to leave.

Somehow we managed to rent a car, a 1950s Renault with the gearshift built into the dashboard, and got back on the road, heading for Tangier. Having conquered the medina, we were filled with just so much self-confidence.

This time there were no larcenous cops to check our papers, probably a good thing, since we had nothing to buy them off with except our sunglasses and a couple of funny hats. After a few hours of driving through the green, sprawling hills of the Moroccan countryside, we stopped at a roadside café for some lunch.

We ate beautiful grilled vegetables and couscous, dominated by confident, oversize artichokes, served with ripe olives and harissa, a chili paste that packed the wallop of a bazooka. We drank cold peppermint tea.

Suddenly Party Horse excused himself and hurried across the street. Something had caught his eye. I had no idea what he was doing, but pretty soon there were people following him into a storefront. A crowd was gathering, and I thought I had better investigate.

He was sitting in a barber's chair, getting a haircut. The entire town, about thirty people, had come to watch.

After he was shorn, and had paid and thanked everyone and shaken every single person's hand, I had to inquire about the sudden urge, while traipsing across Africa, to clean up his coiffure.

"I thought it was a bar," he confessed. "I saw a chair and a counter with some bottles on it and a guy wearing a nice shirt. I got excited and went in to order a drink. After I realized what was happening, I was too embarrassed to say anything, so I just let him go. He did a nice job, don't you think?" I agreed, and got my hair cut there, too.

Back in Tangier, after leaving the rent-a-car on the street to be stolen (since it was easier than returning it), we hired a taxi to take us by the casbah to have some dinner. But first Party Horse insisted that we ride some camels. He had seen them on the beach, and now he was determined not to leave Africa without having his picture taken on one. To confound matters, after a few drinks at the American hotel—where every spy in the world seemingly gathered for happy hour—and a few smoldering hits of hash oil from a pipe I had fashioned out of a banana, he was now speaking in Arabic.

"Jamál!" he had declared to our cabdriver, whose English was perfect. "I must ride jamál!" Somehow Party Horse had divined that jamál was the Arabic word for "camel."

Unbelievably, the cabdriver understood. "No problem," he told us. "I take you to jamál." He aimed the cab toward the center of Tangier.

"No, I said jamál! Take me to jamál! I want to ride jamál!"

"Yes, yes, my friend, I take you to jamál! No problem!"

"Then why the fuck are we going inside the city? Don't try and rip me off. The beach is that way. That's where the fucking camel is."

"Camel? Ahhh. Camel. The word for camel is jamel," he explained. "You ask for jamál. Jamál is young boy."

After living in Spain for almost two years, I made my first return trip to the States, a weeklong jaunt to go to my brother's wedding, but also for a much-needed reality check. It was great to be back, to see friends and family in New York, great to eat decent pizza. I loaded up on dirty-water hot dogs and bagels, and bathed in Budweiser.

I did not expect to get zapped with culture shock, but after being away from the States for so long, even the money seemed exotic.

Snorting coke through a hundred-dollar bill was a nice treat. Nothing else in the world smells like American money, and I relished the musky bouquet of capitalism with the giddiness of a tipsy oenophile presented with a bottle of '84 Haut-Médoc. As a cocaine delivery system, Spanish money is also quite sexy (ditto the old Dutch twenty-five-guilder note), but filthy Yankee lucre has its own pimped-out-Tony-Montana-rock-star-New-World voodoo that will never be beaten by a European banknote sporting a picture of a prune-faced monarch.

At dinner one night my dad asked me uninterestedly how my band was doing, and I told him, "Pretty good. But it's not like we're ever going to be the Rolling Stones or anything." I thought about that for a second, and asked him if he knew who the Rolling Stones were.

"Yes," he sniffed. "They are a *successful* rock group."

Between road trips and recording sessions with the Fuckers, I was still pushing my pen around and had finally broken into the upper stratum of sleaze scribbling for *Hustler*. The world of adult publishing is a small one, and a couple of editors I had known in New York were now in Los Angeles working for Larry Flynt Publications, home to *Hustler*. They invited me to start pitching story ideas.

As I look back from the haughty technological perch on which we now reside, my first article for *Hustler* seems hopelessly quaint. It was for their Sexplay department, an article explaining that *e-mail* could be *anonymous* and that you could use the *Internet* to meet potential *dates*. In 1993, the Internet was just beginning to bubble into the common consciousness, and this sort of sexual subterfuge was seen as wildly subversive. Who would ever have thought it was possible to meet women without leaving the house?

At the time it wasn't even possible to e-mail *Hustler*. I was using my primitive laptop to send my stories via phone line—I had an external modem the size of a humidor and some clunky software that took an hour to send just a few pages to their fax machine. I should have charged them by the foot: a three-thousand-word story would birth fourteen feet of filth, printed out on an inky scroll of old-fashioned thermal fax paper.

My best work for *Hustler* was a story about enterprising twins who ran an amphetamine lab *and* a brothel near the meatpacking district in Hamburg, Germany. It was the perfect setup: drop-dead gorgeous sisters who sold sex, meat, and speed to truckers.

Of course the story was cooked. It was a composite: I knew about the whorehouses, I often ate at steak houses in that part of Hamburg, I had extensive knowledge of the drugs, and I knew some very sexy, very ambitious twins. I simply nudged the truth along a little bit and put them all in the same place.

I also wrote some very regrettable stuff for *Barely Legal*, a *Hustler* spin-off that specialized in young-girl fantasy fodder. *Barely Legal* was a runaway hit, one of the most successful new porn titles in years, and it spawned a slew of imitators, including my old book *Live!*, which had been repackaged (again) as *Live Young Girls*.

When *Barely Legal* started, it had a sort of a tongue-in-cheek cheerleader fetish vibe. Later, it began to look more like *Predator Monthly*. *Live Young Girls* catered to sickos right out of the gate. Even for me, they had gone too far. Porn-star-looking sex bombs in tight sweaters and Catholic schoolgirl uniforms is one thing; underage-looking waifs posing with stuffed animals and candy canes is just wrong.

The last piece I wrote for *Hustler* was about Malasaña, which I painted lovingly as the wildest town in Europe, a mecca for sex, drugs, and rock 'n' roll; a modern-day Sodom for Six-String Hedonists and Big Beat Fanatics. It featured a detailed portrait of a local promoter, an unscrupulous fat Basque man who skimmed money from bands to buy drugs and whores. It was a very good story. And true.

When El Bratto and I had the bright idea to eat the acid and go swimming, we had the beach all to ourselves. The sun was only just poking its nose over the horizon. Now, midmorning, when we were finally ready to come in out of the water, the sun was screaming, and the beach was filled with families—half of them horrified and hiding their children from the psychedelic drug monsters now wading toward them, the other half just pointing and laughing and having a good goddam hee-haw at our expense. We must have looked like a couple of idiots, completely naked (except for our sunglasses) and very confused. It had been a long night. After almost three years, three hundred gigs, and thirty thousand miles under our wheels, I had finally decided to quit the Pleasure Fuckers.

Climbing out of the Mediterranean Sea in Málaga, Pablo Picasso's hometown, I could see where he learned to draw. Everyone seemed to have both eyes on the same side of their heads. When they moved, their bodies clattered into shimmering cubist fractals. Or maybe it was just the drugs. They were good, and strong.

I probably should have just kept swimming out to sea. I was surely the only man any of these Malagueños had ever seen who had been ritually circumcised. Perhaps I was just being paranoid? Maybe they'd think I had been bitten by a shark? No way, José. They'd take one look at the results of my bris and peg me for a Jew in a New York second. Back in Madrid, I had been a source of curiosity and excitement to a small group of adventurous young women eager to experience the wonders of ancient Jewry through the magic that is me. But who knew what the people here, still living in the shadow of the Spanish Inquisition, would think when they saw the Creature from Temple Beth Shalom emerging from the water, drugged to the gills on LSD? I didn't want to wait around for my reviews. Or *la policía*. Now, where the fuck were my pants?

The Pleasure Fuckers had been slotted to play the headline spot at a giant music festival in the desert, but after a torturous evening of waiting, night had turned into day and we were still not on.

There were thousands of people there, and we were scheduled to go on around 3:00 a.m., a good time to be hitting in front of a Spanish festival crowd. Everyone would be peaking, the ecstasy heads, the speed freaks, even the drunks would still be on form. But at four o'clock, we were still about three bands away. The tribulations of playing in Spain. That's when I realized it was going to be a long night. By the time we finally took the stage, at 6:00 a.m., the crowd had thinned and everyone was crashing. We played a short set. I don't remember it being any fun.

It was a dismal end to an event that had kicked off with Turmix pilfering drink tickets from his bandmates. Sick of his bullshit, I could have quit right then. It had already been in the back of my mind.

When we arrived in Málaga after driving through the desert all day from Madrid, the guy in charge had given the band some drink tickets so we could get started while they were still setting up the backstage with kegs of beer. He foolishly gave them to Turmix—ten of them. Turmix gave the four other Pleasure Fuckers one each, and held on to the rest.

This was just petty nonsense, but it was the last straw. Turmix had been shaving money off of gigs for years. He booked the gigs and was generally entitled to a percentage, although I don't know anyone who takes money from his own band. The problem was that he was taking money he had not earned, overpaying himself and underpaying the group. When I first found this out, I went ballistic. I was told, Relax, he always did this. As if that made it okay. And on and on it went. He borrowed sixty deutsche marks from a promoter in Hamburg so he could get a red-light blow job and never paid it back. After that, we couldn't get booked there. Thanks to Fat Boy's fifteen-second hooker fantasy and his misconceptions about his right to other people's money, we were shit out of luck in one of the best cities in Germany.

There had been a somewhat tepid move to keep Turmix on a short leash, but inertia takes on a whole new meaning when you are dealing with a three-hundred-pound man who named himself after a blender. We were on a good roll, and no one wanted to blow it by getting rid of our gimmick.

Now, at the end of the night in Málaga, I just wanted to go to the beach house where the bands were staying and fall facedown for a dose of nature's sweet restorer, sleep, the one thing I did not get a lot of during my career as a Pleasure Fucker.

But at the beach house there were more people than beds, and I was holding a short straw. Someone must have not done the math. Oh, wait. Turmix and his wife had barricaded themselves in a big room that had seven beds in it. After drinking forty-seven pints of vodka and orange soda, he must have confused it for the honeymoon suite at the Fontainebleau.

I was fed up. But there was no use stomping around and waking up the innocents who were passed out everywhere—except for the snoring, it was a lot like Jonestown. As a few more disgusted musicians straggled in to try to find a piece of floor to curl up on, my friend El Bratto and I decided to make the best of it, drop the blotters that someone had gifted us earlier, and jump into the sea and enjoy the morning.

It was lovely. There are those who say the Mediterranean is the toilet bowl of Europe, but I disagree. It is more like the bidet. And I have always had great luck with Spanish LSD, or *tripis*, as they call it. (As in "trippy.") That morning on the beach, before the madding crowd of cubist sunbirds arrived, I had hallucinated dozens of tiny dinosaurs burrowing in the sand. I had the same experience on my sixteenth birthday when I dropped some acid and went to see Johnny Winter in Asbury Park. I figure it must have had something to do with the way the sun hits the water.

The fireworks erupted in the van about halfway back to Madrid.

It is well known to one and all that I hate the Beatles. They ruined rock 'n' roll. The day Bob Dylan got them stoned for the first time was one of the blackest days in history.

This is another line of thought that hasn't done much to make me popular. The Beatles are sacred cows that no one is ever supposed to criticize. I'd be better off talking shit about Jesus at the pope's Christmas party.

But let's face it: *Sgt. Pepper* was a deathblow to rock 'n' roll. *Will you still need me, will you still feed me?* Please. The whole thing sounds like sickly geriatrics singing the sound track for a children's movie—one that was thankfully never made.

"Being for the Benefit of Mr. Kite"? If I wanted to listen to warmed-over show tunes, I'd go out and get a copy of *Thoroughly Modern Millie*. This is exactly the kind of goop that legitimized art rock and paved the way for every crappy progressive 1970s concept record that followed. I can draw a straight line from the Beatles to Genesis and Yes faster than Paul McCartney could scarf up a batch of freshly baked pot brownies.

They have their moments, but for every "Helter Skelter," "Taxman," or "Yer Blues," there is "Ob-La-Di, Ob-La-Da," "The Fool on the Hill," "Octopus's Garden," or some other lilting, unlistenable crud that does nothing but mock the listener for buying into this sham. "Hey Jude" is the most tedious piece of shit ever perpetrated on teenage ears. It sounds like a bunch of drunks singing along with the town retard while he practices his piano lesson.

Before they bought into all of that flower power crap, when they were still playing in Hamburg at the Star Club, boozing and taking amphetamines—drugs that were designed for rock 'n' roll—and delivering three sets a night of Little Richard and Larry Williams covers (before soft-pedaled bubblegum like "Love Me Do" and "Eight Days a Week" took over the show), then you really had something. You can hear a faint trace of that excitement on recordings of their first American tour. That is, when you can hear the band over the screaming fans, who clearly weren't there to actually listen to the "music." When the Beatles came to New York, Shea Stadium was filled with thirteen-year-old girls. That should tell you something right there.

It is amazing how many otherwise irreverent intellects go ape shit when I start in with this line of patter. Reactionaries. If Dave Insurgent were around, he'd have cuffed them on the head and told them to liberate themselves.

So, naturally, I keep on saying it. While I was living in Spain, I put these elevated thoughts into an article for *Ruta 66*, by far the best music mag in Spain. They got more mail for that single article than they had ever received in ten years of publishing—bags and bags of hate mail from sappy Beatles fans whose feelings I had hurt. The editors were delighted. And I just love working as a heel. They invited me to write whatever I wanted. For my next act I reviewed one of my own shows with the Pleasure Fuckers, and you can bet I gave the drummer raves. Naturally, this signaled another whole round of hate mail. "Who the fuck does he think he is??" Even the other Pleasure Fuckers thought I was being a bit cheeky.

Which brings us back to the Pleasure Fuckers' van, now leaving Málaga. Turmix sure looked well rested riding shotgun—he was too fat to sit anywhere else. And he knew I was plenty steamed. Burbling under the surface of my lysergic glow was still the bitterness that there was a thief among us.

I am not sure why I had put up with this for so long, except that the other Pleasure Fuckers were willing to shrug it off, and as a group, as a gang, we needed each other. When the formula worked, we were like an iron fist. The band had become a lifestyle, and from the Canary Islands to Croatia, from Paris to Prague it had been a spectacular ride.

But we had gone about as far as we were going to go, and I was ready to get off the bus, for good. Turmix, taunting me by playing the

Beatles on the dashboard stereo, only expedited the matter. And not just any Beatles—a murky-sounding bootleg of White Album outtakes. It was like a bad dream.

I admit it, I broke my own rule and reacted. But I had lost my sense of humor for Fatty. All it took to push me over the edge was a poorly recorded demo version of "Rocky Raccoon." When we stopped on the highway to get gas, I ripped the cassette from the player and chucked it into the car wash across the street. The sound of it being crushed by one of those big black roller things that squeegee windshields was the best music I had heard in years.

12

HOW TO MAKE
YOUR MONKEY HAPPY

I arrived back in New York with a thousand dollars in my pocket, recompense for my most recent story for *Hustler*. I started in Madrid with a thousand bucks, so I figured I could land just about anywhere in the world with that much money and make a go of it. New York City was never easy, but I'm made of some pretty stern stuff. The first thing I did was get a chocolate egg cream at the Gem Spa—a much-redacted version of the Edison Cure—and then, newly fortified, I trucked over to Midnight Records and talked my way back into my old job.

For the first few nights I crashed with Chandler and his bride, La Gatita Mala, who had gotten spliced in a civil ceremony in an East Village community garden and were now house-sitting an artist's loft on Avenue B. But there was something seriously wrong there. Chandler's drinking was completely out of control. He was slamming bourbon during the day and not making a whole lot of sense. Instead of wearing the glow of newly wedded bliss, he was wearing the stench of a sunlight drunk. And his shrew of a wife offered no support—she had her own money and was throwing it around at trendy bars, places where Chandler would never dream of going. She had hooked up with a horrid posse of leather pants–wearing idiots, all of them blinded by the Bright Lights of the Big City. Every night she ditched her husband to go out on a spree with these spoiled rich kids who slurped overpriced Cosmopolitans and gobbled designer drugs and then spent the next day bragging about their hangovers and the supermodels they had seen at Bowery Bar. They were awful.

I hated her because she knew what she was getting into with Chandler and just didn't seem to care. Eventually her dopey friends drifted on to the next trendy scene, and she began to get the message that no one wanted her here. If you are going to live in New York, it requires a little bit of humility and restraint, which she never had. We exist on top of each other here, and you have to be aware of your surroundings and treat people with respect. This is a town that eschews solipsists. Eventually she just up and went back to Spain, leaving her husband high and not so dry.

Chandler's drinking, which was legend, was beginning to kill him. People loved him and couldn't bear to see him spiraling downward so rapidly. He was a leader among a scene and greatly admired, but no one could help him, except of course himself. It soon became apparent that it was time, too, for him to get the fuck out. He moved to Austin, where Mariconda and Susana had relocated and were doing great.

Mariconda had a good gig cutting video for the local news, and he was sporadically producing local bands. Susana was on her way to a good job at a university research lab. While the rest of us had our heads buried in the recreational, she had actually studied *practical* chemistry in college. And they had a kid.

The night Mariconda's daughter was born, he called me, yammering away as if he had been up all night tweaking on industrial-strength speed. "Sharky, we spent our whole lives, all our time with the Raunch Hands on the road, running around, looking for the next big high, for something stronger to really blow our minds. Seeing my daughter being born was like the best drug I ever took." It was an oddly warm sentiment from a man whose idea of fun is to break a guitar over someone's head.

Chandler lay low in Austin, stumbling through oddball jobs on car lots and construction sites, leaving a trail of bottles wherever he went. For a while, again, we didn't hear a whole lot from him.

George's marriage to Tomoko, sadly, had also skidded off the road. We all should have figured that this was not a marriage made in heaven—the sixty-dollar-a-gram snot dripping out of Party Horse's nose back at the Elvis Presley Wedding Chapel was probably a fair indicator.

I don't know how I was the only Raunch Hand who had avoided getting hitched, but given their one-in-three success rate—good numbers in baseball, but pretty fucking dismal in the love-and-marriage department—perhaps I was being prudent. Hey, I wanted to fall in love. I'm a very romantic fellow, and I wear it on my sleeve, but I know I'm no day at the beach, either. I am an action man and I need an action woman. Preferably one with a colossal superbrain. Anyway, before anything was going to happen, I needed an apartment and probably a job that paid more than ten bucks an hour. The women in New York can be sticklers about that stuff. For now at least, Edison Preferred was in the basement with few takers.

As it turned out, I knew a guy who was looking for a roommate in a ridiculously cheap apartment, an illegal rent-controlled sublet on Seventh Street and Avenue A. My share of the rent would be three hundred dollars, pocket change by New York standards.

You pays your money and you takes your choice. I would be living with a part-time male go-go dancer who—aside from occasional stints shaking his bony ass onstage with a handful of local bands for whom he had become a combination mascot/fetish item—was terminally unemployed.

Unable to gain acceptance in the American workforce, Go-Go Boy had plenty of time to spruce the place up and had gone for Modern American Squalor. Two years' worth of recycling was lovingly stacked up in the kitchen in picturesque disarray—hundreds of beer cans in happy blue plastic bags and enough copies of *The New York Times* to heat a midsize prison camp through a Siberian winter. The bathroom doubled as a laboratory, cultivating some of North America's most exotic mold spores, which prospered in a damp, wet environment, unfettered by chemical cleaning agents. As for decor, Go-Go Boy drew his inspiration from the urinals at CBGB.

I had known Go-Go Boy for years. Everyone did. He was a fixture on the local scene, and actually a smart and funny guy. He had gone to Columbia and had written his dissertation on the Rolling Stones' *Exile on Main St.*, positing that the sixties were only truly over when Mick Jagger sang *"I can't even feel the pain no more."*

I liked him, but the living situation was like *Papillon* meets *Glen or Glenda*. When I came in and turned on the light (a bare 60-watt bulb that usually had a pair of Go-Go Boy's sweaty panties hanging over it to dry), I would be knocked over by a herd of cockroaches stampeding for cover. Their exodus, punctuated by the percussive clicking of their little Cenozoic bodies on the filthy linoleum floor, was louder than the F train. At least I no longer had to clip my toenails—the roaches nibbled on them for me at night. Between the wildlife, the fauna, and Go-Go Boy, who was more often than not passed out drunk on the dirt heap of a couch, decked out in orange high-tops, fishnets, and hot pants, it was not the kind of place I could bring a date up to for a nightcap. Romance would have to wait.

Thanks to having such cheap rent, even making slave wages at the record store, I was able to sock away a few dollars, and luckily I found another rent-controlled sublet from a pal who had moved but wanted to hold on to his lease, since rent-controlled apartments in New York are the world's most precious commodity. This one was twice as much as Go-Go Boy's palace, but still a thousand bucks less than I would have paid without such a sweetheart deal. It was a real honey of a place, too, a garden apartment in the West Village, with a big ol' gas grill out in back, which I promptly named Lucille.

Meanwhile, I was still conducting a hard-target search for a new job in publishing. Porn was not what it had been. Cheap video, a glut of new product, and the Internet—which was showing all signs of being here to stay—were shaving points off the sales of the magazines, which were now doing almost all of their writing in-house and downsizing their staffs. I gave Carmine a shout, but he had nothing for me—the same chimps that were working there five years ago were still firmly installed in their jobs. It was a closed shop. But perseverance and industry bring sure reward. Once again I answered an ad in *The New York Times* and found a new career on the straight and narrow—as a business journalist.

The ad was for *Soft Drinks & Beer*, the leading trade magazine for the beverage industry. Trade magazines are notorious snoozes, but beer and soda pop? All those bubbles? What could possibly be more fun? At that point I would have taken a job with *Floor Covering News* or the *Journal of Human Resources* (both actual periodicals), anything to get back in the game. With *SD&B*, I hit the jackpot.

Jet-setting around Europe to do brewery tours was about as close to rock 'n' roll as I was going to get in a straight job. *Hey Mike, do you want to go to Amsterdam and talk to the people at Heineken?* Okay. *Would you go to Dublin and visit Guinness?* You bet.

What sealed the deal is that they were looking for someone who not only had magazine chops but could navigate Spanish well enough to edit their Spanish-language publication. Somehow I had turned a three-year coke jag into a marketable skill. While I was at *SD&B*, I went to London, Paris, and all over Germany and Italy, and I even made it to St. Louis to visit the Anheuser-Busch Clydesdales and the geniuses who make Budweiser.

I learned a whole headful of beverage-related arcana, all sorts of insider poop about dynamic right-angle transfer in low-friction conveyor systems, polyethylene terephthalate (the stuff they make plastic soda bottles out of), and high-intensity sweeteners. I did a lot of financial stories and had to learn how to speak Wall Street. I spent a great deal of time interviewing financial analysts and CEOs, and I often had to decipher stockholders' reports for, say, Coca-Cola or Cadbury Schweppes and turn them into breezy feature stories.

But the marketing stories were the real powerhouse education, and I began to formulate a theory that magazine marketing shared the same principles as beverage marketing. Beverages, like magazines, were highly affordable luxury items that depended on consumer satisfaction to generate repeat sales. It was so much about the packaging, getting people to pick up your product, letting them discover for themselves just how good you were, and then adding value in every phase of the experience. Ultimately the goal was to create a successful, long-lasting relationship between the product and the consumer.

Innovation was Rule Number One. This was the case with every consumer product, but you were lucky if you could sell someone one iPod a year. Buying magazines and soft drinks had to be somehow benignly habit-forming. This was drilled into my head every day by the best minds at Pepsi, Coke, Sam Adams, you name it. Every top producer had marketing wizards of the highest caliber, and these people never stopped thinking of new ways to grow their brand and make their core products better. Fritz Maytag III, the brewmaster at Anchor Steam Beer, told me, *Every day I try to put something better in the bottle.* I had him sign a photo of himself to me with those words inscribed, and I hung it in my office at *SD&B* and later took it with me when I signed on to run *High Times.*

Unfortunately, this otherwise upbeat gazette of soda pop and beer was run by Ally Alpacka, the single most disagreeable person I have ever met in my life. A hog-bodied Hun of a woman cursed with toxic halitosis—which she treated by chain-smoking Kool 100s in everyone's face (it was incredible how she could actually smoke *at* you)—what she lacked in personal charm she made up for with ill-advised cosmetic schemes built around disco-era blue eye shadow, blush that would have been better suited for a ten-dollar whore, and shit-colored lipstick that someone probably told her "softened her features." It did not. It looked like Willem de Kooning had puked on her face.

Her hair was red like canned borscht, the unfortunate result of years of chemical rinsing, made more ghastly by her insistence on wearing colors that clashed with her head—puce pantsuits and mauve sweatshirts—the kind with sequined butterfly appliqués, straight out of the Golden Girls' spring collection. When she had an important meeting or had to do business out of the office, she would squeeze her rolls of fat into dated pin-striped suits, which she thought made her look corporate and powerful but really made her look like the comic relief in an all-drag production of *Guys and Dolls*.

Ally Alpacka had previously run a few successful trade shows and had somehow managed to put together a team of investors to buy *SD&B*, which she had identified as not being fully optimized, especially in a newly emerging global market. There was a lot of money out there.

Her plan was to build a task force of editors and salespeople and, with the precision of a military strike, become omnipresent in the beverage industry and usher in a new, aggressive era in ad sales. In theory, I liked Ally Alpacka's hard-ass approach to the business. Sadly, however, no one has ever done more to alienate and disillusion talented people who actually liked their jobs and were excited to do good work. As far as joie de vivre goes, it seemed that Ally Alpacka, contrary to every one of her stated goals of running a successful business, was on a mission to stamp it out wherever it lived. She was like a combination of Big Foot and Foghorn Leghorn—to whom she bore an uncanny resemblance—stomping around the office and ruining everyone's day.

She had a huge chip on her shoulder about being a "woman in a man's world," and she would pointedly ask her male employees how they felt about "having a woman as their boss." Which is not only a kick in the nuts to the last fifty years of progressive gender politics in the workplace, but also probably illegal. It did not help that every time she opened her mouth, it sounded like someone stepped on a duck.

All of this was bad enough. Then she decided to start bringing her dog to work, a real Marmaduke of a hound, about as tall as I am, with a jaw the size of a panel truck. Poopsy had the run of the place. If I left my desk for a second, I would come back to find him drinking my coffee. Then, jacked up on caffeine, he'd go tear-assing around the office—he was big enough to knock down a cubicle—and work would shut down until Ally Alpacka could corral him back into his pen. Then I'd get yelled at.

I had little in common with most of the staff—the editors were largely starter chimps with communication degrees from B-list schools, and the ad guys were typically fast-talking gorillas with slicked-back hair and pinkie rings—but everyone was very nice, and we were at the very least able to bond in the shadow of the World's Worst Boss.

The one guy I worried about was Carlito, a potbellied intellectual from Mexico who had come to New York with ambitions of becoming a literary giant à la Jorge Luis Borges. Toiling under the weight of crushed dreams, he came to *SD&B* to be our chief Spanish translator. He believed with every cell in his body that this work was beneath his gigantic intellect, and he was miserable all the time. He looked at Ally Alpacka as the very embodiment of the Evils of American Capitalism, and he would stew at his desk, fomenting his own private Workers' Revolution. The possibility of him snapping and coming to work locked and loaded never seemed terribly remote.

And then there was Frank. On Frank's first day of work he showed up in a dashiki and a tricolored Rasta cap, accented by some sort of smelly hemp jewelry. He was fresh from a stint with Amnesty International, and his was not exactly the off-the-rack uniform of the associate editor in training, but he had apparently got past the gatekeeper by waving his English degree from Rutgers.

Someone had tipped him off about my background, and when we were introduced, the first thing Frank said to me was, "Yeah, man, I heard you played in a band. Do you guys still jam?"

"Listen, hippie," I pressed him, "we do not *jam*. We play *songs*." He thought about that for a while, until he realized that I was just busting his balls, and we became great friends.

Frank is a very intelligent guy, but he always had something to prove. He was rebelling in every direction. This was his first job, a leap for him, since he considered employment of any kind a sellout. He had joined Amnesty straight out of college, ostensibly to help save the world, but more likely to piss off his parents, which is why he kept covering his arms in tattoos.

One night after work, Frank and I were drinking with some of his pals. Mostly they were a nice bunch of Jewish kids from Long Island who followed the Grateful Dead when they were in college and now, freshly sprung, were getting back to their true roots and working for enormous brokerage firms, doing right by their upper-class suburban upbringing, and achieving nouveau yuppiedom in record time. Frank was the iconoclast. He wasn't making as much dough as some of his pals, who thanks to family connections were now swinging at Goldman Sachs, but he was always going to be the Player.

Frank's friend Martin, a Brooks Brothers–wearing no-neck with a pedigree from a long line of Wall Street Jews, was mopping up the Glenlivet and complaining about his car, a cherry red Audi 6. The poor thing, he had grown tired of it. Now he wanted a Porsche. But he didn't know how to tell his folks, who had just bought the Audi for him last week.

"Dude," said Frank, and I knew this was going to be bad, "just report it stolen and get the insurance money."

"That's a good idea," said his friend, "except first it has to be stolen."

"No problem," Frank assured him. "Just give me the keys. I'll get rid of it for you. I know some boys who'll chop it, and then you can call the insurance company." Frank left driving the Audi.

No good was ever going to come of this. No matter how much Frank liked saying it, there were no "boys," and there wasn't going to be any "chopping." For a few weeks Frank tried to find someone to take the car, bust it out into parts, and make it disappear. He asked the various pot dealers and low-level criminals he knew, and they all said, sure, I know someone who knows somebody. There was so much smoke up everyone's ass it was like being at the All-Nude Slo-Cook BBQ championships.

Unfortunately, it was a lot harder to get rid of a brand-new Audi than Frank had prophesied at the bar, and his friend was starting to get pissed off that the car had not been stolen yet. He didn't have any wheels, and he couldn't call it in. What the fuck was going on? Well, for one thing, Frank had taken to driving the car around town, using it as flash to pick up girls and to joyride with his buddies, and he wasn't that eager to let it go. He drove it to work every day and never thought twice about where he parked it, since it was going to be stolen anyway. At one point he even gave me the keys and told me to have my way with it.

Finally, when none of his posse of potheads came through with a connection to get rid of the car, and Martin was threatening to come over and break Frank's legs, Frank started leaving it on the street with the door open and the keys in the ignition.

This went on for a week, and no one came near it. He'd drive it up to Harlem and leave it running, and when he came back, it would be out of gas, but untouched. And giving the car back was not an option. It was just too embarrassing.

And then it happened. Frank left the car on the street in Soho, had a few drinks at some trendy hotel bar, and when he came back, it was gone. He went back into the bar to have a few more and celebrate.

Pretty soon his cell phone rang. It was Martin, who had just received a call from the New York City police, who had impounded the car because it had more than a thousand dollars' worth of unpaid parking tickets on it, all written in the past few weeks. Frank had to go to the impound lot and pay the fine in cash to get the car back.

When he started this caper, Frank was sure he was going to make some fast bread, and now he was out a thousand dollars and he still had the car to get rid of. He finally drove it to a remote location a few hundred miles north of New York City, set it on fire, then walked five miles through the woods to get a bus back home.

Let me tell you a story about two monkeys. Just regular monkeys. Cute ones. The first monkey (Fig. 1) is very sad. Sad and angry. There is an unpleasant monkey scowl on his face. He is suffering from monkey malaise. The other monkey (Fig. 2) is smiling. He is alert and happy and ready to take on the world. This is the kind of monkey you'd like to set up shop with, the kind of monkey you'd like to work next to, the kind of monkey you want in your posse. He is holding a banana.

Fig. 1   **Fig. 2**

Now let's take a closer look at that banana (Fig. 3). What's that? A price tag? Five cents? Hmmm. So the only difference between an angry monkey—one with his mind polluted by evil thoughts of work stoppages and industrial sabotage—and a happy, motivated monkey, who feels empowered and is eager to please, is a nickel? Well, who wouldn't want to spend five cents to have a happy monkey? And that's the moral of our story: it is easy to make monkeys happy . . . almost as easy as it is to make them unhappy.

Fig. 3

Ally Alpacka taught me that. Well, by example. I'm not so simple or naïve that I believe a piece of tropical fruit is in and of itself the Philosopher's Stone of modern management technique, but half a dime's worth of banana every so often can make for some mighty cheerful chimps. Ally Alpacka was surrounded by a gang of misanthrope apes who wanted to kneecap her sorry ass.

She once invited the art and editorial staff out to lunch to "reward" them for the great job they were doing. Of course everyone likes to be taken to lunch, but no one likes to be constantly reminded that it is some kind of *gift*. She had a way of lording it over the place, kind of like Marlon Brando in *The Island of Dr. Moreau*, and made it seem like it was a great act of charity for her to come down from the mountain, and at the risk of soiling her muumuu feed us and let us bask in her mag-nanimous personage, presumably so we would offer her our undying thanks for letting us put out her magazine by continuing to toil obedi-ently in her royal trenches.

Everyone already had their hackles up, but nonetheless we were generally looking forward to having a nice time out of the office. Some of the girls in the production department had actually come to work dressed up for the "company lunch"—when Ally Alpacka announced that instead of going out, she thought it would be "more fun" to have pizza in the conference room. Suddenly her reward seemed like a pun-ishment. Pizza in the conference room? That's what we did when edi-torial meetings ran long, and no one liked it then, either. She could have pulled down her polyester stretch pants and rained drizzling shits over the entire staff and received a warmer reception.

My favorite part was when she really started twisting the knife in the wound with a nauseating speech about how "the company likes to do this for its employees so they know how valuable they are." People were seething, the general perception being that we were worth more than a slice of crappy pizza. Like maybe lunch in a *restaurant*?

I was treated better in the porn business—I wrote a few overheated books and got a cash bonus, not to mention some gravlax canapés and very decent champagne. At Drake, my salary had doubled in two years. All my editors at *Hustler* and *Penthouse* had to do was call me and say "great job," which they never failed to do, and I beamed with pride and made sure my next job was even better. That was my banana. But Ally Alpacka just didn't have it in her cavernous self to be kind without strings attached. She was a pig who wanted to eat all the bananas—and the coconuts, and the pineapples, and the mangoes, and the papayas—herself. It was the single most ungracious performance by an employer since Truman fired General MacArthur.

Except for the *Soft Drinks & Beer* Christmas party, a depressing, low-rent fiasco in the basement of a smelly Irish pub. I still can't believe I put a suit on for it. I shouldn't have even bothered to shower.

Ally Alpacka's speech that day was an award winner. "We had a very good year, thanks to everyone here. And that's why we wanted to have this party for you, as a little bonus." And that was it. That was our little bonus.

13

ESCAPE FROM DOGGIE VILLAGE

I was in love. I fell hard. I felt like I got hit with a sailboat. Or a two-by-four, right to the soft part of my skull. My head was swimming. The sidewalks jiggled like aspic. I was one smitten kitten.

When I got back from Spain, the phone was ringing constantly with calls from people asking me if I wanted to play the drums in their bands—and I would politely tell them to fuck off. I had given up that life, I would explain, to begin work on an avant-garde outer-space ballet to be set on board an interstellar Iberian drug frigate.

After three years of rock 'n' roll warfare and chemical prevarication with the Pleasure Fuckers, I had zero interest in getting back in the van, metaphorically, existentially, or any other which way. No gigs, no pressure, no album to write, no more reindeer games. It was nice just to tool around on the guitar and bang merrily on the piano for no other reason than I felt like it. Eventually, people stopped calling. Which of course made me feel that I was no longer wanted. I suppose you can't have it both ways.

Perhaps that had something to do with why, a year after my return from Spain, I agreed to come out of my premature retirement. The fellow on the phone gave me a sob story about his drummer's having broken his wrist and how they were going to miss their Big Gig at Coney Island High, and how much they loved the Raunch Hands and GG Allin, blah, blah, blah. Well, all right then. But just one rehearsal and one show, and I'm out. Unless Led Zeppelin suddenly decided to re-form, I really had no desire to join a band.

The following week, there I was, waiting outside the rehearsal studio on Avenue B in the bitter cold, cursing myself for agreeing to this gig, when I saw her. She was wearing a tapered red wool jacket with wide lapels (later I would discover that she made it herself); tight blue jeans; and mod, square-toed boots. Her eyes sparkled, even at night. Her dirty blond hair looked as if she had it styled in London, in 1966. She was carrying a guitar. I can still hear the voices in my head—angels singing, harps, fireworks going off, all that good shit. No amount of LSD ever made me that goofy.

When the boys in the band showed up, I reluctantly followed them into the building. I smiled at her, wanly. She smiled back knowingly and walked through the door ahead of me. Zoinks! Turns out she was part of this drummerless gang of punks!

I acted like a complete idiot, stepping all over my tongue, showing off on the drums, acting like a schoolboy who had never seen a pretty girl before. When we took a break, I hammed it up a little on the battered upright that had been pushed into the corner of the studio and got another smile out of her by warbling my way through "Sloop John B." I was like, *gone*.

The gig sucked. They weren't a very good band—I probably should have auditioned them first. _____, the princess who had captured my heart, was an especially lousy guitar player. Lost right from the start, she got tangled in her own cord, accidentally unplugged her guitar, and spent most of the show trying to figure out why there was no sound coming out of her amplifier. She was twenty-four years old and in just thirty minutes had reached the same aurum stratum of "failed rock musician" that had taken me years to achieve. I was gaga for her.

After the show we flirted with each other at the bar and took turns buying each other drinks. I lied and told her she was great and not to worry about the show, it could happen to anyone. And then she left with the lead guitar player.

I love the beginning of *The Postman Always Rings Twice*, when the drifter, who narrates the story, gets a glimpse of the bombshell behind the counter at the greasy spoon he stumbles into, then goes outside and pukes up his breakfast. "I wanted that woman so bad," he declares, "I couldn't keep a thing on my stomach." That is exactly how I felt. I was out of breath for a week.

About a ten days later she left a message for me on my voice mail up at Ally Alpacka's House of Mirth, where she had assiduously tracked me down. She was asking for a date. When I heard the message, I actually swooned.

Turns out that the lead guitar player *was* her boyfriend, but they were done, and she had been thinking about me, too.

I went Camel Walking down the halls of *Soft Drinks & Beer*. I did the Hucklebuck, the Hully Gully, and the Hand Jive, too. I did the Freak, the Freddie, and the Frug. I nearly knocked over a cubicle doing the Locomotion.

Frank looked at me as if I had just lost my mind. It was a fair assessment. "What the fuck is wrong with you?" he demanded before screaming at me to get the hell off his desk, where I was now getting busy with the Mashed Potato.

"Sharky Dance of Joy!" I told him. "She digs me!"

"Well, you look like an escaped mental patient. Knock it off before Ally's dog takes a bite out of your ass."

The throes of new love, those first few weeks of excessive drinking and fucking, made me feel as weightless and giddy as a Spanish astronaut. Every night after work we'd meet for dinner and wind up sitting at the bar for hours, drinking and talking, falling for each other over and over again, and then going back to my place to roll around on the hardwood floor and have some more of that Brand-New Sex. Sometimes we didn't wait to get home and would orchestrate a stealth bathroom tryst between rounds of icy vodka gimlets. We were soaring. On one of our first dates we went to Venice, Italy.

I had to go to Munich on *SD&B* business, a hit-it-and-quit-it trip to attend a press conference and introduce myself to a few captains of industry. I had to be there for only one day and one night, so I said to ____, "Come with me. Munich is a nice old town, we'll drink some good beer, eat a schnitzel, and then we'll get on a train and head through the Alps to Italy or something." She loved the idea and chose Venice as our destination, a six-hour hop from Munich.

Before getting on the train, we stocked up on Bavarian sausages; ripe cheese; some of those gorgeous, oversize, pillow-soft pretzels they use for bread; a few jars of toothy, spicy mustard; a couple bottles of cold, dry Riesling; and lots of heavyweight German chocolate. We had a second-class compartment all to ourselves, and by the time we were ready to tuck into our picnic basket, we had hit the Alps, clickety-clacking across Austria through the Brenner Pass at Innsbruck, and it began to snow. After years of scribbling porn, I had finally scripted a storybook romance.

Venice looks like something from a Jules Verne novel. There is no other place on Earth remotely like it. Perhaps on Mars. There are no automobiles, no scooters, no buses, just water taxis on the bigger canals, and of course the gondolas. For once, the advance press was true: Venice is as off-the-charts romantic as promised.

It was on our second day there that the darkness struck. We had taken a ferry across the lagoon to one of the small islands that float off the coast, and suddenly I found my new love silent and grim. If she were in a comic strip, she would have had an ominous-looking rain cloud drawn over her head. It turned out that she suffered from manic-depressive disorder, and this was my first experience seeing her on the downside.

"I get like this," she told me blankly. "I just want to die. I can't feel anything."

It was overwhelming. Her pallor infected everything around her. Just standing next to her, my fingertips felt cold and my feet were numb.

"You can't do anything," she explained flatly. "You can't cheer me up. Just ignore me."

It was heartbreaking. Eventually, she told me, it would pass. And by the time we got back to New York, it had. Those last few days were rough, but there was no way I was going to bail out on her. She had more brains and more talent and more good logic than anyone I had ever met. I was awed by her unguarded insight into the world around her. There didn't seem to be anything she wasn't interested in learning. A conversation with her could be an adventure.

The dark shadows could swarm over her quickly, but the good times were positively buoyant. We were loving New York City, bouncing between dive bars and cozy restaurants. When it was time to get out— and the secret to living in New York is to leave once in a while, before the noise and skyscrapers begin to close in on you—we took a vacation on Martha's Vineyard. Cruising down their precious Protestant Main Street, blasting Public Enemy and Ice Cube on the stereo—past the overpriced, nautical-themed gift shops selling scented candles and schmaltzy quilts and crafts—we scared the shit out of the pink Izod shirts and Topsiders.

When the sublet on my apartment was up, I moved in with her. It felt right. I put my books on the shelves next to hers—she was delighted that I didn't immediately try to carve out my own space. She began listening to my collection of post-bop noise and insisted that I take her to jazz gigs. She turned me on to some punk rock bands that I had overlooked. She had a large collection of 45s, and sometimes we would stay up all night spinning them. Even our cats got along famously.

_____ began taking antidepressants and went every week to talk to someone, and it really helped. We were growing closer together, and it seemed as if she was leveling out. She had been toying with the idea of going to law school and was beginning to get the confidence that she could do it. She just needed someone to believe in her.

I was ready for a career change, too. After consecutive championship seasons snorting weasel dust for Team Pleasure Fucker, *SD&B* had been the perfect gig to get my head screwed back on. I sharpened up my magazine skills and absorbed every bit of wisdom imparted to me by the marketing wizards who had turned the sugar-flavored bubble-water business into powerful international cartels. Actually, if it had not been for Ally Alpacka's utter lack of couth and guile, I might have stuck around for a while longer. I liked hopping around Europe, and I was becoming pretty slick at the confidence game of balancing editorial integrity with the shameless hucksterism it takes to sell ads. I could have evolved in this job—there was certainly a lot of money to be made running a beer-and-soft-drinks trade mag. Unfortunately, I had hit the glass ceiling as a mid-management chimp. There were no orangutans at *Soft Drinks & Beer*, Ally Alpacka would not allow it. She was the Lawgiver, and she wanted to keep at least a genus and a species between her and the next-closest ape.

After a night of hard drinking with John Holmstrom that saw me railing to him against Ally Alpacka and the *SD&B* experience and ranting about my lust to be behind the editor's desk at the *right* magazine, John encouraged me to contact the *High Times* owners about the newly opened editor in chief position. I should have listened to him more carefully.

Since my column-writing days, John had been promoted from executive editor to publisher of *High Times*. Actually, "promoted" may not be accurate. More like "sentenced."

Most people don't know what the publisher of a magazine actually does. The common perception is that the publisher owns the business. Which is true as far as the "publisher" is the parent company—Condé Nast, Hearst, Advance Media, etc. are all magazine publishers. But what we are talking about is the person with the title of Publisher who is responsible for running the business side of the magazine and is a paid employee. Usually the publisher comes from advertising sales—many publishers were ad directors who came up from the trenches working as salespeople. The publisher is not only in charge of the ad department but also has the final word on circulation, subscriptions, marketing, events, and any nuts-and-bolts issues regarding the actual process of getting the book to the printer and then to subscribers and the newsstand.

There is also an old model of "editor-publisher," where the name at the top of the masthead—such as Flynt or Hefner or Guccione—was also the magazine's founder. You don't see that so much these days, especially in mass-market titles. The entry barrier to get onto the newsstand is just too great; there are too many titles put out by a handful of superpower publishers who will always have the upper hand with distributors. And there is too little rack space to accommodate new titles; it's a finite resource and one of the business's most valuable commodities.

You'd be shocked at how many people who have the publisher's job could not write even the simplest headline. They began as Gorillas and worked their way up to Orangutan but never really quite lost the pronounced eyebrow ridge that defines their primitive skulls. As much as they have climbed the evolutionary ladder professionally, there is almost always something indefinably vulgar about these beasts.

Top editors are extremely business savvy. They know the machinations of every department, and they work closely with the publisher to grow the brand and keep the revenue streams flowing and create new opportunities for advertisers. The publisher is responsible for a magazine's profitability, but the editor is responsible for sales. If the magazine isn't selling, you can bet the owners and the publisher will have something to say about it.

Holmstrom was named publisher of *High Times* after the three previous publishers walked out the door in relatively quick succession, thanks at least in part to the efforts of *High Times* editor in chief Steve Hager and the United States government.

I don't want to suggest that Hager and the government were working in concert. Even the paranoid conspiracy freaks who breed at *High Times* would blanch at that idea, although one of the persistent rumors that has surrounded the magazine since its inception is that it is secretly owned by the feds—founder Tom Forçade was often accused of being a CIA operative.

Once upon a time, Hager was a charismatic and talented editor with real vision and had in fact saved the magazine from near ruin in the 1980s by chasing the hard drugs out of the book. Back then the centerfold was just as likely to be a cordilleran vista of shiny cocaine as it was a slab of North African hashish. Hager made it a positive-vibe pot magazine with an emphasis on cultivation. There is no question that he ushered in the magazine's Second Golden Age after the nascent years of Forçade. But Hager was also not so subtly using *High Times* as a platform to launch his own cult of personality, à la Mao Zedong or Kim Jong Il.

Hager had always embraced old-fashioned hippie dreams and 1960s-style activism. His heroes are Ken Kesey and the Merry Pranksters— they of *Electric Kool-Aid Acid Test* fame—and the Dutch Provos, a proto-Prankster anarchist group that came out of Amsterdam in the early sixties and innovated performance art as street protest. The Provos were famous for baiting policemen into overreacting to absurdist pranks and letting the cops expose themselves as violent and brainless reactionaries. What the cops never got was that the Provos saw them as "essential noncreative elements for a successful Happening." The Provos were a lot like the Yippies in that regard. A lot of the unrest that fueled the Provos' rise to fame as a national movement for antiwar intellectuals and punks could have easily been stymied by just ignoring them.

Which is pretty much what happened to Hager's own troupe of pro-pot activists, the Freedom Fighters.

Often cited as the first sign of Hager's madness was an interview with him that ran in *High Times* in 1990, according to local legend conducted by *himself*—there is no byline, the interviewer is only identified as *"High Times."* Basically an advertisement for Steve Hager and the Freedom Fighters, who would later be featured on the cover of the magazine as well, it was a glaring error in judgment and a laughable paper monument to Hager's ego, which would soon enough swell to megalomaniacal proportions. What would be next, a Steve Hager statue in the lobby? A giant, doobie-puffing Steve Hager float in the Macy's Thanksgiving Day Parade? When I was hired seven years later, people were still cracking jokes about it.

The Freedom Fighters were a good-natured-enough organization—they rode around the country dressed up in vaguely psychedelic Revolutionary War–era costumes and promoted the use of hemp for food, fuel, and fiber. They were harmless and fun and well-meaning, and naturally were embraced by stoned college students and leftover hippies, unfortunately not the sort of constituency that could effect a major policy shift in the upper echelons of government.

The "hemp cause" is an important one. It is nothing less than an American shame that it is illegal to grow industrial hemp, the kind that has little or no THC content. I am not sure that it would save the planet, as Hager and his ilk like to claim—it certainly hasn't beaten swords into plowshares in the parts of the world where it is legal to harvest—but it is an astonishingly useful plant with the potential to make an enormous positive impact on the environment. You can make paper and cloth out of it (the Declaration of Independence was drafted on hemp paper), and it could be an important source of bio-fuel for an ailing planet. The U.S. government actually encouraged farmers to grow it during the Second World War and even produced a propaganda film called *Hemp for Victory*.

Growing hemp was made illegal, along with every other sort of cannabis, in large part thanks to the efforts of an ex–railroad cop named Harry Anslinger who became the first "drug czar" and introduced the Marihuana Tax Act of 1937. Marijuana had been linked by sensationalist newspaper magnates such as William Randolph Hearst to "murder, insanity, and death" and was largely seen as a way to arrest Mexican laborers who were taking jobs during the Depression. Marijuana-puffing African Americans were equally disparaged as wild animals by Hearst's yellow journalism. All of this much to the delight of cotton growers, petrochemical companies, and paper producers—who also had Anslinger's ear—who would directly benefit from the eradication of hemp as an industrial competitor.

No matter what you think about marijuana as a drug, there is absolutely no good reason why growing hemp, which has no psychotropic properties, should be illegal. It is ludicrous to the point of being criminal. Unfortunately, most Americans don't care. Hippie textiles are never going to be a hot topic, no matter how many potheads put on powdered wigs and tricornered hats and run around complaining about the evils of Industry and holding hokeypokey hippie happenings in homage to the Merry Pranksters.

I'm a huge fan of the Pranksters and the Provos. I get it. I embrace certain hippie values. I believe that psychedelic drugs are not only a hoot, but can be a legitimate ticket to mystical experiences and are an invaluable tool to help people examine their values and show themselves parts of their minds—and a reality—that without the trip they would never have had access to. I think Aldous Huxley made a lot of sense. So did Tim Leary on occasion. But he was deluding himself and his would-be followers if he thought LSD was the planet's only hope. I also believe in civil disobedience. But then again, I am not a hopeless pacifist, either. Just take a swing at me and see what happens.

On the cusp of the twentieth century, I would have hoped that someone who spoke as enthusiastically about progressive politics and change as Hager did could have come up with something new instead of simply stealing riffs from his heroes. The sixties were over. Didn't anyone read Go-Go Boy's thesis?

Copycatting counterculture tactics from the past wasn't just uninspired and boring, it was embarrassing. The Provos were influenced by the Dadaists and the Situationist International before them, but the Provos moved forward—adopting the spirit of smart-ass rebellion fomented by their predecessors—and created an original movement that was of their own time.

The sixties birthed a very real, powerful revolution, the urgency of which was dictated by a brutal period in American conservatism that demanded people of conscience to rally together to create a civil rights movement and protest not only a particularly ugly war but a military draft. The original hippies blossomed because the times demanded it.

You can't re-create those conditions, and why would anyone want to? More important, you can't react the same way to different sets of circumstances. If they ever bring back the draft, I'll join the Freedom Fighters in a flash, but you can bet I'll be rewriting the rule book.

Holmstrom was named publisher soon after Hager's self-penned hagiography appeared in the magazine. Before Holmstrom, one *High Times* publisher lasted almost ten years—a record for a company legendary for infighting and rapid staff changes—and then quit abruptly, his exit shrouded in mystery.

The next guy walked into the office only to be greeted by a U.S. government attempt to shut down the magazine. He headed for the hills after just a couple of months.

The government operation was called Green Merchant, and it stemmed from the far-fetched idea that *High Times*, along with indoor pot growers, pot writers, and gardening-supply companies who sold hydroponic growing equipment, grow lights, and the like, were part of a vast criminal conspiracy. The Drug Enforcement Agency went hog wild, using *High Times* as their address book to find gardening-equipment suppliers and manufacturers who had recently discovered a new market selling to indoor pot farmers. But the truth of it was that most of these garden-supply companies wanted nothing to do with pot; they had nice legit businesses selling to tomato growers and equally mundane hobbyists. Sure, the extra dough was nice, but when the fuzz came calling, they cut and ran like Reagan in Beirut, and with them, a whole lot of *High Times* advertising dollars.

The DEA was ruthless in its intimidation, allegedly posing as bikers, Vietnam vets, and "the medically needy"; coming into gardening stores, the majority of which never advertised in *High Times*, asking how to grow pot and then seizing assets under questionable laws that declared perfectly legal products (like run-of-the-mill grow lights) illegal if they were somehow "intended" for illegal use. It was shady and overzealous—one report claims that the DEA raided NASA's horticultural research lab because its name was on a list of customers receiving indoor growing equipment—but it nearly put *High Times* out of business. They never came after the magazine directly, but with the possible threat of criminal conspiracy charges swirling in the air and a Republican administration not terribly keen on playing by the rules in their "War on Drugs"—let's just keep in mind that when they couldn't bust Al Capone for bootlegging, they came in the side door and snagged him for tax evasion.

Much to the credit of the *High Times* ownership, they kept on publishing, filling pages with whatever content they could whip up as advertisers dropped out. It was a heroic effort in the face of an archaic but no less nasty campaign to keep marijuana smokers at the fringes of society. Never forget that the War on Drugs is a war on people.

There was another new publisher after that, but he flamed out pretty quickly, allegedly after getting a good dose of Hager, who has always seen the publisher as a slave to Mammon whose sole goal on Earth was to crush the promise of Hippie Utopia with the lethal tools of Capitalism.

Holmstrom was the perfect man for the job. He had run *Punk* and worked with Forçade, and he had been a *High Times* editor for years. His guts and dedication to the cause were unimpeachable. He lived through Green Merchant and didn't budge an inch.

It took a while, but Holmstrom finally earned the ire of his old friend Hager, if for no other reason than that Holmstrom was now working on the evil business side. Six years later, Hager and Holmstrom, according to the locals who were there to witness this circus, were at each other's throats constantly. The timbre at the office was described as "unbelievably bad."

Hager, for all his revolutionary bluster, had clearly lost his way. Sales were starting to slip. The magazine was redundant and uninspired. His most recent cover had been a photograph of a clog—yes, a *wooden shoe*—stuffed with pot. Just in case you still didn't get the Dutch connection, there was a windmill painted on the shoe.

He was out of ideas and publishing the same magazine month after month, a meandering hodgepodge of pot photos and cultivation tips underscored by the endless bleating of his retro rainbow revival. Not only wasn't it relevant, it wasn't even fun.

The most damning evidence of Hager's departure from objective reality appeared in the November 1997 issue. In an article titled "Whee! The Hemp People," Hager tells the story of how he organized the Hemp World's Fair in Oregon, an event whose "focal point was to be a silent meditation on Sunday, from dawn until noon." Six hours of hippie time-out is not my idea of a party, but then again, I am not the mastermind behind Doggie Village.

Doggie Village is the canine gulag where Hager locked up all the bad dogs that the Hemp People had brought to the fair. At one point in this saga, a couple of children take mercy and free the pups. Thankfully, Hager was on it. "We got a jailbreak at Doggie Jail," he announces over his walkie-talkie. You can bet that when they read that, the collected *High Times* staff had a hearty bow-wow-wow at Hager's expense.

Although not to his face. It's a good thing I wasn't working there at the time—I probably would have left him a box of hemp dog biscuits, or maybe a chew toy shaped like a joint. But no one is allowed to tease Steve Hager. Like Steve Bloom, and a few other hypocrite pot smokers at *High Times* who preached *the mellow,* Hager had an anger-management issue, and he held grudges.

At one point during the festival, Hager the Hippie Enforcer tried to banish a hot dog vendor in an RV to Bus Village, "where he belonged."

> "Nobody wants your Babylon food," I said finally. "Why don't you go solar and sell organic food, or better yet, pack up and leave?" Of course he was making plenty of money and had no intention of leaving . . .

This was about as sound a tautology as when Yogi Berra said, "No one goes there anymore, there are too many people." Anyway, who doesn't love a hot dog? Aside from Steve Hager, that is, self-appointed arbiter of all that is "Babylon."

This is the best part: about halfway through this drama, Hager shifts his point of view from first person, as in "I sometimes had two or three meltdowns standing around yelling," to the third person, and begins calling himself Phoenix, as in, "Phoenix had a sudden urge to test his wings and fly." It's never really explained, but it's obviously the result of some sort of contrived psychedelic epiphany. At the end of the story, Phoenix hallucinates seeing the Beatles hanging out with Bob Dylan and the Tin Man. When he wakes up on a riverbank, he is talking to a dog, just a regular old pooch, although *wise.*

With all the feuding and bad craziness, the *High Times* ownership demanded that Hager and Holmstrom both step aside. I felt bad for Holmstrom—who's a loyal guy and believed strongly in *High Times* both as a company and as a political statement—and how he was marginalized by Hager, whose antiauthoritarian views never left much room for hierarchies and bosses. Except for himself, of course, since like all great dictators, he sees anyone not subordinate to him as a personal threat.

Pushed out of the publisher's office, Holmstrom opted to run the company's then-fledgling Internet site, which was in sore need of attention. Hager, neutered but still on the payroll with the new and largely honorary title of editorial director (he had no office and did not come to meetings), went home to lick his wounds.

And so *High Times* was looking for both a new editor in chief and a new publisher.

"I hope you get the editor's job. I think you'd be great at it," John told me, although it didn't quite work out that way. "Just don't blame me when you're miserable. It's a real snake pit up there. But you'll find out soon enough."

14

NEVER MIND THE DEADLINES

Time was so hopelessly amorphous a concept at the *High Times* Park
Avenue office as to defy Einstein's freakiest models of the continuum
and dwarf even the most far-out Native American philosophies. To get
the three-o'clock editorial meeting started by 3:30, one would have had
to fold the fabric of the universe onto itself and lead the staff through
some sort of cosmic wormhole.

As publisher, the figurative leader of this gang, I worked hard to in-
still temporal concepts that had already been adopted by most of the
modern world: except when you begin to reach the speed of light—a
velocity not likely to be achieved by a staff who did everything *adagio*
and nothing *con brio*—time moves forward at the same rate for
everyone. And so deadlines came and went every month with maddening consistency, just as they had at *High Times* for the better part of
twenty-five years. Editorial meetings, too, came with mundane regularity, held every week at the same time in the same place. If you had a
watch and a calendar and a vague idea of where the conference room
was, you should have been able to nail it with little difficulty.

My old nemesis Steve Bloom was always the last to arrive at these
meetings, usually eating a pile of cookies and getting crumbs
everywhere. Bloom was, like Steve Hager, hovering near fifty years old.
Whereas Hager, through some miracle of lysergically mutated genet-
ics, had kept a fairly youthful countenance, Bloom looked more like
Grandpa Simpson. He had stringy red hair, which—clinging to some

hideously outdated concept of tonsorial protest statements—he insisted on wearing in an anemic ponytail.

After Bloom settled in with his snack, I could begin.

"The next person who suggests putting Bob Marley on the cover is gonna be looking for a new job." I measured the room and waited for a new idea.

Crickets.

Finally, with crumbs all over the place, Bloom said, "I think we can get David Crosby."

Are you fucking kidding me? *David Crosby?* And here I had my heart set on Joan Baez.

It was one of those rare moments of real-life deus ex machina when Ozzy Osbourne's publicist called moments after the meeting broke up. Bloom fielded the call, actually put the woman on hold, and came into my office.

"Ozzy Osbourne wants to be in the magazine."

Ozzy? Seriously? Black Sabbath has got to be the Number One Classic Stoner Band of All Time. This was perfect. While Ozzy didn't have the star power of Zep or Floyd (this was before the Osbournes' MTV show), *everyone* loved Black Sabbath. They might have just as well given away their records free with every pack of Big Bambú. Ozzy was our very own Elvis.

"What are you waiting for? Tell them yes."

Bloom came back a few moments later. A chocolate chip fell from his mouth. The publicist was back on hold. "They say they want the cover."

Ozzy's publicist was smart to call us. At this point Ozzy was just a fucked-up old hangover playing oldies for a souped-up county-fair circuit. Ozzfest was a successful summer touring festival, but no magazine in the world would even consider putting him on the cover in 1999. Except *High Times*.

"Tell them we'd love to have Ozzy on the cover, but he's got to pose with pot. Those are the rules here."

I didn't think they'd go for it; after all, aside from being a notorious drug fiend, Ozzy was notoriously in rehab. He wasn't supposed to be *near* any drugs, let alone pose with them on the cover of a national magazine. But you've got to ask. Unbelievably (after being put on hold for another twenty minutes), they said okay. This was great news. Clear the decks, Big Story in the works.

For a change, there was some real energy in the office. People were genuinely excited. Except for Steve Hager, who, although on forced leave, was not exactly confined to a Fortress of Solitude. He was still contributing to the magazine, calling constantly, and as a longtime favorite of the *High Times* owners (he really did do great things for the magazine before he lost his mind), he had their ear. "Putting Ozzy on the cover," he told them, "will kill the magazine. We're a *hippie magazine*. Ozzy Osborne is *heavy metal*. We'll lose all of our readers. Edison is destroying *High Times*."

Hager's megalomania could never tolerate anyone else editing *his* magazine, and with Ozzy he saw an opening and began a vicious campaign lobbying for his old job back. This was the beginning of a whole world of trouble.

Meanwhile, the photo shoot went great. The studio was dressed beautifully with red velvet curtains, all manner of skulls, daggers, and chalices, a ridiculous throne perfect for the singer of Black Sabbath, and, of course, the "veggies." We had even commissioned a "sweet leaf" pendant to be made by the artist Robin Ludwig, a handcrafted silver pot leaf for Ozzy to wear.

To people in the trade, having your weed in the centerfold is like winning an Oscar, and their stock skyrockets once their product goes prime time, so it isn't as hard as you might think to find a couple of pounds of good-looking pot that can adopt the come-hither pose common to centerfold models everywhere.

I got to the studio a few minutes before Ozzy shuffled in, and when I say "shuffled," I mean it. When he walked, he made the same sound as one of those old Apollo Theater soft-shoe dancers made when they threw a little bit of sand on the floor to get that good scratching thing going. This was about a year before *The Osbournes*, but if you've seen that show, you have an idea of just how damaged Ozzy is. He is the picture-book definition of "drug casualty."

His entourage was a couple of Spinal Tap–looking roadie dudes who were trying to keep him on a short leash, but of course when Ozzy saw a chrome skull filled with bright green buds, he flipped. "Fuck! Is that *real*?" You bet it is, Oz. Wanna try some? His handlers weren't too crazy about Ozzy's getting stoned, but they couldn't stop him from taking a few hits from a beautifully handblown glass pipe.

I took a giddy toke on it myself. I wasn't much for getting stoned at the office, but on photo shoots, loitering around a kilo of bright green bud, it was pretty hard to resist. Anyway, as my high school English teacher told me somewhat cryptically after I got snagged for smoking pot out in the woods behind the parking lot lo those many years ago, "There is a time and a place for everything." I wasn't going to pass up the opportunity to bust corn with Ozzy.

Ozzy put on the "sweet leaf" and posed with handfuls of reefer. He sat in the high-backed throne and talked to the skull filled with pot. Like a heavy metal Hamlet. It was beautiful. Despite the fried synapses, he was a total pro, very nice, good-humored, and easy to deal with. Tony Iommi, Sabbath's nine-and-one-half-fingered guitarist, came by and pushed some weed around for the cameras. It was a dream, the perfect *High Times* photo shoot.

It wasn't long before Ozzy began to get a little claustrophobic (and paranoid) in a room filled with people (and two pounds of illegal drugs), so I herded all nonessential staff and hangers-on to a neighborhood bar.

It was the next day when I got socked with the bill for the pot. Normally, the "product" is "rented," which means "borrowed," with the understanding that someone will buy a few ounces (at about $700 per) and pay for what I call "shrinkage." The dealer weighs the product that is going to be photographed, and at the end of the day he weighs it again. You can expect that a little bit is going to be smoked (don't forget we already bought a couple of ounces for that purpose, but when everyone is getting a little buzzed, they kind of forget that and start confusing the props with their personal stash). And naturally some gets lost after being moved around, from, say, the brainpan of a skull that looked as though it were on loan from Dr. Evil to a tableau of appropriately heavy pipes and bongs. Sure: shrinkage. A bit of shake weed, a few small nuggets.

But not *ounces* of superbly intact buds, the kind of buds you could club a dinosaur over the head with. I think it was the Design Dude, who informed me that I would have to come up with sixteen hundred dollars to cover the bill.

Sixteen hundred fucking dollars? What, was Ozzy eating the shit?

The guy has a rep for biting the heads off of bats and snorting ants, so I wouldn't be surprised. What the fuck happened? It better have not been any of our guys . . .

No, no. It was Ozzy's entourage, I was told. They were stuffing their pockets with weed when they left. Fuck, why didn't they just ask? Boosting the stash was pretty square. No class. We would have pretty much given them whatever they wanted out of pure respect for their boss.

Well of course, now I had to hear it from Wanda the Evil Accountant. Nothing at *High Times* happens without the Evil Accountant getting involved. She is a scandal whore and a busybody of the worst sort, a human speed bump who lives to monkey-wrench the works and shut down the machine. This is the woman who, on the morning of 9/11, screamed at me to "get back to work" while I was trying to locate missing staffers and let families and friends know that we were okay. Now she would have to come up with a check, which someone had to turn into cash to give to the bereft supplier. We did this all the time. It wasn't a big deal, but nothing at *High Times* happens without drama. You'd think I was diverting funds to a Republican fund-raiser.

Hey, I was steamed about going overbudget on the shoot, but shit happens, especially when you're working in a cloud of smoke. At the end of the day we're just going to have to suck it up. Of course, now everyone in the office is talking about the stolen pot (and not getting any work done) and I'm getting the blame, even though I wasn't even there. Whatever, I'm the publisher, I can deal with it. We just scored a major coup with Ozzy Osbourne. Everyone should be tickled fucking pink.

At some point, amid the cacophony of stoned *High Times* editors yammering on and on about all of this (imagine the sound of twenty geese fighting over the last piece of grain), it occurred to me that "Drug-addled Rock Star Pilfers Pot, Chaos Reigns at Stoner Photo Shoot" was an irresistible PR hook. Just like the entire stoner world, the scandal sheets (ditto Howard Stern) loved Ozzy, too, for all the great copy he has provided over the years for things like pissing on the Alamo in drag and committing various acts of onstage carnivorism. There was no way I was *not* going to exploit this. If I didn't, I just wouldn't be doing my job.

When the mag came out a couple of months later, I leaked the story to Page Six, the world's most-read celeb gossip column in my favorite right-wing hate sheet, the *New York Post*. They had always been friendly to *High Times*, at the very least because people like to snicker at a goofy pot mag. I wrote up a one-page press release, exclusive for them, and fired it off. They loved it. I was very careful not to explicitly accuse Ozzy of swiping anything, and to make sure that the tone was humorous, in the spirit of good fun, and in no way accusatory or angry. I spent a lot of time crafting my sound bite. The success of the piece and how *High Times* came off looking would depend on how funny (and hopefully smart) we seemed. But mostly it was just ridiculous— two of the world's most notorious (and absurd) institutions get together, and the weed goes missing. Duh.

The next day the story appeared on Page Six in a featured box with a photo I had provided of Ozzy chewing on a fistful of reefer, the same shot that was used on our cover. We had hit a home run—there we were, our cover on one of the most widely read pages in the entertainment industry. It didn't get any better. A-list celebs pay professional ass-lickers like Lizzie Grubman twenty-five grand a month for coverage like this.

Under the head OZZY: STICKY FINGERS, the story read:

OZZY OSBOURNE sure had fun during his photo shoot for *High Times* magazine. The metal musician appears on the front of the pro-marijuana monthly holding two huge handfuls of pot. But at the end of the day, a prop skull that held the reefer was lighter than before Ozzy arrived. "Let's just say the skull weighed about two ounces less when Ozzy left the studio than it did when he came in," chuckles publisher Mike Edison.

Aside from the fact that I do not chuckle (fat people chuckle, I *laugh*), I could not have asked for more. Howard Stern was talking about it on the air, and the phone lines were exploding: every radio station in the country, it seemed, wanted an interview with me, and I was glad to reply. That week, I did almost thirty interviews, hitting every media market in the country. I kept it light and a little goofy, denied knowing what really happened ("man, it was like *sooo* smoky in that room"), and made jokes about sticky buds. The day before, people were wondering if *High Times* was still being published. After that, everyone knew we were the "Most Notorious Magazine in the World."

But the rank and file at *High Times* were less than happy. "Why'd you have to drop a dime on Ozzy, man?" "Why did you say he stole the pot?" Whoa! *Where did I say he stole anything?* The office was buzzing with mutiny. Hager was howling at the moon. I had committed a capital sin, and they were calling for my head, which meant everyone was calling uptown directly to the law offices of Michael Kennedy, one of the owners of *High Times* and the de facto Capo. He had hired me and would presumably fire me if there was enough pressure from the staff.

Except that Michael was fed up with being bothered by staffers every time the publisher made an unpopular decision—which, of course, is part of the job. But there was zero respect for authority at *High Times*, and trying to do an end run around the publisher had become thoroughly entrenched in the politics of the place, which were ruthless. Truly, this was an asylum run by the inmates.

One of Michael's honey-voiced proxies called me in my office. "Mike," she intoned, like a cross schoolteacher who was going to have to mete out some discipline. She sounded like she had nice legs. "What is going on down there? Everyone is calling us about this Ozzy fellow." I explained what happened, omitting no details. "We understand," she said, "that this man bites the heads off of bats."

"Yes, I have heard those rumors," I deadpanned.

"Then I wouldn't be worrying too much about his reputation," she said. "Thanks, Mike. Good job."

The Ozzy issue was one of the bestselling issues in *High Times* history.

High Times is a family business. Founder Tom Forçade left the magazine to his immediate family, who lived in Arizona, and his New York lawyer, Michael Kennedy. It was Michael to whom, on Holmstrom's recommendation, I had sent my résumé, and he had interviewed me in his office a few days later.

Michael Kennedy is very smart and very tough. When I met him, he was about sixty years old and wore his gray hair brushed back. For an infamously radical lawyer, he had relatively conservative taste in suits and ties, but he was still a very intimidating presence. At one time Nick Nolte could have played him in a movie.

Michael had been Tim Leary's attorney and had worked closely with Yippie leaders, and he had defended Jim Mitchell, the famous porn producer who shot his brother and fellow pornographer, Artie Mitchell. Later Michael became known in more polite circles for representing Ivana Trump during her divorce from The Donald.

One of the stories he loves to tell is about the spoils of one of Tom Forçade's legendary smuggling runs. Tom was somewhere in the swamps of Florida making a transaction, when the police crashed his party. Tom grabbed the profits—a suitcase full of dough—and took off into the woods. Lying low in the mire, he somehow managed to escape the cops and their bloodhounds. After hours of hiding in mud, he buried the dough and got the hell out of there. Days later, when the cops had finally split, he went back and retrieved the suitcase, which he brought to Michael. Of course the money was caked in filth and had to be washed and dried. Michael took a look at the mess and declared, "Tom, we've got a serious money-laundering problem here."

For my interview with Michael for the editor's job at *High Times*, I put on my best suit and painted my chest with a silk tie, circa 1949. I was—as Philip Marlowe says at the beginning of *The Big Sleep*—"neat, clean, shaved and sober, and I didn't care who knew it."

After fifteen years of jockeying with loudmouth porn kings, ranting from my soapbox and proselytizing like a hopped-up preacher on the fundamental American birthrights of protected free speech and unfettered hedonism—after the shopping bags filled with knockout weed and the sheets of brain-twisting acid, after all the insanity and rock 'n' roll, after four continents of gonzo mythmaking and drug-fueled pranksterism, magic buses, political outrage, and tasteless comedy—this was where I belonged. I was uniquely qualified to lead this magazine into the future. I was sure of it.

I had done my due diligence on *High Times*. Not only had I scoured their current issue—the one with Pancho Villa on the cover—but I had gone to the New York Public Library Periodicals Room and made a pretty thorough study of the last few years of the magazine as well.

I was shocked. I had not looked at *High Times* with any regularity since I'd stopped writing my column about ten years prior, in 1989. The later issues seemed unfocused. Not only was there little flair in the writing, but the actual type was unnecessarily small and hard to read. Later I would find out that this was because stories were going into the magazine without being edited, and they were often too long for the space. Sometimes the layouts were confusing—giant bursts of color without much rhyme or reason. Too often the best photographs were tiny—one piece about a fairly exciting summer rock festival droned on and on pointlessly, squeezing out photos that were no bigger than thumbnails. They had taken a story with a little bit of giddyup and slashed its tires.

And then there were the covers. Before Pancho Villa (seriously, *Pancho Villa??*) and the wooden shoe stuffed with pot, the most recent celebrity cover had been George Carlin, who in 1998 wasn't much more than a warmly regarded relic. He would enjoy a much-deserved career renaissance, but it certainly was not on account of *High Times*—he couldn't even be bothered to have a new picture taken for the cover. They ran a tired publicity shot. To say it was amateurish would have been kind. The magazine looked like a souvenir program that someone had left under their chair after one of his shows—in 1974.

I went to meet Michael Kennedy with my copies of *High Times* flagged with Post-its. I didn't want to reinvent the roach clip; there was a reason it had been around for almost twenty-five years. The brand name was indelible and widely respected, but its value had been diluted by retrograde editorial policy and indifference that left it hopelessly dated and listless. *High Times* had become an anachronism. It was the lava lamp of the publishing industry.

One of the worst things about the magazine was that it had become *tame*. What happened to the fuck-you attitude?

It seemed to me that it was one of the very few national publications that had carte blanche to say whatever it wanted without fear of reprisal. Isn't that what the readers expected? They were *outlaws*—it was a drug magazine, for chrissake. If you look at the early issues, it was all there. Every issue felt like trouble brewing. But under the warm and fuzzy hippie hoodoo that Hager had been cultivating, the *Easy Rider* ethos had turned into politically correct gruel for the tofu-and-wheat-germ crowd. What I wanted to know was, *did these crusty Rainbow types Hager was courting even have five dollars to buy a magazine?*

Michael nodded in agreement.

He asked me about my politics and what I thought about drug laws. "I think all drugs should be legal," I told him. "I just don't think this country is ready for it." I went on about the absurdity of locking up pot-heads, of locking up anyone just for getting high. It was the government's job to protect us from bad people, not from ourselves. "And anybody who has the audacity to take a joint away from someone who is dying," I added, "ought to be strung up in the town square and beaten with a stick."

When I was called up for my second interview, I was offered a job—although not the one I thought I had been interviewing for. Apparently, impressed with my marketing plans and passion for taking the magazine forward, they thought I'd make an ideal publisher. At first I demurred. I was an *editor*; I had never been on the business side.

"But, Mike," Michael reasoned, "you know how to work with an advertising department, right?" I did. "You've managed several magazines, and you have a good track record. You know every job on the floor." It was true. Since I'd knocked Jeremy out of the ring to take over *Main Event*, I had watched everyone I had ever worked with like a hawk and had asked a million questions, and mostly everyone was eager to teach me what they knew. If I had to, I could write a story, lay it out, sell an ad on the facing page, and get the whole mess to the printer on time. I'm not saying I could ever be the art director of a magazine or the production director, but I knew the nuts and bolts. I loved magazines. Aside from playing music, it's all I really ever wanted to do. This was an offer I could not refuse.

High Times would be celebrating its twenty-fifth anniversary in just over a year, and they wanted to ramp up business and take advantage of this *mitzvah*. The twenty-fifth anniversary issue needed to be the biggest and best issue in *High Times* history. I was up to the challenge.

And I would have support staff on the business side. John Holmstrom, who had been the publisher for the previous six years, told me frankly that it wasn't rocket science and I would pick it up quickly. Mary McEvoy, the interim publisher after John and Hager were pushed out of the top slots, would still be on staff to help me crunch numbers.

Mary was a fish out of water at *High Times*: she was a publishing professional. A suburban mom who had enjoyed a good career in the magazine racket, mostly as a circulation and distribution expert, she had worked at Condé Nast and had helped on the start-up of maverick *Sassy*, the coolest teen mag ever until it got shut down for its frank shoptalk about masturbation and other "sensitive" topics. All of which gave her plenty of juice in my eyes. Mary was nice, knowledgeable, lev-elheaded, and without ego. She knew what the fuck she was doing and was happy to share her expertise, in direct contrast to our so-called Marketing Witch.

The Marketing Witch was a square who wanted desperately to be accepted by the hippies and, typical of *High Times*, put an undue pre-mium on personal alliances. She was a Hager loyalist and yearned for his approval, and since I was a friend of Holmstrom's, she was hostile to me from my very first day. A mean girl, steeped in a watercooler office culture of treachery and backstabbing, she was pure poison. It would have done me well to shit-can her on the way in.

Michael Kennedy was very clear in my mandate to be "hands on" with the new editor-in-chief they had hired, Paul DiRienzo, who had never worked as an editor of a magazine before. DiRienzo was an unrepen-tant anarchist-hippie with no clue about how to sell magazines, or why, for that matter, that was even important. His background wasn't even in print journalism, it was in nonprofit news radio. Michael and the *High Times* owners felt that his super-serious commitment to hard left-wing politics would balance my damn-the-torpedoes approach to put-ting out a rock concert of a magazine.

In DiRienzo's worldview, selling magazines was for capitalists, and capitalists were pigs. My edict to start thinking about *High Times* not so much as a pot magazine, but as a *magazine*, like a *business*, was writ-ten off as part of a crypto-fascist plot to get in bed with Exxon and McDonald's, arms contractors, strip miners, Walt Disney, and all the other traditional enemies of The People. He was blissfully unaware of where the money even came from to keep *High Times* running, why we needed ads, or how we got the book to the readers. I think he as-sumed that the magazine ran on good vibes and fairy dust and was delivered to newsstands by our team of magical unicorns and dancing bears. He was remarkably lax with editors, contemptuous of deadlines, and bordering on juvenile in his blanket disregard for authority. I can't really blame him for failing so spectacularly—he was com-pletely unequipped to run a day-care center for potheads, much less one that put out a four-color magazine every month.

For his first act as editor, DiRienzo put Dennis Peron on the cover, an elderly gay pot activist who was running for governor of California on some sort of hemp ticket. Dennis was a good guy, definitely the kind of alternative politician we supported, but he wasn't exactly Jimi Hendrix in terms of reader response. Still, you want your editor to edit, and you have to give the new guy enough rope. Not surprisingly, the issue sold miserably. His next brainstorm was to follow up with former Black Panther Mumia Abu-Jamal, a convicted cop killer now doing time on death row, where he had spent most of his time hurling invective and incendiary rants about injustice at the society who incarcerated him. Although he would never say what actually happened the night of the alleged murder, Mumia always maintained his innocence and had become something of a cause célèbre for the radical left.

When I balked at the wisdom of putting a convicted cop killer on the cover, DiRienzo started blabbing to his anarchist pals that *High Times* had been taken over by a suit.

A suit? Well, at least I owned one.

Personally, while I was never part of the "Free Mumia" crowd (like most people, I was never convinced of his innocence), I am all for shoving it up whitey's ass. But I also had a responsibility to the owners of *High Times* to not run the magazine into the ground.

One day, there was even a protest in front of my office—a bunch of DiRienzo's squatter pals picketing *High Times*'s "new fascist regime" or some such anarcho-twaddle. Instead of rallying support for his cause, DiRienzo had embarrassed the entire company by encouraging this rabble. It didn't take long for the story to get out to the mainstream press, who were having a good laugh at our expense.

Michael Kennedy was livid. John Holmstrom brokered a meeting between DiRienzo and me in the hopes that DiRienzo would settle down. Holmstrom had lived through the Publisher-Editor Wars once with Hager, and he didn't want to see it happen again. "Learn to get along," he told us, "or neither of you will last." It didn't work. The next day DiRienzo tried to foment an uprising at an editorial meeting by calling me "the capitalist mutherfucker in the publisher's office."

I was given permission to fire DiRienzo. It didn't take long for the story to show up on Page Six. Under the headline "Smoked Out," DiRienzo was quoted as saying, "I was trying to make it better, but they want a cult magazine." I responded in the same article: "What is he talking about? All we're trying to do is make *High Times* a magazine about getting high, not about getting busted."

I was now publisher and editor in chief, and although the latter title would never be bestowed upon me, I was unambiguously stationed at the top of the masthead with the blessings of Michael Kennedy. I felt very positive. Finally, this was our chance to turn things around.

What was once the Voice of a Revolution was now perceived as nostalgia, a pamphlet for moldy fig potheads, the punch line to a thousand stoner jokes, and the de rigueur set dressing for low-budget reefer comedies.

But *High Times* was still an American icon, and when we took stock of our bona fides, it was immediately clear that the big gun in our arsenal was our large-caliber Don't Fuck With Us Outlaw Attitude. What other magazine could say with a fair degree of certainty that its readership by and large consisted of unconvicted criminals?

As contraband, porn mags were passé. It might be embarrassing to be caught with a copy of *Plumpers on Parade*, but it wasn't a Big Red Flag that said you were doing something *illegal*. No matter how much marijuana had become part of mainstream American culture, taken for granted, laughed at, and considered a key part of the daily diet for University of Florida freshmen, it was still against the law to possess it, smoke it, trade it, sell it, grow it, bake it in brownies, or make Day-Glo suppositories out of the stuff and gently insert them for even the most benign medical necessities. Generally speaking, the U.S. government is a humorless bunch of cocksuckers, and they do not care that you are not hurting anyone by getting high. They put you in jail for that shit.

High Times itself was just this side of being a controlled substance. Buying a copy, or being *caught* with a copy, was a tacit confession to living outside the law, and to a lot of people, that's a pretty fucking sexy notion.

I saw *High Times* as a twenty-first-century bible for good-natured rebels, a Molotov cocktail of druggy hedonism, stoner culture, left-wing and libertarian politics, flamboyant rock journalism, historic and contemporary counterculture, arch humor, pointed satire, fuck-you attitude, righteous indignation, and hyper-smart commentary wrapped in innovation and shrewd design. Tom Forçade had always said that

High Times had "no desire to be limited to being the magazine of substances that people put in their mouth," that it should be the "best magazine imaginable."

If anyone was still on the fence as to whether *High Times* was the sine qua non of outlaw magazines, I would spell it out for them on every cover, right under the logotype, in an easy-to-parse tagline: "The Most Notorious Magazine in the World."

It was a strategy that worked. From that moment on, not only did sales start picking up, but now, anytime we were mentioned in the press, or anytime I was on the radio hooting it up with a morning zoo crew, our tagline was part of the introduction. Everyone in the mainstream media we came in contact with fawned over us. For a while there, we weren't being snickered at for being a tribe of lost hippies, we were being embraced for being iconoclasts and heroes.

I'd get asked all the time how we "get away with it." Get away with what? We're a *magazine*. No matter what kind of bee the administration had in its bonnet, there'd still be some pretty heavy First Amendment concerns about going after the media *just because you don't like the message*. There is nothing illegal about putting out a pot magazine. And after all, we would *never* break the law . . .

Go ahead. Ask me about the centerfold shoots. "We shoot at remote locations . . ." "Oh, you do it in Amsterdam?" "Sure. If you say so."

I did dozens and dozens of interviews on morning radio shows all over the country, and they always asked, Is everyone there stoned? Of course not! How could we possibly put out a magazine if everyone was stoned?

I kept it light and kept 'em laughing—which kept them calling back. And I would never cop on air to the true secrets of *High Times*'s inner sanctum, the 10:00 a.m. bong crew or the 4:20 smoking break, when the entire staff would disappear and come back half an hour later bearing the resin-soaked stigmata of happy-go-lucky stoners. (One good thing I can say about Bloom is that he was usually so stoned after the 4:20 break that if I borrowed a CD from him, he was bound to forget about it.)

For those not in the know, "420" is stoner code for smoking or getting high, or for the ordinance itself, as in "Let's 420" or "Got any 420?" It has become such popular weed-head argot that it has become a big business itself: 420 T-shirts, skateboards, caps, badges, belt buckles, and stickers can be found at any head shop, surf shop, or hemporium, right next to the rolling papers. Four-twenty in the afternoon is the universal stoner time, and at 4:19 the *High Times* staff was like a bunch of railroad workers waiting for the whistle to blow. April 20 (4/20), ditto, is the Secret Stoner Holiday. Unfortunately, it is also Hitler's birthday and the day of the Columbine shootings. In a lot of places (well, "high" schools) it is also "ditch day." There are a lot of potheads who will look under any rock they can for new and positive things to say about their drug of choice and claim that lives were saved at Columbine because a lot of kids skipped that day. (Imagine that headline: MARIJUANA SAVES THE LIVES OF CHILDREN.)

At any rate, 420 is the stuff of myth and legend. The most commonly held belief is that 420 was California police code for a pot bust, although there's not much evidence to support that. Another key to cracking the code is that it is often cited in textbooks and cautionary drug histories that there are 420 separate chemicals in marijuana. And dig Bob Dylan's stoner anthem "Rainy Day Women Nos. 12 & 35," better known as "Everybody Must Get Stoned." Twelve multiplied by 35 is 420, but I'm sure this is just good stoner kismet and not some sort of psychotronic Rosetta stone. Then again, Crosby, Stills, Nash, and Young recorded a bummer of a song called "4+20." Makes one think.

The "truth" behind the legend of 420 was "discovered" by Hager when a group of Deadheads who called themselves the Waldos contacted him and claimed that they had started it. (This is how Hager discovers things: someone tells him.) The story was that in the mid-1970s they would meet every day after school at 4:20 to get stoned. The meeting place was a statue of Louis Pasteur, and they called it "4:20 Louie." The Waldos were big Dead fans, and they used to make flyers to pass out at shows and started including "420" in with the other pothead arcana. Eventually it caught on through the unwashed masses of wandering Deadheads, sort of like a low-level dose of the clap.

Not a bad story, but as usual, Hager took it to mind-boggling, cult-like extremes, flying himself out to California to see the guys and spending hours videotaping them. He told everyone at *High Times* that we would make millions: he, Hager, Grand Imperial Potentate of Pot, was the only one who knew the Truth. Pages in the magazine were dedicated to the Waldos. All other myths and legends surrounding 420 were suppressed. (*High Times* could be a lot like Soviet-era *Pravda* in the way it censored and controlled drug information and propaganda to suit its chemically altered view of reality.) Hager would pontificate endlessly to a captive audience of editors who knew that not to humor him meant getting shit assignments.

"Marijuana smokers are an oppressed people—like Christians!" he would scream at anyone who would listen. He was rabid, taking his rants so far as to rail at a reporter, "We're the Jews! We're going to the concentration camps!" I agree that the fuzz should lay off potheads, who as a group are about as threatening as a playful summer breeze, but comparing scofflaw stoners to Holocaust victims was revolting and did little to gain sympathy for the cause.

According to Hager, "420" was the secret sign marijuana smokers used to identify each other, similar to the way early Christians used the sign of the fish to avoid persecution. It wasn't much of a secret: we peddled enough 420 merchandise to flood a small flea market. Of course, after hundreds of hours editing Waldo videos on iMovie, and casting dozens of pages of shoddily written tales of Waldos heroics (if you consider getting stoned in the afternoon "heroic"), Hager's fantasy of a Waldos franchise and the bucketfuls of cash it would earn *High Times* remain as elusive as an exciting Jerry Garcia guitar solo.

Despite my abject hatred for Ally Alpacka, I had learned a lot from her about setting goals and hitting them, especially in the advertising department. The *High Times* ad director had done a great job with the accounts that he had been managing for years, but at some point he had lost the fire in his belly. He was making good dough and was no longer hungry. I thought it was odd that I had never seen him go out on a sales call. He just sort of sat at his desk waiting for the phone to ring, like a retired cop working the beat as a night watchman in an old-age home.

One day I popped my head in his office and asked him how things were going.

"We're done," he told me cheerfully. "The book is sold out."

I was astonished. Ally Alpacka would have been apoplectic. *You never stop selling.* It wasn't even the ad "closing" date yet. We still had another *week*. Sell another page, and we'll find space for it. For the right people, for the right price, I would rip the book apart on press to make room. A four-page story might have to be cut to three pages to make room for a full-page ad. The Design Dude would rant and rave to anyone who would listen, but that was publishing. All magazines work this way, at least all successful ones. I shook the ad director's cage good and hard, and he got the message. Ad sales went up immediately.

But every month, as the page count changed and the "map" of the magazine was revised to accommodate new advertisers, the *High Times* editors would freak out, demanding to know why we were adding pages, and blaming it on the publisher for scheming to make their lives difficult.

At *High Times*, without forcing a showdown, the writers couldn't even be counted on to cut a few sentences to make a story fit on the page. They would rather pressure the Design Dude into laying out their stories in smaller type, making them nearly impossible to read, than sacrifice one diamond of a word: apparently there was nothing that a *High Times* editor could type that was not worth a million in prizes. Having to cut a whole page—a record review or an update on Michigan hemp activists—to make room for an ad was seen as some sort of modern-day *Kristallnacht*.

Professional editors and writers get it: magazine publishing is a dynamic system, and the book can and does change right up until the last minute. The upside was that if we sold enough ads, we would have to add more pages, and then they would have more space for editorial. That would create a whole new set of problems, since we never seemed to have a "bank"—an inventory of content that could be used to fill holes.

There is a lot of midwifery in magazine publishing that no one wants to take part in—as they say, you never want to see how the sausage gets made. Writers and editors don't want to know about production. Artists and production people don't want to know about the vagaries of the stories we write; they just want them in, and on time. Advertising people don't care about editorial; it's just product. When I came on board, Bloom asked me, "How did you get to be a publisher? You're a *writer*. How do you know about *ads* and *production*?" There was no secret. I just paid attention.

Our one-man ad department needed a shake-up. I hired a new salesman to join the team, and now the ad director really started paying attention. Suddenly he had competition on the floor. Sales continued to climb.

We were going to offer special discounts and packages, incentives for advertisers to take extra space in our big issue and encourage them to stay in for the rest of the year. I wanted "tombstones"—ads that said "Congratulations High Times on Twenty-Five Years." Every buzzer and bell, pullouts, inserts, whatever an advertiser could dream up, we could do it, and we would make the numbers work for everyone.

Our printer, Quad/Graphics, was the best in the business, and its staff was incredible. Its customer service reps knew everything about the printing business, and they worked hard to get us whatever we wanted. How much would it be to have a die-cut centerfold printed on 180-pound laminated paper with silver mylar mirrors? The quote would be on my desk the next day. Potheads love pizza. Could we wrap the magazine in some sort of thermal plastic and enclose a free slice? They would find out for me.

We had been given a fifty-thousand-dollar budget for the *High Times* twenty-fifth anniversary party. *Fifty thousand dollars!*

I was sick to death of off-the-rack magazine parties with lame DJs and one-hour open bars sponsored by some trendy vodka that no one in his right mind would drink if it weren't being poured for free. The *High Times* Twenty-fifth Anniversary Party had to be legendary. It had to be the Mother of All Parties, The Most Notorious Party in the World.

The damage would be done at Irving Plaza, the best venue in town. They had a great stage and a balcony with a VIP section. The band would be the hugely popular hip-hoppers Cypress Hill, who, in the pages of *High Times*, had taught the world how to roll a blunt. We decided on an open bar all night, and not just beer and wine and low-budget swill. Everything was going to be top-shelf. I wanted our guests to feel as though we actually liked them. It was expensive, and it probably fit into someone's category of "Babylon," but it was sure to keep the party going. And of course there would be enough "goodies" to re-launch the Age of Aquarius. Hundreds of joints would find their way to happy kissers. Pot cookies would be catered by stealth pastry chefs. The happy farting sounds of balloons being filled with nitrous oxide would be a call to arms.

It was a massive undertaking. Every detail—the band's contract, their accommodations, plane flights and airport transfers, equipment rental, balloon purchase, the club's fee, the open bar for eight hundred people for six hours, and a million other particulars—took months to negotiate. The calculus needed to divine exactly how much pot we would need to roll seven hundred joints alone would have taxed NASA's best logistical team. Then there was to be food at the party, and sponsorships from rolling paper companies, and tables for activists and hemp clothing manufacturers that needed to be organized. There was *High Times* promotional merchandise that needed to be designed, manufactured, and distributed. Everyone was going to leave with a souvenir. Invites were printed and mailed, with real stamps, hand-picked, depicting either civil rights leaders or eye-popping art. No postage machine bullshit—it was an old-school detail, but the goal was to present *High Times* as a first-rate organization. Everything communicated. No taking the easy way. Despite what anyone had ever heard to the contrary, or the received wisdom and running gags about stoners being fuckups, when we did things, we did them right. At least that's what *I* was selling.

I called a meeting to round up the troops and begin forming a party team to get some idea of what everyone wanted to do, what everyone's job was going to be. We had a lot of money to spend, it was going to be one for the ages.

"So, who wants to help start looking for a venue?"

Silence.

"Who wants to be on the entertainment committee?"

Silence.

"Who wants to help with the guest list?"

Silence, punctuated by a muffled burp or a fart, I couldn't be sure.

"Who wants to roll the joints?"

I do! I do!

And that was the *High Times* party staff, who had been conditioned to ask Not What They Could Do for *High Times*, but What *High Times* Could Do for Them. What they didn't get was that the party was not being thrown *for* us, it was thrown *by* us, for advertisers and the mainstream press. It was to make a big splash and get our name in the papers and on TV. Just like every other big media party, this was first and foremost a publicity event. We weren't dropping fifty grand to entertain a few monkeyshine editors and their stoner pals as a reward for a job well done.

I just kept on truckin'. Despite passive resistance from the staff, many of whom, like Sufi mystics in reverse, had achieved soaring levels of ennui, things were moving in the right direction. The *High Times* twenty-fifth anniversary issue was going to be Bigger than Big—I had been cranking on it for two years and was projecting 150 pages and record numbers in advertising. *High Times* ownership thought I was nuts, but they wished me luck.

The Design Dude was especially dismissive. When I came on board and shared my plans to reinvigorate the magazine, he just walked away, moaning, "Dude, we've been doing this for a long time without you. We know what we're doing." I pointed out that circulation had been slipping and suggested that we needed to take a hard look at *High Times* from all angles and figure out why people weren't picking it up as much as they had been. He shrugged me off. "Whatever, dude."

The Design Dude was a grouchy slug of a man who often looked like he had slept under the boardwalk at Coney Island. It seemed as if his wool ski cap was fused to his head—even in summer, when he dragged through the office in a hoodie and shorts—and his beard always begged for a trim. He looked like Charles Manson, but without the good vibes.

Of all the people in the office, he was the one who bristled most at any suggestion that the magazine could possibly be even a little better, and besides Hager, he was the one staffer most convinced of his own genius.

One thing that always struck me a little bit odd is that he never wanted to go on the press check. But naturally, if the magazine came back from the printer and the colors didn't match the proofs exactly, he was the first one to scream bloody murder.

A press check is exactly what it sounds like: you go out to the printer, roll up your sleeves, and make sure that what comes off the press looks like what you sent them. The pressmen did a good job, but if someone from the magazine was there to help fine-tune it, we could count on excellent results, even on the tricky pages.

Usually art directors or production directors will go on press. Mostly, there aren't any problems, but sometimes it can be difficult getting the colors exactly right, especially since there is so much green in *High Times*. The color proofs we get of, say, the cover, are made with a photographic process, whereas the magazine is printed on a four-color press. Ink on paper will never look exactly like the proof, which is really just a guide. Matching the proofs isn't always easy; there are sometimes "conflicts" on the press. For instance, you'd ideally like to see Ozzy on the cover glowing with the skin tone of a living human. But he is holding a big pile of green buds, which you'd like to see shimmering like a traffic light. If you run the green too hot on press, Ozzy will take on a green cast, too, and look even more like a gargoyle than he does in real life. It's a balancing act, sort of like mixing audio. You can turn up the bass or the snare drum or the vocals, but if you turn everything up, you get mush.

The crucial pages, of course, are the advertisements, because if they don't look like the proof provided by the advertiser, they will raise Holy Fucking Hell and their caterwauling will make the Design Dude's whining seem like that of a petulant little girl. Beyond any affront to their delicate sense of color, they won't want to pay for the ad, and the publisher will have to give them a "make good," which are the two dirtiest words in the whole business.

The ads that were most sensitive at *High Times* were those for the "fake buds" that were always on the inside cover and usually the back cover, often on massive gatefolds.

These were expensive ads, and if their product didn't look bright green and healthy (which could mean having to pull a bit of magenta out of the mix, generally disastrous for skin tones), I would get an earful. And since they ran on the same form—the sixteen-page sheets that were cut and bound to make the magazine—as the cover, where there was often a sallow-skinned pothead who needed the benefit of a lot of ink to look healthy, you had what was known as an "in-line" conflict.

More than any of the other intrigue that swirls around *High Times*, everyone always wants to know what is up with the ads for the fake weed that are peppered throughout every issue, promising the best in "legal highs." They look good, like genuine Thai Stick and top-grade weed, and they have names like Hydro and Wizard Smoke. They also peddle crap like "herbal ecstasy," "herbal opium," and "herbal hashish," and their ads look fantastic—lush and sticky and inviting, just like the real thing. But it's all a load of crap.

Still, people buy this shit and, apparently, a lot of it. There could be more than one hundred pages of ads a year for fake herb, several hundred thousands of dollars in advertising. And no matter how shady the business seemed, it was legal, and they always paid promptly.

There are a few theories as to why this was such a successful hustle: the most prevalent around the *High Times* office is that the bunko weed is sold to gullible rubes and underage unfortunates who think they are going to get high from it, or that it is bagged and sold by unscrupulous drug dealers as is, or used as some kind of hempy Hamburger Helper in order to stretch a little weed into a nice baggie that can be sold for a lot more dough.

The stuff looks good in pictures, but I can assure you it is junk. It's not even pleasant to smoke.

The "buds" themselves are a variety of oddball botany, but mostly common herbs like sage and varieties of hops and dogbane. These plants are pressed and stamped into "buds" and packaged gorgeously. And they aren't cheap: twenty-two bucks for a gram and a half of fake bud, thirty bucks for an ounce of their bottom-line dirt, up to seventy dollars a lid for the "good stuff," which can mostly be bought, sans nifty marketing, for a couple of bucks at a well-stocked herbalist.

There was always a campaign by Hager to get rid of these ads, since they were considered a chink in *High Times*'s otherwise impenetrable armor of high-minded hippie values. Within the marijuana community, there were always rumblings from our detractors, mostly other start-up cannabis mags, who accused *High Times* of being amoral capitalists and complicit in marketing fake drugs to kids. But in all my years at *High Times*, I saw few if any complaints from actual readers about these ads or the products. It is likely that anyone who got suckered was too embarrassed to speak up, but the manufacturers would swear up and down that the majority of the business came from repeat purchases by people looking for legal alternatives to marijuana.

I would have loved to get rid of those ads, but what was going to replace the revenue? There was no way in hell the *High Times* ownership was going to bow to the pressure of a Hager-manufactured pseudo-scandal and chase the ads out, given the kind of dough they generated. Nor were they anything new: ads for "herbal highs" had been in the magazine since the first issues produced by Tom Forçade. They had always been an accepted part of the business. The only difference was that the marketing had reached incredibly sophisticated levels. Nonetheless, Hager would always submit these ads as evidence of my failure as a publisher.

Dumber, though, than even Hager's naïveté to think that we were going to give away that kind of business was Bloom, who would breathlessly show off his complete lack of acumen and savvy to *The Washington Post*, blurting that the ads were a rip-off that didn't get you high. "They're kind of taking advantage of gullible readers," Bloom said. "It's a borderline scam," he added, at once calling *High Times* readers stupid and implicating the magazine in fraud.

And yet the magazine was doing better than it had in years. Ozzy was a home run, and the next two issues I edited proved that it was no fluke.

There were no tricks: every day I tried to put something better in the bottle. I was careful to maintain an editorial balance, to bring in new readers while holding on to our loyal base. I was not turning my back on anyone. I remained faithful to the high quality of grow stories Hager had fostered. One cover I helped engineer was classic—a robust, budding plant shot in front of a spectacular explosion of tie-dye color. I wasn't trashing the old hippie color palate out of hand, I was just trying to expand the repertoire and keep things in perspective.

It was all about balance. Ours was a big tent, and everyone was welcome. The Ozzy issue, for instance, also featured a Hager-sponsored conspiracy story about who *really* killed Martin Luther King—as if thirty-five years later *High Times* suddenly had the scoop. This piece was mocked mercilessly on *Saturday Night Live* in a sketch based on an imagined *High Times* editorial meeting—and they were frighteningly accurate in their depiction of drawling, drooling editors too stoned to do much besides wait for a new break in the Kennedy assassination case. I laughed my ass off. Actually I was flattered that *Saturday Night Live* would even bother to spoof us. Bloom, however, was furious. "Fuck them," he bellowed. "What right do *they* have to make fun of *us*??"

At home, things were alternately very good and very dark. _____ was now fully immersed in her career as a law student and was acing every class, but she was still suffering the extreme highs and lows of bipolar disorder. When she was swinging downward, it was horrible. The least of it would be crippling episodes of self-doubt, and I would take her out to a romantic dinner and remind her that she was a superstar. We always left the restaurant holding hands, but I was always aware that we were walking on thin ice.

Sometimes I would be leaving for the office and she would still be in bed, sobbing, "Maybe today is the day I will kill myself." How was I supposed to react to that? Not go to work? I spent a lot of time lying next to her in silence just so she wouldn't have to be alone with her brain.

There was no way to predict the mood shifts; the disease took her up or down without warning. It was bad. I certainly couldn't tell my friends what I was going through at home, there was no way I would have betrayed her trust. Sometimes she would be very happy and working hard for weeks and weeks at a time without any sign of depression.

We took a trip to Jamaica together on a *High Times* junket. I was looking forward to getting out of New York for a few days with her. Changing the scenery boded well. We'd get into the island groove, eat some jerk chicken, drink some good rum, smoke the ganja, hit the beach.

From the moment we got to the airport, where we met up with the gaggle of *High Times* staffers who had signed up for this pothead perk, it was a stoner clusterfuck, with people forgetting things and losing their tickets, getting lost on the way to the gate, and stopping randomly to admire shiny objects. We were on our way to Jamaica—couldn't anyone wait a couple of hours to get baked? Don't be ridiculous, dude. Standard *High Times* justification was "It's always 4:20 somewhere."

Behind the dust cloud of stoners stumbling to the gate was the Marketing Witch, clacking along in last year's high-heeled sandals and a bright yellow tube top. She quacked at her husband to hurry up—he had a bag on his back and bags hanging off of each arm, and he was struggling with something that looked like a steamer trunk. He looked like the overworked bellboy in a screwball comedy. She sipped contemptuously at a frozen drink while she waited for him to catch up to her at the ticket counter. I felt bad for the poor bastard. The Jews who built the pyramids had a better deal.

When we landed in Montego Bay, we were harassed the second we touched ground by Rastas peddling big bags of dope.

Although it fuels the tourist economy, marijuana is illegal in Jamaica, and I was advised to wait until we got to the quasi-resort where we would be staying. It would be far safer, and anyway, airport weed was strictly *blood clat*, bad news. It was too expensive and never the real deal. Wait for the Lamb's Bread—the good stuff—and then buy a big bag, enough to last the week. Something about the size of a love seat should do it.

The beaches in Negril were pleasant enough, but there was fantastic swimming and snorkeling off the cliffs. We took a one-day scuba-diving class and had a good time scooting around twenty feet under the surface with a torrent of multicolored fish, breathing through fifty-pound tanks strapped on our backs, yet nearly weightless in this other-Earth environment. Since my career as astronaut had been pretty much a non-starter, this was a good consolation prize. And it made _____ happy—she found that leaving our landlubbing lives behind was a nice break from the avoirdupois of law school.

But not surprisingly, she took an immediate dislike to my coworkers. "They don't respect you. It's weird. They don't take you seriously because you're *not* stoned all the time. And for all their One Love hippie talk, they don't even respect this place." She was right. She usually was. Chief Hippie Hager, for example, was particularly cavalier with his code of karma, eating conch fritters and conch sandwiches every day even though there were signs posted everywhere saying not to, because conch had been overharvested and the local population was in danger. "I don't care," he told _____ when she asked him why he was ignoring the eco-warnings. "I'm only going to be here for a few days."

"You deserve better," she would tell me. "When I graduate from law school, I'm going to be making a lot of money. Then I'll be able to take care of you for a change. You can quit this job and focus on writing and playing music." It sounded good. But then, I am often a victim of my own optimism.

15

EXTREME CHAMPIONSHIP
POT SMOKING

I fucked up. I failed. I wanted Happy Monkeys. Instead I got monkeys who wanted to kill me. It's my own fault. I let myself be pushed up against the wall, and I pushed back. But I'm not sure what else I could have done. To not have would have been to admit failure before I even began.

To paraphrase Thomas Jefferson, I firmly believe that he who bosses least bosses best. But this situation was out of control. The magazine was never on time—it was like watching one of those Discovery Channel wildlife shows where they slow the film down so you can see how the animals' legs work.

In the annals of *High Times*, my situation was far from unique. In 1979, Tom Forçade's widow, Gabrielle Schang, moved into the publisher's office and after only a few months at the job took her frustration out in print, scribing a heated opinion page. "When I was invited to become the publisher of *High Times* last year," she snarled, "the magazine was languishing in the clutches of a clique of aging hippies, unable or unwilling to grow out of the burnt-out knee-jerk radicalism of the '60s . . . Frankly, I think they were suffering from amotivational syndrome."

Indeed, the more things changed, the more they stayed the same. Given the short-term memory loss endemic to an organization whose collective reefer habit could have swallowed the Mexican economy, I shouldn't have been surprised that no one felt the slightest tinge of déjà vu.

Our production costs were through the roof, jacked with late fees from our printer, who was becoming increasingly concerned that we were piling on so much stuff at the last minute that they were not going to be able to do the job. We had to stop missing deadlines and put an end to the frenzy that always surrounded the press dates, when the production department would hurriedly try to cobble together a magazine by replacing nonexistent editorial pages with house ads. The tardiness repeatedly pushed the magazine to the edge of missing an on-sale date, which would have been a costly disaster. Michael Kennedy actually suggested that I create a fake calendar and begin lying to the staff about when the real deadlines were, but it was just too distasteful to me to treat a group of allegedly professional magazine editors like children, even though in the winter, when it snowed, work stopped and everyone ran around the office like grade-schoolers hoping to be sprung for the day.

At *SD&B*, a staff of seven—several of whom were out of the office traveling a lot of the time—put out thirty-six magazines a year (twelve issues of *SD&B*, plus six each of the monthly *SD&B International* and *Refrescos y Cerveza*, plus twelve issues of a monthly tabloid targeted to retailers), as well as a yearly trucking and distribution guide, two trade-show guides (not to mention that we organized shows ourselves and were responsible for booking speakers and creating panels, a full-time job in itself), and a heap of special projects like one-sheets, media kits, direct mail pieces, bulletins, and dailies for industry conventions, which were a huge pain in the ass. On top of that we did several special issues in Chinese for the Asian market—they were extrapolated from *SD&B International*, and I shepherded them through a translator and a Chinese proofreader. I can only assume I got it right, since no one ever complained.

It was incredible that a staff of fourteen editors, art, and production people (plus a team of freelancers) could not get out *twelve* issues of *High Times* a year (plus two *Best of High Times*, which were reprints of old issues) on a timely basis and without near catastrophe.

Besides Bloom, and Hager, who was not keeping office hours but was lurking about keeping his presence known, Dan Skye and Steve Wishnia were the other senior editors. Aside from the fact that they both looked like the "before" picture in an ad for Grecian Formula, they could not possibly be more different.

Dan Skye was forty-something and wore his gray hair in a ponytail, Freedom Fighter style. He was a talented writer and photographer, a very good pot journalist, and one of the hardest workers there, as long as it served his best interests. He lobbied vociferously to have his photos on the cover of *High Times*, which were often very good but not always the best choice. Like Bloom, Skye was a chimpanzee who yearned to be an orangutan; he felt that he should be the next editor in chief, and the two of them always seemed to be fighting.

Skye did mean-spirited impersonations of everyone on the staff. I caught him doing me once, and I have to admit, it was pretty good. I think he captured my essence, hyperventilating about making the magazine better and sounding a lot like an old Jewish man who had just discovered a hair in his soup. I wish he had just taken it to heart rather than building a stand-up routine around it. To mock the sanctimonious stoner stylings of Steve Hager, he screwed up his face like a clenched bunghole and babbled incoherent narco-nonsense, like "The herb is a sacrament, it is the goddess of the counterculture." If Hager had caught his act, he probably would have clubbed Skye over the head with a hookah.

Wishnia's hair exploded off the sides of his head in an unkempt symphony of frizz, making him look like some sort of mad scientist who had blown himself up in a failed bathtub chemistry experiment. Also an intelligent guy, easygoing, with an artsy streak and a punk rock past, but he had a lot of trouble articulating his ideas over the roar of aggressive editors who seemed to be in a constant struggle to bully one another into submission. Which is too bad, since he often had good things to say. But because he didn't share the pot-fueled delusions of grandeur the other editors were infected with, he was often drowned out.

One of Wishnia's responsibilities was to copyedit stories before they went from the editorial department into art. Proper copyediting is a rigorous job that requires a fairly anal and exacting approach to grammar and proper usage and what is called style. Maintaining style is one of the cornerstones of good publishing. Unfortunately, with everything running late all the time, he was often browbeaten into being not much more than an expediter of rush-job journalism, and even at the most basic level, the magazine suffered for a lack of precision.

When we say "style," what we are talking about is consistency throughout the book. All magazines have style sheets, which are used as guides to keep, among other things, spelling consistent. For example, *The New York Times* uses "Al Qaeda," *The Wall Street Journal* prefers "al Qaeda." The *High Times* style sheet specifies the difference between Hoffman, as in Abbie the "radical activist," and Hofmann, as in Albert, who is described not so accurately as the "discoverer of LSD." Which is like saying that Eli Whitney "discovered" the cotton gin. At *High Times* they really do believe that acid grows on trees.

Chris Simunek was the cultivation editor. In other circumstances I think we would have become good friends. He had known Dave Insurgent pretty well and had actually played for a little while in one of Dave's later, ill-conceived projects. But while I was at *High Times*, he brought little to the party—a shame, for he was undoubtedly the most talented writer of this lot.

Hager had spoiled Simunek by assigning him to write a series of ersatz *Fear and Loathing*–style stories that usually involved Simunek dropping acid and going somewhere to write about it—Cancún, Memphis, Burning Man, Jamaica. Sometimes the resulting articles were quite good. Sometimes they were overly contrived and uninspired. But unfortunately, that's all he seemed to want to do now, and every story he pitched involved a cache of dangerous drugs and his name on a plane ticket. Nice work if you can get it, but all those sweet assignments had also turned him into something of a prima donna. At editorial meetings, he slumped in his chair and shot down every one else's ideas.

As cultivation editor, his main function was to be in charge of the Grow America section of *High Times*, arguably our most popular and important department. Most of the weedy warlocks who could unlock the profound grimoire of harvesting potent buds had trouble turning their sweet science into comprehensible magazine stories, and Chris was there to straighten them out. I think he resented having to rewrite other people's junk prose, especially that of our on-staff herbalist, Kyle Kushman.

Kyle had been a successful grower himself—and it was Simunek's job to encourage Kyle and turn him into a writer. But Kyle, taking his attitudinal cues from his mentor, once told me that "as long as *High Times* won't give me a raise, I intend to do the bare minimum. I don't want to hear shit about coming in late or leaving early." I was flabbergasted. I suggested that saying this to the publisher was probably not the best road toward a fatter paycheck, and that 30K a year (plus benefits;

five weeks off; surplus centerfold weed; occasional jaunts to Europe, the Caribbean, and beyond; and the local luminary status that came with working at the World's Most Notorious Magazine) was a pretty good deal for an "associate editor" whose remedial English would have otherwise stopped him dead at the door of any community college in the country.

Any other boss in the world would have fired Kyle on the spot for such an ill-advised stump speech, but even as publisher, even with Michael Kennedy's continued allocutions that I had to "be the Boss," I did not have the juice to cut him loose. After the DiRienzo fiasco I was told that there would be no more firings, this was the staff, make it work. And goddam it if everyone on the floor didn't know it, too—the place had more leaks than the Nixon White House. Just as Holmstrom had warned me, the publisher had all the responsibility to keep the magazine profitable and running smoothly, but none of the authority to back it up. It was a management structure designed for failure.

And then there was Pot Star. Pot Star was actually a *High Times* reader who had landed an internship at the magazine and somehow parlayed that into a job, although I'm not quite sure what that job was. On the masthead he was also listed as associate editor, but he was as much of a mascot as he was an "associate" anything. Pot Star was six feet and three hundred pounds (including the funky beardlike thing growing out of his chin) of Texas stoner, and in his early twenties was the youngest member of the staff. I loved Pot Star because he was the "everyman," a *High Times* reader who had landed his dream job of smoking dope for a living. Hanging out with Pot Star, you could get a good feel for a large part of the *High Times* audience, who were mostly made up of like-minded delinquents. I was hoping to groom him into taking a larger role in promoting the magazine.

That was the motley core of a staff that also included a senior citizen who sometimes slept in his office (a leftover from previous epochs, whom no one had the heart to send home); a news editor who was quickly being made obsolete by the Internet; and a few freelance writers and editors who came to meetings, but whose lifestyles would never tolerate anything as bourgeois as a steady job.

There was also a managing editor, whose main job was to traffic stories between the editorial and art departments and was charged with the responsibility for keeping the magazine on time. In my tenure at *High Times*, four different people held that job, none of them entirely successful, since they invariably got sucked into the 420 vortex and fell prey to the hobgoblins and punctuality deficits of the perpetually stoned.

Wanda the Evil Accountant would bellow constantly that it was the production department that was screwing up, since that's where the money was being spent on late fees.

As usual, Wanda had it wrong. The production director, an unreconstructed metalhead named Bobby Black, was the one guy on the floor who had his shit together. Bobby Black wore his hair halfway down his back, blasted a sonic wall of stoner rock from his office, hit the daily 4:20, and did his job remarkably well, especially considering the pressure he was under. The production department is the last link in the chain between the magazine and the printer, and it was his job to collect and prepare all the digital files that needed to be sent to the printer, to keep track of what had gone out and what was missing, and to check the proofs as they came back. If there was a problem, the printer called Bobby Black, sometimes in the middle of the night. His job was not easy, but he kept things moving, a near impossibility given that the staff at large generally considered any sort of schedule an oppressive nuisance.

After my first year at *High Times* as publisher, I recommended to the owners that Bobby Black be given an extra Christmas bonus. Normally, everyone got a bonus equal to one paycheck, but he had been doing an especially great job holding things together as we kept adding pages to accommodate new ads, which also needed a lot of attention to get right. Bonuses were uncharted territory at *High Times*, and at first they balked, but I fought for him and managed to get it through. The owners were worried that if the rest of the staff found out about Bobby's extra bonus, they would feel entitled to one as well, and would be somehow *less* motivated to work. I told them that wasn't bloody likely.

By far my biggest blunder was to deliver faithfully Michael Kennedy's edict that there should be no pot smoking in the office.

When I was at *High Times*, I almost never got stoned during the day. If I busted corn at 4:20, I could pretty much count on having to tussle with an angry advertiser at 4:35. If I wanted to hit my goals, I needed to stay sharp. Actually, by that time I wasn't smoking all that much pot—when it became a staple, it ceased to be special. For me, at least, the novelty of being able to get stoned at work wore off quickly. No matter how much pot you smoked, you were still at *work*. It was a fool's paradise.

But Michael's mandate had nothing to do with discipline or sobriety. It was all about *liability*, and he was adamant about it. When I shared this with the staff, they just laughed at me. "This is *High Times*, dude."

Michael was especially serious that there should be no pot in the office, especially "felony amounts." Does that sound obvious to anyone who ever ran a business? Especially one that made its nut by photographing large quantities of world-class marijuana month after month and was famous for its advice on how to grow same in your bedroom closet? That was legendary for putting snowdrifts of cocaine on the cover and in the centerfold? For the better part of twenty-five years, *High Times* had joyfully quoted local prices and user reviews for every drug imaginable in the always popular Trans-High Market Quotations department, only more recently dropping the hard drugs to focus on superstrains of weed:

> *LSD*—Fresh from the lab, $2–4/tab. Amphetamines—white crosses and black beauties, $2–4. Methaqualone powder—Do-it-yourself 'ludes, $500 oz. *Lebanese hash*—Hello old friend! $130 oz. *Thai sticks*—Beware of Mexican poseurs, $180–$225. *Cocaine*—disco toot, $125/gram. *Yukon Swifty*—Ultra light green nuggets coated in white crystals. This shit smells like a skunk that got trapped in a cotton candy machine. $350/oz.

Given this font of information, anyone with half a brain cell left dawdling in their skulls should have been able to figure out that we were on *someone*'s radar and that discretion just might turn out to be the better part of valor.

But I think what really scared the shit out of Michael were the persistent stories of complaints from the office upstairs. Allegedly, a pregnant woman had said something about smelling marijuana, and when Michael heard this, his business had flashed before his eyes.

I could see the headline now:

PREGNANT WOMAN INHALES MARIJUANA SMOKE FROM POT MAGAZINE, GIVES BIRTH TO FRISBEE.

"Mike, I don't want any pot smoking in that office," he ordered. "You have to be the boss. Tell them." I guess Michael could have told everyone himself—everybody respected Michael. But he's smarter than I am, and he gets to play the Good Cop. After all, he was the Law-giver. I was just an unpopular Orangutan.

The *High Times* crew were masters of stealth smoking. The best of them could have gotten high on the crosstown bus without incident. What made this possible was one of the twentieth century's greatest innovations: the Mute.

Like the No-Bounce Street Hockey Ball before it, the Mute was a revolutionary leap forward in recreation science. The Mute was gim-micked up from a two-liter Pepsi bottle retrofitted with parts from sur-plus Israeli gas masks. You could take a hit from a bong and exhale into the Mute and there would be no smoke, no smell, nothing. It worked like a charm. If the teenagers of the world ever got hold of this technol-ogy, it would undermine parents everywhere. It was brilliant.

The Mute was the brainchild of a marijuana enthusiast with an en-trepreneurial bent who lived in a remote part of upstate New York. His idea had been to sell these contraptions through the classified ads in the back of the book, and he had sent a sample along with his check. When the 420 crew at *High Times* realized that the dingus actually worked, they ordered a dozen of them, and every editor had one sitting next to his desk.

Do you have any idea how many bong hits you have to blow through an Israeli gas mask filter before it gets clogged and no longer works? These things were designed for use in World War III, but the *High Times* cannabis commandos went through them like Kleenex. When the Mutes stopped working and everyone was waiting for a new ship-ment (apparently the Israeli military just wasn't making enough gas masks to meet the demands of the *High Times* staff), they began to fashion their own, inferior models, crafted from cardboard tubes and fitted with Snuggle brand fabric softener sheets held in place with rub-ber bands. Not only did this fail to mask the smell of pot, it also made the office smell as if Willie Nelson were doing his laundry in the con-ference room.

Sometimes it wasn't even the smoke—people would come by with freezer bags filled with buds so stinky that it smelled like a baby was having its diapers changed. Even the elevator reeked. It would be nothing to walk into someone's office and see a dealer breaking up a pound of Purple Haze into small Ziplocs. On payday, the office was like an open-air drug market.

Michael's no-smoking policy was a pipe dream. It was useless. All it had accomplished was to make sure that the daily dopers on the floor hated me. I was now officially a fascist. When Snoop Dogg came by the office one afternoon with a cigar box full of buds, I simply gave up and joined the party.

Another full-scale battle flared when John Holmstrom had the audacity to suggest that we do a story about . . . *professional wrestling*! It was as if he had suggested that we change our tack and apologize to the Drug Enforcement Agency, throw a fund-raiser for the National Right to Life Party, and host a buffet for the entire military-industrial complex. The staff yelled and screamed and kicked so much you would have thought they were all training to be wrestlers themselves. Bloom, one of the only "legitimate" sports fans on a staff of anti-jock stoners, was the loudest opponent. "I hate wrestling, and I don't want it in the magazine. It's fake!" he would bellow, as usual, just not getting it. Wanda the Evil Accountant, who had never met a lynch mob she didn't like, chimed in with her valuable editorial opinion: "I don't think there should be wrestlers in *High Times*," she spat. The way she said it made it seem distasteful, even for a woman who I suspected ate broken glass for breakfast. Even Hager made a special appearance in the office just to fan the flames with his preprogrammed peacenik agitprop and declare that wrestling was "warrior culture," his catchall phrase for things that didn't suit his lifestyle—e.g. alcohol, tobacco, firearms, heavy metal, and processed sugar.

Holmstrom's timing was sensational—Vince McMahon and his World Wrestling Federation had at that moment the most-watched show in cable television history. Their Monday-night broadcast had actually scored higher ratings than the establishment's standard-bearer, *Monday Night Football*. Now if that wasn't a Blow Against the Empire and a sure sign of a Counterculture Revolution, then maybe LSD really did occur naturally, and all you had to do was know where to look.

McMahon had performed something of a miracle. He had admitted publicly that wrestling wasn't "real" and was now calling his business "sports entertainment. " This was a sucker punch to the naysayers and anti-wrestling snobs who had thought that when McMahon coughed up and confessed to the world's worst-kept secret—that wrestling was fixed (God forbid!)—the business would just evaporate. But exactly the opposite happened. Unhampered by local sports authorities who required licenses and state-approved physicians at every event, McMahon had freed himself from miles of red tape and bureaucratic nonsense that had kept his carnival in check. After all, no one was trying to stop Metallica, or the circus, or the Muppets on Ice. It was just show business.

Far from fleeing the arenas, the fans loved it. Everyone already knew that wrestling wasn't "real." They just didn't give a rat's ass. They had the Dostoyevsky-esque Faith.

That year, Vince McMahon became a billionaire and made his debut in the Forbes 400 as well as being featured in *Newsweek*, *Rolling Stone*, and a slew of other "straight" magazines. *The Foreign Object*, I am proud to say, had scooped them all by putting Vince on the cover of our first mimeographed issue, sixteen years earlier.

Obviously I supported Holmstrom. Never mind my own obsession with the art—I wasn't editing the magazine so *I* would have something to read, I was following Ron Ronson's prescript to "know thy reader." It may not have been regular viewing for the elitist urban heads at *High Times*, but I knew there were a lot of bong-hitting frat boys watching TV through a cloud of smoke and rooting for Vince to get his ass kicked, and we could turn them into *High Times* readers if we could just persuade them to pick up our magazine.

This was Vince's other greatest innovation: he was now actually wrestling, further blurring the lines of what was real and what was fake by working a gimmick as the evil boss of his own Wrestling Federation. On his show he made the wrestlers—his employees—literally kiss his ass. Vince would pull down his pants and demand that everyone on his payroll get on their knees and pucker up. It was completely outrageous, a *legitimate* billionaire CEO running around with his pants around his ankles demanding to be treated like some sort of god by his employees. Vince quickly became the most-hated heel in the history of the game.

His main foil was Stone Cold Steve Austin, a beer-swilling, pickup truck–driving ass-kicker who in another era would have been cast as a bad guy. Pitted against Vince, he became wrestling's biggest hero since

Hulk Hogan. Who wouldn't want to see the boss get the shit stomped out of him? It was the greatest gimmick of all time, and you would have thought that the *High Times* staff might relate to it as a parable for workplace rebellion. But perhaps they knew me better than I gave them credit for. After all, I had already used that shtick in *Main Event* and had come out on top. I owe my career to it.

Holmstrom's genius was in finding the pot-smoking wrestler, Rob Van Dam, who was working a "420" gimmick with an outfit called Extreme Championship Wrestling—or, as its fans called it, "E C Fucking W." Van Dam was our guy. He was a flashy, high-flying wrestler who wore psychedelic tights and, sailing off the top rope in some spectacular feat of gymnastics, would declare, "I just smoked your ass!"

ECW was a small promotion that worked out of venues like the old Elks Lodge in Queens, where they turned a thousand-seat theater into an "arena of pain." The shows there were no-holds-barred and out of control: flaming baseball bats wrapped in barbed wire were the norm. Wrestlers would leap off the balcony, twenty feet in the air, to smash their opponents through folding tables that had been set up at ringside and covered in thumbtacks. There was no such thing as a "foreign object"—there was no longer a need to hide weapons. Wrestlers just let it all hang out in the open: street signs, frying pans, snow shovels, fluorescent light tubes, cheese graters, garden tools—there was no end to the creativity that went into thinking up potential new weapons. One night I saw a wrestler busted open with a child's toy lawn mower. Another enchanted evening, a plate of nachos.

"Rob Van Dam is just your average, long-haired, pot-smoking hippie who's always at peace with himself," Holmstrom wrote, "especially when he's kicking somebody in the face!" It was a great bit. The story went on to detail not only Van Dam's athleticism and outside-the-ring pot activism, but his hordes of fans who held up signs that said "RVD 420" and shouted, "Let's smoke pot!" when he entered the ring. It was insane to think that this did not have a place in *High Times*.

Van Dam turned out to be a very humble, intelligent guy, and after the matches Holmstrom and I would get stoned with him out behind the Elks Lodge. (Holmstrom wasn't really a pot smoker, but he always made an exception for his favorite wrestler.) Thirteen years in the magazine racket, and I was still hanging out in parking lots getting fucked up with professional wrestlers. Talk about being true to your school.

The fans at these shows were positively rabid. Not a single one of them was without an ECW T-shirt of some kind. This was no fad, this was a genuine revolution within the industry, much like punk rock had been in its glory days. Eventually, all of the mayhem that was being innovated by ECW was co-opted by the WWE, just as punk rock was absorbed into the mainstream. In fact, short of putting ECW out of business, Vince just wound up buying the entire promotion, and eventually he made Van Dam his champion. Holmstrom's story was a smash. For a change I had backed the right pony.

At home, the mental health index was sinking into the red. _____ had also taken to self-medicating with marijuana, and although it may have mellowed her out in the evenings, it was making her withdrawn and unwilling to deal with our very real relationship problems.

Law school is brutal, like boot camp for shysters. It is an insane way to live for three years. But _____ was acing her exams and fighting her way through her own personal demons on her way to a great career.

When she asked me if I could bring some reefer home, I couldn't say no to her. When you see someone who has been in so much pain, you don't deny them relief. But it put up a cloud between us. She'd smoke and zone out to the TV, then fall asleep. We were barely communicating. Our romantic life evaporated.

I suggested that she lay off the reefer, but she told me it was the only thing that calmed her down at the end of the day. After fourteen hours of studying contracts and torts, who wouldn't want to smoke a fatty and relax?

I suggested that we needed to find a little time to spend together, on *us*, and work on our relationship. She told me that if a relationship was that good, it shouldn't need any work. When I suggested that even under the best of circumstances, this was a wickedly naïve assumption, there were promises that when she graduated, things would get back to normal and we would be able to spend time together and go on vacations and enjoy each other the way we had when we were falling in love. She knew I was making a lot of sacrifices. In the meantime, I just had to be patient with her, law school was rough.

I paid the bills, made sure she had what she needed, and then never saw her for most of the week. Even the cats got short shrift. She wouldn't even take a moment to pet them on the way out the door. She used to dote on them and take time every day to play with them and babble in kitty talk. Now she just pushed them aside. In her focus to get through her day without being sandbagged by her own chemical imbalance, she had turned to ice.

At work I had few friends, but I was still dedicated to righting the ship and was getting good results, at least on paper. Business was strong, and even if the staff wanted to screw me with my pants on, at least to the owners I was still the fair-haired boy.

As we approached the twenty-fifth anniversary, sales were booming, circulation was climbing, and we were going to throw the biggest party of all time. When it was all through, *High Times* would be at a peak of profitability and we would have earned the respect of our colleagues and peers. In publishing circles, we would no longer be forced to sit at the kids' table.

What I didn't see coming was Steve Hager.

One day Michael Kennedy called me up to his office for a meeting. At *High Times*, these executive huddles were often a ruse. There might be some pretension that we were actually "meeting," but the decisions had already been made by ownership and were just being delivered. There was no real discussion.

Unfortunately, a lot of the decision making was based on the knee-jerk emotional impulses of the other owners—Forçade's family—who hid behind the screen and were clueless about what actually went on in the office. They had never asked for *High Times* but had it thrust upon them after Forçade's death, and they seemed a lot more concerned with quelling any employee unrest and keeping things quiet than with running a successful business. Hager was an especially squeaky wheel, and he needed a lot of grease.

For all of Michael's good judgment, his radical proclivities, and his ability to see things with lawyerly logic, he often acquiesced to his partners, who had actually issued a *High Times* mission statement braying that the magazine would become "a model for dysfunctional and currently unemployable persons" and boasting of a "convoluted chain of command." This was the squares stooping to patronize the stoners and what they perceived to be the stoner lifestyle, their ill-conceived attempt at saying "See? We understand." It was unnecessary and disgusting, really, since there is no shortage of talented, responsible people who like to smoke pot.

But they got what they wanted.

Michael began reasonably. "The job is too big for you. It is too big for anyone—being both the publisher and the editor is just too much." He took time to compliment me, however, on how well I had been holding it together. "You've done a remarkable job in turning things around," he told me.

Hager sat with his arms folded. I could tell that it was killing him to keep quiet. Michael continued: "We want to bring Steve back," he said evenly. "This is not criticism of the job you've done; we are very appreciative of your hard work. But we think this is the right time, leading up to our twenty-fifth anniversary, to make a change. You have a party to throw, there's a lot to do. You're doing great with the advertising department. We want you to be the publisher; we know you are going to be a success." Nice words, I suppose, but it hurt. Something I loved was being taken away from me.

I had been foolish to think that I could do it all—it was running me ragged, working late and on weekends, trying to keep a hundred balls in the air—but the magazine was looking and selling better than it had in years. My idea, though, would have been to let me loose on the editorial side, the job I had interviewed for in the first place. That was not going to happen. Once Michael broke the news, Hager was off his leash and he leaped on me like a famished tiger.

"*High Times* is not *notorious*. Dude, that is so *negative*. We should be like a *family magazine*."

I have a lot of difficulty thinking about *High Times* as a family magazine. I offered this: "Since we started running 'The Most Notorious Magazine' line, sales are up. From the very first issue."

Michael cross-examined: "Mike, do you think that's the reason we're selling more?"

"There would be no way to prove that. But it sure as hell didn't hurt. We were right about Ozzy, Steve. We've got to get this magazine out of the sixties. For chrissake, *High Times* didn't even exist in the sixties."

Michael watched us, waiting for Hager's response. The colors in Hager's face were intensifying. He was beginning to look like one of his tie-dyed T-shirts. Finally, out of the dark recesses of his brain, where apparently his frustration with me had been bubbling violently for months, he belted, "YOU CAN'T BE THE EDITOR OF *HIGH TIMES*. YOU DON'T EVEN LIKE THE BEATLES."

There is no way that Michael, who had endured enough lunacy for a lifetime, could have seen that coming. I certainly didn't. He looked at me with a raised eyebrow.

"What the fuck has that got to do with anything? I have to like the Beatles to have this job? Who's the fascist now?" I took a beat and calmly reasoned with Michael: "I don't hate everything they've ever done, but I think *Sgt. Pepper* was a mistake. 'When I'm Sixty Four'? You know, it's just not good music." Michael shrugged congenially. It would have been a hard case to argue against. But Steve wasn't having any part of it.

"You will never be the alpha dog here," he growled. I was becoming very uncomfortable in that room. Hager was prone to drama, and I guess his time spent as the commandant at Doggie Village had really gone to his head.

Back at the office, it was up to me to make the announcement that Hager would be back as editor in chief. "Meet the new boss," I said. "Same as the old boss."

I saw some happy faces, but also a lot that were terrified of Hager's dopehead despotism. He was like one of the apes at the beginning of *2001: A Space Odyssey*, except that, given the chance to toss his bone into the sky and elegantly usher in a gigantic evolutionary leap, he chose to take that bone and club the living shit out of the monkey sitting next to him. Once, he had been a visionary. Now he was just a bully.

The transformation was complete: he had morphed hideously from the mellow marijuana idealist into a sanctimonious creep who didn't run a magazine so much as he did a glassy-eyed auto-theocracy.

There was no talking to the guy. He insisted on being called Phoenix and would babble on incoherently about CIA plots, stoner reality shows he was going to make millions from, and his dream of moving the *High Times* office to Woodstock.

Hager's first move was to strip off my tagline and replace it with the impossibly flaccid "Celebrating the Counterculture." The younger staffers groaned. He was moving in reverse, repositioning the brand without consideration for market viability, contemporary tastes, or how stupid it sounded.

Hager was obsessed with the word "counterculture," and even the most timid of the editors was sick of his myopic definition of it. It was suggested to him that the *counterculture* didn't end in 1970, the *sixties* ended in 1970. At one meeting convened expressly to discuss the highlights of said counterculture, Hager shot down every idea that managed to percolate its way up through the editorial staff. And there were some good ones after the Beatles called it quits: the eighties Do It Yourself grassroots punk movement that had been even more politically pointed than its predecessors, the empowerment of the DJ, the rise of designer drugs, the advent of raves as the new "happenings," and the new wave of grunge music that had exploded out of Seattle. When Nirvana knocked Michael Jackson off the Billboard No. 1 spot, surely that was a great victory for the counterculture: FLANNEL SHIRT–WEARING DOPEHEADS WITH ELECTRIC GUITARS OVERTHROW THE ESTABLISHMENT AND CHANGE MUSIC HISTORY FOREVER.

"Nah," Hager said. "We're not going to do any of that. Anyway, our readers don't like punk."

Never mind *High Times*'s radical rock 'n' roll past, this bit of doper dogma was glommed from the failure of 1997's "Pot and Punk" issue, which stands up as one of the most ridiculous covers in the history of the magazine—of any magazine—Pancho Villa and the wooden shoe filled with pot notwithstanding.

Picture this: a disenfranchised youth, head shaved, looking off into the No Future with a pile of buds on his dome, artfully arranged to look like a bright green marijuana Mohawk. Even if you had no idea how *High Times* readers felt about punk rock in general, you could be sure that they didn't want to look at a picture of an ugly dude with pot balanced on his head. But that was Hager's *High Times*, a binary system—you were with him or you were agin' him. Dissent was not permitted.

Somehow, through all of this and after much lobbying, I managed to score a cherry assignment: for the annual *High Times* travel special, I was to go to Spain to write a long feature story about the pot culture that was blossoming there. Who better than I to report on the Spanish drug scene?

Pot and hashish were decriminalized and smoked everywhere in Spain. Bars were often choked with the smell of the omnipresent Moroccan black. But now, for the first time, high-grade homegrown marijuana was becoming popular. My friends there who knew about my gig at *High Times* were constantly sending me spectacular pictures of their grow rooms.

It seemed as if every town had a cannabis boutique that went far beyond the pipe-peddling head shops of the past, specializing in setups for closet farms that could harvest ounces of sticky buds. Dutch seed companies specializing in superior strains like Northern Lights, Blueberry, and White Widow were reporting booming sales in Spain. There was even a successful reefer magazine, a *High Times* knockoff, riding the trend.

I took off for the trip with plans for a no-stone-left-unturned campaign to interview everyone from shop owners to growers, from hardcore activists to stoners in the street, and, of course, a powwow with the editors of the new Spanish pot mag. My article would be comprehensive and describe not just the relative quality and prices of the standard-issue hash and the new marijuana, but would place the phenomenon in the historical context of a country that had a dictator until 1975. Their cultural revolution hadn't even begun until the 1980s. The scene was exploding.

I was in Spain for seven days. Jorge Cervantes, the *High Times* cultivation expert and columnist, was living in Barcelona at the time. He is an incredibly nice guy and a botanist of no small ability. He introduced me to some key people, and through my own contacts and ability to prattle in the local language, I met a dozen more. I saw spectacular indoor grow operations and an outdoor pot farm in the mountains of Catalunya. Every day I hit the pavement. I shot twelve rolls of film, pictures of buds as well as the new guard of Spanish hippies and stoners—and some very pretty girls in fields of weed. I worked my ass off and came back with the goods.

After a hard week of writing late into the night, when I wasn't busy doing publisher stuff, I had just about completed the story when Hager stopped by my office and casually told me not to bother, they weren't going to use it. "Yeah, just give me a couple of paragraphs. It's only gonna be half a page."

I was livid. What the fuck had I been doing in Spain, running all over the country for a week chasing potheads, when I could have spent my afternoons chasing tapas and chicas instead? Never mind that it had cost the company several thousand dollars to get what they could have had for free—I could have stayed in New York and coughed up half a page with just a few phone calls. This was just passive-aggressive bullshit, Hager's way of pissing on me. Still, I respectfully asked him to read my story and look at some pictures before he made any decision to kill it. Presumably, he had sent me there for a reason—it was an awfully expensive way to get me out of the office for a week, and I had worked my ass off. I set the bar high and brought home the best story of its type.

"No," he told me. "I already made up my mind. You got a problem with that?"

"You don't even want to look at it? Even on the off chance that it might be good for the magazine? I've spent a week writing it. It's great stuff—it is very exciting what's happening there now."

"*Oh,*" he said, in a tone so patronizing that I knew I was about to get hosed with dull wit. But there was no way to anticipate the full meltdown I was about to witness. "So YOU'RE upset? YOU got to go to Spain. And now you're mad at ME??! Well, I guess I'm a bad doggie!" At which point he grabbed himself by the seat of his pants with one hand and began spanking himself with the other.

Again with the dogs. I had never seen a grown man behave like this before, except possibly John Cleese in an old episode of *Fawlty Towers*. Hager paraded himself around the room like that, spanking himself and hopping around, the whole time yelling "Bad doggie! Bad doggie! Edison gets to go to Spain, but I'm the bad doggie!"

I was at a loss for words. I felt kind of sad for him, actually. Something really terrible must have happened back in Doggie Village.

I watched him carry on for a few minutes, until I could not possibly bear it any longer.

"Steve," I finally said, "get the fuck out of my office."

16

BRUTUS WAS RIGHT

Men should never wear open-toed shoes. It is always a mistake. The last guy who did it successfully was Jesus Christ. The year after He died, trendy Romans were already declaring them *sooo* last millennium. All the fashion-forward Citizens of the Empire knew it. Unfortunately, Julius Caesar was never that hip, matching his primitive Birkenstocks with a bedsheet and accessorizing with a bunch of leaves and branches on his head. It is no wonder he was stabbed by the much more style-conscious Brutus. I would have done it myself given half a chance.

I reckon that someone with as much antipathy for the male sandal as I have should never have accepted a job at *High Times*, where the perennial summer footwear is some kind of hemp rope and straw contraption that would have been out of date in an Italian vineyard two thousand years ago. But you take the bad with the good. All I could do to bring these folks out of the wilderness was lead by example in my Chuck Taylor high-tops.

A great victory for the Cause came in the form of a U.S. government–commissioned study about pot that concluded that "marijuana is not a gateway drug"; that it was not particularly addictive (if they had stopped by the *High Times* office, they might have come to a different conclusion); that it had medicinal value; that it was not as dangerous as commonly used drugs like Prozac or Viagra, not to mention alcohol and tobacco—which, they wrote, *were* gateway drugs—nor did it have their same potential for abuse. The report said without ambiguity that everything the government has been telling us about pot was a lie.

Naturally, the very moment the report came out (officially titled *Marijuana and Medicine: Assessing the Science Base*), assholes like "Drug Czar" Barry McCaffrey started back-stepping and demanding more research, denouncing the very report that his office, specifically the White House Office of National Drug Control Policy, had sponsored. We'd seen this before: in 1972 Nixon asked for a report on pot, and when it came back saying that "neither the marihuana user nor the drug itself can be said to constitute a danger to public safety"—and advising that marijuana ought to be at least decriminalized, because turning young people into convicts was a lot worse than having them experiment with pot and letting them grow out of it naturally—he threw it in the trash without reading it, started the War on Drugs, and, unfazed by the momentary interruption, went back to compiling his enemies list.

I called my friend Gretchen at the *New York Post* to see if they were going to be doing an article on it and who the reporter might be. I definitely wanted *High Times* to be part of the story. For a change, we had won some bragging rights.

Things worked out better than I could have imagined. Gretchen, who at the time was the photo editor, said that if we could come up with the right image and get it to them immediately, the story might make the cover and *High Times* would get the photo credit.

I went straight to the Design Dude and asked him what we had in the way of archival shots of iconographic pot leaves—the classic, in-your-face, seven-leaved pot plant that had been the proud emblem of pot smokers everywhere and the inspiration for T-shirts, stickers, and cheap-looking silver jewelry since the advent of the head shop. If we moved quickly, I told him, we could own the cover of the *Post*.

This is what I got: "Dude, I'm kinda busy. I'll check later."

"No, not later, *now*."

Damn, I hated having to be the Boss, but self-important slacker hopheads like the Design Dude forced my hand every goddam time. I was really getting sick of this bullshit. If I had asked him to come to my office to check out a pile of new weed for the centerfold, he would have jumped out of his chair like a mutherfucking bunny rabbit. "News" isn't sexy, but it is how we win the minds of the public, and this was the best shot—the only shot—we would enjoy for a long time. We were not going to miss this opportunity.

After he made it clear that I was annoying him, he gave me the photo, which had been sitting on his desk the whole time. I had the production department scan it, and I e-mailed it to the *Post*. About an hour later Gretchen called back and told me, "You're in. You got the wood."

"Wood" is newspaper slang for the cover.

Later that night I met Gretchen in a bar, and we waited for a messenger to bring us copies of the *Post*'s first edition. The *Post* prints several editions, the last one being the "Sports Final," and depending on what happens during the night, sometimes the cover will change. We were hoping that our pot leaf would make it through until morning. Her cell phone rang. We were good. We'd be on every edition.

About an hour later a messenger came with the paper, fresh off the press. It was the prettiest thing I had ever seen, a giant pot leaf with the headline FEDS GO TO POT: FUROR OVER DRUG CZAR'S PRO-MARIJUANA STUDY. Rendered in a high-contrast silhouette, it could be seen from a mile away. It *screamed* marijuana. And along the side it said, "Photo courtesy *High Times* magazine." Yes! Score one for the good guys.

This was a huge coup—we had basically manipulated the front page of a major metropolitan newspaper. I think the Provos and the Pranksters would have been proud, but back at the office, our success was greeted with the usual lassitude. The Design Dude complained that the photo credit was too small.

But Michael Kennedy got it. The *Post* with our pot leaf was everywhere. You could not walk down a street in New York City without seeing it. He called right away. "Congratulations, Mike. How the hell did you do that?"

"I still have a few friends left," I told him.

"Don't worry," he assured me. "Stay the course."

The timing of the *Post* cover could not have been better. That was the day I was scheduled to be a guest on Al Goldstein's *Screw* spin-off TV show, *Midnight Blue*.

Midnight Blue was a staple on New York cable television. It was on several times a week at midnight and was seen by a surprisingly large audience, a silent majority who would never cop to watching smut on television. It did not hurt that the advertisements—so numerous they threatened to overwhelm the actual program—were lurid X-rated teasers for "escort services" catering to every possible racial proclivity. Anyone channel surfing after midnight was likely to stop and gawk, at least for a few salacious moments. Between the graphic come-ons for hookers and phone-sex lines, Al would rant and rave, jiggling like a hastily constructed marionette whose strings were being pulled by a palsy victim, tearing into politicians and celebrities with an incredibly foulmouthed stream of venom and humor. It had turned him into a popular cult figure in New York. Every time he opened his mouth, it was a lawsuit waiting to happen.

Al had been asking me to come on the show for some time, and I had been looking forward to it. It was damn fine luck that the day we were taping, I had a prop as good as the *Post* with our pot leaf on it. And I brought the Pot Star with me—if he was going to be the face of *High Times*'s future, I wanted him to get used to being on television.

Pot Star looked fabulous in a gold lamé Oriental smoking jacket and outsize rose-colored sunglasses, like the psychedelic kingpin of an intergalactic drug cartel. With his dreads tied back behind his head and sticking out every which way, he was an outer-space acid guru preaching the gospel of *High Times*. And Al was a gentleman. Just back from Amsterdam, where he had been a guest of *High Times* at our Cannabis Cup event—where awards were handed out for the best strains of marijuana—he put his sewer mouth in park and demurred to Pot Star's expertise. "I can't distinguish the high between Purple Haze and White Shark," he asked, uncharacteristically humble. "Am I unsophisticated?"

"It's hard to tell the subtle differences. It takes a certain palate to discriminate," Pot Star told him, playing the connoisseur card. "You can stick your nose in the bag and smell it and check the density of the buds, see if they're too dry or too wet, or not cured properly, which leaves it with a leafy taste . . . The problem is people give you pot and you're walking around with a trash bag full of weed, and you smoke thirty joints a day . . . I wake up in the morning, and the first thing I do is take a few bong hits, and then I go to work. I smoke all day long. I'm constantly stoned."

Between every segment there was a bumper cut from *Reefer Madness*, shots of American flags, fishbowls filled with bright green pot, gardens, indoor grow rooms, and a montage of Amsterdam coffee shops and marijuana rallies in Washington Square Park. Our Web address flashed on the screen repeatedly while Peter Tosh sang "Legalize It." It was like science fiction, a TV ad from an advanced civilization where pot was legal. And it looked a fuck of a lot better than anything that had ever come out of the *High Times* video department.

I spoke about how *High Times* reached a wide diversity of marijuana enthusiasts. Pot Star gave good advice about beating a drug test (if you can't stop taking drugs, drink tons of water and never give your first morning's urine). Al talked about how he uses pot to slow time when he's having sex. And then we showed off our pot leaf on the cover of the *Post*, and the Jews did their shtick:

AL: Today is a great day. Look at the cover of the *Post*.
ME: When the *Post* wants pot, they come to us . . .
AL: You guys have been right all along. The government is as full of shit about drugs as they are about masturbation.
ME: So, Al, does masturbation lead to harder stuff? Does it lead to fucking?
AL: Not in your case.

After that bit of vaudeville, Pot Star demonstrated his joint-rolling prowess and twisted a banana-size hooter, which we smoked like Hopper, Fonda, and Nicholson sitting around the campfire in *Easy Rider*. Al looked right into the camera and delivered the coup de grâce: "Mayor Giuliani, you piece-of-shit scumbag, I hate your fucking guts. I'm gonna smoke this joint—it is an illegal act. Fuck you."

Don't forget that before 9/11—when he somehow seemed to be everywhere at once, shining with an uncharacteristically empathetic presence (and before he shed the last vestige of humility and decency and turned himself into an international celebrity, and the terrorist attack into a profit stream, by exaggerating beyond the pale what his actual leadership role was, earning the ire of cops, who already hated him for greedily taking all the credit for lowering New York crime stats, and the firemen, who wanted nothing to do with him after he began promoting his political future by shamelessly glomming on to their glory and tragedy)—he had already overstayed his welcome by showing his true colors as an unapologetic prig and power-mad megalomaniac. He was convinced that government had the right to silence its critics—he made a ludicrous attempt at banning protests from the steps of City Hall; his administration withheld public information from journalists; repeatedly refused permits for demonstrations (and was repeatedly ordered by the courts to issue them); and vainly and illegally slapped gag orders on cops and city employees critical of it. Eventually the Giuliani administration lost *thirty-five* First Amendment cases brought against the city. Few people in American history have held so much contempt for Freedom of Speech.

The most famous of these cases was his attempt to evict the Brooklyn Museum from its premises, claiming that it had no right to exhibit "offensive art"—in this case Chris Ofili's painting *The Holy Virgin Mary*, which used elephant dung within the composition, a reference to traditional African rituals and materials. (Incidentally, in the same exhibition, Ofili had another work with the names of Cassius Clay, James Brown, Miles Davis, and Diana Ross written on clumps of the very same stuff, and no one seemed to mind.)

Giuliani took the position that He as Mayor had the authority to decide what could be shown in the city's museums. (Incredibly, he never actually saw the painting; he had only heard about it secondhand.) He went so far as to create a "decency committee," much like the Reich Chamber of Culture, whose job it was to suppress "degenerate modern art" under the Nazis, or the Taliban's Agents for the Preservation of Virtue and Elimination of Vice. Both the state supreme court and the appellate court hammered Giuliani as a tyrant. He was the most recent in a long line of Republican hypocrites trying to legislate morality, and much hated for his efforts. The stick up his ass was costing taxpayers millions of dollars in frivolous lawsuits.

It did not help his deluded posturing as a vessel of Catholic virtue and family values that he literally paraded his mistress around New York while he was still married (he took her as his date to the St. Patrick's Day Parade, an act so crass that the *Daily News* said it was like "groping in the window at Macy's"). He only later informed his wife (his second) of his intention to separate from her—at a public press conference. She sued him for divorce, citing adultery.

Our interview with Al lasted forty minutes, but each week they showed only one five-minute blast of us between the hooker ads, so it took two months to show the whole thing. Since *Midnight Blue* ran the same show twice a week, we were pretty much saturating the late-night sleaze market. It seemed that everyone had caught at least a glimpse of it. During its eight-week run, I could not walk anywhere in Manhattan without someone stopping me to shake my hand.

And we were the cover story of *Screw* that week, a vividly executed Peter Max–style celebration of the weed, illustrated by regular *High Times* contributing artist Steve Marcus. Inside, the best parts of our interview had become a feature story, along with photos of Pot Star, Al, and me toking and mugging for the camera with the front page of the *Post*. The cover of a recent issue of *High Times* was reprinted, along with our Web address and a poster for our twenty-fifth-anniversary bash. At the time, *Screw* circulation was fifty thousand a week.

One might think that for this groundswell of good vibes and an act of televised civil disobedience in the face of a common foe—Giuliani was also arresting pot smokers at an unprecedented pace, to "run them through the system," and had become the sworn enemy of anarchists, punks, hippies, liberal intellectuals, and civil libertarians—we would have been treated as conquering heroes.

Instead, I caught the full force of a verbal shit storm from the Marketing Witch, who had seen this as some kind of opportunity to bury me once and for all.

"You're disgusting," she barked. "How can you go on that show with *that pig*? Why did you have to bring Pot Star?" She liked Pot Star. We all did; he was the company freak. He had just boasted on television that he smoked thirty joints a day, but somehow I was corrupting him.

In fact, Al Goldstein had been a longtime friend of *High Times*; not only had he just returned from the Cannabis Cup, where he was a VIP, but his picture was featured in our coverage of the event. If the Marketing Witch had bothered to look inside the magazine she was responsible for selling, she might have known that. Actually, if she knew anything at all about *High Times*, she certainly would have known that in the 1980s Al was proudly listed on the our masthead as a contributing editor, and he occasionally wrote the magazine's long-running Sex column, where he would alternately whine about his "small Jewish dick" and brag about his "storybook sexual encounters." Not atypical of these adventures: "I was on a Greyhound bus headed to see Barry White at the Westchester Premiere Theater. My young female companion led me down the aisle bisecting the bus's marijuana-saturated interior to the little bathroom in back. There, while bumping from side to side, my young lady friend proceeded to suck me off, doing a wonderful juggling act as my balls bounced off her chin and smacked against her nose."

Back in those days, no one shied away from the ribald and the ridiculous. Mick Jagger even got in on the act, jokingly offering to fellate Tom Petty in a famous 1980 interview.

> HIGH TIMES: Tom Petty gets up there and just stands there and just sings his songs . . . he emanates sex and has a lot of charisma by just standing there.
> MICK JAGGER: I know what you mean. I'd suck his cock afterwards.

But over the years the tie-dyed revisionism and hophead hypocrisy that had become the hallmark of corporate hippiedom had infected every level of the *High Times* hierarchy. So outraged was the Marketing Witch that I was dragging our *dope magazine* into the gutter with Al that she went so far as to call Michael Kennedy to complain about the show and to let him know that I "kept pornography" in my office. This new drama mushroomed until I was accused of creating an "uncomfortable work environment."

This was no joke, it was a potential sexual harassment case, and Michael treated it with the appropriate gravity. No matter the motives or veracity of the accusation, Michael had no choice but to have a sit-down with me and Wanda, the acting human resources officer. A complaint had been made, and they needed a record of it to show that it had been taken seriously and dealt with accordingly.

I was aghast. It was astonishing how low the Marketing Witch would stoop. This was not some catty junior high school feud; it could quickly turn into a lawsuit.

It did not make me feel any better that Wanda, with whom I had tangled since taking the job, was there in a potentially decision-making capacity, but she put any personal feelings she held toward me aside and handled this with the utmost of professionalism and discretion, for which I was grateful. The Marketing Witch, however, knew nothing from such virtues, and as I walked down the hall past her office to Wanda's, where I was presumably being called to the gallows, she cackled at me, *"You're gone."*

There was no way to combat her vitriol without really stepping in the shit and making it worse for myself. But I didn't want to fight back. There was absolutely no way I was going to take that bait. For all of my shortcomings, which are vast, I have always strived to comport myself professionally. Michael Kennedy agreed. "I cannot imagine you behaving inappropriately," he told me.

I was particularly aware of gender politics and the rules that governed the workplace, *because* I had worked for adult magazines, not in spite of it. At Drake we had many more women on staff than there ever were at *High Times*. (Aside from the managing editor, who worked in strictly a functionary position trafficking everyone else's stories, Hager never hired female editors.) Working for a sexually explicit magazine, one had to be especially aware of and courteous to female coworkers, and even in such a highly charged environment, we never had any problems.

"We publish a very adult magazine," I suggested to Michael. "I would expect people here to be sophisticated and mature enough to handle all sorts of free speech." I was not being glib. I could not have been more serious. "And I would never have anything of a blatantly sexual nature in plain sight in my office," I added. "It's not my style, and besides, I know better."

Michael nodded but didn't say anything. Wanda, too, was mostly silent. Michael asked me what sort of pornography I had in my office. I showed him the copy of *Screw* that featured *High Times*. Far from any sexual images, the cover offered a goofy psychedelic painting of a fat guy smoking a doobie. It looked a lot like an outtake from *Yellow Submarine*, and it was absolutely relevant to our magazine. Actually, it could have easily been mistaken for the cover of our magazine. I also had a copy of *Penthouse*, their thirtieth anniversary issue, which we were looking at as we planned our twenty-fifth-anniversary issue. It, too, was absolutely germane to our work. In place of the traditional centerfold model, the cover was an elegant white, with a reproduction of their "gold key" logo. It was about as prurient as an ad for air freshener, and frankly, I have no idea why they even thought it would sell.

Michael told me to put them out of sight and to stay out of the Marketing Witch's way. He looked disgusted. I was asked to be discreet and not discuss this with anyone on the floor, but of course the Marketing Witch had already seen to that, blabbing to everyone. At the time, no one said anything to me directly (much later I would hear all about it), but I was getting a sympathetic vibe from a good part of the staff, who knew that a line had been crossed.

I disobeyed Michael Kennedy for the first and only time and stuck my head in the Marketing Witch's office. I wanted to apologize to her myself. "I'm sorry," I told her, doing little to conceal my sarcasm. "When you are in charge of promoting a drug magazine, you don't get to claim the moral high ground."

This was the bad time. Back at home, the curtain was about to come crashing down. There was no escape. Work, relationship—how could I have failed on such a Goliathan level? My friends told me that I cared too much. That I had to stop leading with my heart. No one else at *High Times* was as invested in the magazine—why should I be? It hadn't occurred to me that one of my greatest assets could also be my greatest weakness.

They told me I should ditch my girlfriend and move on, they could see I was unhappy. Of course they weren't aware of what was really going on, what with the suicidal mornings and the subzero communication breakdowns. Naturally, _____ never wanted anyone to know about her precarious mental balancing act, and I always protected her.

Bipolar disorder is a nasty disease. I know a lot of guys who would have headed for the hills and written her off as loony tunes, but despite the motocross course of emotions and high-wire acts of mania and depression, four years later, I was still gaga. I missed spending time with her terribly. I couldn't wait to get our romantic life back on track. I didn't want to be with anyone else.

All of the day-to-day drama and the demands of her juris doctor had taken a severe toll, but the worst thing, it turned out, was that as she gained self-confidence, she became so eager to be part of this new group at school and hook a blue-ribbon gig at a high-octane law firm that she betrayed her own values and the person who loved her most. She had become everything that she had hated when I met her: a cold-hearted opportunist, a careerist social climber.

Law school and psychotherapy had robbed her of a soul. "I don't feel anything," she told me at the end. "I can't. If I did, I'd never be able to do this."

When it came to graduation time, she sandbagged me, and viciously. A year before, she had said that she didn't want to go to graduation; it didn't jibe with her punk rock sensibility. It made sense—neither of us went in for all that pomp and circumstance. The plan was to escape together and take a deep breath.

Somehow that plan changed. I got wind of it when she told me that her parents were coming for the ceremony.

Her parents? What the fuck? For three years of law school they didn't do shit for her, although her father was loaded. I even had to cosign her student loan. The only thing she ever got from her old man was vague warnings about New York City. Never mind that this was the guy whose idea of paternal sweet talk was to tell his daughter that she was never going to make it as a lawyer. Maybe that's why she needed him there, to prove that she was on her way. Okay, I got that. I still had some unresolved issues with my father, who I felt never took me seriously, either.

I told her I didn't realize that she was even going to graduation. "Of course I am," she told me. "Are *you* crazy? After all that, you don't think I want to go and get my diploma?"

"Well, then I certainly want to go, too," I told her. "We've been through this together."

"I only have two tickets," she told me. "You said you didn't want to go."

"*You* said you didn't want to go. And I supported that. I thought we were going to go away? What happened to that?"

"I changed my mind," she told me in the smug tone of a child who was holding all the marbles for the very first time. "I never made you any promises. There are no promises in life. We have nothing in writing."

I wanted to puke, but I was empty. I had already given her everything I had, emotionally, financially, spiritually, every which way. I was drained. When we started out together, I knew she was a comer, but she had no idea of her own self-worth. Her old boyfriends, she had confided to me, never made her feel attractive. They never even told her that she was pretty. I had actually met a couple of them, and they were controlling creeps. One of them had even made her cat crazy by trying to toilet train him, and it took a lot of love to sort that cat out, too. Ours, she delighted in saying, was the first healthy relationship she had ever had, and she had finally broken through the wall of low self-esteem. She told me that I made her feel special, as if she could do anything. Finally, she said, she knew who she was.

_____ was graduating with honors. She was in the very top tier of her class, a *Law Review* editor, and she had been recruited by a powerful white-shoe litigator whose pedigree would insure a stellar career. I was so proud of her. Her future looked bright indeed. Unfortunately, I wasn't part of her plans.

The day of her graduation, a day we should have been enjoying together, basking in the First Rays of the New Rising Sun, was one of the saddest of my life. I watched her get dressed to go out. She was so beautiful, and for a change, she was very happy. She didn't seem to notice that I was gray with depression.

"I'll meet you afterward," I suggested meekly. "I'm sure there will be a party, and your parents will want to go out . . ."

"You can't come," she told me flatly. "Don't you get it? If anyone finds out that I live with a guy who works for *High Times*, they'll think I'm a pothead. It could hurt my career."

Fucking hypocrite. Never mind that she was smoking more dope than I was and that I was buying it for her because she had no dough. When I was first named publisher of *High Times*, she had been so happy for me and had boasted to her friends about my cool new job. Through my tribulations there, she encouraged me as best she could, although her enthusiasm had been on the wane as she got deeper into school. I assumed it was just a product of her topsy-turvy brain waves and an ungodly workload. It hadn't occurred to me until then that she had sold me out for a corporate lifestyle.

"Look," she told me as she finished putting on her lipstick. She always wore a muted red, "crystal amethyst" I think it was called. It was the perfect color for her, and it always drove me nuts. I was heartsick watching her get all dolled up to go receive her accolades.

"You've done so much for me, but I can do it on my own now. I mean, thanks, but I don't need you anymore."

The one inarguably good thing in my life at the time was the Raunch Hands, who had started playing again, sporadically re-forming to do garage-rock festivals. The year before, we had played Cavestomp! in New York. This year we were jetting to the Las Vegas Shakedown, with two dozen other bands of our ilk. This was soon after ____ moved out. When I realized that she had a piece of coal where her heart used to be, I encouraged her to follow her dark muse. I believe I said, "You go. The cats stay." She didn't even pretend to care. It didn't take long to realize that I got the best of that deal.

Cliff Mott and I left for Vegas the night before the Shakedown began so we could check out Little Richard and Chuck Berry, who were appearing at Caesars Palace, just a hop, skip, and a spectacularly failed jump from where my old pal Evel Knievel had smashed his skeleton into kindling.

Chuck's part of the show, typically, sucked. For the first couple of songs I thought the band was out of tune. They sounded awful. And then I realized that Chuck kept changing the key, leaving a very confused pickup band struggling to keep up with his whims, which seemingly had no good musical reason other than to be difficult. To make matters worse, he kept stopping songs to look at his watch.

Little Richard was another story. His band was a well-oiled rock 'n' roll machine: two drummers, two bass players, two guitar players, full horn section, and Little Richard's grand piano front and center. He strolled onto the stage to a hard-pumping vamp, wearing what is best described as a purple chiffon shower curtain. His hair was about three feet high, and he had on more eye makeup than GG Allin and Alice Cooper combined. He looked awesome. With the help of a couple of younger, more masculine bandmates he stood on top of the piano and signaled for the music to stop. He had something very important he wanted to share with the audience.

"WHOOOOOOOOOO!!!!" he squealed. "I AM THE BEE-YOO-TEE-FUL LITTLE RICHARD!!!" He gave the band the signal that it was okay to continue, hopped off the piano, and began banging away at a positively pugilistic version of "Bama Lama Bama Loo." It was strong stuff.

After that he slid through a set of greatest hits, whooping and hollering and only occasionally stopping to proclaim his greatness or make some sort of vital non sequitur. "Look at my hands!" he screamed. "Aren't they *bee-yoo-tee-ful*?? Can you believe I once had to wash dishes? *Me*?? The Georgia Peach??!! WHOOOOOOOOO!!!" or "I am drinking Gatorade because I want to be like Michael Jordan! Isn't he lovely? I want to be just like him!" I think someone might have wanted to mention to Richard the high probability of that ship having already sailed, but there was no stopping him, and thank God for that. Rock 'n' roll cures all ills.

Indeed, the Raunch Hands' Las Vegas vacation was turning into exactly the prescription for what ailed me. Another good shock to my metastasis of brokenhearted gloom was a chance rendezvous with a girl I knew from Los Angeles, an old Raunch Hands fan in town for the Shakedown and also on the rebound from a bad breakup. She had driven out with a couple of girlfriends with whom she was sharing a room. I convinced her that was no way to spend a weekend in Vegas, and certainly no way to get over the guy who had dumped her, and quickly installed her into my suite at the Rio so the healing could begin.

In the morning we repaired to the patio to drink Bloody Marys with all the other lunatic musicians and fans. It was quite a scene, truly *la dolce vita*: fifty or sixty tattooed punks slurping frozen drinks and smoking dope in the kidney bean–shaped pool out behind the casino while a flock of scantily clad cocktail waitresses fluttered around them taking orders and hustling for tips.

We were playing the next night, and Mariconda arrived just as I was buying a solid rock of an eight ball from an enterprising cabdriver who was convinced that I should buy a bag of Vicodin from him as well. It was sound advice. You should always listen to the cabdrivers in Las Vegas. They *know*. Mariconda and I smashed up the coke with a Bible the Gideons had thoughtfully left in my room just for that purpose, and we were off to the races, ready to throw the fireball.

The Raunch Hands show was a triumph. Chandler, especially, was devastating. He sang like a champion and commanded the action as if he had something to prove. And he did—even in the depths of alcoholism he is a man who knows his own self-worth, and he did not come to Vegas to fuck around. He looked positively arch in aviator Ray-Bans and a New York Police Department VICE SQUAD T-shirt, which came in handy later when a couple of Las Vegas cops knocked on the door of his hotel room. There was a full-tilt fiesta in progress, and everyone dove to cover up whatever ordnance they were smoking or snorting, but when Chandler opened the door and the Vegas cops saw him in his NYPD blue, he gave them his best version of a fraternal wink and nod. They went for it hook, line, and sinker and didn't bust up the party.

After that, he disappeared. It probably didn't help that in the lobby of our hotel was Three Mikes' Discount Liquors, open twenty-four hours a day. We sent out a search team for him but came up empty. (I'm sure it didn't help that our search team was assembled from a coterie of drunk and wired musicians who had been up for three days.) But when we got to the airport two days later, we found him passed out by the gate, under a chair, the very apotheosis of a professional rock musician.

Still, he was a mess. Breakfasting on speed-rack vodka didn't help. He did the right thing and moved to Maine, near where he was from, to enter a rehab program. His friends were behind him one hundred percent. It's just amazing that more of us didn't need to join him.

My last night in Vegas I went to see Tom Jones with my new roommate and one of her girlfriends, who had just gotten out of jail for armed robbery. The conditions of her parole prohibit me from telling you any more—I'm not even sure she was allowed to be in Las Vegas. You can file that adventure, too, under Top Secret Action.

When I got back home and the glow of Vegas finally wore off, I realized how crappy things still were. Nothing had changed. _____ was gone. The only thing she had left behind was her guitar amplifier, with a note saying she would come get it later. I gave it to some kids down the street who were starting a band.

And I was still getting the shit beaten out of me at work. But no matter how bad it was or how much I wanted to anesthetize myself, I still had to show up in the morning and do my job. You can't let the bastards get you down, and I took my responsibility as publisher very seriously, as did my employers. No matter how much bullshit I was getting from Hager and his editorial rabble, I had received a raise every year I was there. Circulation was up twenty-five percent. Advertising pages were up every quarter over the last. Michael Kennedy asked me what the secret was, and there was no secret: every day I challenged myself to put something better in the bottle. I was never satisfied. And I didn't freak out whenever there was a problem.

Of course, there were always problems.

Every magazine office was under pressure at deadline time. The stress could be incredible. The industry was rife with legends of people sleeping in the office when it was time to close the book. Advertisers dropped out without warning. New ones came in at the last minute. Stories changed constantly. There were production glitches. And then, just when you got the book out the door and you thought it was safe to go into the water again, there could be problems on press, although not every magazine had to go scrounging for 180,000 packs of missing rolling papers like I once had to. (They were to be polybagged with the book as a giveaway—the manufacturer who had promised 200,000 packs of papers sent only 20,000 and by way of explanation offered a coy "oops." I had to renegotiate the entire deal in an hour, but the book got out on time.) It was all part of putting out a magazine. We did it every month. You just had to roll with it. Panic is for amateurs.

For someone who had been working at a magazine for more than ten years, it was amazing how little Wanda, now back to her default position as the Evil Accountant, actually knew about publishing. There was no solution for which she could not find a problem.

With the increase in ad sales, our production costs went up proportionately—more ads meant more prepress work and more pages. But it also meant more revenue. There is a formula we followed—we'd project how many ads were going to be in each issue and then make the map based on an ad-to-edit ratio of about 40–60. If it got close to 50–50, we'd add pages. You always needed to place ads against editorial, preferably on right-hand pages, which advertisers coveted. When I started at *High Times*, we were running a 108-page book, plus covers. We were now up to 128 pages, and not only was the revenue up accordingly, it was a better product. The Plop Quotient was high— when you dropped it onto a table, the *plop!* of the slick cover resonated nicely.

Wanda the Evil Accountant was not impressed. Our conversations went something like this:

WANDA THE EVIL ACCOUNTANT: Mike, this month our production bill is $8,000 more than last month.
ME: Yes, we added pages to make room for $36,000 worth of new ads.
WANDA THE EVIL ACCOUNTANT: But our production costs went up $8,000.
ME: Yes, because we have $36,000 of new business. We're $28,000 to the good. If these advertisers stay in, that's $336,000 of new business on the year. And I expect it to climb; there is a lot of momentum.

WANDA THE EVIL ACCOUNTANT: But our production costs are up.

And so on.

The anniversary issue was everything I said it would be—the biggest issue ever, an all-time record in advertising. When I tossed it on my desk, it plopped like a London broil.

Mary McEvoy told me to watch my back. "You're a threat to these people," she warned me. "You work too hard. They're afraid that you make them look bad. They had it a lot easier before you came in."

But by then it was too late. Michael informed me that my position as publisher was untenable. "They don't respect your authority, Mike," he told me. "We're going to have to make a change."

I had done everything I was asked to and delivered everything I had promised, but I had failed to win the hearts and minds of my staff. I could not possibly have done worse in that department. It didn't help that I was strapped with a shrew like the Marketing Witch and an agent provocateur like Hager, but the fault lies squarely on my shoulders. My management style was inappropriate for this team. That I *had* a management style was inappropriate for this team.

The worst part was the humiliation of having to carpetbag my stuff down the hall from my corner office, and the absolute glee of certain staff members who thought they had won some kind of war. There was a new publisher coming in; the announcement would be made in a few days. His name was Ski, short for a polysyllabic train wreck of a Polish surname, and he was a good friend of the Marketing Witch. Oh, joy. After that meeting I heard her in the hall braying to anyone within earshot of how she had finally brought me down. I didn't say a word. It was enough to know that her karma was fucked forever.

But Michael Kennedy made it very clear that I was not being fired. They didn't want me to leave. In fact, not only did they want me to stay, but they wanted me to write my own ticket and come up with a new job description, maybe get back to doing some stories. And they wanted to pay me a bonus for the job I had done as publisher, well known to all the citizens of Gotham as the key to a Happy Monkey.

I'm a pretty good negotiator, and when I took the job as publisher, we had made a handshake agreement that if I increased revenue and hit my goals, I would be compensated above my salary. The publisher was the final word in advertising, but since I was not a salesman and not entitled to a commission, I would have to get my piece at the end of the day. Michael and his colleagues were good to their word, and they cut me a check for six thousand dollars. Not enough to change my lifestyle, and about half of what it should have been, but unprecedented in *High Times* history, and it went a long way toward reestablishing some goodwill between the Trans High Corporation and myself. That year, including some Penthouse Letters I had written to goose my lack of a real sex life, I banked almost ninety thousand.

I would have liked to just walk away, but I wasn't going to tank a good paying job until I had something else lined up. I was not thrilled that I would have to come to work every day and face a gang that had worked hard to neuter me, but I was enjoying having some money for a change. Pretty soon I was going to put a down payment on an apartment. But none of it mattered. There was one more thing I had to do: make the *High Times* movie.

How could it possibly fail?

17

THE HOLY TRIFECTA OF SLEAZE

When I sleep at night, sometimes it is hard to tell if my dreams are coming from inside my brain or if I am more like a radio antenna, picking up images and transmissions from space. At least in space no one can hear you scream. Whatever Mick Jagger was taking so that he couldn't feel the pain no more, I wanted some of that.

I was looking at failure on either side of me and trying to cut a swath down the middle with an increasingly toxic mélange of drugs and madness. It was self-medication at its very worst, binging with Party Horse on cocaine, vodka, beer, and whatever else we could get our hands on. And we all know what that leads to: doomed Las Vegas weddings with overweight Elvis impersonators and blind North African road trips in search of silly hats and hash oil.

I was grappling with bouts of mania, confusion, desperation, and loneliness; depression, reckless irresponsibility, and a profound inability to confront reality; intellectual disorder and malaise; drug-induced euphoria, dementia, and hysteria; frenzy, lunacy, and pyromania; obsession, regression, repression, and pronounced procrastination, not to mention frequent borderline-psychotic episodes of mumbling under my breath and laughing out of context. But I still had to go to work every day. Ironically, my job insured that I kept one hand on the wheel at all times.

Out of the line of fire, at least I didn't feel as if I was constantly dodging bullets at the office. Still, I had few friends there. Holmstrom had finally had enough and officially resigned after thirteen years as a full-time staffer. There was little joy in Mudville.

My new job was Director of Editorial and Marketing, an absurd title that was supposed to encompass a broad area of responsibility that included marketing and promotion as well as special editorial projects designed to help leverage ad sales and create synergy between the magazine and our website. Or at least that's what I told my employers.

It was not a bad gig in theory, never mind that in the history of magazine publishing the words "editorial" and "marketing" had never appeared together in a job title. And I was now free to do some writing. I was planning a trip to Mississippi to try to find out if bluesman Robert Johnson had been smoking the local homegrown on the night, as legend has it, that he made his pact with Satan. Marijuana grew wild in the Mississippi Delta, and I knew there was an untold story there. I was going to find it.*

I had my own department, of sorts, and successfully marginalized as I was, Hager mostly stayed away from me. I didn't have to answer to anyone besides the new publisher, whose main goal, it seemed, was to play nice and keep his job. Turns out he was a powder puff. A nice guy, but soft. He was in way over his head.

---

*It was unlikely but entirely possible that Robert Johnson was toking on one of Satan's cigarettes the night, as legend would have it, that he went down to the crossroads to sell his soul. The results of my trip were inconclusive, but I did score a largely untold history of blues and reefer. Untold, because as Gatemouth Brown professed (while we were smoking a joint on his bus), "Everybody smokes pot, but you gotta be careful about what you sing out in this world . . . you can put yourself in a helluva spot."

Johnson's stepson, Robert Lockwood, Jr., says that although he never knew Johnson to smoke marijuana (they were both whiskey drinkers), it wouldn't have been the least bit odd. "Young people smoked it. Everybody smokin' it," he told me, talking about the Mississippi Delta in the 1930s, where as a teenager he learned to sing and play the guitar from his itinerant stepdad. "Shit, it was there when I got there," he said. Taj Mahal, who also has a strong interest in blues and cannabis, told me that Mississippi John Hurt once explained to him that "marijuana was around, but whenever we had some money, we bought some good gin. It was growing wild, but it was a cheap high." Taj also laughed that Hurt would "smoke up your stash" if you were foolish enough to leave it out.

When bluesmen left the rural South for the city, they took their love of the weed with them. Marshall Chess said that Little Walter was "always high, drunk, coke, grass, whatever. We used to record him when he was high." (Lockwood says that when Walter was shot on a Chicago street in the 1950s, they had to pry a handful of joints out of his clenched fist before they brought him to the hospital and chained him to the bed.) I also heard tales from the guys in Canned Heat about getting stoned with John Lee Hooker ("Reefer was definitely part of his life"), and Muddy Waters so loved his herb that he burned one before playing for Jimmy Carter at the White House.

Ski was a middle-management guy with no real connection to the *High Times* lifestyle. After me, they wanted a publisher who didn't fancy himself a creative mind, just a wonk who could keep an eye on the business. He did his best not to rock the boat and to lie low, listening to crappy prog rock records in his office, which were his major touchstone to stoner culture. I think once upon a time someone tossed him a Buzzbee at an Emerson, Lake, and Palmer concert. I have no idea why he was hired. Mary McEvoy summed it up right away: "He's not going to move the dial."

But he was smarter than I was in at least one department: when Michael Kennedy told him he didn't want any pot smoking on the floor, Ski nodded yes and then ignored him. The quotidian cannabis consumption skyrocketed, and where I had been vilified as *High Times*'s version of Papa Doc Duvalier, Ski was lauded as the Willy Wonka of Weed.

Everyone told Ski, *Get along with Hager and you won't have any problems*. Of course, getting along with Hager meant letting him have his way, and it didn't take long before sales started slipping again. I watched in awestruck disgust as all the gains we had made under my watch evaporated, but as proprietary as I felt about *High Times*'s success, it was no longer my problem. I had other wieners to roast.

A few weeks before the twenty-fifth-anniversary party, the people at Irving Plaza were starting to get cold feet. They knew what went on at a *High Times* party, and as publicity about our shindig began to pop up in the press, they had legitimate concerns about appearing on anti-pot bully Giuliani's radar screen. There was a risk involved in throwing this party, and I had to know that if there was going to be pot smoking— and we all knew that there was going to be not just pot smoking, but ganja intake on an industrial scale—then they reserved the right to pull the plug at any time.

When I told Bloom that there had been some concerns raised, his reaction went something like "Tell them to go fuck themselves, they have *reggae* bands there all the time, and now they have a problem with us? Fuck them, we're going to have our party and do whatever we like." I opted for a more anodyne method of negotiation, and after a lot of back-and-forth and sweet talk with the club and counsel with Michael Kennedy, we decided to forge ahead and cross our fingers. Last-minute jitters came with the territory.

Irving Plaza was packed, start to finish. Eight hundred people drank, smoked, ate positively ass-kicking marijuana cookies, danced to Cypress Hill, and generally mopped up whatever intoxicants we whipped at them. Mostly, though, I worked—greeting guests and running around with a walkie-talkie to make sure that everything was running on schedule and that there were no problems. Everyone who wanted a cookie or a balloon filled with gas got one, even if I had to chase it down myself. Even though I had been pushed to the fringe, it was still my party.

When you throw an event of this scale with a team of potheads, even if they aren't doing any work, there is going to be some confusion. Some hippie artists brought with them, unsolicited, a giant neon pot leaf that they had made. It looked good, but they put it on the stage without checking with anyone, and I had to ask them to move it, because as anyone who knows anything about electrical fields will tell you, neon emits radio frequencies that can seriously fuck with wireless microphone systems. Like, for instance, the one Cypress Hill was going to be using. Of course when I explained to them why we had to find a better place for it, they told me not to worry, it was cool where it was, man, and I shouldn't be so uptight.

A lot of people showed up who were not on our list, and my walkie-talkie squealed constantly.

"Mike, one of the Ramones is here, should we let him in?"

Oy.

"Mike, Woody Harrelson just headed up to the bar, thought you might want to get your photographer."

That was more like it. But when we got there, he was being mobbed by some seriously uncool stoners who pretty much chased him out of the party.

When Michael Kennedy arrived, I was there to greet him and lead his flock of middle-aged *High Times* owners up to the VIP section, where we had reserved tables for them so they wouldn't have to tussle with the unwashed masses. I guess I shouldn't have been surprised that those tables had been taken over by indolent staffers and hangers-on, who, given the endless boundaries of their entitlement, naturally thought the tables had been reserved for them. Just once more I had to be the Evil Boss and piss off the staff so that the people who had actually ponied up the fifty grand for this fiesta could sit down and knock back a few highballs.

I was also introducing Ski as the new publisher and explaining with a tight smile to everyone that I was just moving down the hall so I could get back to editorial work. It was a terribly unpleasant position to be forced into. But I did right by Ski and my employers, and I kept my mouth shut when Hager got onstage to receive accolades for an issue and party he had precious little to do with. I swallowed so much pride that night I felt food-poisoned.

Our photographer for the party was the great Dave Allocca, one of the top celebrity shutter hounds in the world, self-proclaimed master of the grip-and-grin snapshot.

I had met Dave through Gretchen at the *Post*—he shot for them all the time, his stuff was all over Page Six. One night Gretchen and I were watching a TV documentary about paparazzi and celebrity photographers. As the *Post* photo editor, Gretchen was featured in the film, which shadowed several photographers as they tooled around New York City from event to event—galas, premieres, award shows, etc.—trying to get the crucial star pic that would make the papers the next day.

Most of these guys are just starfuckers, in the business because they want to get close to the celebrities, with whom they have a twisted love-hate relationship. They chase movie stars all day and then scream that they all suck because celebrities are a bunch of stuck-up assholes. I'm sure many of them are, but Dave just never seemed to care, which is why he's so good at his job. He wasn't trying to make friends, just get the picture and get the fuck out. He wasn't impressed with anyone.

In one scene in the documentary, Dave wheels into a charity event wearing a tuxedo and a camera around his neck. He sees Jerry Seinfeld, says, "Hey, Jerry, can I get a picture?" Jerry says, "Sure." Dave takes the pic, says thanks, and is out the door in fifteen seconds to get the picture to the paper. He has zero interest in hanging around. On his way out, another photographer is arguing with the security who won't let him in. He is cussing and spitting about what an asshole Jerry is. Apparently he had been following Jerry for days and Jerry wouldn't give him a shot. And it's no small wonder—the guy is clearly a sociopath harboring some sort of vendetta against the rich and famous.

Dave's idea of driving in New York City is to do a pirouette on Death's incisors. He rips through Times Square traffic dodging cabs, bike messengers, pedestrians, the whole time screaming at everyone to get the fuck out of his way. He's an old-school New York newspaper guy, hustling like a maniac with zero regard for anything but getting the next picture and hitting the deadline. He isn't really a paparazzo, because he isn't a stalker. He never takes a picture anyone doesn't want taken, which makes him a popular guy with the superstars he is always snapping. The Rolling Stones took Dave on tour with them, and his kids were dressed in clothes Tommy Hilfiger had sent over as a thank-you for some pictures Dave had given him.

At one point he gets a flat tire and lets loose with a string of expletives that would have made Dolemite blush like Raggedy Ann. After letting his aneurysm run its course, he gets out of his car, right in the middle of Broadway, to fix the flat. He doesn't want to get his tux dirty, so he takes it off and throws it in the backseat.

Up to this point, Dave, despite his hard-boiled edge and press credentials, looks like a nice Italian boy from New Jersey. Which he was, once upon a time. When he pulls his tuxedo shirt off, it turns out that he's covered with tattoos and he looks more like a refugee from the Hells Angels, especially with a tire iron in his hand. He changes the flat in five minutes, puts his tux back on, and is off to snap Bill Clinton.

"Who the fuck is this guy?" I asked Gretchen.

"Oh, shit." She laughed. "You have to meet him. You guys will totally hit it off."

It turned out that Dave loved nothing better than pot, punk rock, and professional wrestling, and we got on like a house on fire. Right after we met, he flew straight back from covering the *Vanity Fair* Oscar party, to come to Queens with Holmstrom and me to get stoned with Rob Van Dam in the parking lot behind the Elks Lodge. On the way, we stopped at the White Castle on Queens Boulevard. Chomping on double-cheesers en route to the Arena of Pain, Dave flipped on the stereo and the Cramps came oozing out. "Edison," he said, "we just hit the Holy Trifecta of Sleaze." Turns out he was a Zen master, too.

Now he was working the *High Times* party. He got a photo of Joan Jett posing with the blowup of our magazine. I would have preferred if we had been able to pull some A-list movie stars, but who doesn't love Joan Jett? The next day that picture was everywhere, and that's all you really want from a party like this—some pop in the papers. Dave would continue to be my secret weapon, keeping us in the press whenever we had something we needed to make noise about.

The party was an unqualified smash. Even my biggest detractors congratulated me. I am sure I was the only person there who did not enjoy it.

Toward the end of the night I went up to the office in Irving Plaza to pay the bill. I had been carrying a check for seventeen thousand dollars around with me all night, which would cover the lion's share of our tab. I would pay the balance the next day. I also had a large cash tip for the bar staff, and I gave the owner a rare Zippo lighter with the old *High Times* logo on it as thanks for being part of the magazine's history. He told me that it had been a perfect experience and we were welcome anytime.

When I went back out into the club, it was empty. I was completely alone. So I went home. There was nobody there, either.

The *High Times* movie was written by Victor Colicchio and Nick Iacovino. Vic was the cowriter of Spike Lee's *Summer of Sam*, and this was going to be his next big project.

I met him at the Stonys—the *High Times* film awards.

The Stonys were Bloom's idea, and I applauded it. I thought it was a perfect publicity ploy and a good opportunity to make friends with some Hollywood types who might come around to realizing that *High Times* was a great vehicle in which to promote their films. One of our biggest problems was getting celebrities to be in the magazine—usually some worrywart of a publicist would freak out at the mere mention of our name. But the truth was that we hit a very good, very targeted audience, and for the right film or star, we were a great place to be seen.

In typical *High Times* style, having a good idea was not enough. Egos would have to flare before anything could happen. In the months leading up to the Stonys, the magazine was sorely neglected while Hager made elaborate plans to film the show and then make millions from broadcasting it. Of course that never happened.

Meanwhile, Bloom spent his time guzzling popcorn and salty snacks in dark screening rooms. At the outset, Bloom, never one to trouble himself with the trappings of humility, not so subtly anointed himself the *High Times* Film Czar, a pothead potentate appointed to decide what were the best "stoner movies." No debate was encouraged, and the criteria remained vague as to what would qualify a film to be nominated for a Stony. Even the definition of what constituted a "stoner movie" was problematic. Did there have to be actual pot smoking in the film to qualify? What about *Fantasia*, or the Marx Brothers' collective oeuvre—longtime favorites of the Alice B. Toklas crowd looking for a dose of *divertimento subversivo*? Unfortunately, Bloom had little knowledge of the history of film or the aesthetics of cinema, tools that the clever critic puts in his belt before proclaiming himself a pundit, stoned or not.

While the would-be movie *machers* put all their energy into the Stony Awards, magazine sales were drifting. Ski should have fired a cannon across the bow and reminded everyone that the point of having a *High Times*–branded awards show was to sell more magazines, and if the book suffered because of the event, they were killing their own cause before they even got started. Except that Ski was on the Nice-Nice Train to Happy Hagersville, and there would be no firing of cannons, only the gentle cupping of hippie balls while the magazine gasped for air.

But the event itself went well and was generally well received despite the ponderous nature of a four-hour awards show served up in a cloud of smoke. I had encouraged Bloom and Hager to keep the show down to two hours, which seemed like plenty of time to get the point across without turning this into a slacker ordeal ripe for ripping by whatever press we could gather (my job was to promote the event), but potheads are not known for brevity or efficiency, and the show lumbered on. Still, we won some good publicity—Dave Allocca came through again, and his photo of Tommy Chong and the Toxic Avenger made the entertainment pages. Even if we made zero contribution to the canon of film criticism (why did I still cling to the hope that *High Times* might be taken seriously by anyone?), Bloom had done a good job. Everyone especially liked the awards themselves: chrome-plated bongs with trophy-shop plaquettes that said STONY on them.

It was during the intermission (at the two-hour mark) that Alison Thompson and Victor approached me to talk about making the *High Times* movie. Because I had eschewed the diurnal pothead activewear of T-shirt and jeans, opting for raiment more apropos to an awards show— vintage art deco tie, black suit, black shirt, blue wing tips, gray-blue fedora—they naturally assumed that I was the serious-minded side of *High Times* and that they would have a better chance of having a lucid conversation with me than with someone who was wearing couture copped from the *High Times* merchandise table.

It always paid to dress up a little. When I had meetings with people out of the office, by phone or e-mail, they generally assumed that the guy from *High Times* would be lax with facial hair management issues and wearing leftovers from the Summer of Love, so they would try to appear cool by showing up in a LEGALIZE IT! T-shirt or some other badge of reefer-headed hip. When I made the scene clean-shaven and sporting a suave-as-fuck tie, I immediately had the upper hand. It never failed.

Victor Colicchio is a magnetic guy. He has an easy way about him for a guy who grew up in the deep Bronx, where he got the inspiration for *Summer of Sam*. He is also an actor and had a couple of small goombah roles on the big screen. He does a nice job in Woody Allen's *Bullets Over Broadway* and is part of Henry's crew in *Goodfellas*, besides acting in *Summer of Sam* and a plethora of TV cop shows. He also does a ripping Tony Curtis impersonation, which he picked up when he was working as a stand-in for the genuine article on *Naked in New York*. I liked him immediately. I think everyone who meets him does.

Victor's script was excellent. This was exactly the project we needed to take *High Times* to the movies, much like *National Lampoon* had done with *Animal House*. There were a lot more people out there for whom the brand resonated than who actually read the magazine, and this was a great opportunity to reach them.

High Times Potluck, as it would be titled, was not your typical stoner comedy. Something like "Cheech and Chong meet the Sopranos," *Potluck* would be an upbeat caper flick that centered around a middle-aged Italian mobster who discovers the magic of marijuana. The film follows a suitcase filled with pot as it changes hands—from an honest artist dealing to make ends meet, to the creeps who rob him, to the mobster, to a band of punk rock chicks who give it back to the mobster, who tries to sell it to another dealer so he can get some dough to give to the punk rock girls because he has taken a shine to their singer.

It was very shrewd, and the conceit of the suitcase passing from hand to hand anchored a large ensemble cast that would finally come together at the end of the film at a giant New York City marijuana rally, making it the *It's a Mad Mad Mad Mad World* of pot. The entire film was to be shot on location with a gritty urban look. In fact, this would be Alison's first time directing anything like this—she was a documentary filmmaker who had shot for *National Geographic*, and she wanted to exploit her talents to show off New York City as a stark landscape inhabited by its own indigenous wildlife.

It was a no-lose situation for *High Times*. The deal was structured so that we had no capital investment in the picture. Most of the money—a million-dollar budget—had already been raised, and now with *High Times*'s name on it, there would be a fresh buzz about the project to get the next round of financing. All we had to do was provide our name, marketing support, and some consulting in our area of expertise, and we'd get a cut on the back end. Bloom and I would share an executive producer credit.

Vic and his team had put together a first-rate cast and crew. Michael Green, the director of photography, had worked on every Woody Allen film since *Radio Days*, as well as on a slew of other features, TV, and commercials. Paul Bernard, the assistant director (and also one of the film's producers), was at the top of his profession and had just finished a string of gigs including *Mars Attacks!*, *Three Kings*, *Any Given Sunday*, and *The Patriot*, all enormous jobs. That they could get people of this caliber to work on a *High Times* film was a testament to the power of our brand. Everyone worked for minimum pay because they loved the project.

The cast was a combination of unknowns, well-respected hardly knowns, and a few ringers, including Stony superstar Tommy Chong, and Jason Mewes, famous for his role as pothead deluxe Jay in the Jay and Silent Bob films. Frank Gorshin, who played the Riddler on the *Batman* TV series, was in. Dan Lauria, who is probably most famous for his role as the dad on the TV show *The Wonder Years* but has done a shitload of television and theater, played the mob boss. He is an extraordinary actor. When he gave his Big Speech at the film's climax, an overwrought soliloquy on the meaning of "family," half the crew cried openly. Sylvia Miles, who had received Academy Award nominations for her supporting parts in *Midnight Cowboy* and *Farewell, My Lovely*, burned a hole in the screen as a crazy old lady who taunted her criminal children into a life of crime so they could buy pot for her glaucoma.

The lead roles—Frank, the Mafia hit man, and Jade, the sexy young punk rocker—were played by Frank Adonis and Theo Kogan.

When the casting began, Alison asked me if I had ever heard of a band called the Lunachicks. Heard of them? I was one of them! Theo was their bombshell singer, and the rest of the girls were on to play her band. Theo had been in a few films (she was Cool Tattoo Girl in *Zoolander*, and Prostitute in *Bring Out the Dead*), but this was her first starring role.

Frank Adonis was a veteran. You can see him lurking in the background in Scorsese's tough-guy epics *Goodfellas*, *Casino*, and *Raging Bull*. He was in *Wall Street*, *King of New York*, and *Bad Lieutenant*, and was exceptional in *The Eyes of Laura Mars* as Sal Volpe, the role that brought him to Scorsese's attention.

The rest of the cast—fifty-eight speaking parts—was filled out by an ensemble of up-and-comers and local luminaries. It was an enormous talent roster. Vic had written an incredibly ambitious screenplay that was not going to be easy to execute in a shooting schedule of thirty days.

Making Bloom a "producer" may not have been the best idea, but we were counting on him to use his connections as *High Times* music editor to help pull together a killer sound track for the film. Obviously the music was going to be a crucial element to marketing this movie, and he was making Big Promises.

But it went right to his head, and he began showing up every day during filming, swaggering behind the cameras and asking everyone—actors, crew, whomever—if they wanted to *smoke*. These people were working, and there was no way they were going to toke up in the middle of shooting a feature film. It was no wonder people made fun of *High Times*. The only surprising thing was that Bloom still didn't get it.

"I wanted Bloom barred from the set," Victor told me later. "He was disruptive. He didn't know when to speak or when not to interfere. As he was watching scenes, he was rewriting things—and he wanted us to refilm them! People were complaining. There was a conscious effort to lie to him about locations."

Was it Jim Morrison who said that the logical extension of living in America was to become God? I posit that a logical extension of living in New York City is to be in a movie. I scored big with my role as Stabbing Victim.

We shot my scene after midnight on Bleecker Street, a block from CBGB. We had a spring-loaded knife that was going to be stuck in my thigh by one of the Bad Guys as I came around the corner. I was playing a witless tourist who was in the wrong place at the wrong time. I'd hit the ground, and the cops, including Vic, who played the lead detective, would have to stop chasing the thugs to keep me from dying.

There are three things I have learned from professional wrestling: *sell*, *sell*, and *sell*, and when it was time to do the bit, I was determined to make it look like the Crime of the Century. I was in the moment, as Marlon Brando might have said, and when I took the knife in my leg, I hit the sidewalk hard.

Alison called cut. "That was great, Mike. Let's do it again. I want to see a little more of your face when you hit the ground."

I did it again, this time falling with my face cheated toward the camera, contorted in pain. That was no act; the sidewalk came up fast and took a bite out of me.

"Great, Mike. Let's go one more time."

We ended up doing it six times from different angles, until my entire side was bruised purple from taking the bump. I earned a nice round of applause from the crew, many of whom had been advocating the use of a fake rubber sidewalk.

The next shot was a bloody close-up. Up until now there was no "juice." By way of special effects, I was to hold the blood bag in my hands, and when the knife went into my leg, I would grab the wound, pop the bag, and the blood would start flying. Since there was no duplicate wardrobe to change into, we had only one shot to get it right. In went the knife, I hit the pavement one more time, and the claret was tapped. It was a good mess.

Even though I got stabbed in the thigh, thanks to a tricky angle, onscreen it looked like I took the knife in the balls. Which would cause some considerable groaning from audiences and some worried looks from potential paramours who would require personal assurance that my equipment had been left in perfect working order.

By the time we finished my stunt, it was 4:00 a.m. and I was rawboned and covered in gore. I had a great time filming the part, a real dream come true, but now all I wanted was to go home and drink a cold beer in a hot shower. I hailed a cab and told him where I lived.

The driver took a look at my hands and leg, saturated with stage blood. "Look, buddy." He recoiled. "I think I oughta take you to the hospital." I still had a little left in me. "No," I gasped, still deep inside the character of Stabbing Victim. "Must . . . go . . . home . . . must . . . feed . . . cats." Much accustomed to nutcases climbing into his hack, he just shrugged and took me home. I tipped him well.

Back at the ranch, the rancor smoldered unabated. There was actually a contingent, led by Hager, who sometimes seemed to be rooting against the success of the film, presumably so he could say "told you so" and use our failure to leverage his own mishmash of a project. I think he felt that if we succeeded, he would never have a chance at making his own movie, when in reality, if this film did what it was supposed to, it would open the doors to all sorts of projects.

At some point during the production Vic made a not so subtle appeal to Hager's ego and put him in the film, which succeeded in getting him on board. But after he saw that it was only going to be a walk-on cameo, he went back to hating the movie. It didn't help that I was the one who was shepherding the project along from the inside.

Vic seethed. "Ski says not to deal with you because you won't be here for too much longer; you are making too much money. And Hager has a problem with you bringing the magazine into the future—it's like he is accusing you of some scientific experiment, like cloning humans."

I was stoic. I wanted to see this film happen, but Vic was getting sick of dealing with the *High Times* merry-go-round.

"I have a hard time understanding any of these guys. When I first brought in the script, I heard a big complaint that we don't represent the 'stoner community.' How could we make a movie without the 'hey dude' dudes? So we wrote them in. And then I get accused of stereotyping pot smokers! What annoys them one day pleases them the next, and vice versa. We have meetings and we talk all day without anything being discussed. It's like being in *Groundhog Day*. The same shit happens over and over and over again."

Meanwhile, production moved along, but it was becoming clear that Alison was the wrong director for this film. She was great with lions and tigers, but not so much with people. And she knew virtually nothing about pot. She didn't speak the lingua franca of the daily doper—she couldn't roll a fatty, navigate a hookah, or pick the Allman Brothers out of a police lineup. She didn't know Cheech from Chong, let alone the difference between *indica* and *sativa*.

What she did know was that if she got behind a film written by the screenwriter of *Summer of Sam* and tagged with the *High Times* brand, she had a shot at making a splash with her first feature. Alison came to the table with a good bit of the financing for the film. Given her experience filming in the jungles of Africa—and Vic's vision of presenting New York City as some sort of wildlife preserve for untamed artists, punk rockers, and hippies—she got the job, with the caveat that Vic would be in the backseat helping her drive. Which was a plan architected for disaster.

No director wants to be told what to do, and it wasn't long before she was feuding with Vic. She needed his input but didn't want the cast or crew to know that he was the "man behind the curtain," so she insisted on creating a complicated series of codes and signals that they would use whenever she needed his help, or when Vic needed to contribute. It was a huge distraction, and she had a hard time bringing to the screen the energy required to pull off a *High Times* cops-and-robbers doper flick. The chemistry between the principal characters, Frank and Theo, never boiled as much as it fizzled.

Frank is deceptively subtle—you can't see him act—which is why, or so I have been told, Scorsese keeps coming back to him. As a Mafia hit man, he is a stone-cold killer who buries his emotions. Theo, on the other hand, is a beautiful, exuberant rock 'n' roller who needed to work into her role the same zest she brings to her band. But as a less-experienced screen actress, she fell into Frank's rhythms, and Frank, used to painting with a more ethereal palette, didn't deliver the big performance that an upbeat pot comedy demanded. Many of their scenes together fell flat.

Jason Mewes, too, needed a good kick in the ass. As a pot dealer, he came off a bit too creepy, sniffling and rubbing his nose like he had drug problems more worrisome than the wacky tabacky, but for some reason Alison didn't twig to it. Jason has great charisma, and it was a coup to get him, but he didn't shine anywhere near the way he was supposed to.

Still, there was a lot to like about this film, and if Alison had concentrated on making a *good* movie rather than a *great* movie (she reminded me more than once that Orson Welles's first picture was *Citizen Kane*), I think the end result would have been more even. There were a lot of miscues and mistakes just from overreaching.

But the good parts are terrific. The mob guys were particularly endearing. It was a great group of crusty old men mostly sitting around the social club grunting at one another, and the whole film seems to perk up whenever they are on-screen. The Big Finish, at the pot rally, packs a good punch, when the various threads of the plot come together, centered around Frank's reunion with his drag queen son, whom he has finally forgiven for his transgressions. It is an unapologetically happy ending: the gangsters have traded their guns for ganja, and all is right with the world. Cue the music, *bada-bing badda-boom*, and everyone leaves the theater ready to bust some corn.

I was on the set every day as a "consultant." As part of my job I rolled more than four hundred joints—trumpet-shaped spliffs, New York pinners, bombers that looked like snakes that swallowed dogs, seven-paper monstrosities, and an armory's worth of basic, *prêt-à-fumer* doobies. That was probably the best job I ever had.

I helped Alison plow the depths of stoner nuance as best I could, and I rounded up an arsenal of handblown glass pipes and bongs. I was even able to find a working Buzzbee.

But my biggest contribution was the ChroniCaster: a fully functional bong-guitar to be wielded by Tommy Chong.

Originally the *Potluck* script had called for Jimi Hendrix's guitar to be given away at a raffle at the pot rally, but that seemed a bit too on the nose, and anyway, the Hendrix family was sure to have something to say about it. I suggested we make a *High Times* guitar. We had already created one for a contest—a bright green number with a rhinestone pot leaf below the bridge, luthiered by a madman named Joe Naylor, who runs a company called Reverend Musical Instruments out of Eastpointe, Michigan, near Detroit. I called him up, and when he heard that Tommy Chong could be wailing on his next creation in the *High Times* movie, he faxed me his idea for a "bong-guitar," which was to the first *High Times* guitar what the space shuttle is to a slingshot: an engineering masterpiece. Much more ambitious than my original idea of retrofitting a pipe onto an existing design, this would be made of Lucite, front and back, and the body would be like the chamber in a bong. The bowl of the pipe rested on top of the body, and smoke was drawn through surgical tubing, magically filling up the clear guitar. But the best thing about it was that it was actually going to be a bitchin' guitar—the design called for a pair of screaming P-90 pickups, locking tuners, and a rosewood neck. It would be the ultimate rock 'n' roll prop, on a par with Iron Maiden's giant monster mascot, Eddie, or with Pink Floyd's inflatable pig.

When I explained to Vic and the producers that we had a custom-made bong-guitar coming, they were floored. There was only one problem. By the time Joe and I had worked out the nuances of the ChroniCaster, the film was already in production, and now the script would have to be rewritten to accommodate the new gimmick. Even though there were a few days before we had to shoot the guitar, there were scenes that had dialogue to establish the Quest for the Chroni-Caster, and we were shooting them *that day*. Not only would we be fucked if we shot a scene with characters talking about a guitar that didn't show up—as far as everyone was concerned, it was still in the dream stage—the dialogue to set up the ChroniCaster had to be written in half an hour. It didn't help that no one knew what the thing would actually look like. All I had was the drawing Joe had faxed over, which was more like the lunatic sketches of a dime-bag da Vinci than the blueprint for anything that could conceivably be built by anyone lacking access to the Jet Propulsion Laboratory. It inspired little confidence.

I told everyone not to worry, I had everything under control. "I'm not like the others; you can trust me." They bought it. But meanwhile I was praying that the guitar would show up when it was supposed to. I mean, Joe seemed like a reliable guy, but what the fuck did I know? People who get excited about building bong-guitars are a breed apart.

Vic immediately sat me down on the set with him (in those big director's chairs you always dream about), and we started writing new lines for the principal stoners, who were going to be bugging out about the guitar, for the camera, in just a few moments.

STONER NO. 1: Dude, that's no ordinary guitar.
STONER NO. 2: It's more like a bong with strings!
STONER NO. 1: You can play it . . .
STONER NO. 2: You can smoke it . . .
TOGETHER: You can play smokin' it! It's the ChroniCaster!

It wasn't Paddy Chayefsky, but I understand that William Faulkner had a similar experience during his Hollywood days. Ten minutes after we had written those lines, they were coming out of the actors' mouths. It was scary, an oddly Zeus-like feeling. I learned more about filmmaking that day than I did in two years at NYU.

Joe Naylor, it turned out, was something of a wizard. The Chroni-Caster showed up on time, a jaw-dropping, one-of-a-kind pimp-my-guitar masterpiece. Never underestimate the impact of a fully functional, hot-wired bong-guitar.

Unfortunately, the Whoa! Factor of the ChroniCaster died hard when Tommy Chong refused to play it live for the cameras. He's a very good guitar player, but he didn't want to take chances on flubbing the part, and he insisted that it be overdubbed.

The impact of the ChroniCaster came from the fact that it wasn't a trick—some mad genius had built this contraption for the movie and it actually worked. Tommy needed to *sell it*. It still looked pretty cool, filling up with smoke while Tommy posed with it, but with the sound obviously added later, it just didn't deliver the "Holy Shit" moment it should have. Weeks later we screened a *Potluck* video teaser in front of a stoned test audience of a couple hundred people, featuring a demonstration of the ChroniCaster. I showed it front and back, so everyone could see how it worked, and then smoked from it while I fumbled through a few riffs. There was an audible, gushing, spontaneous exclamation of "Cool!" when the guitar filled up with smoke, and afterward I was swarmed with people offering me fat Baggies of the stankiest buds if they could just try it themselves.

Tommy later told Vic that he thought the film was going to be some slapped-together piece of shit, and if he knew that Vic had written *Summer of Sam*, he would have prepared differently. Fuck. If Tommy Chong—a guy whose fame peaked when he drove an ice-cream truck made of weed—didn't take *High Times* seriously, we probably didn't have much of a chance with Hollywood at Large.

Somehow I was still around when it was Stony time again the next year. Even if the paranoia and hedging of bets by *High Times* was undermining *Potluck*, I was still living my dream of producing a drug film.

My main job remained director of editorial and marketing, still not a bad gig, since no one had ever figured out what that meant exactly. I made it up as I went along. I went to New Orleans for Jazz Fest wearing a *High Times* press badge, a triumphant return ten years after my whirlwind tour with Wally Wang. It was a good trip—I gobbled some mushrooms on a party boat, ate alligator pie for breakfast, and spent my afternoons in the Gospel Tent.

I wrote a few record reviews, mostly of stuff I needed free copies of; scribbled an obituary for Frank Sinatra ("beyond hopeless romantics giddy with bone-dry martinis and spurned lovers drowning in last-call whiskey shots with the bartender, Frank resonated with macho in the styles of Jim Morrison and Iggy Pop, who started their careers by re-inventing Sinatra's signature crooning and spanking it with fistfuls of blotter acid and electric guitars"); and composed a snarky denunciation of prog rock, which to me seemed like easy pickin's, but got Ski all up in arms because it skewered the bloops and bleeps of the synthesizer dorks he so cherished.

I produced a *High Times* CD of jam bands and worked on licensing a Spanish-language version of the magazine, which was a dismal failure. No one at *High Times* could figure out why we would possibly want to publish a magazine in Spain. And I worked on the award shows, writing press releases and generally trying to drum up some interest in the mainstream press.

This year's Stony Awards were more like an experiment in social entropy than any sort of Happening. I was standing in the lobby of the theater trying to get a handle on things when David Peel, the folksinging guerrilla and *Potluck* star (his 1972 album *The Pope Smokes Dope* was produced by John Lennon), burst in off the street with his scraggly troupe of grimy Greenwich Village relics, strumming and singing his signature song-cum-chant, "Have a Marijuana." It was a din of dysfunction, disruptive, and frankly disgusting, a live-action diorama depicting all at once everything that is wrong with hippies, folk music, and reefer.

Guest of honor Dan Hedaya (who, among other things, played Richard Nixon in the pothead political farce *Dick*, and Alicia Silverstone's father in *Clueless*) got one look at these animals and headed straight for the door. Hastily exiting the theater and turning the corner, he nearly knocked over his fellow thespian, would-be *Potluck* star Jason Mewes, who was whiter than the ghost of Hamlet's father and puking violently in the street. This did nothing to ameliorate Dan's fears that he never should have accepted the invitation to the Stonys in the first place. I have never seen a man so horrified. Against all odds, Dave Allocca, truly a magician, managed to wrangle them together for a human-looking picture, which made the paper the next day. It helps to hire people who know what the fuck they are doing.

Around this time I was starting to think that a comedy was the wrong line of thinking, and we should have made a disaster flick. I'd often heard tales of the Curse of Tom Forçade: that the chaos that always seemed to cast its spell on *High Times* was his phantom spirit rattling the cages. John Holmstrom used to say that *High Times* was Forçade's last great prank: he never intended it to be a legacy, and now everyone was suffering for what the founder intended as a grand practical joke.

There was a TV camera there that night, a local crew looking for an interview with one of the semi-luminaries who was probably backstage huffing some centerfold weed. They asked Hager, who was running the show, if he could find someone for them to talk to, but he had no idea where anyone was. True to form, he melted down and started yelling at me. Except this time it was in front of a TV crew.

"You're my publicist!" he screamed, like a spoiled heiress. "Do your job!"

I was livid. The television crew was mortified. If they had decided to have some fun and push "record," we would have had a Hindenburg-size PR disaster on our hands. I can only hazard that they were too shocked at Hager's behavior to tape this episode and fire it off immediately to *America's Most Embarrassing Home Videos.*

That was the tipping point. Right then I knew I was going to have to find a new job. I never even understood where this animosity came from. What ever happened to the archetype of the "laid-back stoner"? I was sick of taking it on the chin from this asshole. I did what I had to do so the TV people got what they needed, and then I got the fuck out of there and went across the street to the Mars Bar to steel myself with several fistfuls of bourbon.

I was fired soon after that. But not before Ski was let go. My take-no-prisoners approach to publishing had made the company a boatload, but at the expense of the idyllic editorial dystopia that somehow trumped the bottom line. Ski's laissez-faire approach to shepherding the magazine kept everyone happily grazing on the greenery, but business drooped like a drunkard's dick. He was not invited to stay.

The new publisher—this would be the third in the four years since I came on board—made his entrance dressed in pale yellow slacks and a pale yellow V-neck sweater, what I imagine he thought passed as white-boy hip-hop chic. He claimed to be some kind of marketing whiz. He looked like a stick of butter.

The Stick of Butter wasted little time in calling me into his office. Wanda the Evil Accountant was there. I knew what was happening. You can smell these things from a mile away.

I was plenty pissed off—but not for being fired. I would have fired me, too. Had I not been handcuffed coming in, I would have chopped a few heads and staffed up with people loyal to me. As it was, I was number two on the masthead, and he wanted his own guy in there. That made good Machiavellian sense. Unfortunately, he was a classless turd who had the idea that he could treat me like an idiot. That's why I was pissed off.

"Mike, this isn't personal."

"I know it's not personal. How could it be personal? You don't know me."

"Mike, frankly, for what you're making, I could hire two college kids . . ." I loved this logic—they keep giving me raises and bonuses, then fire me because I'm making too much. And then to suggest that a couple of unformed children could possibly replace a professional who had been successfully mining the underbelly of magazine publishing for fifteen years? Whatever. But that's not what set me off.

The Stick of Butter pushed a heap of legal documents at me. "Mike, I would appreciate it if you signed these papers." Now *that* was crazy. Did he really think I was going to sign something handed to me by the hostile publisher of a dope magazine without reviewing it carefully? I used to be the hostile publisher of a dope magazine. I knew all too well the kind of shit we tried to pull.

"Are you fucking out of your mind? You really want me to sign something without reading it? Get me Michael Kennedy on the phone right fucking now. Michael has been my lawyer for the last four years, and he would have had my head on a plate if I even thought about signing something without reading it. Don't tell me it's not personal and then try to fuck me. Do you always fuck strangers? Are you some kind of whore? Get me Michael Kennedy on the phone right fucking now."

Wanda the Evil Accountant nodded toward the phone. What I said made sense.

While Margarine Man called Michael, I took a look-see at the papers. They were trying to cheap out on a severance package, which was typical Wanda parsimony. She hated paying anyone, even though accounts payable was her job. It was no wonder she was miserable all the time.

A meeting was set with Michael for later in the week, and I was politely asked to pack and get the fuck out of the office. On the way home I stopped in a cliché and got shitfaced.

A few days later at Michael's office, I was, once again, clean, shaved, and sober, just like the first time I had met him.

"Michael, with all due respect, this severance package is unacceptable."

He was gracious but hesitant. He ducked and weaved and said there wasn't anything he could do about it, which of course was bullshit. Michael did not become a successful lawyer because he was a pushover.

"Michael, you are the one who taught me that everything is negotiable—and never to take the first offer."

He rope-a-doped some more.

"I really don't know what we can do for you . . ."

"Michael, look, you told me I had job security."

"When did I say that?"

"On October 13, in the tenth-floor conference room, at around three-thirty in the afternoon. Michael, you also taught me to always take notes."

He sat back and sighed. After 9/11 the entire publishing industry had fallen into serious trouble, and Michael had made a special trip to the office to talk about it with the staff. There were going to be hard times ahead, he warned, but he also told me that if I continued to bring value to the company, as I had, my job would always be safe.

A few days later he called back with a new offer, which I accepted. The guys at *High Times* might not dig it, but sometimes it pays to get up in the morning and put on a suit.

Whether it was vanity or intellectual laziness or fear of being exposed as having run out of ideas, or some combination of future phobia and refusal to accept the present, refusal to grow up, and refusal to accept that most of the innovations of the counterculture—from hippie fashions to rock 'n' roll to organic food—had been co-opted by the mainstream, Hager had doomed *High Times* to the ignominy of insignificance. In a postmodern world, it was shocking that *High Times* was unable to reference anything but its own history. Instead of embracing success, the staff was threatened by it. They could always sell magazines to potheads and closet farmers, but when it came to inserting themselves vertically into American culture, they were soft. No one took them seriously. It made me profoundly sad.

I was sick of having my heart broken. It was time to get out of town for a while and blow all the bad shit out of my head. I flew to Spain, to Las Fallas, a festival where they set a town on fire and everyone drops acid and watches it burn. Living well, after all, is always the best revenge.

18

NARCISSISM AND DOOM

1. Sex magazines
2. Beer magazine
3. Pot magazine

That's not a résumé, that's a crime scene. I didn't even bother to list my years working the wrestling beat. I was in enough trouble already—why gild the lily?

Once again, I needed a job. I still had *Screw* magazine on speed dial, so I gave them a shout. They might be in the market for a smut peddler with a pedigree.

My old gun-toting pal Chip from Drake days was now the managing editor and in charge of hiring writers—Al Goldstein mostly sat in his office and ordered overpriced electronic gadgets from the Hammacher Schlemmer catalog. I figured if Chip saw me floating in the gutter, he might buy me a bottle of wine.

It was no charity—he desperately needed someone to review the mountainous pile of pud pullers that were threatening to take over the office. He had been writing the reviews himself, and it had finally begun to hurt. Man of Steel that I am, I took the gig immediately and began writing under the name Lord Zeppelin.

It is harder than you might imagine to find someone to critique porn movies, at least someone sentient, who still had his sight after years of chronic self-abuse. I occasionally reviewed these clarion calls to auto-stimulation back in the *Cheri* days, but it was never my favorite part of the job. Mostly the stuff I had to watch wasn't all that interesting. I was working in a den of filth every day, and all I really wanted to watch was *The Sorrow and the Pity*, anything just to bring me closer to the planed edge of reality. But if this is what it would take to pay the bills, I was game.

Pornography is an illusion painted as reality, more fantastic than any James Bond movie or *Star Wars*. The sex in these movies doesn't exist. You could be the best-looking cable repairman in the world, carrying twelve inches of salty lunch meat in your shorts, but there is no way on God's Green Earth that you are ever going to end up having your mind—or anything else—blown by a raven-haired, double-breasted mattress thrasher with bee-stung lips, welcoming thighs, and a dewy pudenda who answers the door in a diaphanous kimono and nine-inch heels, caressing a bottle of baby oil. You have a better chance of becoming a Jedi knight and destroying the Death Star.

What's really scary about the porn movie business is just how geeky the fans who watch this crud really are. It may not be surprising that hard-core porn fans often suffer from a lack of social skills, but what you probably don't realize is that they could go toe-to-toe with Comic Book Guy or a dozen tribble-loving Trekkies in their knowledge of their hobby and its mind-melting minutiae. Fucking by its very nature is a repetitive business, but you can bet that porn fans, *real* porn fans—not guys who "look" at it once in a while—can pontificate endlessly on the Rubik's Cube of multi-partner variations with *Kama Sutra*–like authority, and discuss the subtleties of double penetration with the verbal alacrity of Gael Greene deconstructing dinner at Le Cirque.

Thankfully, the *Screw* style does not cater to such gentility. Reviewing seven volumes' worth of *Omar's Anal Adventures* for our special Black History Month issue, Herr Zeppelin effused, "Omar spunks so much spizzle in this jizz-fest you'd think he had a jar of Hellman's hidden in his ass!"

While I was toiling under the weight of a pseudonym as heavy as Lord Zeppelin, progress on *Potluck*—I was still involved in the project as a producer, and still tight with Vic and the filmmakers, who encouraged my involvement—continued to be rained on by the dark clouds at *High Times*. The Stick of Butter wanted nothing to do with it and, conspiring with Hager and his cabal of cotton-mouthed cohorts, finally gave the production an official vote of No Confidence. The message resonated: if *High Times* wasn't going to get behind its own film, you can bet your last jazz cigarette that no major distributor was going to, either.

Bloom continued to advocate for *High Times* to support the film, but he had dropped the ball and ended up getting exactly none of the bands he had promised for the sound track. Without a killer soundtrack, a stoner movie was like pancakes without syrup—hard to swallow.

No matter how stoned you were, *Potluck* was never going to be a *great* movie, there was just too much gone wrong with it, but it had a fun, easygoing vibe and won some minor accolades on the festival circuit. At the New York International Independent Film and Video Arts Festival it took the audience award for Best Feature, and in Atlantic City it scored the jury prize for Best Comedy.

I was even invited to speak at a screening of *Potluck* at the NYU film school, and there was an article about me in the school paper with the headline DROPOUT PRODUCES POT FILM. I was quoted as saying, "Education is the biggest sham in America. I encourage everyone to drop out of NYU." The kids ate that shit up with a spoon (although I don't think any of them actually took my advice). Sixteen years after Dave Insurgent and I were laughed out of our production class for pitching punk-rock zombies and the Great Spliff of Knowledge, I was being bombarded with questions from a roomful of future Spielbergs who wanted to know the secret of my success (and what was up with the fake weed in *High Times?*).

But the reviews were brutal. *The Village Voice* said, "The movie's egregious buzzkills—hazy plot, jarring non sequiturs, pointless pothead-celebrity cameos—defy even herbally-enhanced viewing." The *Toronto Star* offered, "First-time Australian Director Alison Thompson . . . really doesn't have a clue what she's doing." After a brief theatrical release, the film went straight to DVD.

As a movie producer, I had a bright future behind me.

The two hundred bucks a week I was getting from Al Goldstein and *Screw* to keep America up to date on the state of the video squack market was just about paying for my beer and helping to fund an Internet dating habit I was slowly developing. But my savings account was wilting like the last rose of summer. Unfortunately, the market for thirty-something editors was not blossoming in the post-9/11 zeitgeist. A lot of magazines had purged their staffs, and senior editors who survived the cuts were holding on to their jobs with the same sanguine sense of propriety that a pit bull takes to a pork chop. It was a lousy time to be in the magazine racket.

My mom let me know that she was appalled that I was back in the skin trade by clucking her tongue and sighing heavily, which is how Jewish mothers signal displeasure to their children. As a tribe, they would make an excellent subject for a treatise on sociolinguistics. But she was unambiguous in her offer of support: after harping about how I should find a new career ("Maybe you can teach English?"), she told me to call her if I needed anything, that I could count on her.

Both my parents had remarried and were a lot happier, but my mom was wearing it especially well. She's a neurotic Jewish mother who had her heart torn out when her world began twirling violently off its axis—she didn't sign on to be a single mom, she was looking forward to a life of bar mitzvahs and baby showers. I should have been married by now and giving her brilliant grandchildren with sparkling blue eyes for her to dandle on her knee. For the first time she was being genuinely supportive. I welcomed it and it was the beginning of a much-repaired, healthy relationship.

My father, however, was always somehow able to make me feel as though the dismal American economy was somehow my fault.

At least Grandma was happy that I wasn't working for "that dope rag" anymore. Sex magazines were much better (I was always honest with Grandma about what I did, she deserved no less)—at least *sex* might lead to *children*.

Mostly Grandma wanted to know if I was seeing anyone, and did I ever speak to "whatshername, that lawyer you were living with." I wasn't, and I didn't. Grandma suggested that I try the Internet.

Being the booby prize in a drunken dance contest was far preferable to trolling cyberspace for hard-luck cases, especially on the advice of my eighty-five-year-old grandma. But the old trout made some sense.

My first foray into the cesspool of Internet dating was a little reconnaissance on a Jewish dating site—I figured I owed Grandma at least that much for all the pills I swiped from her when I was a teenager.

By way of jumping into the abyss, I skipped the Internet part of the ritual mating dance and took a flyer on one of those "parties" that these cyber-yentas were always hosting, figuring the worst-case scenario would be two hours of free booze.

Someone (I think it was Al Gore) once described twenty-first-century America as "a culture of narcissism and doom," and it was all there at the event I attended. The place was lousy with brash whores and mousy little bitches. And the women were even worse. Louis Vuitton bags, French nails, and Atkins casualties bathed in sickly sweet perfume circled the room like vultures, while dickheads in khaki Dockers made snappy patter and tried to impress each other, reliving their frat-boy days at Zeta Beta Tau by ordering watered-down kamikaze shots at the bar.

There are few things scarier than a thirty-nine-year-old single Jewish woman cruising a JDate mixer in four-hundred-dollar Manolo Blahniks that are slicing her feet into pastrami, except for maybe the forty-year-old male virgin sulking in the corner to a soundtrack of diluted hip-hop spun by a DJ wearing a tricolored Rasta yarmulke and in desperate need of a bath. I fled that scene like Moses hauling ass out of Egypt. But I am nothing if not compassionate, and it gave me the idea to use my connections at *Screw* and teach a class in how to haggle with a hooker with a minimum of hassle. (By the way, do you know why Jewish guys like to look at porn movies backward? They love the part when the hooker gives the money back.)

Undeterred, I put an ad-for-self up on a slightly hipper dating website. I wrote "I am as comfortable in jeans as I am in a little black dress." That's how most of the women's profiles read, so I figured what they were looking for was a man who felt the same way. Within a week my mailbox was filled with the dewy scent of hopeful responses.

It's amazing how many women there are in New York who just want to get drunk and fuck. *Three.* And they were really quite nice. We went out and charmed each other and got sloppy and went home together and then never saw each other again—I am assuming because we were both too embarrassed, although it could just as easily have been because they weren't impressed with the rectitude of my moral compass after twenty-eight margaritas. It must have been all that salt.

Even though I can be a little bit slutty when the mood strikes, I am hardwired to be a gentleman, and I always insist on picking up the tab on a first date. You know in the first five minutes (five seconds?) whether you are ever going to get together, whether it is that night or on the third date, but to bail capriciously on dinner after the first cocktail would have just been uncouth. Say what you like, but I'm no cad. People have feelings, and I never want to be in the position of hurting someone else, except, of course, on purpose.

This ontology was costing me a couple of hundred dollars a week. At least the profile I posted was honest—I may have rounded up my height and rounded down my weight, but that was just for the sake of dealing in whole numbers. Some of the women I met had misrepresented their weight by entire zip codes.

A good, steady job remained elusive, but one remaining benefit of the life of a freelance porn slinger was that there was time to get back into the music, and the Raunch Hands managed to pull together a two-week tour of Spain. Watching porn tapes for a living was making me a little edgy. Literally or figuratively, I was ready to throw the fireball.

Chandler's experiment with clean living was still on shaky ground. He had been bouncing dangerously between recovery and recidivism, but he assured us that he was okay to get back in the van. Mariconda and I had a little powwow before we left: we promised that there were to be no more bags of mystery pills on this jaunt, and no excessive day drinking, either, just our regular short beers for breakfast and however many bottles of Rioja were reasonably needed to wash down some typical Spanish lunch—say, four. Or maybe five, if it was paella day. And then maybe one, but *only* one, of those kooky coffee-and-brandy concoctions. But that was it until sound check. Unless we were holding some coke, and then perhaps a small line. But only as a *digestif*. After all, we weren't animals. We made no promises that we'd stay sober, but agreed that we'd try at least to wait until the sun went down before we started to get seriously weird.

Predictably, after ten straight shows, the wheels came off the cart and we defaulted to our reprobate instincts. When Norah from the Pleasure Fuckers joined us for a few gigs, we were doing shooters and bumps in the van at 140 kilometers per hour on the way to the club.

It was a good tour, especially the show in Madrid, which was a spectacular homecoming for us. It seemed as if the whole city was there. But Chandler wasn't ready to rejoin the Raunch Hands yet, and after the tour he wound up back in rehab. It would be a while before we saw him again.

I had also begun my own band, the Edison Rocket Train.

Originally, the concept had been to call the group the New York Sheiks. I was out from behind the drums, hollering and slashing away at the guitar, often with a bottleneck slide, and wearing a kaffiyeh, the traditional Arab headdress.

My persona of the Original New York Sheik was based on a rich subculture of blues singers, matinee idols, and bad-guy professional wrestlers. Never mind Lord Zeppelin's highbrow critical analyses—unifying these disparate strands of popular culture was clearly my greatest scholarly achievement. My personal string theory.

Although the image of a sheik now all too frequently conjures waves of hatred, back in the 1920s and '30s, to be a sheik meant to be a supercool dude, a ladies' man, a player, a pimp, a badass mutherfucker, the very symbol of virility. That's why prophylactics were called "sheiks." In those days, Rudolph Valentino, as Sheik Ahmed Ben Hassan, was the most poweful potentate of the silent screen's dreamy-eyed lovers, and that's where the Mississippi Sheiks, a famous prewar country blues combo (who wrote "Sitting on Top of the World," later covered by Howlin' Wolf, the Grateful Dead, and Cream, among others), got their handle. As far as I know, they didn't dress up like actual sheiks—they were a street band whose wardrobe would have fit in just as well in a cotton field—but Sam the Sham and the Pharaohs ("Wooly Bully") loved to parade around looking like Egyptian acid casualties, and even Elvis took a sheik trip in *Harum Scarum*. It was a time-tested gimmick. Like I always say, if it's good enough for the King of Rock 'n' Roll, then it's good enough for me.

The greatest Sheik of them all, of course, was the original fire-throwing Sheik from Detroit—the most feared professional wrestler of all time—and in fact the first song we did was a stomping rewrite of "I Like to Hurt People," the title song from a documentary about a movement to ban him from the ring. The weird thing was that when I put on the Sheik outfit, I sang better.

But mostly we were a filthy blues band, albeit with punk rock tendencies. I was sick to death of what "blues" had become—shucking and jiving for yuppies drinking Lite Beer, a shopping-mall version of down-home Chicago, the soundtrack to an endless commercial promising "good times and good friends." It's what I call the Happy Horseshit Hour, and it made me want to kill myself. The last time I was in a blues club in Chicago, the band was so slicked up, "soulful," and "funky," they would not have sounded bluesy if you ran over them with a hearse in a graveyard at midnight.

With Satan mixing the sound.

To whip the band into shape, we played every Thursday for months at Handsome Dick Manitoba's bar. Manitoba was himself a former professional wrestler turned rock 'n' roll legend, and he fronted the proto-punk heavyweights the Dictators. He fed us beer and cognac while we worked out our set in front of an audience of confused dipsomaniacs.

Everybody loved the New York Sheiks, but after 9/11 it became very clear very quickly that any sort of Middle Eastern imagery was going to be a marketing disaster of New Coke proportions, never mind that our posters advertised "Terrorists with Telecasters" and asked the musical question, "If you have a bomb in your car, do you have to fasten your seat belt?" I lost the kaffiyeh in a big hurry and replaced it with a leopard-skin fez and fistfuls of Mardi Gras beads. And thus, the Edison Rocket Train was born.

When I was in the South chasing that devil weed for my blues story for *High Times*, I had spent a few days with T-Model Ford and RL Burnside, the last of the great Mississippi bluesmen. I drew a lot of inspiration from that trip, not least of all from eating goat sandwiches at Otha Turner's picnic and drinking liters of moonshine corn liquor, what my friend Amos calls "the poor man's LSD." That ain't no joke. Drinking that White Lightning will make you speak in tongues and see all sorts of crazy shit. It delivered unto me a great vision.

The first thing I did was get rid of the drummer's cymbals—I wanted to hear both hands on the drums—and I hired a full-time maracas and tambourine shaker who called himself Omar, King of the Maracas. He was a kickboxer slumming as a downtown rocker, and he was the only one I could find with enough stamina to shake maracas for forty straight minutes while I did the snake dance and wreaked havoc on my guitar, occasionally smashing it into a giant Chinese wind gong I had bought for no other purpose. The whole thing sounded like an overamped tent revival meeting, what we called Go-Go Gospel and the Shakin' Beat.

We forged our sound from field hollers, spirituals, work songs, New Orleans second-line dance beats, *Fun House*, and a new wave of Afro-

Futurism I had instigated, based in part on World War I–era manifestos that advocated the destruction of all past art forms. I had begun experimenting with a two-string guitar of African design—played through a very aggressive fuzz box–echo machine combination—and spouting Sun Ra–inspired gibberish, spinning stories about black men in silver spaceships. This would be the basis of my solo show, which I would later take to Europe.

When I had the idea to drip some retro-future space oddities onto the first Rocket Train record, *Yes! Yes!! Yes!!!*, I called Jon Spencer and asked him if he'd come on down and play the theremin on a couple of tracks.

The theremin is a primitive synthesizer of sorts that is played without actually touching the instrument. It has one or two antennae, *elements*, and as you move your hands close to them, it begins to wail. It all looks very mysterious and dramatic. (Geeks take note: the theremin is based on the principle of heterodyning oscillators, triggered by the capacitance of the human body, kind of like the way radio reception can change when you move around the room.) The theremin is featured on scads of science fiction soundtracks, such as *The Day the Earth Stood Still*, the *Star Trek* TV show, and a handful of pop songs. The Beach Boys' "Good Vibrations" is probably the best-known song featuring the theremin. "Hand Jive" by Lothar and the Hand People is a good one, too. Jimmy Page uses one in the psychedelic part of "Whole Lotta Love." With his band the Blues Explosion, Jon had made the theremin one of his signature riffs, and he took it to new levels of showmanship and vindictive noisemaking, dueling the damn thing nightly in a ferocious battle of Man vs. Machine. I had always been a theremin enthusiast, but I didn't want anyone to think I was ripping off shtick from the Blues Explosion, so I went right to the source. Jon said he'd be glad to come down to the studio and make a racket.

I had met Jon a few years before in Madrid when he came through on tour with the Blues Explosion. We had been traveling in similar circles—Crypt Records was the label behind both the Raunch Hands and the first Blues Explosion disc—but for some reason we had never met before that. After I moved back to New York, we wound up being neighbors and became close friends. We had a lot in common, least of all that we were a couple of Ivy League dropouts who still clung with childlike optimism to the belief that in rock 'n' roll there was salvation.

I was frankly in awe of the Blues Explosion's ability to mangle John Lee Hooker riffs and James Brown beats into something viciously twisted and still sound distinctly punk. Rock 'n' roll had lost a lot of its swagger. Most of the stuff that people were calling indie or alternative was a load of self-consciously introspective, weepy, whiny crap, suspiciously Beatles-influenced melodies retro-engineered for alt-punk shlubbery. There was a lot of droning, navel-gazing nonsense cluttering the airwaves. Everyone had the same advantages of forty years of rock 'n' roll before them to draw on, but the Blues Explosion stood out in sharp relief. They seemed to adhere closely to Ezra Pound's mantra to "make it new." Phil Spector used to talk about people who made good records and those who made contributions. The Jon Spencer Blues Explosion was in the second group. Having Jon play on my record was the best thing that could have happened—I wouldn't have traded him for Beck, Bono, and two Foo Fighters to be named later.

The Rocket Train played a lot in the East Village, in bars like Manitoba's and Otto's Shrunken Head, a mutant punk-rock tiki bar on Fourteenth Street. I had a matching silver cape and shirt made for me—I figured if Elvis, Sun Ra, Mick Jagger, James Brown, Superman, Screamin' Jay Hawkins, Dracula, Evel Knievel, and Liberace all had capes, I should probably get one, too. Our music spoke for itself, but I always like to shake a little glitter on the pie.

I was never happier than when I was screaming the blues and generally making a spectacle of myself. We played at the Baby Doll Lounge, a topless joint in the financial district. We made it as far as Austin and New Orleans and did a string of shows at the Asbury Lanes, a rock 'n' roll bowling alley on the boardwalk in Asbury Park, New Jersey, where we actually set up on a stage in the middle of the lanes and people bowled around us while we played. Mostly we played in any bucket of blood that would have us. After the show it was always the same. The bartender would come over and shrug. "You guys would have made some money tonight, but you drank so much, you owe *us.*"

We played CBGB's thirtieth-anniversary show with the Dictators, a cherry of a gig, until ____ had the temerity to show up. I knew exactly when she arrived, because the temperature in the club dropped ten degrees in five seconds, and it was already winter, and bitter fucking cold. When she moseyed on up to me after the show, as if everything were just ducky, I felt like vomiting all over her designer shoes (her taste had changed dramatically since we lived together), and I cursed the day I met her. She was by far the worst hangover I have ever had, including the day after a particularly nasty evening of speed trials when I suffered a small stroke at a Yankees game and was blind for almost thirty minutes.

I should have told her to fuck off, but I took the high road and was civil, bordering on nice. And then I walked outside of CBGBs to get some air and didn't even notice it when I stepped in a giant, icy puddle, right up to my knee.

The bad vibes didn't end there. *Screw* was tanking, and I was out of another gig.

Al always said that *Screw* had been a success not because of his talent and vision, but in spite of his tendency to fuck everything up. After years of flying-by-the-seat-of-his-pants porno prosperity, it finally bit him on his gigantic ass. Sales were plummeting, mostly since free alternative weeklies like *The Village Voice* had become a major source for hooker ads. No one needed to cough up the three bucks for *Screw* to score a pay-for-play floozy. Even the Yellow Pages were taking ads for "escort services" and "out-call massage." Of course the Internet had dealt the biggest blow to the print porn business, and Al, already an anachronism, was in no way equipped to ramp up *Screw* technology and compete in the twenty-first century.

Screw still managed to sell ads, and cash was coming in. The World's Greatest Newspaper still had a loyal following of readers who expected to see the usual hatchet jobs of celebrities and politicians bent over and taking it the hard way. Unfortunately, those joyous pages were being pushed out of the book to make room for Al's endless rants about his son, who was about to graduate from Harvard and had disinvited Al from the proceedings, figuring that having a Fat Loudmouth Pornographer starring as the paterfamilias was not going to play well on their tony Cambridge campus, even if it was the very same FLP who had been sporting the hefty tuition tab for the past four years. Al was livid. He disowned his son as a bastard and began speculating vociferously in the pages of the magazine who the kid's real father was: Osama bin Laden? David Berkowitz? Rosie O'Donnell?

It was funny at first, but he was relentless, and sales continued to drop. No one wanted to read about Al's petty family squabbles. He didn't seem to care. He was like Lenny Bruce, obsessing his way to the grave.

Screw was down to one part-time editor who was translating Al's nearly incomprehensible rants—left late at night on the office answering machine—into the weekly editorial page. But that was about it. The guts of the book were being filled up with still pictures from freebie porn videos and articles picked up from past issues. No one wanted this crap. Lord Zeppelin's career died hard.

Al yelled and screamed like a classic paranoiac. Everyone was out to get him. Even if that were true, it wouldn't have mattered. He was determined to destroy himself. He was spending as if he had won a shopping spree from a game show, buying giant plasma TVs in bulk, laptop computers, limited edition Nike sneakers, and humidors filled with Cuba's finest, not to mention pouring money into the sizable restaurant, hotel, and plane ticket habit that kept him bouncing between his New York home base, his Florida compound, his Los Angeles pied-à-terre, and his "smoke-easy" in Amsterdam.

He bought a dozen high-tech vacuum cleaners, and when he went to someone's house for dinner, instead of a bottle of Chardonnay, he'd bring a vacuum with him as a gift. Beyond any Dada absurdity, it was just the latest sign that Al's mental health was about to supernova.

A former assistant, egged on by Al, filed a harassment charge. The trial was an enormous mistake, but it was Al's last go-round in his favorite venue, the courthouse.

What Al never realized was that this was *not* a First Amendment trial, it was a tawdry piece of shit, a misdemeanor that never should have seen a jury. Of course Al managed to turn it into a circus. His Free Speech laurels were unimpeachable, and the promise of his outrageous behavior pulled a decent crowd of reporters, but no matter how much he yelled and screamed and preened for the press pool in his red, white, and blue leather biker jacket, it was not for the noble cause. It was just about a foulmouthed nutcase in a beef with an assistant.

Al could never control his vitriol, and it could turn personal and ugly very quickly. He is incapable of being calm, he needs a fight, he needs friction to survive. Pissing off Al is a terrible thing to do unless you want to find yourself featured in the pages of *Screw* and on television, the target of a Fuck-You on *Midnight Blue*. In this case, he was dropping the bomb on a young woman he had unceremoniously fired on the phone after she fucked up a rental car reservation. Al left several repulsive phone messages for her, calling her, among other things, a "smelly cunt" and a "lowlife scumbag." She also found herself an unwilling media star in the Goldstein empire, starring in a *Midnight Blue* segment called "The Losers of My Life," which also showcased a couple of Al's ex-wives who now own beautiful houses thanks to him. Al was charged with twelve misdemeanor counts of harassment and aggravated harassment.

He had definitely fucked himself. His assistant wasn't the kind of public persona who had to sit back and take this shit. Unfortunately for her, though, no one was buying her babe-in-the-woods routine, either. Before she took the job, she had been warned repeatedly by Chip and by Kevin, *Screw*'s longtime art director, that Al was a foulmouthed monster and a human minefield, that they ran a smut factory, that transvestite hookers came running in and out of the place all the time, that they filmed an X-rated TV show in the office next door. On the stand, when she tried to play coy and only reluctantly admitted that she knew "it was geared toward adults," there were audible guffaws from the jury.

Al might even have had a chance if he didn't take to featuring District Attorney Charles Hynes, whose office was trying this case, in *Screw* every week. Al mailed him copies, personally.

"Did you or did you not," the prosecutor asked Al at the beginning of the trial, "write an editorial advising hijackers to crash their 767s into the office of the DA?"

Al went beserk and started screaming, "That is speech! I will not be silenced!" He got what he wanted when Judge Danny Chun ordered the bailiffs to take him away in handcuffs. By the end of the trial, Al was showing up tanked to the gills on Valium and Lord knows what else, wearing mock prison stripes with a cartoon ball and chain around his ankle.

The next issue of *Screw* featured Hynes "sucking Chink cock"—another classic *Screw* cut-and-paste job that left nothing to the imagination—and Al began telling anyone who would listen that Judge Chun "makes a nice lo mein but puts too much starch in my shirts."

Even Howard Stern, King of the Loudmouths, told Al to cool it with the Chinese food and laundry jokes when he had him on his show during the trial.

Yet Al was winning the support of the press pool, which was growing daily. He fawned over a *New York Times* reporter who had written a glowing profile of Al, telling him, "I want to thank you . . . I'd like to fuck you in the ass, you small-cocked Jew faggot." The reporter was delighted by the attention. Al charmed female reporters with promises of expert cunnilingus and condominiums in Florida. No less than Jimmy Breslin, perhaps the greatest writer in the history of New York newspapers, took it upon himself to remind a crowd of ink-stained wretches that Al is there "for you."

Al's main line of defense was that, yes, he was an asshole, but not a criminal. The jury, after deliberating for days, finally delivered a verdict: they agreed, he was an asshole.

The technical differences among them remain elusive at best, but Al was found guilty of six charges of harassment and not guilty of the other six. He was facing two years. He told reporters that he would like to be sentenced to "community service at Nathan's," the famous Coney Island hot dog joint.

Al's legal bills were towering. And *Screw*, now more of an anti-Hynes tract than a magazine, was officially out of gas. *Midnight Blue* was yanked off the air, as he wasn't paying his bills to the cable company. His New York apartment was gone. His place in Los Angeles, gone. The Amsterdam flat just a resin-soaked memory. His Florida mansion—fifteen rooms built around a giant statue of a hand giving the middle finger, the last great symbol of New York Jew Largesse— would eventually be sold to keep Al drowning in pints of Häagen-Dazs, his preferred method of treating the diabetes he suffered from.

Al's conviction was later overturned. But by then he was living in the office, where he slept among boxes upon boxes of brand-new sneakers, hermetically sealed humidors, piles of books and unopened CDs, a flat-screen TV the size of a bedsheet, and a phalanx of vacuum cleaners waiting for dinner parties.

Even more shocking, after years of working his gut as a pillar of who-gives-a-fuck hedonism, Al decided to give up girth as a gimmick and had his stomach stapled. He dropped a hundred pounds in no time, but it had no effect on his mouth. He continued to rage a verbal shit storm against his son—so vile that when a good-hearted rabbi heard Al ranting on late-night radio, he took it upon himself to go to the *Screw* office and beg him to find forgiveness and make peace with his child. Still wearing the stitches of his surgery, Al greeted the rabbi shirtless, with pus dripping from the sutures.

Soon after that, the New York marshals came and locked up the office. Al owed months of back rent. *Screw* was bankrupt and taken into trust by the state of New York, which was now, by default, in the porn business.

Meanwhile, the news out of *High Times* was no less bizarre.

The Stick of Butter was gone; he, too, had failed miserably. Bobby Black told me that the Stick had rarely come out of his office, apparently terrified of the inmates at the magazine. If there was a production problem, Butter Boy would send Bobby an e-mail even though the production office was only about ten feet away.

It did not help that Hager, left to his own devices, had continued to turn back the clocks to the Summer of Love. No surprise, Modern America had little interest in his jingly-jangly Renaissance fair of a magazine. Circulation would eventually drop to a mere hundred thousand, probably the lowest it had been in thirty years, 60 percent down from when I was steering the ship. It had to be one of the most colossal negative turnarounds in the history of magazine publishing. He was relieved of his office as well.

In fact, along with Butter Boy, most of the editorial staff was cut loose, although somehow Bloom dodged that bullet—he was probably out shopping for cookies when the purge came.

There was a new editor and publisher, and they had a Master Plan for Renewed Success: *they were going to take the pot out of the magazine.*

Far from being a panacea for the sins of the past, this seemed like sure evidence of drug-induced insanity. *Take the weed out?* Why not take the tits out of *Playboy* while they were at it?

The whole world had finally gone topsy-turvy. The new editor and publisher was Richard Stratton, a Forçade crony who had done eight years for pot smuggling and later produced several well-received documentaries. Calling the current version of *High Times* nothing more than a "pamphlet for potaholics," he set a mandate for reform and hired John Mailer (son of Norman), formerly one of *People* magazine's most sexy personalities, to be his executive editor. Their idea was to turn *High Times* into a lifestyle magazine "celebrating freedom."

"I don't believe we should be throwing *that* in people's faces," John Mailer sniffed to *The New York Times*, referring to the very product that had been featured on almost every *High Times* cover in the last twenty years. This should have disqualified him for the job on the spot. Showing his own premium blend of bravado and naïveté, Stratton also vowed, "The ads for fake pot have to go."

Conspiracy theories abounded. Why would they do this? Why would Michael Kennedy and the *High Times* owners knowingly crash their business?

But Stratton and Mailer were resolute, talking about the new audience they were going to attract and the new advertising dollars that would follow. It was hard to figure. I never thought of Michael Kennedy as the kind of guy who would trade the family cow for a bag of magic beans.

If you told me that I'd be spending my summer vacation studiously attending Bible meetings with the Jews for Jesus, I probably would have carved out your eyes with a rusty mezuzah and filled the holes with hot deli mustard. But it was my own choice. I wanted to be there. I needed to hear their message.

I was not looking to be saved. I was on a deep undercover assignment for *Heeb*, the upstart Jewish culture magazine for which I had also covered the Goldstein trial. My new job was to rip the sheet off of these creepy messianics and expose them as the dangerous religious cranks I knew them to be.

Heeb was the brainchild of Jennifer Bleyer, a brilliant Columbia grad who had once published a fanzine called *Mazel Tov Cocktail*. She started *Heeb* on a whim by dashing off her idea for a Jewish counterculture mag to Stephen Spielberg's Joshua Venture, a foundation set up to fund creative Jewish social projects. Somebody there liked it: they came back with a check for sixty thousand dollars to start the magazine. I had seen an ad looking for contributors to *Heeb*, and I replied immediately.

The name *Heeb* itself was just goofy and irreverent enough to create a swirl of media attention, and it was a hit right out of the gate, getting a ton of ink and coverage on everything from CNN to Howard Stern. Jennifer was the real deal, fearless and idealistic.

I loved writing for *Heeb*. Jennifer had assembled a very bright staff of lefty intellectuals and like-minded save-the-world types. She even had an editor from *The New York Times Magazine* look at my Goldstein story ("Appetite for Destruction"), and it came back with a few insightful comments and a thumbs-up. It was incredibly rewarding and encouraging to be edited by someone at such a high level of the game. It was nice to be doing some real journalism for a change—it had been a while since I wrote anything that didn't involve a giant bag of pot or a horny housewife.

My Jews for Jesus opus began in a New York City subway station on a brutally hot summer day, when I let one of their slack-jawed zombies "broadside" me with some of their icky pamphlets. One of them featured a picture of a Jewish star and a pig, proclaiming that "Jesus is so powerful that he can make us pigs kosher to God." As if special dispensation for a bacon cheeseburger would add souls to their flock.

As directed, I called the number on the pamphlet and asked for Tuvya Zuretski, whose real name, I later discovered, is Lloyd Carlson.

Before we go any further, let me say that I am okay with Jesus. I don't agree with everything He said, but when have I ever agreed with everything Anyone has said unless I was bombed and thought it might get me some action? His message seems sound to me. Kindness. Peace on Earth. He stood up for whores and lepers. He looked like a rock star. And rumor has it, he turned water into wine, a damn fine trick in anyone's book. I figure he has precious little to do with the Moral Majority, the Ku Klux Klan, the Spanish Inquisition, Miracle Whip, or the intolerant Bible-thumpers that play Republican politics like a high-stakes game of Smear the Queer. Blaming Jesus for that crew would be like blaming the Grateful Dead for having fans who smell bad.

The Jews for Jesus are not Jews at all. They are Christian evangelicals, fundamentalists, part of a large group of "Messianic Hebrews"—zealous missionaries peddling cut-rate salvation—trying to "complete the Jews," which is one of the conditions for End of Days and the Second Coming of Christ. There are more than four hundred of these groups in the United States, mostly funded by the Southern Baptist

Convention, but Jews for Jesus is the only one with a catchy name brand, as well known for its cheap alliteration as it is for its oxymoronic controversy.

The lies these people tell are mind-boggling in the extreme. Their meetings are awash in gore and idiocy. The worst of this Holy Roller yammering is a particularly foul view of the Holocaust as some sort of blood sacrifice so that the Jews could atone for their sins. This was somehow linked with a lesson in How to Destroy Satan, an ill-founded tale based on the metaphor of killing a snake. "You have to crush its head," they told me. "You can't just cut it in half. If you cut it in half, do you know what happens? You get two snakes." I'm no herpetologist, but I knew there was something specious in this reasoning. "It's true," I was assured. "They're just like worms."

Adam and Eve, of course, is a story to be believed without qualification. "Well," I offered, "last night I was watching *Conquest of the Planet of the Apes*, and it got me to thinking about evolution . . ."

This is not what they wanted to hear. Monkey talk would not be tolerated.

"Science only has *theories*, and they are always *changing*," they explained to me gently. "You need *proof*. The Bible was written four thousand years ago and *it hasn't changed*." And there you have it, friends. QED. Case closed. So, was I ready to accept Jesus as my savior?

Not even an All-You-Can-Eat Pigs-in-a-Blanket Buffet and the promise of condomless sex with a disease-free shiksa porn star would have gotten me to go back into that theological kook house. I may be a cheap Jew, but salvation is one thing I am not going to be buying wholesale.

19

HOWLIN' WOLF VS. THE ALIENS

The emergency room in a Spanish hospital is no place to spend a Saturday night.

My first Rocket Train solo tour of Europe ended in disaster, with my hand twisted like a failed experiment in abstract expressionism—broken, dislocated, and throbbing like an earthworm at the end of a fishing hook.

The tour started as a lark. Some friends in Toulouse, France, who put out a fanzine called *Dig It!* wanted me to bring my new band over for some shows, but there was no way I could afford to bring the whole Rocket Train at the time. I jokingly said I'd come by myself and busk in the Paris metro. It seemed like a good way to kill time between jobs.

Somehow, this idea made sense to them. They told me to bring just a guitar; they'd book me into small bars. "Everyone knows you from the Raunch Hands and the Pleasure Fuckers. Do five small gigs, and you'll make enough to pay for the plane fare and have a great time."

By the time I arrived in Paris, I had a full-scale outer-space blues revue simmering: Mike Edison's Interstellar Roadhouse. I based the show around my two-string super-fuzz diddley-bo guitar and the theremin, now officially referred to as the Rocket Tone Generator. I belted away at Delta blues, spirituals, and greasy R & B, showering the whole mess in a patina of bargain-basement psychedelia and neo-futurist psychobabble. "When wars are fought with guitars," I spumed between blasts of outer-space noise and high, whining riffs on the slide guitar, "I shall be the New Electric Samurai!!!"

The idea of playing a few bars just for kicks quickly turned into a ten-date tour that took me as far south as Valencia. My old friend El Bratto—last seen high on acid and treading water in the Mediterranean—was booking the Spanish part of the tour. He's a nice guy but a bit of a *bobo*, and he got the dates screwed up so I wound up scheduled to play two towns on the same night. Seeing as they were both potentially good gigs—the Raunch Hands always did well in both towns—I figured what the hell, we'll rock Gijón, which was an earlier show anyway, and then we'll haul ass over to Oviedo, an hour down the road, and do some damage there. It was a colossal mistake.

Leaving Gijón sucked. It was the perfect Rocket Train audience at the Louie Louie café, a relatively sophisticated bunch who got off on old R & B and blues as much as the punk rock spirit, and totally fell for the outer-space blues routine. I wanted to stick around, I was having a great night. I could have found a wife in that crowd.

Some nights it was tough. A lot of crowds, especially younger audiences, just want to be blown away with volume and speed. Not that there is anything wrong with that, but ultimately I was working a one-man blues show, no matter how far-out it got. There were still plenty of fireworks and high-energy rhythms—one magazine called it "Howlin' Wolf meets *War of the Worlds*"—but it was definitely not for children looking for a sugar fix.

Unfortunately, the crowd in Oviedo was made up of teenagers who were already shitfaced by the time I got there, and they were expecting me to lead some kind of mosh pit. To make matters worse, in accordance with the traditions of the laziest Spanish pueblos, they hadn't even bothered to set up the sound system.

When I did show up and tried to get things happening, they didn't have the right kind of plugs, and someone had to go look for an adapter while someone else tried to find a mic stand. I ended up duct-taping the mic to the back of a chair. It was a mess. I should have just gotten in the van and gone back to Gijón.

By the time I played, I was fairly drunk, but the crowd was completely fucking blotto and already starting to slam dance before I even played a note. There's not a lot to do in that town, and this was their big night to blow off steam.

I worked my ass off, skipping the weirder part of the show and jumping on tables and playing versions of "Pills" and "Subway Train" and whatever else I thought might work. Eventually I won them over, but it was a sick gig. It was *wrong*. What started out as a winning night had turned into a nightmare, and I was thoroughly pissed off and drowning my anger with Pantagruelian doses of Jim Beam. It wasn't long before I was completely out of my skull, and trying to show off for the last pretty girl in the bar, I attempted a cartwheel out front in the street. Another bad idea. I crumbled like stale coffee cake, crushing the fingers of my left hand when I landed. I could hear the knuckle, the one that ties my palm to my little finger, pop like the cork in a bottle of cava.

I knew the tour was over right then. I managed to make it back to El Bratto's house, where he gave me some kind of Spanish dummy pill. He figured I'd sleep it off and we'd make the show in Bilbao the next night. Thankfully, it was the end of the run and after Bilbao, there was only one more show.

I woke up the next day, and my hand was swollen like a cantaloupe. El Bratto took one look and said, "Cheezis, Sharky, your hand is broken!" Yeah, no shit. That's what I've been trying to tell you. I can't play tonight. "I didn't believe you, I didn't really think you'd miss a gig." Seriously. I have to go to the hospital. Now. "Nahh, you don't want to do that. The hospital is no fun. I have a friend who is a doctor. I will call her."

And so we trudged over to the town doctor's office—apparently her son had taken the horse and buggy for the day, so she wasn't making house calls. She smelled a little bit like oatmeal, as old people sometimes do, but she was really quite nice. She took one look at the melon at the end of my arm and said, "Your hand is broken. You should go to the hospital." I had my second opinion.

"Okay," El Bratto acquiesced. "We'll go to the hospital. But first we are going to have a barbecue."

"What the fuck are you talking about? Let's go . . ."

"Sharky," he reasoned, "your hand is already broken. It is not going to get any more broken if we have lunch first. It would be *una lástima* to waste such a nice day. Look, we have some nice chorizo, and *hamburguesas*. Have some wine, have some beer, smoke a joint, have some more pills, you'll feel better. We'll go when the sun goes down. We're gonna be at the hospital for a while, we should eat first."

There was a certain irrefutable Spanish logic to this.

When we got to the hospital that evening, the X-rays showed what I knew all along: Tab A was no longer inserted in Tab B, and they had to put Sharky back together again.

Here's one thing you should never do: call a doctor bad names when he is trying to forcefully pop your bones back into place without the benefit of anesthesia.

This guy's specialty was medieval quackery. He made some pretense of shooting my hand up with a dismal numbing agent—water, I think—and, without waiting for it to take effect, had his Nurse Ratched of an assistant grab my elbow while he yanked at the other end and tried to push the bone back into place. It was like some kind of sick tug-of-war, with Yours Truly starring as the rope. I would have been howling if I had not taken the NY Yankees cap off my head and gagged myself with it.

"*Pensaba que todos los norteamericanos eran duros, como los vaqueros en las películas.*" He pushed me.

"*Oye, carcinero, yo pensaba que todos los españoles eran simpáticos, como en las películas.*"

With that, he gave my arm a tug that would have ripped the knickers off the Statue of Liberty, and my knuckle popped into place with an audible *ca-chak!* I thought I was having one of those mythical acid flashbacks they used to warn you about in seventh-grade health class. I guess I should have just been grateful that he didn't start bleeding me with leeches.

They wrapped my hand in a cast that might as well have been fashioned from a roll of toilet paper and a few packs of Big Bambu and sent me on my way with some Advil. *Advil?* I was fucking furious, but they would not give me anything stronger.

"Sharky," El Bratto offered, "you should not have called him 'butcher.' He didn't like that."

There was only one thing to do: take El Bratto, who had hung out with me for six hours in the hospital, out to dinner. I, of course, am never much motivated by food or drink, but I would pretend to have an appetite so as not to offend him.

I began by waving off the usual table wine and ordering the good Rioja reserva. In the States it would have been at least forty dollars a bottle in a restaurant, but in this family-owned *mesón* in the hills of a mining town, it was about ten bucks, twice what the boss had paid for it.

In Asturias, the region of Spain we were in, besides wine, the thing to drink is *sidra*, unpasteurized hard apple cider, with about half the alcohol content of beer. So we got a case of that, too. The main thing about the *sidra* is it needs to be *aerated*. When you pour it, the mouth of the bottle should be a minimum foot and a half away from the glass. It's not that easy to hit the glass without splattering the stuff everywhere. Locals and professional waiter types can hold the bottle over their heads and the glass behind their backs, down by their knees, and not miss a drop. But it's a trick you have to learn by practice, so working through a case of cider involves quite a bit of splashing around. It is just another one of those things that makes Spain so special. It's as if they *want* you to make a mess.

We sharpened our teeth on a *cazuela de mariscos*, a seafood salad of octopus, shrimp, calamari, and whatever else was lurking about that day, and some *paté de cabracho*, made from, so I have been led to believe, nothing but the finest red scorpion fish. It is delicious. For dinner we each had the *cachopo*, another typical *plato asturiano*, which is basically a ham and cheese sandwich, except instead of bread, they use a couple of thick steaks.

After that, I was understandably beginning to feel a bit peckish, so I ordered the *especialidad de la casa*, the famous *paletilla de cordero*, the ingredients for which are the hindquarters of a lamb, and fire. It comes on a giant slab of wood, looks like it was prepared by cavemen, and is frighteningly toothsome. Not to mention, messy. We had the usual round of flan, apple liqueur, and *carajillos* before going back to the house to smoke the rest of the hash and drink whatever bourbon and beer was left over from the barbecue. Then, purely out of spite, I threw the Advil away and cleaned out El Bratto's medicine cabinet. I slept well that night, but goddammit, I should have been in Bilbao. In twenty years, that was the first gig I had ever missed.

I was supposed to be in Toulouse the next night, and I was not going to miss another show. Rock 'n' roll is the best job of all time. You don't get to call in sick. I wasn't sure what I was going to do exactly, but I was formulating a plan: if I could find a length of pipe just the right size and could somehow attach it to the underside of my cast, I could use it as a bottleneck slide and play guitar sitting down, sort of like a makeshift lap steel. It had just the right elements of Rube Goldberg and Hound Dog Taylor, and I thought it could work. Toulouse was going to be my end-of-tour party. I had started there, and I needed the circle to be unbroken. It was a free show at a bar, as much a fete for me as for everyone who had been so supportive and had encouraged me to come over and make a racket. There was no way I was not going to play.

Also, I had a date with a big breast. Well, a duck breast, actually, the highly prized *magret de canard*, a thick slab of meat as rich and satisfying as any strip steak you'll find in New York or Kansas City. The ducks in France are well fed and content. The restaurant had been booked for weeks, and I would have hated to disappoint the chef, who lives to see the delight I take snarfling his handiwork.

I called ahead and explained that I was flying on only one wing and that we were going to have to recruit a few musicians to back me up and also figure out how to jerry-rig my busted hand so I could at least make a go of it. One of the guys from *Dig It!* was so concerned that I get the right piece of heavy metal to strap to my arm that he took his sink apart, nearly flooding his apartment, until we found the perfect length of copper pipe.

The show was a smash, if a bit sloppy. The place was packed, and there were people out on the street who could not fit in the bar to see the spectacle of a one-armed man attempting to reinvent the slide guitar. Frankly, it hurt like hell, and I have no idea what further damage I was doing to myself, but it was an experiment in sound and orthopedics (orthophonics?) that no one there is likely to forget. Everyone was very appreciative that I did not bail simply on account of a few shattered bones. I played half a dozen songs sawing away at the two-string fuzz monster and the six-string Earth guitar, before going a cappella for a few drunken field hollers and then bringing on some friends to end the tour with an old-fashioned version of "Louie Louie," with all the dirty words left intact and plenty of mangled French patois.

After the show we drank to this and that until it was time to go. I went straight to the airport from the club in a car filled with shitfaced Rocket Train fans.

By that time I was clearly out of my senses and capable of pretty much any kind of savagery. Someone should have alerted Homeland Security—especially since when x-rayed, the briefcase I carry the theremin in looks like nothing less than what it is: a series of small packages (echo machine, various fuzz boxes, etc.) wired to a primitive radio receiver. I saw it on the screen and *I* wanted to arrest and torture me.

When I got to New York, I went to a *proper* doctor, a *New York* doctor with a wall full of expensive-looking diplomas and a Jewish-sounding last name. He took one look at my mangled paw, marveled at the free-form engineering masterpiece that was my cast, and snorted, "Who was in charge there, Frank Gehry?"

It is important to have a surgeon with a sense of humor. He immediately cleared his schedule and told me not to go anywhere, he was going to operate that afternoon. One more day healing in the position it was in and he would have to rebreak my hand before resetting it.

God bless him, he shot me up with so much anesthesia I couldn't feel my face, let alone my hand. It took two hours to insert three steel pins in me, reconstructing the mess at the end of my arm until my fingers and hands lined up in a way that looked less like modern art and more like something that belonged on a human being. He sent me home with a jar of real painkillers. I promptly went to a sushi bar and washed them down with a bottle of sake, the most recent version of the Edison Cure. Like I say, you've got to be flexible.

I had worked for so many magazines that were meant to be *read* with one hand, it was only fitting that I was now going to have to write with just one. Unfortunately, I didn't have a whole lot of work.

I was done with *Heeb*. After four issues, Jennifer had decided to move on. She was sick of the headaches and the hangers-on, and in the first year she had pretty much accomplished all that she had set out to do with the magazine, which was basically to see if it could be done against the odds. Having achieved that, she did not want to be tied to it forever.

She left the book in the hands of Josh Neuman, one of the associate editors. Josh shouldn't have been in line for such a responsible position, but he was the only one who could afford to do a full-time job with paltry compensation—Jennifer had been eking by on an honorarium and a part-time job, but the magazine was not making enough money to actually pay salaries—and he became the new editor by default. He asked me if I would be the editorial director, second on the masthead, and help him shape the book, since he had almost no magazine experience beyond being a *Heeb* sycophant. I agreed. I would still have plenty of time to pursue other gigs, and *Heeb* was an excellent reference. I loved working with Jennifer; she set the bar high and got great work out of me. I still felt loyal to the magazine, even though she was gone.

Armed with an inheritance and plenty of free time, Josh had made the improbable evolutionary leap from Junior Chimp to Lawgiver, but he still desperately needed an Orangutan on board, someone who knew what the fuck they were doing.

As it turned out, Josh may have asked me to be his editorial director, but he sure as hell didn't want any editorial direct*ing*. All he wanted from me was to doctor the rough-and-tumble features he had solicited and make him look good.

Josh broke every single rule of being a good e-in-c: he put himself on a pedestal and didn't return calls or e-mails from writers or freelancers. He didn't respect his staff. He was inflexible and did not accept criticism. He panicked at every deadline and acted like a bully. He certainly did not encourage creativity, and became married to every idea he had.

It's important to have the balls to throw out your first idea and look at things from different angles. You can always come back to it, but if you fall in love too quickly, it gums up the works and nothing ever evolves. It takes patience and a nurturing spirit, and you can't be afraid of being trumped by someone else in the room. Magazines need strong leaders, but just like being in a rock 'n' roll band, it is a cooperative process. Josh was clueless. Jennifer had never acted like the Lawgiver, even though it was her magazine. She didn't have to. Everyone respected her, and she listened to her team. She made everyone feel important.

Even though Jennifer was no longer working on the magazine (she went on to write for a far more successful Jewish publication, *The New York Times*), she was still on the *Heeb* masthead as founder and was supposed to be acting as an adviser. *Orangutan Emeritus.* But it didn't take long before she refused to have anything to do with Josh, whose ego-tripping was out of control. I sometimes wondered whether his main reason for running *Heeb* was so he might have a shot at fucking

Jewess comedian Sarah Silverman—an admirable goal, but not one that was likely to be achieved by acting like an insane person. It was kind of like John Hinckley trying to score with that Foster girl.

The last straw was the despicable cover story about Jesus Christ that Josh insisted was going to stand as a monument to his genius. I was appalled.

Generally speaking, when I say that something has crossed the lines of taste and civility—or rather, that something is such an egregious example of bad taste that *my* sensibilities are chafed—flags go up, the band stops playing, and everyone stands around with their mouths agape, worried that whatever it is must be *really* bad and we are all going straight to Hell.

I took one look at the photo spread called "Crimes of Passion" and said, "You Have Got To Be Fucking Kidding Me." I could not have been more serious. The Holy Virgin Mother with pierced tits? Oy fucking vey. I wanted no part of this.

Mostly, I was offended by the story because it wasn't funny.

Allow me to recap: I have proudly penned some of the most pernicious trash ever foisted on the reading public. I wear the stench of the most noxious publications in the history of American letters like a red badge of courage. Thanks to me, an entire generation of college students knows how to score a bargain blow job from a crack whore. I took great pride in chronicling the smelly sex lives of the homeless. I lauded *Omar's Anal Adventures*—seven volumes of them!—with a glee usually reserved for children's birthday parties. I have scrawled, *sans souci*, prurient tales of incest and cherry-popping too rough even for circulation among the United States' maximum-security prison population. I have championed race-baiting and misogynist wrestlers, and I have peddled to America's youth magazines loaded to the teeth with illegal drugs. Not limited to spreading filth in the free press, I was a willing participant in GG Allin's scum-rock porno freak show. I think I carry a fair amount of gravitas in this department. There is not much that shocks me. So when I call "cut," people usually listen.

The *Heeb* photo spread—an "irreverent" portrayal of Christ's last moments on Earth—was humorless, void of parody or satire, dull, and a careless waste of all the "smart capital" Jennifer had built into *Heeb* as a hip and progressive magazine. As well executed as it may have been, the photo spread carried no philosophy, no message, no irony, no meaningful text, just a thick-tongued reaction to Mel Gibson's *Passion of the Christ* movie, which *wasn't even out yet* and which *no one had even seen*. We were getting dangerously into Giuliani territory: prior restraint, mob rules, bandwagon hopping, and all sorts of free speech issues that the editor of *Heeb* should feel a duty to defend.

If Josh wanted to go after Mel Gibson (preferably *after* seeing the film), he could have nailed him to a cross and shoved up his ass one of those silly hats the pope is always wearing. He could have shown Mel tea bagging Woody Allen or popping a Steven Spielberg–shaped ginger-bread man into an Easy Bake oven. He could have had Mel singing "Edelweiss" while peeing on Whoopi Goldberg, or he could have por-trayed Jerry Seinfeld buggering Braveheart with a marble rye. *Anything*, as long as it showed *some* sense of humor.

And when did Jesus and the Virgin Mother become the targets of such vitriol? We were supposed to be mocking intolerance, ignorance, and bigotry, not *faith*.

Before turning *Heeb* into his vanity project, Josh taught philosophy at a local college, so he should have known a thing or two about "con-text." We were a Jewish magazine. We didn't poop on Jesus' mom. That was a job for the Brooklyn Museum.

Of course Mel is a venal anti-Semite and deserves no less than a fourteen-pound matzo-ball suppository. His movie isn't much more than a gory, hate-filled propaganda reel. All Josh was doing was giving Mel some legitimacy by getting in the muck with him. Spoof him— brutally, caustically, venomously—and show him that you are smarter than he is. Measure your response with humor. What could be more Jewish? Follow the sooth teachings of Rabbi Dave Insurgent and *liber-ate yourself*.

Josh desperately wanted to be seen as "cutting edge," and for his ef-forts, *Heeb* earned a sharply worded rebuke from the Anti-Defamation League, admittedly not a group known for its sense of humor, but now *Heeb* was skirting dangerously close to embracing the same intolerant ideology with which it wanted to do battle. Josh would brag that he wanted *Heeb* to be a big-tent pop culture magazine, albeit a Jewish one, but on his first issue he flew straight into a black hole of racism and fear and painted himself into a corner as a knee-jerking twat. It was infantile.

A lot of people were surprised that I quit a relatively high-profile gig on principle—*Heeb* was such a media darling—but fuck it, I have my standards, and anyway, I was all grown up and really had no business playing in the sandbox with spoiled children.

Eventually Jennifer cashed out and sold the magazine to Josh, but by that time she had also had enough of his bullshit, and they communicated only through their lawyers. The magazine continued, but with little spark.

For a while I worked for *index*, a gorgeously produced art and culture magazine. It was oversize and printed beautifully on thick matte paper. Every issue was rife with high-end fashion ads: Armani, Gucci, and Marc Jacobs were in every issue. Tom Ford used us to road test his most controversial images. It was a different world from *High Times*, which was always infected with ads for cut-rate gardening tools and dehydrated urine samples that you could use to pass a drug test.

The magazine was run by artist Peter Halley, one of the wildly smartest people I have ever met. In addition to being an incredibly successful painter—he came up in the 1980s East Village New York art scene with a highly conceptual string of "neo-geo" minimalist paintings and constructions—he ran the painting department at Yale University and was a well-regarded critical thinker, much influenced by Michel Foucault. He ran *index* out of his painting studio, a large loft in West Chelsea, something like Andy Warhol's old Factory, but without the sex and drugs. Which should have been the first clue that something was seriously amiss. But I needed a job, and the magazine was magnificent.

I was hired as publisher—with editorial responsibilities—a path I had gone down before with less than sterling results, but I could not say no to the money, 60K a year. I didn't last that long.

Peter was a white-knuckle ex-smoker. He still had a vicious habit, but now he satisfied his jones by chewing through boxes and boxes of extra-strength nicotine gum. Which may have done wonders for his lungs, but not so much for his blood chemistry. He always seemed on the verge of boiling over. Some very talented people were terrified to work for him. He was freakishly involved in the minutiae of the magazine, maniacally driven to tinker with every word until it hit some inexplicable note of Neoplatonic perfection. Production halted until he had his way with every caption, every hed, every blurb; even casting the table of contents became an endurance contest, a decathlon of short-form prose.

I agreed with him about the level of precision he demanded, but since he was usually off in New Haven or at a gallery opening in Germany or Korea, he was never around, and the magazine just sat there waiting for his arrival, when he would freak out and start tearing up pages and screaming.

To do my job, I had to brace him. I understood that he was overwhelmed with Yale and his art, but he was fucking up deadlines, and he was going to have to get it together or we were going to be missing press dates and there would be no one to blame but himself. The people at *index* worked twelve-hour days and weekends; there was no lack of work ethic there. I was as dedicated to the deity in the details as much as he was, but he had to learn when to let go and get the book out the door. Peter finally told me that I was *too professional* to work there.

Well, now I had truly heard it all. For once, I had nothing to say. He invited me to contribute as a freelancer as much as I wanted.

As a freelance editor I went from making five thousand a month to five hundred, but at least I was finally able to enjoy my job, mostly writing the front section of the book, six short interviews every issue.

It was an incredibly diverse group of people whom I spoke with for *index*. Gus Van Sant was a bit tepid and didn't open up until I started in with the geekazoid film school lingo, but John Waters was as witty and smart and observant as one would imagine. We talked about Phil Spector's hair. Chatting with Udo Kier—one of my all-time favorite actors, who played Dracula and Frankenstein in Andy Warhol's sleazy art-house horror films and speaks lugubriously cadenced English with a strong German accent—was like getting tipsy on really good, really sticky schnapps. I made frequent excuses to call him. Will Shortz, the editor of the *New York Times* crossword puzzle, gave me some hints on how to become an answer on his page (change my name to Eno or Ono), and offered his favorite palindrome, the longest one in English that makes "moderate sense": T. Eliot, top bard, notes putrid tang emanating. Is sad. I'd assign it a name: gnat-dirt upset on drab pot toilet.

Got that?

I spoke with fashion impressarios Kate Spade, Norma Kamali, Hedi Slimane, and agnès b. Bret Easton Ellis, whom I had not been looking forward to interviewing owing to the nasty impression I had of him, left over from the era of brat-packing eighties cokehead clubbing when he came up, turned out to be wickedly charming, tremendously funny, and self-effacing. Kim Gordon from Sonic Youth told me a nice story about scaring some challenged schoolchildren by smashing up their instruments at Neil Young's annual charity event. (Sonic Youth's instruments, that is, not the children's.) Björk was a snooze. Singer-songwriter Cat Power was sweet and shy, as you would expect. But storm-trooping chanteuse Diamanda Galás shocked me (shocked *me!*) with her wonderful and well-developed hatred of the Beatles. Hip-hop mogul Russell Simmons told me "fuck the police," but it didn't seem to have a whole lot of tooth behind it. He was calling from his car while en route to visit his pal Barbra Streisand. The absolute highlight of this run was when Amy Sedaris invited me to her apartment, made me cupcakes, and introduced me to her pet rabbit.

And then one day Peter killed the magazine. I guess he was overwhelmed by his painting and academic careers colliding with the various degrees of angst and stress he brought to the rest of his life. It was too bad; *index* was just one issue shy of its tenth anniversary. There was a big issue and a party in the works. And then, *nothing.* Over a decade, *index* had cultivated a very dedicated, very influential following. But it went out with a whimper, not a bang. Like so many other things in the magazine business, this made little sense.

The year after I left my full-time gig at *index*, I made about fourteen thousand dollars, roughly the amount that I would put on my Master-Card that year. And I had burned through my savings. No one else wanted to hire a *High Times* and *Hustler* veteran, especially one approaching forty who had already made up his mind about how the world should be run.

But I started to get called for an increasingly strange series of odd jobs, including creating a bio and press kit for the family of Frank Zappa, who were about to embark on a tour called Zappa Plays Zappa, featuring Frank's kids Ahmet and Dweezil. The whole thing was designed to look like declassified FBI files, complete with black bars censoring the most sensitive material.

While I was putting it together, I mentioned to Ahmet that I used to be the publisher of *High Times* and I remembered when he had his comedy radio show.

"Oh," he said guardedly. "Were you a guest? I remember we had someone from *High Times* . . ."

"No," I reassured him. "That was the editor, Steve Hager."

"Oh, thank God," Ahmet sighed. "I thought I was going to have to fire you. We figured a guy from *High Times* would be a natural, but he was the least funny person we ever had on the show."

And then Frank from *Soft Drinks & Beer* called. Having failed as a car thief, he was now a big shot in the marketing business, and he wanted to hire me to help write a comedy show about a deodorant that was supposed to make young men irresistible to women.

Frank had been working for a guerrilla marketing company, a logical enough leap after all the wisdom that was imparted to us at *SD&B*. One night he was in a bar telling someone about a campaign he had been working on, marketing toilet paper to college kids at rock concerts. It was a revolutionary departure from the old model of Mr. Whipple pitching two-ply to housewives. After all, who used more toilet paper than the dudes who went to Ozzfest?

The guy Frank was telling this story to turned out to be some sort of literary agent who encouraged Frank to write a marketing book. And so he did. Now he had a book, which made him an expert, and being an expert, he was in demand and had landed a six-figure gig with some slick marketing outfit in Chicago. Their client, the deodorant that made men irresistible, had hired a Famous Comedian who "tested through the roof" on college campuses (Frank really said that, "tested through the roof") to be their spokesman. He was going to go on a tour of colleges with a busload of "T & A" (and no kidding, that's really what they call the models) and give a "class" in why everyone needed the product. Frank and I were going to take their existing ad materials and shape them into some kind of routine for the Famous Comedian. For this I would be paid a rate of a thousand dollars per day.

Frank flew to New York and got us a hotel room. We barricaded ourselves in, began a decent drug collection—green buds, white powder, amber liquor, Xanax, Valium, Ambien, and a shitload of ice and beer—and sent down to room service for a large supply of grapefruits, club sandwiches, Snickers bars, beef jerky, and Gatorade. We weren't leaving until the show was done. Apparently, there is a lot of money in selling deodorant to horny eighteen- to twenty-four-year-olds.

I told Frank that if we were really going to do this right, I would need a piano. I was only joking. I didn't really want a piano, but I felt as if we were trapped in some deranged Neil Simon set piece, and I wanted to see just how far I could push things. Moments later, Frank was on the phone with the manager of the hotel, demanding that one be sent up immediately.

After three days, the room stank like a zoo, but we had a show written, which ended with a faux commencement speech: "Friends, scholars, distinguished guests, horny, incompetent freshmen . . . Tonight, you are going to get laid!" The client loved it, the Famous Comedian loved it, and now, thanks to us, there is a whole new wave of fresh-smelling frat boys contemplating the finer points of date rape.

It was around this time that I also began working for Jon Spencer and the Blues Explosion as their Minister of Information.

Jon had distilled the essence of rock 'n' roll—as performance, as rebellion, as the hellfired covenant of deliverance—into one semi-autistic outburst—*BLUES EXPLOSION!*—which he would shout at the beginnings of songs, in the middle of songs, on top of overwhelming blasts of rhythm and guitar noise, whenever he had the fever. It was his signature riff. My job was to get that shudder-and-shake rock action into print, something a record company publicist could use to blast through the clutter of a million other press releases and knock out jaded hipster journalists who were too cool to get excited about anything.

So we just went over the top rope, yelling and screaming, testifying to the Knife-Twisting Gospel of the Blues Explosion, ranting about New Strains of Psychedelia and the Coalition of the Rocking. We worked dozens of e-mail blasts, Web postings, and press releases, and we got a lot of good hits. It would also get me into some hot water.

Tom Waits had invited Judah and Russel, the other two-thirds of the Blues Explosion, to back him up for an appearance on the *Late Show with David Letterman*—without Jon.

It was an inspired call. While Jon tended to use his guitar like a rocket launcher, Judah worked from a gritty formulary of razor-blade twang, Telecaster thump, and swampy Southern soul. Russell kept a monstrously huge big beat. And they were big Tom Waits fans. They would be joined by Tom's bass player, Larry Taylor, also a musician of tremendous depth, who had been in the original Canned Heat.

The plan was twofold: get the message out and keep the underground hype machine bubbling by dropping a thermonuclear propaganda bomb on Blues Explosion fans; then grab a picture of Tom with Russell and Judah and send it out with a tongue-in-cheek press release ("Tom Waits Blues Explosion?") to the mainstream press and see if we couldn't get it picked up by some Big Rock Mag. Given the cachet of Tom Waits and the Blues Explosion working together, it should have been a slam dunk.

Jon encouraged me to write a crazed conspiracy rant to use for the Blues Explosion website and as an e-mail blast to their fan list. This was at the same time, the run-up to the 2004 election, when Dan "I Know a Fair Amount About LSD" Rather was turning himself into a national laughingstock and about to be bounced from CBS (the network on which the show would air) for going hook, line, and sinker for false memos regarding George W. Bush's dodgy military record.

Why is Jon Spencer being replaced with Old Man Waits? One CBS staffer told us that "the network douche bags are running scared . . . and Letterman doesn't want to take a chance on Jon blues-exploding anywhere near the studio . . . This goes a lot deeper than Dan Rather" . . .

I'd like to think it was a model of gonzo paranoia and situation comedy. Except that the record company publicist—who was probably working for ten other bands that day as well and had little understanding of the Blues Explosion (she kept asking if they could play with B.B. King, you know, because it's *blues*)—jumped the gun, grabbed the copy off the Blues Explosion website, and, without reading it, pasted it into an e-mail and sent it out as a straightforward industry-style press release. It took about five minutes after that for the Blues Explosion manager to call me, horrified. Tom Waits, or at least his people, were furious. We were going to have to "contain" the problem. I explained that it was just the usual fireworks, that it was written for fans who were in on the joke, and what sort of dimwit would have sent that out as a legitimate press release without reading it first? It was not our policy to call the network who was hosting us "douche bags," at least not in official communiqués, and especially not before the actual taping. There were a few hours more of panicked phone calls—at one point the show was going to be called off—before things finally calmed down. But the photo op was shot to hell. There was no way Tom was going to have his picture taken with Judah and Russell, who were absolutely slamming playing behind him. Oh well. It was a cute idea.

When my hand had finally healed and could withstand the impact of Throwing the Fireball, I was summoned to Austin for the Raunch Hands' twentieth-anniversary show.

It may have been our four millionth gig (I had been in the band for only fifteen years, so technically I was still "the new guy"), but it was a coming-out of sorts. Chandler was sober and had been sober, and it looked, brilliantly, as if this time it was going to stick. This would be his first show truly clean.

Chandler had hit rock bottom so many times I am not sure how he ever climbed out of the abyss. It took a lot of strength.

He had been beating the shit out of himself with a torrent of bad liquor and pills. He looked like hell, he made little sense, he smelled bad, and he was losing the battle.

He stayed on my couch for weeks without moving, just pushing a pen hopelessly around the same clue in the same crossword puzzle for hours, drenched in self-doubt, vodka sweat, and depression. Then he left for a treatment program in Phoenix. He told me that before he went to Phoenix, he had experienced an odd moment of clarity, and he could hear the Death Rattle. He had a choice to make—you *always* have a choice—and he chose to live.

Starting young, Chandler had romanticized a drinking life until it almost destroyed him. Fortunately, he discovered in time that he didn't have to get loaded to bring the soul. He could devastate an audience with focus and raw talent. Chandler is a gifted singer, and when he starts shouting the blues, people line up and testify. Instead of emerging reformed and reenergized, he could have easily joined my other dead friends. Now he was regaining the respect and admiration of people who had written him off as a has-been drunk. There was an excitement about him no one had felt since the Raunch Hands were the Next Big Thing, eighteen years before. The good part of his mind was open, working at peak form, and the music started flowing through him like Big Water at a hydroelectric plant. This was rock 'n' roll as Savior. Chandler didn't need to drink, he needed to sing. It was the more powerful force.

Also moving forward, George had a new fiancée, an especially interesting development, considering he was still technically married to Tomoko. In the eyes of Fat Elvis, God, and the state of Nevada, those Vegas marriages are no joke. After ten years, either George still couldn't figure out how to negotiate a no-fault divorce across the international date line, or he just liked to keep the new wife-to-be walking on eggshells. He offered no clue as to whether he was practicing some sort of advanced relationship hoodoo, or if he was just being lazy.

I was still single and still creatively unemployed. It was a good time to get to work on a new Rocket Train record. Jon Spencer had some time off from the road, and he generously offered to produce.

It was during one of these sessions that the Big Blackout hit. No ordinary power failure, this was a complete collapse of the power grid that left not only New York but large parts of Connecticut, Pennsylvania, Ohio, Michigan, and Canada without electricity for days. Hundreds of flights were canceled. Cell phones didn't work. More than fifty million people were affected. Detroit and Toronto were out for the better part of a week.

In the studio, Jon and I were listening to the playback of a song when the lights went out. The emergency fire lights went on, and the tape went *wha wha whaaa whaaaa whaaaaaaaaaa whaaaaaaa* . . . Had we been recording at the time, we would have had the blackout on tape.

After we went out to the street to see what was going on and realized that not only was the neighborhood down, but the entire city as well, Jon headed home to take care of his family. My first thought was to get to the bar near my house. The ice would be melting, and I had some legitimate concerns about the beer.

It was a real wingding of a blackout party. The entire neighborhood was there, along with dozens of people who had been stranded after work when the subways stopped running. Everyone was in a great mood. Of course, by Day Two the novelty of the situation had faded like a cheap suit and even normally resilient New Yorkers were getting cranky sweating it out—it was the middle of August, and hot. Another big problem was that without power, no ATM machines were working, and everyone seemed to be running out of cash. Of course credit cards weren't working, either, and New York could have easily turned into a city of hunters and gatherers. But the first night, spirits were still running high. Compared with what we had all been through in the recent past, a blackout was like a Swiss picnic. When evening fell, the bar was lit with candles, and I found myself sitting next to a Very Pretty Girl who had given up trying to get back to her place in Brooklyn.

Meanwhile, I had a freezer full of food at home that was now involuntarily defrosting. A local grocery delivery service had been offering fifty dollars' worth of free food as a bonus with your first order, and I had decided to take it in pork chops. Big ones. Double-cut monstrosities that looked as if they were drawn by Dr. Seuss. When it became obvious that the power was not coming back on anytime soon, I began to fear for those pork chops.

There was no electricity, but at least I had a gas oven that was still working. I explained the gravity of the situation to the VPG and asked her if she would like to join me for a meat party. Fortunately, she shared my concerns.

Sometimes the stars line up and I catch lightning in a bottle, and sometimes it takes a large-scale disaster to make the Top Secret Action happen. We spent the night cooking the pork chops by candlelight and generally making a mess. When day broke, there was grease everywhere.

20

I HAVE FUN EVERYWHERE I GO

It just wouldn't be a Rocket Train tour if I didn't end up in the emergency room.

It was early, so the hospital in Strasbourg, France, was still pretty calm. Later it would be crawling with broken drunks and football hooligans, but right now there was only a teenager who had skateboarded headfirst off of his roof. And me. My face was busted wide open from taking a bad bump in my European debut as a professional wrestler.

This was my first return to the ring since I took over *Main Event*. A twenty-year hiatus! This was Bigger than Big! I ended up flat on my back, being sewn together by a French doctor. At least he was no butcher. The scar might even look *good*.

Wrestling is one of the few things I can always count on. It is the least self-conscious of all art forms. Wrestling never worries about how silly or absurd it looks. Wrestling does not discriminate. Everyone is invited to the party. It has never let me down.

In many ways, those are the very same reasons why I had initially been so attracted to *High Times*. Once upon a time, they didn't give a damn what the Establishment thought, and they never would have been caught pandering. Few other magazines lived so far out on the fringes that their very existence was a big Fuck You to the straitlaced and the square. Abbie Hoffman once said that "sacred cows make the tastiest hamburgers." Unfortunately, *High Times* turned vegetarian a long time ago.

It was no surprise that the idea to take the pot out of *High Times* was a dismal failure. No one wanted it. I heard that sales were so low that they were selling ads for cash at fire-sale prices just to meet the payroll. It took only a few issues of that farce before they fired the new publisher and editor, stuffed the magazine full of bright green nuggets, and slapped a banner on the cover screaming THE BUDS ARE BACK!

Eventually they brought Hager back as well, which, after being fired and rehired so many times, makes him something like the Billy Martin of pot. Bloom was put out to pasture and given the traditional outcast's outpost of "editor at large." Apparently there was no love lost between those two, either.

It seemed as if they were playing it Safer than Safe. The covers were knocked off, note for note, from covers that had been successful in the past, and they generally featured the subversive floral arrangements of the old school. It probably wouldn't be long before they dug up old Bob Marley's corpse for an encore. Except that somewhere along the line they had picked up a taste for dumbed-down stoner populism, like an idiotic "Miss High Times" contest featuring lurid photos of young women posing suggestively with buds and bongs ("Why you should vote for me: I have great boobies"), and they had pumped out a string of inane "sex and pot" issues featuring porn stars on the cover. Which was, frankly, *shocking*. Aside from defying the rampant pornophobia that had infected *High Times* so rabidly when I was an inmate there, this was exactly the kind of doper juvenilia that Hager had always railed against, and it ran directly contrary to the Earth Mother goddess worship he preached as his counterculture catechism.

And then, far beyond any previously acceptable level of pothead prurience, even for the most puerile of stoners, out of nowhere appeared a story about a "buttbong"—which is exactly what it sounds like: a dildo-shaped water pipe used to smoke pot out of someone's butt. In this case, it was an "adult film actress" who had just got back from filming a reefer-mad fuck flick at *High Times*'s sacred Cannabis Cup event in Amsterdam. The story left nothing to the imagination: "After a quick lube job, she inserted the bong into her ass . . ."

Had Hager really sold his soul to the devil? Surely *this* was Babylon.

I asked one of my more coherent former coworkers, "How the hell do you guys justify all that porn you're putting in the magazine? They would've put my nuts in a vise."

"It's okay if the hippies do it," he explained to me. "You couldn't have done it—for the same reason that only a virulent anticommunist like Nixon could go to China."

Screw may be the sleaziest magazine ever published, but especially by comparison to *High Times* it was always giddily, Socratically self-aware. With *Screw*, you knew what you were getting yourself into—we did not lure you in with silver bells on our toes and then, without warning, clop you on the side of the head with a buttbong. When I was asked to become the new editor in chief of *Screw*, I agreed immediately.

I have often been asked how come I never pursued a gig at Condé Nast or one of the bigger magazine publishers. Henry David Thoreau summed it up well: "Beware all enterprises that require new clothes." Anyway, I never thought they would have me. The upper stratum of magazine publishing was never too keen on hiring dropouts, especially those who come with rap sheets riddled with first-degree wrestling and pornography offenses. I don't know why, but they just don't consider that art. I would love to write for *The New Yorker* (eventually someone is going have to make the Shouts and Murmurs page funny again), but working there? Doing what? It doesn't seem like it would be a whole lot of fun. And it's not likely they'd put me in charge—there or at any of the blue-chip rags that clutter the prime real estate on newsstands and at supermarket checkout counters. In an industry where celebrity access is the coin of the realm, I am probably not the guy you want fronting your business. Publicists have too much power—anger one of their hotshot clients, and you can say goodbye to all of them. Sooner than later I am going to piss someone off, and then what are you going to do?

Editing *Screw* was license to ill and the culmination of a modern-day Abraham Lincoln story. Far below the dingy confines of the mail room, I had started my career at *Screw* on the filthiest part of the street, peddling reviews of open-window peep booths and massage parlors. Now I had the big corner office.

After Al Goldstein's first harassment trial, his self-immolation had continued unabated. He learned nothing from the experience, or from his tidal wave of legal bills. Almost immediately he found himself starring as the defendant in another potentially avoidable harassment case, this time involving an ex-wife whose home phone number he ran repeatedly in the pages of the magazine. For that trick Al spent nine days in jail on Rikers Island and a week undergoing psychiatric evaluation. Soon after, he was thrown off of an airplane for allegedly making lewd remarks to a stewardess, and he was busted for allegedly shoplifting at a Barnes and Noble bookstore. His friends tried to help him, but he was quick to bite their hands. He worked briefly as a "greeter" at the famous Second Avenue Deli in Manhattan, where he had been a regular for years, only to be fired for sleeping in the basement. He spent time in a homeless shelter until the maverick stage magician Penn Jillette came to his rescue and rented him an apartment on Staten Island. Improbably, he got married again, to a woman forty years younger than he. Not surprisingly, it was a disaster, and he ended up sleeping on his new father-in-law's floor.

All of this was tragic to anyone who knew Al as the larger-than-life porno king who could be as articulate and charming in person as he was offensive on his TV show. But he seemed set on destroying himself. When his business was going down in flames, his reaction was to max out his credit cards on extravagant dinners and wildly expensive but ultimately useless electronic gadgets. While *Screw* burned, he fiddled, and then continued to set fire to bridges in every direction. It was hard to feel sorry for him.

Meanwhile, *Screw*'s longtime art director, Kevin Hein, had been approached to become a partner in buying the magazine out of hock and relaunching it, and he asked me if I wanted the editor's gig. I would be only the second editor in chief in the magazine's thirty-four-year history.

Kevin is an Orangutan of the First Order. He is a master of cock-in-mouth composites, a regular Kandinsky with cut-and-paste hatchet jobs. Not only did he have the magic touch with the scissors (he was chopping heads long before the advent of Photoshop), he actually enjoyed it. Tell the man that this was the week we were going to turn Tom Cruise's narrow white ass into a Hollywood dick depot, or strap a dildo on Hillary Clinton and bung it up the rump of the Republican *du jour*, and he would take to it like Chief Wiggum to a jelly doughnut.

He took pleasure not only in the absurdity of the job, but also in the Pranksterish chutzpah in which it was intended. He had learned from the Lawgiver, Al Goldstein, to whom we remained loyal in spirit. After almost two thousand issues of *Screw* (thirty-five years of weekly publication) Al would not speak to us or acknowledge that *Screw* could exist without him, but we still subscribed to his original vision and had no desire to radically change the editorial formula, only the business plan.

Unfortunately, Kevin's partners were gorillas of the worst sort, the kind who resented the other, smarter apes. They were gung ho going in, ready to let Kevin and me lead the magazine, but once the office was set up and the magazine was coming out regularly, they spent all their time fighting over the coconuts.

They had bought *Screw* for a song, but that song was about all they had. Before they made the deal, I suggested to Kevin that whatever they paid for the magazine, they would need that much again to build a world-class website as well as for publicity and promotion. But they were all in, and there was no money left. The magazine did well right out of the gate, we re-energized the old package, and the circulation leaped from 5,000 per issue, where Al had left it, to 20,000 in almost no time. But once again, as a circular for hookers in a world of free alternative newspapers and a thousand websites all offering the same services, it was never going to go the distance without a radical change in strategy.

This not-so-dynamic duo came on board with great promises—they had been in the smut racket for years and would be behind-the-scenes businessmen, while Kevin ran art and production and worked to restore the magazine to its former glory. But it turned out that their idea of how a magazine is distributed was the old model—it falls off the back of a truck. There was little accountability. They did not want to hear about national distribution (*Screw* was available only in the New York tri-state area, where the local advertising came from) or expanding the demographic, or going glossy, or the Internet, or any other modern publishing solutions. It was the worst sort of bush-league bullshit. These guys were so dense they didn't understand why they *even needed an editor*. They boasted that they *owned* the magazine, and *they* never read it, so what was the point? They had no time for foolishness such as a business plan. After six months they still had not hired a full-time ad person or a webmaster. It wasn't much use trying to get these guys to think beyond cash-on-delivery ads for cut-rate call girls—just as quickly as we had ramped up the circ, they started cutting corners, skimping on the editorial budget and circumcising our roster of freelancers. When asked at a strategy meeting where they'd like to be with the business in a year, Knucklehead No. 1 said, "I wanna make a lot of fucking money," and the other said, "I wanna get laid."

We were doomed. I knew it couldn't possibly last with these clowns running the business, and I stayed as far away from them as possible. But even with our limited resources I was having a blast. I adopted the pseudonym Charlie Mordecai, and every two weeks (we were now bi-weekly) Kevin and I would conspire to drop a bomb on the newsstands. I looked forward to going to work every day—in fact, some days I'd wake up so inspired and gifted with such felicity of phrase that I could effortlessly cast a cover line that succinctly captured the very gestalt of *Screw*—MAUREEN DOWD'S FILTHY QUEST FOR COCK was one of those happy riffs—before even getting out of bed, and then I would skip happily all the way to work.

Since her fame will surely fade as quickly as her cheap dye job, allow me to remind you that Mo Dowd is (or maybe *was*, by now) the superannuated *New York Times* reporter and author of the shrill hate screed *Are Men Necessary?* in which she writes, "Deep down all men want the same thing, a virgin in a gingham dress." Which, of course, is complete bullshit: what all men want are virgins who act like whores. Everyone knows that. Most men don't even know what gingham is.

Dowd liked to march up and down Broadway sporting the kind of red fuck-me pumps generally preferred by D-list fluffers, carrying her Pulitzer Prize like a bludgeon and screaming Stone Age salvos at any-one who would listen that *men just don't like smart women*. "If there's one thing men fear it's a woman who uses her critical faculties," wrote Mo, who likes to use her brain as an albatross to explain why no one with any horse sense at all will walk to the altar with her, and who ad-vises women to dumb it down so they can wangle a man.

Not exactly a credit to her race, her book flattered no one and set new extremes in gender bashing, insulting at once several generations of women's libbers, post-Donahue males, the Democratic Party, and the vast majority of sentient human beings. Somewhere there are suf-fragettes rolling in their graves. In our eyes, Dowd was a sexist pig marked for death.

In addition to Dowd, we tore into celebrity frauds (DAVID BLAINE, MASTER OF SHIT: WORLD'S WORST MAGICIAN ALMOST DIES—CLOSE

BUT NO CIGAR!), and pretentious hacks (THE KKK TOOK MY BABY AWAY, CAN'T THEY DO SOMETHING ABOUT JOSH NEUMAN?). Courtney Love, Dick Cheney, Michael Bloomberg, Katie Couric, and the stars of *American Idol* all felt our wrath. Madonna was a regular:

FORGIVE ME FATHER, FOR I AM TALENTLESS: The usual gang of idiots is already up in arms at Madonna's oh-so-shocking stage show, of which the only thing shocking is the palpable lack of imagination. Hasn't she been prancing around in slut clothes and rosaries since day fucking one? She's a one-trick pony, about as edgy as chewed bubble gum and as musical as a vending machine. This year's model features the forty-something soccer mom "singing" from a giant crucifix adorned with disco mirrors. As stage props go, this one looks like it belongs in the Mall of America. Cruddy heavy metal bands with backdrops of pentagrams painted on bed sheets are more threatening. She is tired, pathetic, a bore. Perhaps after she sells out her tour she'll confess, "I haven't had a thought in my head since the first time I sucked off Sean Penn, and that idea blew." We hate her and hope she falls off her stupid cross and breaks something.

But we weren't always locked into attack mode. One unblushing cover line read YOU LOOK GOOD. HAVE YOU LOST WEIGHT? BUY SCREW. When Ronald Reagan croaked, we gleefully whipped up a gala edition in his honor: SPECIAL ISSUE: REAGAN, MONKEYS, AND PUNK ROCK! It was everything I had ever dreamed of.

In a lighter mood, "Russian Volleyball Sluts," "Zero Gravity Swingers," and "Super Horny Sex Women Go Blow Job Crazy" also met with great public approval. That last one seemed to *leap* off the back of the truck.

Our best work was our patriotic broadside for the 2004 Republican National Convention, which was held in New York City at Madison Square Garden, right up the street from our offices.

JOHN KERRY IS A BIG HOMO!—we screamed on the cover. And then, in a red, white, and blue banner: SCREW SELLS OUT, WELCOME REPUBLICANS!

You had to figure that these out-of-town swine were all big-money pervs, and it was going to be a boom time for our advertisers: chicks with dicks, enema specialists, discipline freaks, cross-dressers, and all the other hard-to-find indulgences that right-wing moralists go for when they hit Sin City.

Inside the magazine we featured a spirited four-page eyepopper called "The Manchurian Cocksucker" that showcased John Kerry fellating George W. Bush under the Yale University Skull and Bones logo (the word balloon in Bush's mouth read "Mission Accomplished"). Also featured were Arnold Schwarzenegger terminating Ralph Nader's consumer-friendly, ultraliberal bunghole; fat-ass Bolshevik muckraker Michael Moore spilling his seed in Fox newsboy Bill O'Reilly's craggly face; one more compromising picture of Our Fearless Leader, President Bush, this time being terrorized, *but gently*, by ass bandit at large Osama bin Laden; and future secretary of state Condoleezza Rice, her martini-glass tits chilling in the breeze (demurely capped in patriotic, star-spangled pasties), wearing a beauty-pageant sash that read MISS NEGRO CONGENIALITY 1967.

Sometimes it was hard to tell if we had gone too far. We were just trying to have some fun at the expense of, well, everybody. But after a million manufactured celebrity squack shots, unreality ran high, and it was impossible to tell if we had crossed some sort of line. We were simply too close to the material to be a fair gauge anymore.

One day we asked John Holmstrom—also a *Screw* contributor—to stop by the office so we could get his opinion. He took one look and said flatly, "You guys are going to jail." We were delighted—it was the nicest thing anyone had ever said to us.

The triage nurse moved me right along. It was only about an hour before I had my face stitched up and was on my way.

Strasbourg, a picture-book Alsatian city where everything looks like it is made from pretzels, was hosting the Wrestling Baby Blast Festival, two nights of garage punk and grappling. An old warehouse had been turned into an Arena of Pain, with a huge rock 'n' roll stage at one end, a wrestling ring at the other, and a long bar that ran down along the side. Eight-millimeter loops of old Mexican wrestlers were projected on screens that hung from the ceiling joists.

It had been twenty years since I stomped Jeremy in the pages of *Main Event*, and I was still on a career trajectory that could only lead to someone getting hurt, most likely me. It was exciting.

The first night of this bloody weekender—I was headlining the rock 'n' roll part of the show with the solo version of my Rocket Train act—I nearly died after an ill-advised stage dive during an impromptu version of "The Crusher." I wound up crowd-surfing my way back to the stage, strangled by my own mic cord.

Somehow I walked out of there alive, and the next night I was enlisted to act as ring announcer, no little feat, since my French was still pretty much limited to ordering the *magret de canard* and feigning modesty with pretty girls. No matter, I reasoned, my raison d'être being to interfere in every match and help the heels cheat their way to victory.

The Europeans had a fair handle on this wrestling business: there was a decent roster of gimmicked-up rock 'n' rollers ready to rumble, punks dressed as Red Cross workers standing by with a stretcher, a transvestite timekeeper, and the sexiest, most bosomy cheerleaders on the planet dancing between matches.

They came close to the American ideal of my noble sport, but like someone who has learned to play the blues by listening to Led Zeppelin, they missed a few things. They had the taste but hadn't mastered the flavor. I looked around for a guy in a zebra-striped shirt. No luck. Apparently, I was also the referee. This created an interesting conflict of interest—I was to introduce the wrestlers, then help the bad guy creatively carve up the babyface, and then count the poor fucker out and send him on his way. A referee would have been a nice detail, but what the hell? I could do this.

I entered the ring in full Rocket Train regalia—silver cape, matching boots, leopard-skin fez, and wraparound shades—what the Grand Wizard might have worn to a punk rock wrestling blast if he bought his clothes at a thrift store on Mars.

I got into a pretty good groove clobbering the good guys with the mic, or garroting them with the cord and jamming a stiff thumb to the throat when they fell out of the ring (the dreaded Oriental Spike, banned on five continents). Then I delivered the three count and called for the bell. What a racket! The girls danced between matches, and I strutted around and kissed them, like the Marquis de Sade on a bender.

The final match of the night featured Looch Vibrato, an animal who is also one of France's fiercest guitar players. His band, the Magnetix, a duo that also features his sexy cavewoman girlfriend Aggie Sonora, had been backing me up on that tour, and now I was managing his entrée into a brave new world of headbutts and neckbreakers.

Looch was booked into a handicap match against two of the ugliest men I have ever seen, a couple of goons covered in green paint who called themselves Les Hulks. Looch was going to chew on these guys like breath mints.

Unfortunately, traditional tag-team rules had not loomed large in these so-called Hulks' study of professional wrestling, and when the bell rang, they immediately double-teamed Looch and forced him into the corner, where the timekeeper thumped him on the head with the hammer he had been using to ring the bell. They were cheating! I had no choice but to interfere.

I jumped into the fray, turned to slug the timekeeper, and caught the bell straight in the face.

Did you know that when you get hit in the face with a big brass bell, you actually see stars and little tweety birds? I always thought that Bugs Bunny made that shit up.

I still had enough sense to check my nose (not broken) and my teeth (mostly intact), but I was juicing plenty. There was blood everywhere.

At this point, I've got exactly two things on my mind. First, I must look absolutely gorgeous covered in all this blood and I hope someone is taking pictures. Second, It's clobberin' time!!! I pulled that underhanded no-good cross-dressing timekeeper through the ropes and laid him out with an old-school, Memphis-style Hanging Fist Drop.

But in another second those filthy Hulks were on me. It was chaos in the ring: wrestlers were coming out of the dressing room to brawl, and even the cheerleaders were back in the ring, jiggling their tits. The crowd was going nuts—people were screaming, beer was flying. It was awesome.

Clearly the script called for Looch and me to pound the green guys into paté and then dance giddily around their supine bodies. But apparently, no one had told *them* that. I drove Hulk No. 1's head into the floor with a thundering Skullcrusher, but he had the audacity to get up. I was dripping blood on him and trying to mentally transmit the Big

Finish. Actually, I was just screaming. "Stay down mutherfucker . . . let me pound you on the head a few times and then get your ass on that stretcher . . ." But he wasn't having any of it. I was beginning to get light-headed from the loss of blood, and starting to wonder if it wasn't me who was going out in an ambulance. Looch, who had nearly decapitated Hulk No. 2 with a vicious Lariat Clothesline, was finally fed up with Hulk No. 1's French insouciance and flattened him with a hard elbow to the brain. I counted to three and declared Looch the winner.

The crowd was nearly rioting now. Although our match was more State Fair than Madison Square Garden, for Strasbourg, this was an unprecedented cultural revolution.

There was still the small matter of my face, which was in sore need of repair. My top lip was split in two by the impact of the bell, and I was dripping red stuff like a busted pomegranate. Before I knew what was happening, I was being helped out of the ring by a paramedic (a real one) and taken to the hospital.

The doctor did a fine job. He suggested that it might be best if I gave up any aspirations I may have harbored toward growing a mustache, but the scar was going to be a handsome souvenir indeed. I gave him fifty-five euros for twenty-five stitches and a tetanus shot, a bargain any way you looked at it. And then I hitched a ride back to the arena and joined the party already in progress. There were some cheerleaders there who were concerned about me.

I felt like a champion, just waiting for my belt.

ACKNOWLEDGMENTS

Brain-busting *gracias* to Jeremy Tepper; Sharky's Machine; Carmine Bellucci and everyone at Crescent (Drake) Publications; GG Allin (RIP); Michael Kennedy and *High Times* magazine; the Pleasure Fuckers y su pandilla en Malasaña y mas alla; *Hustler* magazine; Dave "Grip and Grin" Allocca; Gretchen Viehmann and Melch; Victor Colliccio and the cast and crew of *Potluck*; Amos Harvey; Joe Naylor and Reverend Musical Instruments; Manly, the World's Strongest Cat, and "God's Own Kitten," Sebastian; Max Lenderman; Peter Halley and *index* magazine; Jennifer Bleyer and *Heeb* magazine; Tim and Micha Warren (Crypt Records); Larry and Leslie (*Carbon 14*); NASA; *Dig It* 'zine, Human Bretzel Records, Wrestling Baby Blast, and the Magnetix (France); El Bratto; *Ruta 66* magazine (Spain); Eric Danville; Chip Mahoney; Paul Armstrong; Saori Kuno; Nancy Huff; Handsome Dick Manitoba; Screaming Lord Overdrunk; Dave "Viking" Pederson; KGB bar; David Smith at the New York Public Library; Sweet Joey Valentine and all past and future members of the Edison Rocket Train; Page Six and the *New York Post;* the irrepressible Paula Kakalecik Manzanero; Eisenberg's Sandwich Shop; and to everyone who was part of this book or somehow contributed to these savage tales—the doctors, dealers, bartenders, and random punks, musicians, promoters, fans, editors, writers, and anyone I am shamefully forgetting, subconsciously repressing, or dutifully omitting—thank you. I hope you had as much fun as I did.

Special piledriving appreciation and huzzahs to John Holmstrom and *Punk* magazine; to Kevin Hein, Al Goldstein, and *Screw* magazine;

to Jon Spencer and family, and the Blues Explosion; and to my favorite chimp, Cliff Mott.

Lots of crazy Sharky Love to my brothers in arms, the Raunch Hands: Mike Mariconda, George Sulley, and Mr. Michael Chandler.

My unwavering, spine-crushing gratitude goes out to the A-Team: my agent, the redoubtable Jane Dystel, and her posse at Dystel & Goderich; my mutherfucking pit bull of a lawyer, friend, and consigliere, Blaine "Three Box" Bortnick; *Mad* man Rick Tulka; and everyone at Faber and Faber/FSG who worked so hard to make this book a reality (special thanks to kopy kats John McGhee, who helped keep the edges sharp, and the late, great Robert Legault, a post-punk proofreader without peer; Jessica Ferri, the great facilitator; Aaron Artessa, a design dude with a positive 'tude; *publicista suprema* Kathy Daneman; and those crack legal eagles and defenders of free speech, Mark Fowler and Diana Frost)—but above all, to my editor, Denise Oswald, a woman of vast intelligence, good taste, patience, and wit. If there is any coherence or grace evident in this story, blame her.

I am especially grateful to my dad, who has provided much more than the unwitting comic relief that peppers this saga, and my mom, who has been no less than spectacular in her support. While I am certain she loves me enough to root for me no matter what, I am hoping she knows me well enough to skip the book and go right to this page.

This book is lovingly dedicated to the memory of my friend Dave Insurgent.

INDEX

A NOTE ABOUT THE TYPE

This is the famous Fairfield typeface. We know of no font produced by any other publisher that costs so much to lead and kern. Our exclusive Faber and Faber printing process produces a taste, a smoothness, and a readability you will find in no other font at any price.

Rudolph Ruzicka, who originally designed Fairfield for the Linotype company in 1937, based it on the forms of Venetian Old Face fonts, as well as on the designs and details of Art Deco. Its fineness of stem and serif, counter and curve, made it ideal for erotic fiction, where a gentle but firm interface between text and reader is essential. Fairfield gained a loyal following among late-twentieth-century pornographers looking for a high degree of transparency in their printed work, and continues to be championed by liberal intellectuals, wrestling pundits, and absurdist poets, whose readers demand a typeface that is easy to read while stoned. John F. Kennedy was known to be fond of it, and used it frequently in official correspondence.